NOT ONE DROP

NOT ONE DROP

Betrayal and Courage In the Wake
of the Exxon Valdez Oil Spill

RIKI OTT, PHD

CHELSEA GREEN PUBLISHING
WHITE RIVER JUNCTION, VT

Chelsea Green Publishing is committed to preserving ancient forests and natural resources. We elected to print this title on 30-percent postconsumer recycled paper, processed chlorine-free. As a result, for this printing, we have saved:

5 Trees (40' tall and 6-8" diameter)
2 Million BTUs of Total Energy
498 Pounds of Greenhouse Gases
2,397 Gallons of Wastewater
146 Pounds of Solid Waste

Chelsea Green Publishing made this paper choice because we and our printer, Thomson-Shore, Inc., are members of the Green Press Initiative, a nonprofit program dedicated to supporting authors, publishers, and suppliers in their efforts to reduce their use of fiber obtained from endangered forests. For more information, visit: www.greenpressinitiative.org.

Environmental impact estimates were made using the Environmental Defense Paper Calculator. For more information visit: www.papercalculator.org.

Project Manager: Emily Foote
Developmental Editor: Joni Praded
Copy Editor: Susan Barnett
Proofreader: Helen Walden
Indexer: Christy Stroud
Designer: Peter Holm, Sterling Hill Productions

Printed in the United States of America
First printing, October 2008
12 11 10   2 3 4 5

Our Commitment to Green Publishing

Chelsea Green sees publishing as a tool for cultural change and ecological stewardship. We strive to align our book manufacturing practices with our editorial mission and to reduce the impact of our business enterprise in the environment. We print our books and catalogs on chlorine-free recycled paper, using vegetable-based inks whenever possible. This book may cost slightly more because we use recycled paper, and we hope you'll agree that it's worth it. Chelsea Green is a member of the Green Press Initiative (www.greenpressinitiative.org), a nonprofit coalition of publishers, manufacturers, and authors working to protect the world's endangered forests and conserve natural resources. *Not One Drop* was printed on 55-lb. Natures Natural, a 30-percent postconsumer recycled paper supplied by Thomson-Shore.

Library of Congress Cataloging-in-Publication Data
Ott, Riki.
  Not one drop : a true story of promises, betrayal & courage in the wake of the Exxon Valdez oil spill / Riki Ott.
    p. cm.
  Includes bibliographical references and index.
  ISBN 978-1-933392-58-5
1. Exxon Valdez Oil Spill, Alaska, 1989. 2. Oil spills--Environmental aspects--Alaska--Prince William Sound Region. 3. Exxon Company U.S.A.--Political activity. 4. Alaska--Politics and government.
    5. Cordova (Alaska)--History, Local. 6. Exxon Valdez (Ship) 7. Green movement--United States. I. Title.

TD427.P4O8288 2008
363.738'2097983--dc22

                    2008034121

Chelsea Green Publishing Company
Post Office Box 428
White River Junction, VT 05001
(802) 295-6300
www.chelseagreen.com

A portion of the sale of this book goes to nonprofit organizations in oiled communities.

Dedicated to:

The loving memory of my father, Frederick Ott,
my hero, mentor, and friend.

The community of Cordova in Prince William Sound
for its rich teachings in the art of civic discourse,
democracy, hope, and courage.

And the oiled communities in Kodiak Island, the
Kenai Peninsula, and the Alaska Peninsula: Ahkiok, Chenega,
Chignik, Homer, Ivanof Bay, Karluk, Kenai, Kodiak, Larsen Bay,
Nanwalek, Old Harbor, Ouzinkie, Perryville, Port Graham, Port
Lions, Seldovia, Seward, Soldotna, Tatitlek, Valdez, and Whittier

for all we have been through together.

---

*"No problem can be solved from the
same consciousness that created it."*

ALBERT EINSTEIN

A NOTE TO THE READER

This book tells the history of the *Exxon Valdez* oil spill and the events leading to it and away from it from the point of view of the town arguably most
affected by this slice of history: Cordova, Alaska. Not surprisingly, the story
believed, embraced, and perpetuated by ordinary people is at odds with the
corporate lore—the dominant story of these events. Like Howard Zinn's *A
People's History of the United States*, this book reflects events from the trenches,
not the corporate boardrooms; from the people who pay an overlarge share of
the risk of our society's oil dependency, not from those who reap an overlarge
portion of the benefits from it.

I lived this slice of history, much of it in Cordova. However, this is not my
story so much as *our* story. The manuscript reconstructs from interviews with
the author, court records, Congressional or other testimonies, official reports,
studies and surveys of residents by visiting social scientists, investigative media
stories, the local news, and personal reminiscences captured in approximately
annual—and quite detailed—"Dear Everyone" letters. So as not to distract the
reader from the story, annotations are not marked within the text, but readers
who seek more information on a point will likely find it in the endnotes.

The one place where I have taken full liberty of creative reconstruction
is during conversations with my friend, Linden. I did not whip out a pencil
and pad during our hikes, campouts, or numerous teas. But we have had the
discussions portrayed in this book—or very similar talks—for over twenty
years as we tried to make sense of very confusing times. The intent of these
passages is to convey critical information in a straightforward way—and this
book carries endnotes to document the information, not the dialogue. As I
was limited in number of characters for this book, our dialogue often carries
other voices of Cordova, whose names also show up in the endnotes.

All this said, this story is still only my truth—history told through my
lens and life in Cordova. But I believe it accurately portrays larger events and
deconstructs a great deal of corporate lore.

—Riki Ott

CONTENTS

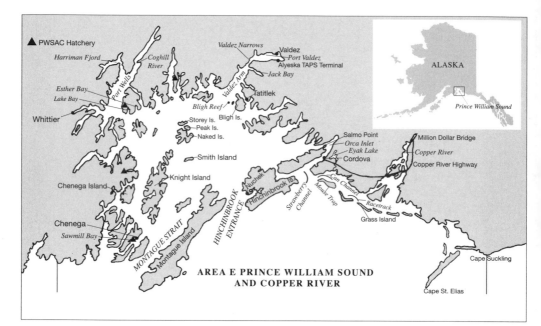

**AREA E PRINCE WILLIAM SOUND
AND COPPER RIVER**

▲ PWSAC Hatchery

Harriman Fjord

Coghill River

Valdez Narrows

Valdez
Port Valdez
Alyeska TAPS Terminal
Jack Bay

Esther Bay
Lake Bay

Port Wells

Valdez Arm

Tatitlek

Bligh Reef

Whittier

Bligh Is.

Storey Is.
Peak Is.
Naked Is.

Salmo Point
Orca Inlet
Eyak Lake
Cordova

Million Dollar Bridge
Copper River
Copper River Highway

Smith Island

Knight Island

Nuchek

Strawberry Channel

Can Channel

Mouse Trap

Racetrack

Chenega Island

HINCHINBROOK ENTRANCE

Hinchinbrook Is.

Grass Island

Chenega

Sawmill Bay

MONTAGUE STRAIT

Montague Island

Cape Suckling

Cape St. Elias

ALASKA

Prince William Sound

North Slope

Prudhoe Bay

Arctic National
Wildlife Refuge

Fairbanks
North Pole

ALASKA

Glennallen
Sheep Mountain ▲
Anchorage
Valdez
Kenai

Chitina

Cordova

PRINCE WILLIAM SOUND

Cook Inlet

Seward

Goodnews Bay

Bristol Bay

Kenai Peninsula
Homer/Seldovia

Juneau

Alaska Peninsula

Shelikof Strait

Kodiak

GULF OF ALASKA

False Pass

Chignik
Perryville

0   100   200   300mi

N

FOREWORD

The grounding of the *Exxon Valdez* and the resulting oil spill in March 1989 was a terrible tragedy. Arguably even more tragic was the Supreme Court decision in June 2008 to reduce the punitive award against Exxon to $507 million, a mere ten percent of the original jury's verdict. These two tragedies should, however, serve as a warning. We the people must demand that such travesties of justice are never again repeated.

As Riki Ott points out, the first of these two tragedies demolished habitats, killed millions of fish, animals, and plants, destroyed communities and families, wiped out businesses, and resulted in untold human suffering—as well as causing the severe economic and ecological losses that made headlines around the world. The second tragedy not only took away the possibility that some of the problems had a chance of being solved, it did something that ultimately may be far more devastating. The Supreme Court decision sent a chilling message throughout the world that was eloquently expressed by the people most impacted, those of Cordova, Alaska. In words painted on placards to post on the walls of willing businesses they announced: GUILTY UNTIL PROVEN WEALTHY and CORPORATIONS WIN. It is up to us—citizens, consumers, parents—to make sure that this message is reversed.

Not One Drop tells some of the personal stories behind the *Exxon Valdez* calamity. As I read about the lives of these people and the land they call home, I kept thinking about my nine-month-old grandson, Grant. I bounced him on my knee and wondered what sort of place he will inherit from us when he reaches my age, six decades from now. If we continue on this path, if we allow corporations to wreak havoc on environments and societies, if we subscribe to a judiciary system that perpetuates these crimes (there is no other word for them), and if we elect representatives who are too cowardly or corrupt to implement policies that support our best interests, then the prospects for Grant and all his brothers and sisters around the globe are indeed grim.

There is an alternative. More than anything else, Riki Ott's amazing book should serve as a call to action. In her closing, after pointing out that Cordova is a community and that she is proud to be from "*that*" town," she states, "somewhere in our story, there are lessons to break the falls of other communities and to speed their recovery so that, community by community, we can work together to rebuild a nation that, too, has stumbled."

Exxon, like most corporations, is driven by a single goal: to maximize profits regardless of the environmental and social costs. Like the others—whether they sell oil, tennis shoes, or pharmaceuticals—it is a hierarchical organization, not democratic. However, the marketplace is largely democratic. We the people still have the power to determine which corporations will make it, which must change, and which will go under. We exercise this power every time we shop—or choose not to.

Our history books are filled with examples of civil rights, labor, and consumer movements that have brought corporate giants to their knees. In recent years, organizations like Amnesty International, MoveOn, Common Cause, the Clamshell Alliance, and Co-op America have profoundly impacted boardroom policies. Rainforest Action Network (RAN) alone has forced Boise Cascade, Kinkos, Staples, Home Depot, Citigroup, JP Morgan Chase, Goldman Sachs, McDonald's, and Mitsubishi to adopt policies aimed at conserving fragile forests. RAN announced in 2008 that it would set its sights on Exxon; it recognizes that when a critical mass of car owners become educated enough to refuse to buy gasoline from Exxon, it will have to change its ways—or close down.

The same can be said for every industry. If enough of us decline to buy clothes made in sweatshops, Nike and its peers will have to transform those sweatshops into legitimate factories where workers receive a fair wage, health care, and retirement benefits—or go out of business. We can—in fact, we must—repeat this process with all the goods and services we purchase. As Riki Ott affirms, "democracy is like a campfire; it needs to be constantly tended or it will die."

The way we vote during the election process is important. Our president and representatives affect the makeup of the Supreme Court and the laws that guide regulatory agencies. We need to insist upon a greater separation between government and corporations, including the implementation of policies that prohibit the "revolving door" that allows executives to become the regulators of the industries they once served and then to return to those industries after their government tenure expires. We need to dramatically shift our concept of corporate personhood, rebalance corporate and individual rights, and restructure how cases like that of the *Exxon Valdez* are heard.

However, we must understand that corporations and their lobbyists have the power to influence even the most determined politicians. We must recognize that major shifts—the end of the Vietnam War, clean up of polluted rivers, enactment of equal opportunity employment laws, removal of trans-fats and hormones from foods, movement toward organic foods and renewable energy, and so many others—occurred because a critical mass of us demanded action. The political and legal changes resulted only after enough of us insisted that they happen.

We have entered a period of history that is not unlike the time when city-states became nations, except today the power is being transferred from nations to corporations. Until recently, we could look at the planet as 180 or so countries; a handful among these influenced most of the others. Now we might better envision the planet as those same 180 or so countries, but they are surrounded by massive corporate clouds that circle the globe. These multinational corporations position themselves above the laws of any specific nation; they often pay no taxes; they form partnerships of convenience—in China, Russia, Iran, South Africa, Brazil, or whatever country best serves their immediate interests. If they do not like the laws of one nation, they move (as Halliburton moved its corporate headquarters from the United States to Dubai) or sell themselves to a foreign entity. They appear to be invincible. But they are not.

Even the most powerful corporations are vulnerable to us—we who buy their goods and services. They cannot survive unless we vote for them in the marketplace. We in the United States represent less than five percent of the world's population and yet we consume more than twenty-five percent of its resources. Our language is the language of commerce and diplomacy. Our art, music, literature, TV, and films reach people in the most remote corners of the planet. We are the global trendsetters. This position gives us power and also imposes on us the responsibility to take leadership. The job of forcing corporations to change their ways falls upon each and every one of us.

We the people have been very successful at forcing corporations to clean up polluted rivers, change their hiring practices, alter policies toward cutting rain forests, and implement changes in so many other specific areas. It is now time to take our demands to a new level. We must insist they modify that single goal that drives them. In order to serve our own self-interests, as well as those of Grant's generation, we must mandate that the new goal be: to make profits but only while creating a sustainable, just, and peaceful world.

More than any time in history, we live in a highly integrated and interdependent world. We are connected through the marketplace, global mass media, and the internet. My grandson cannot hope to grow up in a sustainable, just, and peaceful world unless every child born in Africa, Asia, the Middle East, and Latin America has that same expectation—and it is realized.

The irresponsible exploitation of human and natural resources is a failed experiment. It has taken us to the brink of catastrophe. We see the results of such reckless polices in the melting glaciers, genocide, rising food and fuel prices, diminishing resources, an increasing trend for desperate people to turn to terrorism—and in the tragedy of the *Exxon Valdez*.

Cordova, Alaska is a microcosm. By allowing Exxon to get away with the outrageous crime it has committed against a community that represents us all and by supporting such actions at the gas pump, we are accomplices. *Not One Drop* demands that we chart a new course. Riki Ott has given us amazing stories. She has documented a most significant event in human history. Above all else, she has served notice that we—and our children—deserve better.

We must fight this battle on many fronts. It is imperative that we convince Congress to reverse the Supreme Court decision in the *Exxon Valdez* case and that we work to change the laws governing corporate responsibility. And it is essential that we—you and I—recognize that we have a responsibility every time we fill up at the gas pump. Ultimately, the power rests with each and every one of us.

As you read the following pages, allow your heart to break. Imagine Cordova as your home and Prince William Sound as your backyard. When you set the book down, make an absolute, iron-clad commitment to join other men and women who are determined to create a world that future generations will want to inhabit.

JOHN PERKINS

PREFACE

"I refer to Prince William Sound as one of the two most beautiful places on earth. I leave it to each of you individually to decide what the other one is. We all have a Shangri-La in our hearts and minds. Think of yours when you contemplate what has happened to ours."

DON MOORE,
Cordova City Manager

The *Exxon Valdez* disaster was more than an oil spill in Prince William Sound, just as Katrina was more than a hurricane in New Orleans, 9/11 was more than buildings collapsing in New York, Chernobyl was more than a nuclear meltdown in Ukraine, Bhopal was more than a poisonous gas leak in India, and Love Canal was more than toxic contamination of a neighborhood in Niagara Falls, New York.

Each of these disasters caused loss of life, contamination of the environment, and damage to property. Loss of these visible things was measured in dollars, and the amount was relegated to the courts to decide. But such tangible losses are only the tip of the iceberg of harm in disasters. These disasters so thoroughly disrupted peoples' lives that entire communities became dysfunctional. This type of harm is not yet measured in dollars, so it is invisible in the court system and on corporate accounting ledgers. It is not invisible, however, in the affected communities.

The *Exxon Valdez* disaster became the proving grounds that these so-called invisible losses exist and are especially prevalent in accidents that involve high-stakes, adversarial class action litigation. Damage to social networks is as real as physical and economic damage. Further, this intrinsic damage is more devastating to people and communities than are the tangible losses. Why? Because relationships and the associations that spring from them—friendships, marriages, family stability, community unity, and even national harmony and international peace—are more important than money in sustaining a civil society. The relationships *are* the civil society. When relationships weaken, the glue that binds people together dissolves: community life unravels and becomes chaotic.

Not One Drop is about what happened in Cordova, a small fishing community in Prince William Sound, after the oil spill. What happened in my adopted hometown is not unique. Disaster trauma has happened in other communities. It will happen in many more. Sociologists, the scientists who study the behavior of individuals and groups in society, warn that disasters coupled with complex litigation will become more prevalent in the twenty-first century because of unintended side effects of our technologies. They predict that even natural disasters spawned by global climate change—such as more frequent and intense fires, floods, and hurricanes—will result in litigation over things once considered "acts of God." The Cordova story shows why communities and governments should better prepare to lessen the impact of future disasters on people's lives.

There is an unfulfilled need among the spill survivors to have other people understand what happened to us. While there are other dimensions of recovery, such as litigation closure and restoration of the natural environment, certainly one large part is a collective feeling that we are not isolated in our experience, but understood. This story is an attempt to fill that need.

In telling this story, I draw on my own experiences and those of others through personal relationships and local lore with literally hundreds of scientific studies to buttress this tale. The trauma and healing experienced in our personal lives was mirrored in the larger community. As within, so without, the ancients taught. And so it was after the spill.

Writing was not easy, as it forced me to relive the disaster. Spending time in wild Alaska was my tonic for dealing with stress—birding and biking on the vast Copper River Delta, hiking into coastal rainforests or high along alpine ridges, canoeing beaver-engineered streams, berry-picking, preparing salmon for canning, snowshoeing in deeply quiet forests, ice-skating on silt-scoured-smooth glacial lakes, building bonfires, camping out. Mostly I embraced the wild alone except for canine companions; sometimes I shared these adventures with my friend, Linden, and her family. I was hungry for the calming energy of wetlands and woods, streams and sea, mountains and meadows. The energy was deeply therapeutic.

This book fell naturally into four parts. Part 1, Promises (1968–1989), introduces the reader to pre-spill life in the Alaska fishing community of Cordova, commercial fishing, Prince William Sound, the Copper River Delta, and the uneasy relationship between the commercial fishing industry and the oil industry. The broken promises by BP (British Petroleum), Exxon, and ARCO are spliced into the story as I track the history of air and water pollution from Trans-Alaska Pipeline System (TAPS) operations in Port Valdez.

Parts 2 and 3 follow the community through eleven years from the spill in 1989 through the ten-year anniversary (or "memorial" as Cordovans prefer) in 1999. Part 2, Betrayal (1989–1993), were dark times of eroding personal and family relationships, intense fears about spill impacts, gnawing uncertainty about lingering harm to the ecosystem, deepening worry over secret high-stakes science and litigation, and growing debt. Cordova degenerated into a "corrosive community," scientists' lingo for a town so polarized by trauma, stress, and fighting that collective decision-making and recovery grind to a halt. Part 3, Courage (1994–1999), starts a slow path to healing as townspeople began to understand the lingering oil damage to the Sound and community and to then work together to resolve problems and rebuild community.

During these eleven years, the oil industry turned as slippery as a bar of wet soap, fighting in court and political arenas to limit financial damage from the spill and liability for future accidents. The battle for control turned epic—and Hollywood—with a covert surveillance operation on industry critics, mass firings of whistleblowers, congressional audits, legal actions, and more, all under relentless political pressure to deliver more oil from Alaska's North Slope.

Part 4, New Beginnings (2000–2008), condenses the oil spill legacy into four seminal teachings and applies these to the other of the "two most beautiful places on earth"—the special Shangri-La in *your* heart and mind. All the teachings lead to the same point: the power to recover from disaster and heal communities deeply divided by issues begins when people come together to focus on what they share in common, rather than on what divides them. Growing a democracy starts at home with individual actions.

Ultimately, the spill story is a parable for the twenty-first century of people growing through trauma to realize that all we really have is each other—and that this matters.

ACKNOWLEDGMENTS

My deepest thanks go to the publishing team at Chelsea Green, who challenged me to turn a "nice collection of facts" into a human story—and who then had the patience and wisdom to wait for me to deliver that story. My thanks go to Margo Baldwin, president and publisher, for keeping the faith, selling and reselling the book, while waiting; Shay Totten, former editorial director, who prodded me to take time to write essays and commentaries during revisions to help keep the *Exxon Valdez* story in the news; Joni Praded, current editorial director, who helped weave innumerable threads into a solid story; copy editor Susan Barnett, who added the final spit and polish to the manuscript; and managing editor Emily Foote, who orchestrated production on an impossibly tight schedule.

Apologies to the many individuals, especially Dan Lawn, Stan Stephens, and Patience Andersen Faulkner, among others, who played central roles in the spill drama or aftermath, yet whose characters were edited out of, or whose roles were greatly reduced in, this telling of the story. It is my sincere wish that each of you will someday share your story to teach future generations the need for constant vigilance and the importance of taking action.

My heartfelt thanks go to my friends whose characters were conscripted for this story. An especially *big* thanks to Linden O'Toole for carrying the voices and feelings of many townspeople in her character portrayal, while also sharing her intimate personal story; to Danny Carpenter for his wry humor, steady support, and keen observations; to Lisa Marie Jacobs for her ability to find humor in the worst of times and her poignant insights into human nature; and to the spill children, Malani and Makena O'Toole and Zak Jacobs, among others, for teaching me what is real and what is important.

Thanks, too, go to the "home team" reviewers, Barclay Kopchak and Susan Ogle, for their labor of love for the community in helping craft this story to reflect the larger Cordova story.

I am also grateful for, and extend my thanks to, the many people in Cordova who shared their experience and insights in public or private as each added to the telling of this story; the sociologists Dr. Steve Picou and Dr. Duane Gill, and their colleagues and students, who fell in love with Cordova while working to measure and quantify our loss; the documentary and feature film crews who worked to document this disaster and social crisis so that the story could be shared as a lesson for other people and communities; the students and interns who explored specific elements of the story; the librarians who tracked down miscellaneous facts and papers; the Alaska Forum for Environmental Responsibility and Alaska Community Action on Toxics, and their funders, for providing support; and several donors for personally supporting my work.

And finally, I am forever in debt to my father for his constant encouragement and love. The only way to repay him is to pass it on to others. *Salud!*

INTRODUCTION

In mid-April 1985, I joined my skipper on the frozen shore of Goodnews Bay in western Alaska, where we readied his boat, the *Magi*, for the 1,500-mile journey to Prince William Sound.

I was fresh out of graduate school with a master's and doctorate in marine pollution. I had signed up, on the spur of the moment, to crew on the *Magi*, a commercial salmon-fishing boat in Alaska, because, after thirteen years of academics, I needed a break. My *soul* needed a break. Something major was missing in my life. I didn't know what, but I intended to give myself the summer to sort things out before I started a career, most likely as a professor or research scientist, I figured, to fulfill a childhood dream.

When I was thirteen, growing up in Wauwatosa, Wisconsin, in the late 1960s, I had a transcendent experience, triggered by dying robins falling out of the trees. When I asked my father why this was happening, he placed a bird, quivering and shaking uncontrollably, into my cupped hands as he explained about the neurotoxin DDT. Transfixed by the bird's blank stare, I wanted to know more—and I wanted the world to be safe again for robins.

So did my father. He was a practical conservationist with a passion for birds and children. He was equally at ease with a hunting rifle or a pair of binoculars and a bird book. He reasoned if DDT was bad for robins, it was likely bad for his children as well. At the time, I didn't know that my father had been among the last students of Aldo Leopold, a visionary conservation leader. In my world, he was an ordinary paper salesman who loved his family, his friends, his community, and all creatures, it seemed. When he sensed something to do, whether it was add a new exhibit at the museum or zoo, help save robins or other birds, or protect Wisconsin's rivers, he would gather friends and raise funds to do it. He taught compassion and common sense by example, but mostly he taught "doing" through the art of civic engagement and acting on one's convictions.

My father gave me Rachel Carson's *Silent Spring*, which I read as well as, in short order, all of her other books. I decided to become a marine biologist like Carson. Meanwhile, my father and his friends used Carson's science to sue the State of Wisconsin in 1968 with the fledgling Environmental Defense Fund. The scientist-lawyer team prepared their court briefings and motions at our dining room table. I raced home each day after school and sat quietly, watching the adults do their homework and soaking up the atmosphere of intense concentration and high-energy brainpower. *I* wanted to do research, writing, and science!

My dad and his friends prevailed: In 1971 Wisconsin banned DDT. The rest of the nation followed suit in 1972, the year I graduated from high school.

I set out to find an ocean and a college. A path opened for me to study oil pollution, which I pursued, over the next thirteen years, in four countries and at five universities on coasts of three different seas. When I finally graduated with a doctorate in marine toxicology from the University of Washington, I decided I could spare just one summer in my headlong rush toward a science career. Alaska was so close and beckoning so loudly. I arranged for a former housemate to take care of my dog for the summer and I headed north into an Alaskan spring.

It sounded like heavy artillery fire the night the ice pack broke up in Goodnews Bay. By the next morning, the place was transformed. What had been a bleak flat snowy landscape was now a dark wide-open bay with rafts of colorful sea ducks, decked out for spring breeding. I itched to grab a bird book, but we were too busy. The snowplow had arrived.

Unceremoniously, the front-end loader shoved the fishing boat, *Magi*, across the hardpack snow. The boat's aluminum hull screeched like fingernails dragged down a chalkboard. We slid into the bay. Elegant king eiders scattered out of our way as we headed south to open water.

We nearly collided with our first gray whale. On the rolling sea surface, it appeared as a flat smooth long lump, trailing an oily sheen. I yelled out, "*Whale!*" The skipper cranked the wheel hard over. After that I was on whale watch—and boat watch as the herring fleet was moving around and up Alaska's coast in hot pursuit of the same thing as the whales.

Our stormy ten-day passage took us across Bristol Bay, through steep-sided False Pass, along the rugged mountainous coast of the Alaska Peninsula, through Shelikof Strait, along the steeply forested eastern shores of the Kenai Peninsula, and into the calm waters of Prince William Sound. Finally, we rounded Salmo Point in Orca Inlet and spotted our destination—Cordova.

I stood on the open deck instantly transfixed by the small fishing port, buzzing with activity and nestled at the base of snowy mountains, glistening in the sun. I felt such a strong resonance with this place that I could hardly breathe. I thought, "*Whatever it takes, I'm staying.*"

That summer I sorted some things out. Right off I realized: right place, wrong skipper. But I had signed on for the summer and I kept my word, biding my time. One morning at 2 A.M. while I was mending our net on the dock in Whittier, three kayakers glided silently past. I hailed them, and one took me up on my offer of Neapolitan ice cream.

Danny Carpenter was a sea kayak guide. Danny had a kind handsome face, deeply tanned, with dark brown eyes and long eyelashes. He was my height, stocky, with heavily muscled shoulders and arms. He radiated a quiet confidence and easy manner. We talked until the sun slid to the east and back up in the sky.

A month later, I rented boats from Danny when my sister and a girlfriend joined me for a two-week sea kayak trip in Harriman Fjord and Port Wells. Our first day out, I shared my big news—I was going to buy a salmon drift gillnet permit and a boat and move to Cordova. I hadn't figured out any details, but they always seemed to take care of themselves.

Ten days later when we camped at the U.S. Forest Service's Harrison Lagoon cabin, plans for my big move were well under way. By coincidence, Danny and a bevy of male clients also found their way to the cabin that same night. The small cabin provided a cozy shelter from the summer storm and the two brown bear sows with cubs roaming the area.

Danny and I found a corner in the small cabin to talk while my girlfriends regaled his customers with our adventures. As I listened to his pleasant voice, I suddenly heard myself say, "I'm going to buy a fishing permit and boat. Do you want to crew for me next summer?"

A grin broke across his face, flashing silver from a capped tooth. "Sure."

Later that fall, I determined that my resources fell far short of what was needed to buy a $59,000 gillnet permit, a $45,000 used boat, and about $20,000 of miscellaneous gear, everything from $2 picking hooks to $4,000 nets. So I offered Danny a raise—an equal partnership in my venture. He accepted. Why not? We literally had nothing to lose except our lives, but that didn't occur to either of us. I had nothing saved from my student years, and Danny had worked alternately as a sea kayak guide during the summers and in a ski shop most winters, spending his money as fast as he made it.

We pooled our lack of fortunes through Ott and Carpenter, Incorporated, O.C. Inc., or "Otter Confusion" as Danny immediately dubbed it. We borrowed money from two banks and Danny's friends and closed the deal on our boat, the *Ambergris*, already in Cordova, just four days before our boat ride north left the docks in Seattle in April 1986.

Craig Blau, the seasoned skipper and owner of the *Elfin III*, watched as we loaded a mountain of fishing gear on his deck, along with skis, a kayak, windsurfers, camping gear, and a sewing machine. All he said was, "I thought you kids were gonna' go *fishing*."

The parting shot from our frazzled marine insurer, who'd had enormous difficulty placing us with underwriters because of our lack of experience and choice of fisheries, was, "Just don't sink your boat your first year! I'll never be able to place you again!"

My years of theoretical education were over. My practical education was about to begin.

ABBREVIATIONS

ACAT	Alaska Community Action on Toxics
ACWA	Alaska Clean Water Alliance
ADEC	Alaska Department of Environmental Conservation
ADFG	Alaska Department of Fish and Game
AFER	Alaska Forum on Environmental Responsibility
ARCO	Atlantic Richfield Company
BP	British Petroleum
CDFU	Cordova District Fishermen United
CFAB	Commercial Fisheries and Agriculture Bank
CRWP	Copper River Watershed Project
EPA	U.S. Environmental Protection Agency
EVOS	*Exxon Valdez* Oil Spill
FEMA	Federal Emergency Management Act
HAZWOPER	Hazardous Waste Operator
MARPOL	Marine Pollution Convention
NMFS	National Marine Fisheries Service
NOAA	National Oceanographic and Atmospheric Administration
NOL	Net Operating Loss
OPA 90	Oil Pollution Act of 1990
OSHA	Occupational Safety and Health Act
PAHs	Polycyclic Aromatic Hydrocarbons
PTSD	Post-Traumatic Stress Disorder
PWS	Prince William Sound
PWSAC	Prince William Sound Aquaculture Corporation
RCAC	Regional Citizens Advisory Council
SEA Program	Sound Ecosystem Assessment Program
TAPS	Trans-Alaska Pipeline System
TAPL Fund	Trans-Alaska Pipeline Liability Fund
VOCs	Volatile Organic Carbons

PART ONE

PROMISES

(1986–1989)

"Give me a firm place to stand and I'll move the Earth."

ARCHIMEDES

"The moment one definitely commits oneself, then Providence moves too. All sorts of things occur to help one that would never otherwise have occurred."

WILLIAM HUTCHINSON MURRAY
Leader of the 1951 Mount Everest Expedition

CHAPTER ONE

A PLACE TO STAND

1986

"If my mother could see me now, she'd *kill* you!" Danny glared at me from across our towline, stretched taut and spitting beads of water as it disappeared over the bow of the *Ambergris* into the churning sea.

It was our fifth salmon opener on the Copper River Flats. A strong storm surge had sucked us into the dreaded breaker patch on the west side of Grass Island. The other end of our one precious net—all that we had been able to afford—was hard aground on the beach, sanding down fast. We were trying to tow it off. Flying spume hurled by a screaming fifty-knot wind stung our faces. Behind us, thunderous breakers as tall as two-story houses collapsed with a *woof!* of air that shuddered our fiberglass hull. Our diesel engine whined and strained in full reverse, as we dodged steep walls of water.

Suddenly, a breaker reared up directly behind us. It lifted our five-ton, twenty-seven-foot boat, light as a feather. We surged forward, surfing straight down the wave face. We shot past our towline. At the base of the breaker, the pointed bow of the *Ambergris* dug into the water. The boat broached violently, rolling on her starboard rail. Almost over. Almost. As I clung to the net reel, I could see Danny's boots dangling in the air as he hung on to the front helm. The hissing white furry-foam of the spent breaker was only inches from my head on the other side of the rail.

Then, miraculously, the *Ambergris* found its center and righted itself. Danny and I crashed to the deck, then scrambled up and stared into each other's eyes, searching for some security, something to say that we were all right.

"That would have been fun in a kayak!" Danny yelled over the screaming wind.

"That would have been fun on a windsurfer!" I shot back.

There was a loud thudding noise. The *Ambergris* shuddered violently and its engine died. The towline was wrapped in our propeller. We were dead in the water and each wave pushed us steadily toward the beach. My stomach clenched.

We held each other's gaze. *Who would have the lifesaving idea to get us out of this mess this time?* Each twenty-four-hour fishing period had turned into an epic adventure during which quick wits, steady nerves, and good luck had saved us to fish another day.

"Hand me that knife," Danny shouted, pointing to the knife taped to the base of the net reel for emergencies. He tied it to his kayak float vest and carefully worked his way around to the stern, balancing on a narrow rail on a wildly bucking boat. He ducked out of sight on the transom, then pounded on the hull, giving me the signal to raise the outdrive unit.

I leaped onto the fish holds, through the cabin door, and pressed the tilt button, counting the seconds. After six, Danny pounded again. Enough! Through the open cabin door, I watched the lumpy seas against the steady shoreline and felt them pitch and roll our boat. Time slowed to a crawl.

More pounding! Danny had cleared the towline from the propeller. I lowered the unit and fired up the engine. The *Ambergris* shook and clattered from a bent prop as we rode the seas back to the end of our net, catching the towline and making it fast to a cleat.

Then we saw the other end. About a third of our 900-foot long net was sanded down on the beach. We looked at each other, then, remembering the advice given to us by one sage Flats veteran, we simultaneously yelled, "*It's only a piece of string! Cut it!*"

We left our only net to its fate as we worked our way out of the jaws of the breaker patch and to a safe anchorage in the Grass Island channel.

We found our net the next day during the closure, stretched its full three football fields of length on the beach about two miles from the anchorage. During our walk down the beach, we found a boneyard of broken hulls and pieces of other boats that had not survived the breaker patch. Wordlessly, we shook the sand and stiff fish carcasses out of our net.

Then we hatched a plan. We cut our only net into three pieces and, with the help of another couple who had stayed out for the closure, we carried each shackle of gear, weighing close to 200 pounds, across the soft sand dunes to the anchorage. Three times we made the trip through the glaucous-winged gull colony with scores of birds pelting us with oily droppings, with the driftwood yoke biting into taut shoulder muscles, and with feet sinking deep into loose sand. Three times. Then we sewed our net together and, at high tide, we reeled it back onto our boat.

As we motored into the Cordova harbor three days after the fishing period had ended, Danny said, "I don't think we should do anything, and I don't think we should do that very fast."

This incident proved to be our rite of passage into the fleet of 500 fishermen. Our tenacity—and the fact that we had "he-manned" our net across sand too soft to land a plane—had impressed a tough crowd. Friendships grew as acquaintances, even strangers, started giving us sound advice. Our local knowledge increased exponentially. We began to believe we might actually live through our first season.

Spring Reds and Kings on the Copper River Flats

From mid-May through mid-June we fished for king salmon and red salmon on the Copper River Flats, a seventy-mile strip of remote coastline to the south and east of Cordova. The Flats are the seam between the 700,000-acre Copper River Delta and the Gulf of Alaska—wide-open ocean all the way to Hawaii. The Delta sprawls at the base of the Chugach and Wrangell-Saint Elias Mountains, a region containing the greatest coastal relief on Earth with some peaks towering nearly three miles high. The largest network of ice caps and glaciers outside of the Polar Regions and Greenland constantly worry the range, slowly eroding the peaks like giant slow-moving bulldozers. This mountain range is the greatest source of sediment into the Pacific Ocean from all of the Americas.

The Delta is built from sand and silt—mountain dust dumped when the Copper River abruptly slows its headlong rush and empties into the sea. At the frayed seaward edge of the Delta, the sea and river carves and reworks the sand into a maze of braided sloughs. Long shore and tidal currents take the sediment load and mold it to form a series of barrier islands like long running stitches that separate the wetlands from the sea.

There are no navigational charts for this area. It is impossible to pin the constantly shifting barrier islands to a spot on a map. The National Oceanic and Atmospheric Administration (NOAA) nautical charts simply end at Cape St. Elias on the eastern side of the Flats and start again at Hinchinbrook Island on the western side, leaving a big hole in between. The hole is filled by the highly coveted and often hard-won "local knowledge."

Our most precious tidbit of local knowledge was shared by the fisherman who had patiently taught us to hang our first net. It was a single sheet of paper, showing a U-2 satellite photo of the Flats. Notes were scribbled across the map—wavy lines for breaker patches, "X"s for sunken boat wrecks that would snag fishing gear, little anchors for safe deep holes tucked up behind the islands, and local names for fishing spots, some with warnings like "The Mouse Trap—stay away!" The bar crossings—the deepwater channels between the barrier islands—were also labeled with notes. "Strawberry—AVOID." "Grass Island—west side only."

Danny and I added to our local knowledge by following other fishermen—"seagulling" they called it—to learn the safest commute to the fishing grounds for small boats. "The Can Channel" eliminated the need to go across Strawberry Bar, which claims lives nearly every year. Young, cut spruce marked the channel like poles in a downhill ski racecourse. I plugged the spruce pole locations into our Loran as Danny fought to keep the *Ambergris* steady in the wash of wakes from thirty boats all racing along at top speed. The "Racetrack" was so narrow that boats zoomed along single file, swerving and weaving around the buoys that marked the course. These channels were passable only around high tide.

The tides added a whole other dimension to fishing. Four times a day there are huge tidal exchanges that completely change the landscape. Channels full of water at high tides empty in the space of a few hours. Mean sea level can drop by up to eighteen feet during semimonthly spring tides around the new or full moon, leaving behind acres of flat sand—and sometimes fishing boats stranded like monuments until the next tidal cycle. One fisherman's boat, the *Curlew*, grounded so far out of the channel on a spring high tide that it stayed there on the sand flats for six weeks until the tides were high enough to float it again.

We were warned about the spring storms. The trough of low pressure that forms in the Gulf of Alaska each winter begins to disintegrate in May. But even in dying, the trough can birth vicious storms—cyclones—within hours, too quickly to be detected by the NOAA weather satellites that sweep over the area every six hours. The year before, when I had crewed, one killer storm sprang upon the fleet unannounced. It went from flat calm to blowing over 100 knots within an hour. The storm caught the fleet fishing near Cape Saint Elias. Half a dozen men were lifted from sinking boats by Coast Guard helicopters. Four days later, a couple of the abandoned boats were found drifting by Hinchinbrook Entrance about 100 miles west of the Cape.

Fishermen turn these harrowing incidents into funny stories, which are swapped in town during closures. Paul Swartzbart, who had been at the Cape, joked, "When I tried to pick fish from my net, the wind tore at my rain gear and flapped the hood against my face so hard it about knocked me out. Then it pulled my jacket right up over my head. I couldn't see a darn thing! I think if it's blowing over eighty, just forget rain gear. Pick in the nude!"

Fishing the Flats is tricky business. Your competition one minute could be your rescuer the next. Ric Schultz has fished the breakers longer than most in the fleet. Most people who dared to fish the breakers where the fish ran hard would have a bad scare, feel lucky to survive, and learn to fish elsewhere. The town has more than its share of widows. But Ric fishes the beguiling area known as the "Mouse Trap" year after year, despite having spent the better part of one afternoon in the surf, then on the beach, while breakers mauled his overturned boat. Ric had to charter a plane to get the dog, which refused to get on the rescue boat. During one closure he told a story: "First, this guy corks me and steals my fish, and then he expects me to rescue him when his boat flips!" Ric did. Such rescues would be considered heroics elsewhere, but on the Flats it is just another story told in town during closures.

Fishing couples are rare. When we delivered our fish to waiting tenders on the ebb tides, we were often asked, "Who's the skipper? A boat can only have one skipper!" But on the *Ambergris*, neither of us knew enough to be skipper, so we took turns. The agonizing decision of where to fish could be worth thousands of dollars—or maybe your life.

Whoever's turn it was to be skipper would head for a spot and set the gear, quickly backing the boat to lay out the net, while the deckhand or crew guided armfuls of flying cork line, lead line, and web off the spinning reel to prevent a backlash and ripped gear. Then the skipper would watch the net for snags and dangerous drift. One could cover quite a distance on a hard flood or ebb. The crew could fix a bite to eat or grab a quick nap.

When the skipper called to pull the set, the roles immediately swapped. Whoever had made the set now acted as crew to pick it, pawing through the nylon strands, rubber-gloved fingers flying, to untangle the silvery supple salmon from the web. Meanwhile, the new skipper scanned for a position for the next set or prepared to run back a couple miles to the old spot. This way we managed to fish around the clock, twenty-four hours or thirty-six hours, or however long the fishing opener was.

I quickly learned that one of the main fringe benefits of fishing is watching wildlife. Orcas patrol the outside beaches for unwary seals and sea lions, which in turn hunt for salmon. Noisy glaucous-winged gulls hover in tight flocks and take turns plopping into the water after silvery hooligan. Dark lithe jaegers chase clumsy gulls to steal their fish. Graceful white Arctic terns, swift and fast, make clownish puffins seem even more ungainly. Small charcoal storm petrels flit and fuss near the sea surface, completely at home with the waves. I learned to watch for shearwaters as harbingers of storms. These big, dark, graceful seabirds appear just before big blows like vultures circling to find a kill. When storm winds follow, shearwaters play at the turbulent sea surface, gliding just above lumpy waves and swells.

It is small wonder that marine insurers consider the Copper River Flats to be the most dangerous salmon fishery in the world, but I loved it all—the moods of the sea, the energy of the storms, the dynamics of the fishing fleet, my partner, and the creatures going on about their business. I felt connected to something way bigger than myself, something real.

Closures and Community

During closures we commuted back to town—four to six hours or more if the weather was bad or the tide was wrong. Once back in town we switched from tide time to town time. We delivered iced fish to the seafood processors, scrubbed the fish holds, and took showers at the Copper River Fishermen's Cooperative, "The Co-op," where we sold our fish. We usually pulled the net off the boat onto the dock and stretched it its full twenty-three-foot depth, stacking the cork line and lead line at either end. I mended the net while Danny tinkered with the engine, hydraulics, or other pieces of equipment that needed endless attention. It was a division of labor that suited both of us. I liked working with the mending needle and gossamer twine, weaving new strands of web where harbor seals or Steller sea lions had torn fish from the net. I found I grew quickly frustrated in the confined, stinky engine room space with the rusty too-hard-to-turn nuts. It didn't seem to bother Danny. We ate out, always alert for rumors of who caught fish and where. We slept on our boat in the harbor to save money and keep an eye on who was doing what.

One of the best ways to figure out what was going on in town and out on "the fishing grounds" was at a Co-op salmon barbeque. It was one of the few places where highliners, rookies, tendermen, net hangers, and net menders all mingled—and everyone was in a good mood. The Co-op was always looking to recruit members, so the barbeques were frequent.

The five-year-old company was owned and operated by fishermen who believed that bled and iced fish would fetch a quality price. The Co-op usually matched "grounds price," the competitive price offered by the other seafood processors to fishermen on the fishing grounds. Then in the spring, the Co-op kicked back to its members any profits from the previous season's fish sales. The rest of the fleet tolerated the Co-op with its disproportionate number of "eggheads" or highly educated (most townspeople thought overeducated) folks, because it usually drove up the grounds price for the benefit of all. The Co-op's pioneering niche market efforts led to Copper River reds and kings becoming a household name in Japan, where the fish commanded premium prices.

Wives and children usually came to the barbeques. That made a world of difference for me. Fishing was mostly a world full of men. I didn't realize how wearying that was until one day when I was grocery shopping. I was standing in the produce section looking over the lettuce when I suddenly realized that I felt completely relaxed and peaceful. I froze so as not to chase the feelings off and focused on my surroundings. Women were all around, chatting away to each other—and *not* about boat engines, fish, or weather. After that, I made a point to befriend women in town.

I struck gold with Linden O'Toole at a Co-op barbeque. She and her husband Sam were usually mending gear on the docks during closures with their toddler Malani, baby Makena, and dog Sparkle. While Linden was teaching me how to sew a patch into a net, she and I made the happy discovery that we were both eggheads who had escaped the urban grind.

Linden had literally hiked away from nearly completing a doctorate in natural resource planning and management at Virginia Tech. After studying human use patterns in Colorado and Montana wilderness areas, her restless feet drew her north to Alaska, where she worked in Anchorage as a state land use planner. Drawn to wilder areas, she moved on and rented a tiny cabin at Sheep Mountain along a particularly beautiful stretch of the Glenn Highway. There, between alpine tundra and a shrub-spruce forest, overlooking the upper Matanuska Valley, and flanked by the Talkeetna and Chugach Mountains, her heart found peace.

She earned money for simple needs by contracting on and off with state planners on a scenic highway study and herring fishing in Cordova. Like me, she loved the freedom and self-regulated pace of the fishing lifestyle. Linden met Sam, light of heart and full of music, at the Talkeetna Bluegrass Festival. He, too, shared the fishing bug.

Now, the couple was saving their earnings from crew jobs and net mending to buy a seine permit and boat to fish together as a family. When not fishing, they traveled the state to music festivals, spending falls and springs at Sheep Mountain and winters in Hawaii, camping on beaches distant from tourist haunts. The O'Toole family became a nucleus for friends to gather to share stories, laughs, food, and music at the Co-op. When Sam reached for his guitar, others pulled instruments from net lockers and trucks. Music and song filled long twilight nights as children danced and played in net piles.

Sometimes there was enough time during closures to explore town. Cordova is the hub of Area E, the state fish and game management unit that includes the Copper River Flats and Prince William Sound. The town has one of the largest boat harbors in the state. Nearly 60 percent of the fishermen who held limited entry fishing permits for Area E lived locally, which is unusually high in Alaska. The small community of 2,500 doubles in size when out-of-town fishermen return, often with their families, and the major fish processors bring in crew to work the "slime lines," processing herring, salmon, halibut, and cod. Nearly half of the town's workforce is directly employed in fish harvesting or processing. Most of the town's other businesses provide goods and services for the fleet—groceries, restaurants, bars, fuel, outdoor clothing, and all manner of parts for boats, engines, and nets. One can easily find an O-ring seal for a hydraulic motor or a U-joint for an outdrive unit, but not a bra, not in Cordova.

For six months from April through September, the community is a nonstop buzz of efficient action, spinning like clockwork around the needs of the fishing fleet and the processors. Millions of pounds of seafood are harvested during this time, brought into town, processed into fresh, fresh-frozen, or canned salmon and other products, and shipped out of the roadless seaport by air or sea to buyers worldwide.

The fisheries bring tens of millions of dollars into town. By 1987, when the federal government first included Cordova in its annual ranking of the nation's seaports, Cordova rated among the top ten in harvest value, sharing this distinction with much larger seaports like New Bedford in Massachusetts, Kodiak and Dutch Harbor in Alaska, and gulf ports in Louisiana and Texas. The community and state capitalize on the seafood harvest by sharing a raw fish tax of 3 percent of the harvest value. This tax contributed about 15 percent of the town's general fund revenues.

To help stabilize personal income and community revenues, Cordova fishermen successfully lobbied the state legislature in 1974 to enact several bills aiding development of salmon hatcheries, which were seen as a way to overcome the vagaries of the cyclic wild salmon runs. Startup of the hatcheries in Prince William Sound was a huge cooperative effort. The cities of Cordova and Valdez each contributed $5,000 as seed money. Most fishermen voluntarily contributed two cents per fish from the Flats and three cents per fish from the Sound, and processors matched the fishermen's contribution.

By 1986 when Danny and I entered the fishery, the state and the new nonprofit Prince William Sound Aquaculture Corporation (PWSAC or "piz-WACK") were each operating two salmon hatcheries, while the private Valdez Fisheries Development Association operated another one. The aquaculture system collectively produced eighteen million pink salmon in 1987, making it the largest salmon ranching program in the world.

Summer Fishing in Prince William Sound

In late June, Danny and I made the move, along with most of the fleet of 500 gillnetters, to fish "the other side" of Area E—Prince William Sound. The Sound and the Flats are a study in contrasts.

The Sound is a glaciated fjord system about ten times the size of the Copper River Delta. The 3,000-mile coastline is deeply crenulated, intricately carved by icy fingers of past glaciers. Seventeen great tidewater glaciers remain from the past age of ice. Each descends abruptly from the towering Chugach and Kenai Mountains to the sea. Great plows of past ice had furrowed the sea bottom to depths of over a mile in some places, such as off the northwest end of Knight Island. These temperate glaciers are fed by tremendous snowfall—400 to 800 inches annually in the mountains. High and highly variable rainfall at sea level—over 300 inches annually on part of Montague Island—produce a lush temperate rainforest of Sitka spruce and western hemlock, stretching from the rocky coast right up to the timberline at 1,500 feet. The shoreline drops off sharply into fathoms and fathoms of water, nearly eliminating the worry over snagging gear.

The Sound is one of the most tectonically active regions in the world and has been for some time. The main entrance to the Sound is an eight-mile gap between two large rocky islands, Montague and Hinchinbrook, rafted into place by a migrant tectonic plate from a distant past. The trembles and quakes are reminders that ancient creative forces still percolate deep under the earth's mantle.

On Good Friday in March 1964, the most violent earthquake ever recorded in North America—9.2 on the Richter scale—was centered in the northwest corner of the Sound. This sudden shift of tectonic plates rearranged over 100,000 square miles of the earth's crust. Parts of Montague Island shot up thirty-five feet, while Harriman Fjord sank six feet. Chenega Island slid over fifty feet to the south. Seventy-five lives were lost across the

Sound as tsunamis swept through the area. Chenega was obliterated and lost 30 percent of its population within four minutes of the first tremor. The industrial heart of Valdez was destroyed—its harbor, waterfront, and downtown area. Valdez and Chenega were both relocated and rebuilt. Cordova and the other two communities in the Sound were spared wholesale destruction, but the Copper River area was uplifted and became too shallow for seine boats to fish.

In the Sound, the gillnet fleet first targeted red salmon, returning in pulses in early July to a few major lake systems like the Coghill River drainage in the northwest Sound. After the Coghill run, most gillnetters stayed to fish the lower-priced pinks and dogs. The fleet spread out, fishing near beaches with wild pink streams or where migrating pinks and chums swept around headlands. It was a volume fishery, a lot of picking for the money, but many fishermen preferred the low-stress option to adrenaline-charged fishing on the Flats all summer.

We became festive when the fish and tide weren't running hard. Once we set our net at slack ebb, rowed our dinghy to the beach, scrambled up a hill, and picked blueberries in a muskeg-covered meadow while watching the *Ambergris* fish. The former owners of the *Ambergris* had told us, "The angels sing at Coghill." We heard them that day up in the meadows.

Pinks are the smallest of the five salmon species and the dominant species in the Sound—and had been even before the hatchery system artificially boosted their numbers. Unlike the few larger red salmon streams, there are about a thousand small wild pink salmon streams, often so small that a person hiking in the woods could easily just step across them. Many of these streams are in the southwest Sound, where over 75 percent of the streams had become too steep for salmon to ascend after the land had been pushed abruptly upward by the '64 earthquake. Wild pink salmon, and some of the larger chum and silver salmon, adapted to the too-steep streams by spawning instead on intertidal beaches where the freshwater met the sea.

The seine fleet targets the schooling salmon—the pinks and dogs—near the hatchery entrances. The gillnetters usually kept clear of the seine fleet. The *Ambergris*, a gillnetter, is half the length and a fifth the tonnage of the seine boats. Further, seine skippers, with their four-man (rarely women) crew and two-month season, pack attitudes. Once, when we fished a rocky headland near the Esther Island hatchery, we watched a purse seine operation. The heavy seine was laid out in a blur of flying corks and black web as a

crewman in a small sturdy jitney—packing the same horsepower engine as
our boat—pulled one end of the net directly from the back deck of the seiner,
while the two boats roared away from each other. Working together, the seiner
and jitney kept the heavy net perpendicular to the rock wall of the beach as
fish built up on one side of the net. Then the two boats pulled the ends of the
net together into a big circle of web. The crew quickly closed or "pursed" the
bottom of the net, corralling the milling fish. Then the crew hauled aboard the
seine and its payload of salmon with much commotion.

There was plenty else to watch besides seiners because, like the Copper
River Flats, the Sound pulsed with life. I found the birdlife fascinating with all
of the different shapes, colors, sounds, and behaviors. Birds were constantly in
the air or on the water—and busy! The Sound is thick with bald eagles—3,000
by official counts or about the same amount as in the entire Lower 48 at the
time. I watched them swoop on the sea surface and pull out wriggling salmon
with clenched talons. Black-legged kittiwakes, Arctic terns, and some of the
gulls hurtled their bodies from on high, diving into schools of juvenile herring
or salmon. Other gulls, sea ducks, cormorants, pigeon guillemots, and loons
dipped, dabbled, or dove from the sea surface and left glistening swirls of tiny
bubbles in their wakes. Horned puffins popped to the surface like buoyant
corks, their bright orange and yellow beaks clamping small fish. Harder to spot
were the shy marbled murrelets that whizzed out of the coastal forest at dusk to
feed and whizzed back at dawn—feathery bullets reaching speeds of 100 miles
per hour. One would never guess that marbled murrelets are one of the Sound's
most abundant seabirds with an estimated population of 550,000.

Marine mammals were everywhere. About 3,000 sea otters lived in the
Sound. We could tell when the adult females were foraging underwater for
clams, sea urchins, and other delicacies by the mewling and sharp cries of
pups left floating on the surface. Harbor seals, sea lions, and porpoise pursued
herring and salmon. Once a pod of porpoise chased a school of wild pink
salmon into our net. It surprised all of us. That calm sunny July day erupted
as our net danced, alive with fish, while porpoise catapulted into the air like
popcorn to avoid the web wall.

We learned there are two types of orcas, each with distinct sounds. The
whistling, moaning "resident pods" frequent the Sound and fish for herring
and salmon. The "transient stocks" roam the North Pacific and occasionally
sweep through the Sound, hunting for seals and sea lions with machine gun–
like staccato clicks. We always knew when orcas were coming—seals and sea
lions swarmed at the surface, heads underwater, listening to the whale sounds.

With resident pods, seals and sea lions just went on about their business, but with transient whales, the hunted would clear out. Some friends witnessed orcas attack and devour an adult sea lion. One showed me what was left after the mayhem—quarter-sized bits of skin and fur.

We mostly stayed on our boat in the Sound during closures, as did many other fishermen whose families joined them for the summer. My parents visited, sharing our life and the Sound. One evening, my father sat contentedly on a buoy ball on deck, nursing a scotch on a chip of glacier ice and surveying half a dozen glaciers at the head of Port Wells. Recalling high school days in Europe, he mused, "This is like fishing in Switzerland!" We rafted with other boats and had deck parties with grilled salmon or rockfish, while children swung on buoys and climbed around on the boats long into the sunlit evenings. We set shrimp pots, sport-fished, and explored the bays, beaches, meadows, and forests of a wilderness the size of West Virginia.

The other four communities in the Sound took some looking to find, like needles in a haystack, but more than just mountains and sea separates these communities. The Alaska Native villages of Chenega in the southwestern Sound, and Tatitlek just east of Bligh Island, are in a cultural world of difference. The villagers draw from the sea part of their spiritual foundation. Yet "subsistence culture" is a too-simple English phrase for the intricate weaving of generations through time with stories, dance, hunting, gathering, and sharing wild foods. Villagers from the Sound often visit relatives in the Native Village of Eyak, subsumed by Cordova, to strengthen their cultural bonds through potlatches and ceremonies.

In the two other towns in the Sound, Whittier in Passage Canal to the west of Cordova and Valdez to the north, life is largely divorced from the Sound's natural rhythms. The only way in or out of Whittier was by boat or train. The train floods an assortment of sports fishers, cruise ship tourists, sea kayakers, sailboat guides, and visitors into town, and then ebbs them back out again like the tide. Danny and I and other fishermen swelled the tide when we caught the train to Anchorage during closures. Whittier's 300 residents are indistinguishable in this constant shuffle of humanity, and I assumed that many existed by catering to it.

Valdez has a different flavor altogether. It was, and still is, a company town, made rich by taxing and catering to the oil industry. The northernmost ice-free port in Alaska, Valdez is the terminus for the Trans-Alaska Pipeline System (TAPS) that stretches all the way to the North Slope and Prudhoe Bay. The consortium Alyeska operates the 800-mile pipeline and terminal on behalf of seven oil company owners—but only three really matter. BP (British Petroleum), Exxon, and ARCO (Atlantic Richfield Company) owned over 90 percent of the oil delivery system. The terminal, imposing and foreboding with its collection of machinery and buildings, sits across the bay and dwarfs the town of 3,500. Huge tankers slide silently in and out of the port as they come to load oil.

In Valdez, the tide is oil and it is always a flood tide; it never ebbs. Valdez taxes the tide—or at least the property that the tide flows through, including the terminal and some of the pipeline within the city's limits. A few businesses in Valdez depend on the Sound for fishing and tourism, but this is a trickle compared to the revenues from the oil stream. Twice in its history Valdez had a raucous frontier nature—once during the 1898 gold rush and again during pipeline construction in the 1970s. After the town rebuilt from the 1964 earthquake, it lost much of its gaiety and, when life settled back down after pipeline construction, things became almost somber. Oil is serious business.

Fall Silvers on the Flats

With great trepidation, Danny and I returned to fish silvers on the Flats in mid-August, "fall" in Alaska. To our huge relief, it was nothing like spring fishing. Silvers only ran on the flood and some of the best fishing was "Inside," back between the barrier islands in a myriad of sloughs, not out in the open sea. We learned how to time a low-water set so we wouldn't get swept out to sea by the last of the ebb. We learned to wait for the tide to turn, pushing fish out of eddies and holes into the slough channels where we drifted.

Day and night lost all meaning—what mattered was flood or ebb, a pulse of water that reversed every six hours. On ebb tides we slept fitfully, listening to the rushing silt-laden water rasp our anchored hull inches from our heads. At low water and on flood tides, we fished. During quiet early mornings, we often fished in dense fog, feeling our way slowly across the shallow channel and listening for growling engines of nearby boats. By September, darkness returned after months of daylight. During night fishing, the fleet transformed into a study of lights—red and green running lights, tiny white masthead lights for boats anchored or fishing, and even tinier white buoy lights to mark the end of a net. But the real show was on clear nights when fluorescent lime green northern lights arced and danced in star-studded skies.

When the trough of low pressure in the gulf regained its winter fury and the fall storms started in earnest, Danny and I called it quits for the season. We had barely broken even, but we hadn't sunk our boat. By late September, we joined the main exodus of fishermen leaving town as we headed to different parts of Alaska to find winter work so we could afford our fishing habit.

CHAPTER TWO

POLITICS OF OIL

1987

The *Ambergris* floated easily on the gentle swell undulating our cork line that stretched to the beach. It was June 1987. Our second season had started much like our first with plenty of heart-pounding, adrenaline-rushing forays to literally write home about. The only difference was that this season we were catching fish, lots of fish. Family and friends loved hearing stories of our misadventures.

But the excitement of the early season had passed. With the first spring storms, we had regained our sea legs. The spring bird migration had waned as millions of western sandpipers and dunlins, like swarms of black ants on the beaches, pressed further west and north to start families. The baby harbor seals had grown strong and smart enough to avoid being swept out of their safe shallow nurseries into the open sea where hungry orcas had waited, patrolling the coastline. Even the orcas had moved on. I was restless. I needed new stories to tell.

"Maybe we should go try a breaker set. I need something exciting to write about."

Danny was scanning radio channels and watching for boat movement to gain clues as to where the fish might be this opener. Without lowering his binoculars, he said, "Maybe you should try writing fiction."

Instead, I got involved with fishing industry politics.

Getting Involved

It started innocently enough. When we pulled our boat out of the water in fall, I decided to stay in Cordova through the winter and see what I could do to repay the good fortune we received from the sea.

I found a place to house-sit for the winter. It was an A-frame, originally built by materials flown in by helicopter. The cabin perched high on a hill about three miles out of town with a spectacular view of Orca Inlet and the

Heney Range. The half-mile road up to the cabin was not maintained in the winter. The cabin was drafty, poorly insulated, and completely exposed to the southeast, the direction of winter storms. There was an outhouse, but no running water. There was a wood stove, but no wood.

Danny was highly skeptical. I protested, "I want to live like real Alaskans."

"'Real Alaskans live in trailers,'" he quipped, quoting a TV ad. He went to Anchorage and, anticipating my arrival soon after the snow flew, found us a place to live and reclaimed his job in a ski shop.

I settled into the winter routine and made an important discovery. After the bustle of the summer season, after the out-of-towners left, after most of the processors closed for the winter, the community breathed a collective sigh of relief—and started to unfurl its soul. There were evening potlucks where friends shared stories, music, and food—salmon, halibut, deer, moose, and wild berry jams and pies. The community was like an extended family with an easygoing atmosphere that wore like a favorite pair of jeans. It just felt good. Winter was a time of renewal, a quiet time to restore one's spirit, participate in community activities, and work on political issues.

Just about everyone in town attended the annual fall town meeting. The only place large enough to hold the town's 2,500 people is the high school gymnasium. I squeezed into a spot in the packed bleachers and gazed in wonder at the sea of people filling the seats on the playing courts and every square foot of bleachers. Swarms of children raced around the aisles. White-haired elders, some in wheelchairs with oxygen tanks, sat with their families. I felt my chest tighten with a strange sense of civic pride. This was democracy in action! People had come to speak, and listen, and most importantly, be part of the decision-making process that defined the community's future. People clearly cared about each other and the community. The love and commitment were palpable. This was one of the things I had missed in other places—a sense of belonging and caring like I had learned in Wisconsin from my father. Here was a whole community of doers. For the first time ever, I felt I was home.

In September, I was elected to the board of the Copper River Fishermen's Cooperative and appointed as its delegate to the board of United Fishermen of Alaska (UFA). As an organization of organizations, UFA is a powerful political voice for Alaska's commercial fishing industry, representing about 18,000 fishermen—drift gillnetters, set-netters, seiners, long-liners, crabbers, and trollers. I knew virtually nothing about commercial fishing politics—and very little about politics in general. But I figured I could learn.

I attended a board meeting of the Cordova District Fishermen United (CDFU) to learn about political issues of concern to local fishermen. Eight burly bearded fishermen were packed into a small ten-by-sixteen-foot office overlooking the harbor. The secretary was squished behind a desk littered with files and ashtrays. I squeezed into the circle, listening as the group discussed local gear issues, the statewide threat posed by finfish farming, amendments to the federal Marine Mammals Protection Act, and what to do about Alyeska.

"Alyeska? What's going on at Alyeska? Maybe I can help there," I ventured. Eight faces turned toward me, each etched with a mixture of scorn and disbelief. "I have a master's in oil pollution and a doctorate in sediment pollution," I said defensively. Expressions changed to incredulity.

"I nominate Riki Ott for the board of directors," said CDFU president Bob Blake, a local and longtime political dynamo, widely respected for his dedication to fish politics. Bob was also the lobbyist for the City of Cordova in Juneau, Alaska's capital. "Second," said Ross Mullins from somewhere deep behind a bushy white beard. Within moments I was on the board.

Bob, swarthy with black hair and a trim beard, was the lead on Alyeska issues. He quickly briefed me. "We're convinced they're polluting the water in Port Valdez from that ballast water treatment plant and that they're going to hurt our fisheries," he said. "Christ, they could be polluting all of Prince William Sound for all we know! We've been saying so for three years now, but no one listens to us. The Alyeska scientists and lawyers—they won't even talk to us."

Bob placed a foot-high stack of papers on my lap. "Here, read these. Then call Chuck Hamel." He pointed to a phone number scrawled across the top page of an official-looking document with no further explanation. "There's an EPA hearing on Alyeska's discharge permit November 5 in Valdez. You can write our comments and testify at the hearing." He heaved a deep sigh of relief. "I'm going moose hunting."

Apparently, it was my turn to be "it."

A Wake-Up Call

I did my homework.

It turned out CDFU's history was all tangled up with that of the young state, the discovery of the largest oilfield in North America, and the oil companies that sought their fortunes on Alaska's North Slope. Bits and pieces of the story were in CDFU's archived boxes of testimony, hearings, and news clips. Ross and his wife, Sheelagh, shared their story, filling in the gaps.

Ross had moved to Cordova to fish in the mid-1960s, just a couple years before ARCO struck black gold in Prudhoe Bay—and a couple years before he and Sheelagh had married. It was the largest oil discovery in North America, and it cemented oil's lead over commercial fishing as Alaska's chief money earner—a lead oil had held for just a year. Millionaire real estate developer Governor Walter Hickel aimed state bulldozers north from Fairbanks and turned them loose to blaze an overland road across tundra, river, and mountain straight to the North Slope oilfields to open up the Arctic for oil exploration. Oilmen flowed up the Hickel Highway.

Ross's interest in what happens when big oil comes to town heightened. In January 1969, he followed newscasts of a catastrophic oil well blowout that spewed over 200,000 gallons of black crude into the blue waters of California's Santa Barbara Channel. Images of dead and dying oil-coated wildlife horrified the nation. Ross was stunned to see people using straw—*straw*—to try to soak up the oil on stained beaches. He was incredulous that oil spill cleanup technology was so primitive. Then, just nine months later, the tank barge *Florida* ran aground in Buzzards Bay, Massachusetts, and spilled 185,000 gallons of heating oil. Ross and Sheelagh watched the news—taped in Anchorage and flown to Cordova a week later—showing marshes and beaches near West Falmouth plastered with oil, dead lobsters, scud, and cod.

For Ross, these oil spills were a wake-up call. It was then that he launched a slowly mounting battle to protect Alaska's waters and his own livelihood from similar catastrophes. But not everyone equated oil with danger. Alaska had just netted $900 million by auctioning off 450,000 acres adjacent to Prudhoe Bay—enough to cover the state's operating budget for over four years. Hickel's successor, Governor Keith Miller, called the sale "the rendezvous of our dreams." State politicians were acting giddy. The big three oil companies operating on the North Slope—British Petroleum (BP), ARCO, and Humble, a subsidiary of Standard Oil of New Jersey (now ExxonMobil)—had announced their choice for an oil transportation route: an 800-mile pipeline along the "Hickel Highway" from the North Slope to the ice-free Port Valdez. They planned to ship oil by tanker through Prince William Sound.

And right there was where Ross had a problem. He thought the all-land route through Canada might be a better option for fishermen; it would keep oil out of the Sound altogether. Ross found that CDFU's executive director, Harold Hanson, had written a few letters to the Miller Administration, voicing concern that this project be "done right." The state's responses, he said, "were just platitudes: 'Don't worry, everything will be fine.'" Ross was certain that things "weren't likely to be fine without a hell of a lot more oversight."

Knute Johnson, the president of Cordova Aquatic Marketing Association, was more receptive to Ross's concerns: he sounded an immediate alert to area fishermen. More than 100 fishermen jammed a meeting hall. They needed money to fend off the advances of big oil. They unanimously voted in a self-assessed one-cent levy on each fish they caught. Then they set out to build a war chest.

Ross and Knute immediately began working full-time to block the pipeline route to Port Valdez and reroute it through Canada.

Our Way of Life Is Threatened

After the 1970 fishing season, Cordova fishermen redoubled their efforts. Ross and Sheelagh gathered information about the spills in Santa Barbara and Buzzards Bay. Max Blumer, a well-known geochemist at the Woods Hole Oceanographic Institute near Buzzards Bay, had found that spilled oil migrated through beach sediments and caused lingering harm to sea life at very low levels of oil.

In mid-January, Sheelagh, sitting with a sick baby in Anchorage, watched television images of another California oil spill from two Chevron tankers colliding under the Golden Gate Bridge. Even at one-tenth the size of the Santa Barbara blowout, spilled oil wreaked havoc, killing birds and coating shorelines. Sheelagh's take on the situation was this: "If you guys don't get off your arses and *do something*, we're going to end up in a real fix."

The proverbial last straw for the fishermen was the draft environmental impact statement for the pipeline, released by the U.S. Interior Department just three days before the California spill. The 246-page document devoted only two pages to the threat of marine pollution after stating that tankers posed more of an environmental threat than a pipeline. Ross testified at Anchorage hearings about the need for baseline data in Prince William Sound so, in the event of a large spill, scientists could determine damages to fish and wildlife. He felt that no one in Anchorage listened, but in all, thirty-seven volumes of public comment from around the nation were generated during the two-month public comment period and most of it was critical of the project.

That winter CDFU sent Ross and Knute Johnson, among others, to

Washington, D.C. to try to get at least some tacit support from the Alaska congressional delegation for the alternative Canadian route. Only the single Alaska congressman offered them hope that their concerns would be considered. That was Nick Begich, who died in a small plane crash near Whittier the following year. Senator Ted Stevens, now renowned for his relentless support of the oil industry, told the fishermen that he was assured not one drop of oil would touch the waters of Prince William Sound—words that the fishermen would remember.

Faced with the prospect that, as one fisherman put it, "our way of life is threatened and nobody seems to give a damn," the fishermen played their last card. They filed a lawsuit against the federal district court, claiming the U.S. Department of Agriculture broke its own regulations by leasing too much land to the oil companies for the terminal. Their legal challenge followed on the heels of two others. One, filed by five Alaska Native villages in the proposed pipeline corridor, claimed that the oil companies had failed to honor a promise to hire Native contractors in trade for an agreement by the Natives to waive their land claims to the proposed right-of-way corridor. The second, filed by a coalition of environmental groups, claimed the federal government had not adequately considered alternatives. These three lawsuits were consolidated and became the first major test of the 1970 National Environmental Policy Act. They also launched an era of oil-related litigation that would raise hopes, crush dreams, and continue to pepper the court system to the present day.

Cordova fishermen quickly became unpopular in the young state. "You don't want oil?" growled Democratic Governor Bill Egan over the telephone one day to Ross Mullins. "Then I won't give you any goddamned oil! I'll block off all shipments into Cordova! See how far your fishing boats will get!"

The *Cordova Times* editor, a proponent of oil development, began a statewide smear campaign. "Fishermen were made to look like a bunch of agitators, almost like communists," Ross recalled.

By January 1972, a federal judge had ruled that the U.S. Interior Department was in compliance with all environmental requirements. The Cordova fishermen appealed, but political forces had already begun to slowly extinguish other sparks of opposition. Alaska Native land claims, valued at one billion dollars, would be paid from royalties on oil production. Public comment on the final environmental impact statement was largely quelled by limiting public access. The nine-volume tome was strategically placed at only seven locations around the country—and only accessible during office hours of government agencies.

Over the next year, the U.S. District Court of Appeals reversed the lower court's decision, ruling that the pipeline project could not be approved until Congress amended the Mineral Leasing Act to allow more land withdrawal for the vast farm of oil holding tanks in Port Valdez. Ross said, "Our lawsuit had them stymied."

Promises for Permits

Oilmen turned to Congress for support. Company officials gushed promises like oil from the Santa Barbara blowout. Alyeska promised to "build the best engineered pipeline in the world." Further, Alyeska promised, "(T)he most up-to-date equipment for containment and recovery of the oil will be available at the terminal." ARCO fleet captain Emery Winkler testified, "that all steps will be taken to insure that the most up-to-date navigational and marine procedures will be followed in tanker operations planned for this area." BP's L. R. Beynon promised that the "best equipment, materials, and expertise, which will be made available as part of the oil spill contingency plan, will make operations at Port Valdez and in Prince William Sound the safest in the world." Beynon also assured Congress, "We have adequate knowledge for dealing with oil spills."

In private, oilmen were saying other things. Exxon's Ken Fountain told lobbyists, "I don't care if every goddamn fish dies, get that [authorization] permit. . . ."

The Nixon administration also pushed strongly for pipeline approval, assuring Congress that newly constructed U.S. vessels carrying TAPS oil to U.S. ports would have double bottoms and segregated ballast systems that would allow only minimal amounts of oily water to enter Port Valdez.

For fishermen, this was a critical pledge. Fishermen knew that TAPS tankers would take on millions of gallons of seawater after unloading millions of gallons of oil at distant ports. Seawater acts as ballast to stabilize empty tankers on the return voyage. In most older single-hull tankers, the seawater ballast becomes contaminated with residual oil as it sloshes around inside the tanker's cargo holds. This creates millions of gallons of oily ballast water that have to be emptied before oil can be loaded. The oily seawater then needs to be treated to remove oil before it can be discharged into the ocean. In newer tankers, clean seawater is carried in specially designated ballast holds separate from cargo holds.

The Nixon administration's pledge meant only minimal oily seawater would be created by tanker operations. Significantly, the administration also pledged a tanker ballast water treatment facility "to eliminate as much oil from these wastes as technologically practicable" prior to discharge into Port Valdez.

By November 1973, the pipeline battle was over. In a tiebreaking vote cast by Vice President Spiro Agnew in the U.S. Senate, Congress passed the Tran-Alaska Pipeline Authorization Act. It had taken a national energy crisis, heavy-handed limits to public access, and two acts of Congress to authorize the pipeline project—and the final bill included an amendment by Alaska's senators foreclosing further court-ordered delays and judicial review based on environmental laws.

Cordova fishermen were stunned. Congress had authorized the massive pipeline project *based almost entirely on promises and assurances made by oilmen.* Very few promises had been codified into law.

"In a sense," Ross observed, "when the government took the TAPS project out of the venue where citizens could influence it and just arbitrarily went ahead with it, the government assumed a moral obligation to oversee the pipeline and protect the people from TAPS spills."

Fishermen soon learned there is no institutional life to promises.

Once the oil companies had their authorization permit, they launched an aggressive campaign *against* double-bottom tankers. Within two years, the Coast Guard changed its mind and no longer supported double-bottom tankers. Oilmen also began to renege on other promised safety measures.

Fishermen turned to the state for support, and eventually, Alaska passed a law giving Coast Guard–like authority to state agencies to regulate tanker traffic and control port pollution. That law mandated some safety features that would stave off boat collisions, but only encouraged others—double-hull tankers and segregated ballast among them. It also prohibited discharge of oil and ballast water in state waters and established an incentive tax on shippers. The more safety features shippers incorporated and the better ship they had, the less money they had to contribute to the Coastal Protection Fund.

This new law essentially codified oilmen's pre-pipeline promises. However, the oil companies sued the state to overturn it. And they prevailed. The fishermen watched helplessly as the legislature eviscerated the state's regulatory framework for oversight, slashed the state budget for environmental monitoring, and eliminated all funding for tanker and oil terminal safety inspections.

The state only appealed one decision, insisting that Alaska had a right to regulate ballast water discharge. The move was successful, but this meant the state now shouldered responsibility for enforcing Alyeska's compliance with federal discharge permits and laws. Fishermen were skeptical that the state would fulfill this mandate.

By the mid-1980s, virtually all of the other protections promised by oilmen in trade for public trust and authorizing permits gradually eroded, along with the promised vigilance by oversight agencies.

The promise of double-bottom tankers? Gone. BP blatantly converted three of its double-bottom tanker charters, the *Prince William Sound, Tonsina*, and *Kenai*, to single-hull tankers by drilling through the inner cargo walls to access the space in the double walls and carry more oil.

The promised state-of-the-art vessel traffic control system? Gone. The Coast Guard, under pressure from the oilmen to cut costs, replaced its top-of-the-line radar system with a cheaper one that didn't fully cover the area of operation in the Sound—but Coast Guard personnel, rather than a more expensive civilian team, could maintain the downgraded version.

Coast Guard training standards for pilots responsible for shepherding the huge tankers safely through the Sound? Slashed because of oil industry pressure.

Coast Guard minimum crew size standards? Slashed because of oil industry pressure to save money on the new highly automated tankers.

The promised "best equipment, materials, and expertise" for oil spill contingency plans? Gone. Cheaper equipment was substituted, equipment shortfalls were routine, and spill drills were conducted sloppily and infrequently.

Fishermen soon learned that oil companies had found other ways to cut costs to maximize their profits.

Midnight Dumping Grounds

For Cordova fishermen, loss of the promised double-bottom tankers increased the likelihood of oil pollution in their fishing grounds. Single-hull tankers substantially increase the risk of spills during grounding and collisions. They also create a huge risk of contamination. In acknowledgment of fishermen's concerns, the ballast water treatment plant was one of the few promises that was actually mandated by the pipeline act.

The ballast water treatment plant in Valdez was, in theory, designed to remove most of the oil from the seawater ballast before it flowed into Port

Valdez. But was the treatment plant working as designed? The answer required monitoring of daily discharge and enforcement of water quality standards.

I knew part of this history from my academic training. After the Clean Water Act passed in 1972, scientists all over the country had worked to determine "safe" levels of oil and other chemicals that could be discharged into the nation's waterways without harming wildlife or the millions of people who swam, fished, and boated in rivers and along seashores. The EPA eventually established water-quality standards for oil with the caveat that each state could set stricter standards to further limit the amount of poisons entering public waters.

Alaska had passed the most stringent state standards for oil in the nation in 1979. Oilmen hadn't objected, but they didn't need to: the state and the EPA poked a hole in the law.

To help oil companies meet the state standard, the EPA with Alaska's blessing authorized a small mixing zone for the ballast water-treatment plant. Mixing zones are loopholes in the Clean Water Act. They are zones where industry is allowed to legally pollute public waterways—as long as the poison is diluted enough to meet water quality standards at the mixing zone boundaries. In other words, in mixing zones "the solution to pollution is dilution." The state and federal regulatory agencies assumed Alyeska would have no trouble meeting the state's water quality standards at the edges of the mixing zone. But just to make sure, the EPA hired one of the world's leading experts on ballast water and oily sludge treatment to monitor the treatment plant discharge.

That consultant was Dr. Ihor Lysyj ("LEE-see"). Lysyj was part of the Ukrainian diaspora to the United States and Canada during World War II. He was talented and honest, with an engineer's mind for details and precision. Lysyj found that oil, grease, heavy metals, and other pollutants were entering the receiving waters of Port Valdez in uncontrolled quantities. In other words, Alyeska was illegally polluting Port Valdez. No enforcement action was taken. Instead, the EPA and state renewed Alyeska's discharge permit on the condition that it fix its technical problems and stop polluting the port beyond what was allowed by law, and they increased the area that Alyeska could legally pollute by sixteenfold to accommodate the runaway hydrocarbons—letting Alyeska legally pollute an even larger area of the port where Cordova fishermen seined.

By the mid-1980s, fishermen noticed a blue haze of air pollution in Port Valdez. Ross compared it to "like when you're driving on the New Jersey

Turnpike and you get near Bayonne." According to fishermen, the natural gas fumes were just tremendous. They joked about not lighting any cigarettes. Fishermen were even more concerned about what they couldn't see. How much oil was being discharged into Port Valdez?

In early 1985, eight years after oil started flowing down the pipeline, CDFU's Bob Blake met up with Chuck Hamel, the same man whose number Bob had scribbled on the EPA documents he had handed me with a heavy sigh of relief when I first was seated on the CDFU board.

In his animated aggressive style, Chuck Hamel immediately fired a volley of taunts at Bob. "'They're polluting your water. They're polluting your air. Nothing's working right over at the terminal. Noticed the blue cloud over the terminal? The vapor recovery system—forget it. Those incinerators are just flaring—they're not burning the hydrocarbons like they're supposed to. The ballast water treatment plant is recycling sludge—before they dump in your port. And sludge isn't the worst of it. I've got documents that show those tankers are bringing up all kinds of hazardous and toxic waste. Your port's become a midnight dumping grounds for the whole West Coast tanker trade. You know they're not required to monitor every compound coming out the discharge pipe. No one knows what's coming out—or if it's safe!'" Hamel had documents to back up his claims.

The CDFU board read Hamel's documents with growing anger and dread. The promised state-of-the-art ballast water treatment plant had called for incineration of oily sludge—a black goo of toxic and hazardous substances such as polycyclic aromatic hydrocarbons (PAHs), phenols, and heavy metals. Only treated seawater without sludge and with very low levels of other oil pollutants was supposed to be discharged into Port Valdez. But according to Hamel's documents, the sludge incinerator was never built. Ihor Lysyj, the EPA consultant, calculated that in eight years of operations the plant should have produced enough sludge to cover four football fields three feet deep. Ross said, "We realized there was only one place the highly toxic sludge could be—in the bottom of Port Valdez."

Sludge or not, a general air of complacency had settled over Alaska. That same year every single Alaska resident—man, woman, and child—received a $1,000 check from a trust set up to hold 25 percent of the state's revenues from oil-related mineral leases and oil royalties and disperse dividends to the public. Most residents and politicians fell into step with the oil industry's drumbeat. "There was no way anyone was going to listen to us anymore," lamented Ross.

It didn't take long for CDFU and Chuck Hamel to initiate another lawsuit. This intensified ongoing investigations by federal and state regulators. Soon, the EPA confirmed the fishermen's suspicions and some of Chuck Hamel's allegations. Lysyj compared Alyeska's sludge-handling operations to "vacuuming your house, dumping all the collected dust back on the carpet, and then starting the whole process over again." The EPA ordered Alyeska to stop recycling sludge through its ballast water treatment system and into Port Valdez—and continued its investigations.

That was in 1985, just two years before I showed up at my first CDFU meeting and Bob Blake handed me the paperwork on the latest twist of this saga.

I was sitting in the A-frame in front of the wood stove. Sunlight was streaming in through the windows. Outside, sparkling fresh snow blanketed the foothills of the Heney Range. And on the floor in neat piles were Bob's stack of papers and other documents I had collected. I had read everything and spoken with some of the key players. It was time to act.

Nervously, I picked up the telephone and dialed the number Bob Blake had pointed out to me a couple of weeks earlier.

CHAPTER THREE

PRELUDE TO DISASTER

Across the country in Alexandria, Virginia, a pleasant male voice answered my call. Chuck Hamel had a disarming manner, and within minutes this consummate wheeler-and-dealer and I were talking as if we had known each other for years. He had turned to brokering Alaska pipeline oil after making millions negotiating the resale of oil leases on Alaska's North Slope; but he had lost his lucrative independent oil shipping business after a spat with pipeline owners. Mad about his loss, he had turned to brokering insider information. He had won the confidence of Alyeska employees at the terminal who wanted safer working conditions. He obtained documents from company insiders and aired Alyeska's dirty secrets on air pollution, water pollution, and the dearth of quality maintenance with Congress and the national media. It was a dangerous game for Chuck and the Alyeska employees.

We became day traders, swapping information over the phone. Chuck needed help understanding the science to leverage his claims about pollution. I needed help understanding how the terminal was designed to work so I could offer recommendations to improve operations. Our daily routine lasted, with the exception of summer fishing, for a year and a half, right up to Exxon's big spill.

Escalating the Fray

What I learned from Chuck I passed on to the CDFU board and incorporated into testimonies at various hearings. The mandate of the board was clear: "Just fix the problems at Alyeska and don't paint us green." Commercial fishermen viewed their concerns as separate from those of environmentalists. My first hearing—while Bob Blake was moose hunting—was in Valdez, where the EPA would receive testimonies concerning Aleyska's ballast water discharge permit.

The night before I left to testify, I called my father for advice. A veteran board member of several community and statewide conservation organizations, he had been following my new political activities with great interest. "How do I deal with oil industry attorneys, scientists, and the press?" I asked him. "Stick with what you know," he cautioned. "Stay in your field."

During the six-hour boat ride to Valdez, I worked on my testimony, spreading out papers on a table. As the crew of the M/V *Glacier Spirit* hovered around me, someone blurted out, "Are you testifying for the fishermen?" Surprised, I nodded. "You've *got* to talk with our skipper!" They led the way to the wheelhouse, excitedly presenting me to a tall, solidly built man, bald with a white Abe Lincoln-style beard. His piercing blue eyes twinkled as he offered a meaty hand in greeting. "I've heard about you from Chuck."

Stan Stephens and his family operate the largest locally owned charter boat business in Alaska. Stan spends winters in North Pole near Fairbanks, where he and his wife raised their three daughters, and summers operating out of Valdez. Stan is widely respected for his honesty, integrity, and community service. He regarded the pipeline people as good neighbors and usually included positive commentary about tanker terminal operations during his daily summer charters. But lately he had become worried about all the claims, investigations, and press. His attitude was straightforward, like the fishermen's: "If the terminal isn't working right," said Stan, "let's find out why and fix it."

At the Valdez council chambers the next morning, about half a dozen people had taken time off from work to listen as first the state, then Alyeska, testified about why there were—or weren't—environmental problems created by terminal operations.

The tense mood in the room relaxed when it was the public's turn to testify. As I stepped up to the podium, the black-suited Alyeska officials sitting in the front row, and their support entourage of scientists and lawyers in the middle row, all stashed their notebooks under their seats. When I announced my credentials, the people in the first two rows swooped down to retrieve their notepads, while the public and state officials sitting in the last row broke into excited grins. For half an hour I spoke about what was wrong with terminal operations, what could be done to fix the problems, and why the state should not grant Alyeska's request to relax the state's water quality criteria.

After a long day, I called my father in Wisconsin and gleefully told him that my testimony had surprised everyone. "Surprise only works once," he counseled. "They'll be ready for you next time." I was too naive to suspect what this might entail.

I plunged deeper and deeper into the political arena. Soon I joined some thirty fisher-mostly-men on the board of the United Fishermen of Alaska—the largest coalition of commercial fishermen in the nation at the time. Just months before, the tanker *Glacier Bay*, en route from the Alyeska terminal to Kenai, had hit a submerged rock and spilled 207,000 gallons of crude at the peak of a record sockeye return. Following in its wake were closed fisheries, fouled gear, and lawsuits—along with a heightened awareness about our need for better spill response. Not surprisingly, the event also ushered in heightened efforts by the oil industry to limit its liability for future spills.

Back at the A-frame, I decided to fill the long winter by sharing what I knew about marine oil pollution and what I had learned about problems and fixes at the tanker terminal with the public. People from Rotary clubs to high schools were receptive to ideas to improve Alyeska's operations to protect Prince William Sound. Even politicians listened because Alyeska's track record of pollution and safety issues was raising red flags in a heated congressional debate to open the Arctic National Wildlife Refuge to oil and gas leasing and development. I was deeply satisfied with my work, which I saw as advancing fishermen's concerns to protect the environment.

Just Plain Livin'

To counterbalance the mental challenge, there was the physical challenge of "just plain livin'" as one local put it. I split and stacked three cords of wood—waterlogged spruce, which took a lot of fussing and coaxing to burn. My wood stash lasted until midwinter, well after the cabin and hill were piled high in deep snow. The grade was too steep for a snowmobile to pull up a toboggan-load of wood. So I hauled up five cords by toboggan a few logs at a time, mushing myself up my packed access trail. This was in addition to hauling up groceries and out garbage, up clean laundry and out dirty clothes, and up anything else I wanted and out everything I didn't. I even hauled snow for water.

When Danny realized I was determined to stay, he visited. Once he brought a new pair of telemark skis and patiently taught me to carve turns at the local ski hill, but he had no patience for politics. For the first time in a life packed with activities and housemates, I lived alone. I learned to slow down and soak up each moment. I started to notice things like my heart pounding as I pulled loads uphill, my muscles tightening as I swung the splitting ax, the smell of homemade soup cooking or bread baking, the awe of northern lights dancing and swirling, the lonesome hunger of coyotes howling in the foothills across the valley, and the strength of winter storms shaking the cabin.

Before spring 1988, the O'Toole family moved to Cordova and rented a small home. My afternoon visits often turned into evenings punctuated with meals, music, movies, and stories. Linden and Sam were in hot pursuit of an elusive salmon seine permit for Prince William Sound. They felt that living in their remote cabin at Sheep Mountain hampered this effort. The fishing dream had spread to the children. One night Sam said sturdy two-year-old Makena, sound asleep, had sat bolt upright in bed and declared, "My daddy is a wisherman and I'm gonna' be a wisherman too." Then he had collapsed back into sleep.

With the lengthening daylight and arrival of fishermen, the pulse of life in town quickened. Danny and I took a chance and bought a king net—a large-mesh gill net designed to catch king salmon. It was a net we would only use once—ever as it turned out—before Alaska wildlife managers banned king gear. But it was a memorable "once."

We set in a narrow gutter near Pete Dahl slough, spooling out only part of our new net to avoid ebbing out of the channel as we waited anxiously for slack water. As the current eased, we spooled out more gear. And waited. When the first king hit, we thought it was a seal. The head shot up into the air amid a shower of spray. Then another hit. And another. We watched in amazement. The kings slammed into our gear, churned the silty brown water of the slough white, and sent spray six feet into the air. When the net quieted down after an hour, we picked the gear and found we had won the lottery. The payout was a fish hold full of beautiful thirty- to fifty-pound fish, metallic gray with hues of white silver, blue, and a pale rosy blush. When the bounty was safely in our fish holds, we danced on deck to celebrate our fortune.

Our luck held through the season. One slow August evening in the Sound, we ate a leisurely dinner while our pink net soaked at the entrance to Lake Bay. Twilight deepened as the fleet moved offshore for their night sets. Our cork line started to jiggle like it was possessed. Entire sections of it suddenly sank out of sight. Huge schools of hatchery pink salmon were moving into the bay. We picked our net all night under a sky ablaze with neon green swirling northern lights. A constant rain of fish roiled and jumped all around us. We filled our holds, we filled net bags on top of the holds, and finally we put in our scupper plugs and filled our deck to the rail with silvery bright salmon. As the dusky sky gave way to the dawn, the bay grew quiet. The loon we called Dawn Patrol broke the stillness with its tremulous call as it winged out to the

Sound. The *Ambergris* slowly waddled her way to the tender like a very pregnant woman. News of our delivery woke the fleet into a frenzy of activity, but everyone else was too late. The fish had moved into the inner bay, which was closed to fishing.

We ended the season like we began—by taking a chance on another net. This time it was a deep silver net, one we specifically designed to target the first return of silver salmon to the Esther hatchery. Only one other fisherman in the fleet thought to build a deep silver net. The gamble paid handsomely with almost all the fish tangled in the bottom third of the net—twenty feet below where other fishermen's nets ended.

In late September, we celebrated our first "broom season," according to fishing tradition. We anchored the *Ambergris* behind Spike Island where no one could see us from town, strung crepe paper and balloons from the radio antennas, tied a broom to the rigging, and took pictures. After all, we didn't expect to break $100,000 every year.

We were money ahead for the first time. We had put in more hours during the four-month fishing season than an office worker clocks all year. We could afford to play for the winter. We could afford anything, it seemed. I bought two plane tickets as Christmas presents for my parents to visit during the first annual Shorebird Festival in early May 1989. Danny and I took a vacation together in Hawaii to mull options. Danny decided to let go of his ski job, but I wanted to stick with my volunteer work. Danny was dubious about my growing political involvement. He saw no end in sight and he was uncomfortable sharing our relationship with the Godzilla-like presence of Alyeska and the pipeline owners.

After our trip, we parted company for another off-season. Danny spent the fall and winter in Roswell, New Mexico, bird hunting and spending time with his boyhood friends. I returned to the A-frame for another winter. At least this time I knew enough to stock up on six cords of dry seasoned spruce well before the snow flew.

Hot Water, Hot Air

Once I settled back into the cabin, I regrouped on oil issues. In August, the state had listed Port Valdez as a toxic impaired waterway under the Clean Water Act. Federal researchers had found that bottom-dwelling fish from Port Valdez were contaminated with low levels of hydrocarbons.

Fishermen thought the pollution stemmed from Alyeska's oily wastewater discharge. Alyeska had installed a biological treatment system, which relies on bacteria to literally eat oily pollutants. Experts had stressed that this system was the least suitable of all possible options and warned that Alaska's cold temperatures slowed the bacteria, meaning that oil particulates would pass through the system largely unchanged. However, it was the cheapest option.

According to Alyeska's tests, the system worked well. Alyeska's consultants reported 100 percent compliance with the discharge permit. However, the state environmental conservation supervisor in Valdez found fault with Alyeska's lab tests, discovered errors in Alyeska's field tests, and determined that oily discharge *exceeded* permit levels 73 percent of the time.

Water pollution was only half of Alyeska's problem. In recent years it had been found guilty of two criminal counts of air pollution. *The Anchorage Times* reported that its much-touted incinerator system functioned correctly just 6.2 percent of the time over a seven-year stretch. The other 94 percent of the time, the incinerators emitted over 100 tons per day of volatile organic compounds (VOCs), the same carcinogenic and toxic oil pollutants found in the wastewater discharge. Even when working properly, the incinerators released over 43,000 tons of VOCs per year or nearly half of the nationwide VOC emissions from marine-loading facilities. This was more than the equivalent of the *Exxon Valdez*, spilling uncontrolled into the air every year. It was the third largest source of the carcinogen benzene in the country.

Yet in August, the EPA abruptly closed its four-year investigation on Alyeska air quality with no enforcement action. The agency claimed that most of the alleged permit violations at the Valdez terminal were "unintentional record-keeping errors or equipment problems, not a devious scheme to fool regulatory agencies or pollute the environment."

Fishermen didn't believe it.

That fall, I represented fishermen on yet another issue: the use of dispersants in oil-spill cleanup. The Alaska Regional Response Team was still hammering out its guidelines for dispersant use, and it was a prickly issue. Dispersants are chemical products, largely manufactured by oil companies, for use on oil spills. They act like dish soap to break up surface oil slicks into tiny droplets. In a limited range of sea conditions, wind and wave action drive the toxic oil-chemical mix into the water column, where it is diluted and dispersed. Decisions to use dispersants involve trade-offs: the chemicals are toxic to fish and wildlife in the water column, yet they offer the hope that the bulk of the spilled oil will not reach beaches.

Part of the problem is that dispersants are only 10 to 15 percent effective in cold water with viscous Prudhoe Bay crude as thick as molasses. Fishermen had trouble justifying dispersant use when the risk to fish was so high for such a slim chance of protecting beaches. Fishermen wanted oil-spill cleanup to focus on physical removal of oil from the sea. Oilmen pressed for liberal use of their chemical products. Government regulators and scientists navigated the choppy waters of debate.

Finally, after months of work, we reached consensus. Dispersants should be banned, we agreed, in shallow and near-shore zones that served as nurseries for marine life. They should be allowed in the Sound's deepest waters only when no mechanical cleanup was possible; and, in the waters in between, they should be used only with approval from the Coast Guard, which had to consider seasonal sensitivities, such as the presence of young salmon or the return of herring ready to spawn. The Alaska Regional Response Team would officially approve the plan two weeks before Exxon's spill.

On A Roll

The O'Toole family became my emotional salve for the draining political work. They were positive and upbeat. And I loved the kids' fresh outlook on life. Over a shared dinner one night, Linden told how earlier that fall Malani had watched Sam suit up to fish in the teeth of a gale. The elfin four-year-old looked outside and saw tall spruce trees twist in the wind as rain lashed against the window. Turning to her father, she had thrust her small clenched fist in the air and proclaimed, "Charge out!"

"That's what we're doing now," Linden concluded, "Charging out and trying to buy a seine permit. We've written letters to every permit holder in the fleet, but everyone is holding on, speculating the price will just go up by spring."

The 1988 Alaska fishing season yielded a record $46.4 million, with Japan paying top dollar for all species of salmon. A single Copper River sockeye salmon was worth more than a barrel of North Slope oil; pinks were worth over a dollar a pound. The catch boosted Cordova for its second straight year into one of the top ten seaports in the nation based on harvest value. Predictions of strong returns for hatchery pink salmon and strong spring returns for herring caused confidence to soar. Commercial fishing permit values in Area E skyrocketed. Salmon gillnet permits fetched prices of $185,000, over triple what Danny and I had paid for ours in 1986. Salmon seine permits shot upward of $250,000—and weren't for sale, as Linden and Sam had found out.

Oilmen also had a banner year. Production from the Prudhoe Bay oilfield peaked at 2.1 million barrels a day, providing for just over 12 percent of the annual demand in the United States. Production and pipeline operations had created a cash cow for major pipeline owners BP, ARCO, and Exxon with a return to investors nearly double that of other oil companies.

The oil bonanza flooded into state coffers, providing eighty-five cents of every dollar of Alaska's general operating budget. This was more than enough incentive for the state to look the other way when it came to enforcement action. The state slashed the budget for oversight and monitoring of pipeline operations, including the tanker terminal, to below the 1981 level. Even back then, ADEC supervisors had warned it was spread too thin to adequately oversee the terminal and tankers. The state also ignored warnings that Alyeska was ill prepared to respond to even a moderate spill.

Hungry for more oil and anticipating a decline in North Slope production, the State of Alaska and the oil industry pressed ahead with its concerted drive in Congress to open the Arctic National Wildlife Refuge for oil and gas development. National conservation organizations drew a firm line in the tundra to protect the "Serengeti of the North," a nineteen-million-acre wilderness rich with wildlife and the critical birthing grounds of the Porcupine caribou herd that sustained the indigenous Gwich'in People.

Oil trumped caribou in the first Bush administration: U.S. Fish and Wildlife Service supervisors quashed a report by field staff that oil development at Prudhoe Bay disrupted caribou migration and breeding, as well as threatened millions of breeding waterfowl with pollution of critical wetlands. A subsequent congressional oversight hearing into the matter did not slow down oil proponents. They were on a roll.

Countdown to Disaster

In January 1989, CDFU and United Fishermen of Alaska voted to conditionally oppose oil development in the Arctic National Wildlife Refuge to leverage congressional attention on the North Slope oil industry's breach of public trust and trail of broken promises. Earlier that month within a two-week period, two tankers loading at the terminal had leaked oil from hull cracks, a notorious problem in the North Gulf coast trade. The spills were significant—the *Thompson Pass* leaked 71,000 gallons (1,700 barrels) and the *Cove Leader* 3,000 gallons (70 barrels). The smaller spill occurred during a storm and made a mockery of Alyeska's response efforts. Oil easily escaped the booms and washed up on nearby beaches. Fishermen realized that if oilmen could not contain and clean up spills right at the terminal where the response equipment was stored, the odds were high that if oilmen could not clean up a spill in Prince William Sound. Oil industry and agency response to the *Glacier Bay* oil spill in Cook Inlet had also proven woefully inadequate. Members of five UFA organizations from the Kenai Peninsula were fighting oil companies and contractors in court to recover financial losses from that spill.

As the delegate for CDFU and UFA on oil issues, I spent the entire month of February on the road, echoing the concerns fishermen had already been expressing for two decades. At an oil spill conference in San Antonio, Texas, I sat in a room packed with international delegates to listen to a panel of experts heatedly debate the emotionally charged issue of whether or not to use dispersants after an oil spill. Oilmen advocated use of these chemicals, while independent experts questioned the wisdom of adding more chemicals to the environment without clear evidence that the chemicals would work without causing more harm than the oil alone. A Nigerian delegate finally implored of the panel, "My country only wants to know this: Should we use dispersants or not? I have been coming to these meetings for twenty years. I am afraid I will get shot if I return another year with no answer!" I hoped his fears were ungrounded, because there was no clear answer.

Meanwhile in Cordova, Linden, Sam, and their friend Rick Steiner signed a purchase agreement and leveraged their entire combined savings as earnest money for a prized $300,000 salmon seine permit. The seller even threw in his old wooden seine boat. They planned to rename it the *Blue Note*, in keeping with the priorities of their new joint venture, the Forever Fun Fishery.

On March 23, Stan Stephens asked me to speak to the Valdez community's Oil Action Committee. The scheduled speaker, Mike Williams from Alyeska, canceled at the last minute to attend Alyeska's big annual safety awards banquet that evening at the terminal. Strong gusty winds kept small planes grounded all day and billowing clouds choked mountain passes. Stan arranged a teleconference.

At 7:00 P.M. I pulled on my Sorels and heavy parka, stoked the fire, and headed outside. I careened downhill in my toboggan, bounding across the hardpack. A quarter-mile walk to my bike, a two-mile ride to town, head down, pumping into the wind. For the next two hours I sat alone, speaking into a teleconference microphone and staring at empty chairs around the table while imagining a room full of people seventy miles away listening. I repeated the warning that I had given before.

"Given the high frequency of tankers into Port Valdez, the increasing age and size of that tanker fleet, and the inability to quickly contain and clean up an oil spill in open water of Alaska, fishermen feel that we are playing a game of Russian roulette. When, not if, 'The Big One' does occur and much or all of the income from a fishing season is lost, compensation for processors, support industries, and local communities will be difficult if not impossible to obtain. . . ."

It was late in the evening before I finally headed to the cabin, tired but happy with the Valdez reception. As I trudged up the hill to the cabin, I relaxed, soaking up the quiet energy of the now still night.

At 9:16 P.M., in the middle of my talk, the tanker *Exxon Valdez*, fully loaded with fifty-three million gallons of crude oil, departed from the tanker terminal. About ninety minutes later, the tanker captain, Joe Hazelwood, asked for and received permission from the Coast Guard vessel traffic control to move from the outbound tanker lane to the inbound tanker lane to avoid icebergs.

The radio communications between the Coast Guard and the tanker were taped, as usual. The captain's slurred speech—slow and guttural with frequent misstatements—was thought, later during the investigations, to reflect perhaps too many drinks at the popular Pipeline Club in Valdez before sailing.

The *Exxon Valdez* turned due south and kept going—passing into and then right out of the tanker lanes altogether, for reasons that would later be debated at government hearings, in courts of law, and by the media. At 11:39 P.M., the captain retired to his cabin, compounding a mounting series of errors.

A little before midnight, the ship's lookout, seaman Maureen Jones, reported the flashing red light of Bligh Reef broad off the starboard bow. If the ship had been in safe waters, this light would have been off of the ship's port or left side.

The third mate tried to take corrective action, then called the captain to report that he thought the vessel "was in serious trouble."

It was too late.

PART TWO
BETRAYAL
1989–1993

"Oh, what a tangled web we weave,
When first we practice to deceive."

Sir Walter Scott, *Marmion*

CHAPTER FOUR

TAKING A STAND

1989

A little after midnight on March 24, 1989, James Kunkel, the chief mate on the *Exxon Valdez*, pounded on the second mate's door, fully awakening him with the icy words, "Vessel aground. We're fucked."

The tanker carved a deep groove into the rocky bottom where the reef caught the hull. Rocky fingers scrapped off bottom paint and rolled it into putty-like globs the size of Ping-Pong balls. The reef tore through the roughly inch-thick steel single hull, ripping open eight of the tanker's eleven cargo holds. Jagged hunks of metal littered the reef. Some were the size of a pickup truck bed. Some were arm-length and rolled into twisted tubes.

At 12:27 A.M., Captain Joe Hazelwood radioed the Coast Guard in Valdez to report: "We've fetched up hard aground north of Goose Island, off Bligh Reef. And, uh—evidently, we're leaking some oil and we're going to be here for awhile."

According to a chronology compiled later by the Alaska Oil Spill Commission, by then 115,000 barrels of oil—4.1 million gallons—had gushed from the stricken tanker.

At 3:35 A.M., ADEC's Dan Lawn and two Coast Guard investigators arrived on the scene. Lawn later told the *Anchorage Daily News* that oil was roiling out of the ruptured hull so fast that it was two feet higher than the surrounding seas. He said, "It was kind of like a boiling cauldron, rolling up, boiling and cooking" around the ship. As he climbed up the pilot's ladder, he looked down to see "a wave of thick black crude flowing from the ship into the night."

Moments after boarding, a Coast Guard officer radioed Valdez, "We've got a serious problem. She's leaking and groaning. There's nobody here. . . . Where's Alyeska?" Alyeska was the primary party responsible for initial spill response. When informed that a tanker was "possibly aground" on Bligh Reef, Alyeska superintendent Larry O'Donnell ordered a subordinate to check things out. Then he went back to sleep—for an hour nap, he later insisted.

At 4:00 A.M., a Coast Guard officer went to the bridge to point out to Captain Hazelwood, who was smoking a cigarette, that that probably was not a "prudent activity" in the explosive, hydrocarbon-rich atmosphere. The officer, Mark Delozier, later described the odor of alcohol on the captain's breath as "very, very noticeable" and "very intense." Blood samples taken nine hours after the grounding found Hazelwood was legally drunk, but on whether the drinking occurred before or after the accident, or both, the record is silent.

By 5:30 A.M., Alyeska estimated that 242,000 barrels of oil—10.1 million gallons—had escaped into the sea.

At 7:00 A.M., Jack Lamb, the acting president of CDFU, knocks loudly on my cabin door. When I fling it open, he says quietly, "We've had the Big One."

Present in the Past: Valdez

Medical experts say that disaster trauma is stored in memory with no time tag other than "present." No matter what else of significance happens in a person's life, trauma memory is able to trump it all in an unguarded moment. The intensity of emotion that floods over me when I uncork the bottle storing this genie is as real as when it happened twenty years ago. I am "present" in the past with a jolt of adrenaline and a searing surge of white-hot anger. I am ready for action. The story is all there to tell, but it would fill volumes. The bits that I have chosen to share are just that: single frames of a very long movie.

In Cordova, word of "The Big One" spreads like wind-blown wildfire as family, friends and fishermen who live Outside called in disbelief. But well before the town fully awakens to disaster, I am on my way to Bligh Reef with bush pilot Steve Ranney and local sea otter biologist Chuck Monnett.

We fly out Orca Inlet in silence and round Knowles Head to find a surreal scene. The Chugach Mountains glow pinkish white in the winter light, framing the placid deep blue waters of the Sound. Juxtaposed against this beautiful calmness lies the stricken tanker, blood red and bleeding inky black. We fly into a swirling bluish cloud of hydrocarbons, boiling from the slick into the air. The strong vapors make our heads and stomachs reel. We ascend to clear air and buzz the borders of the amoeba-like slick before flying to Valdez to refuel.

I thought, "Where is everybody? Where are the crews working to contain and clean up the slick? Where are the skimmers? The booms? The waste oil loading barges?" It was nine, ten, hours now since the tanker had grounded. The government-approved tanker spill contingency plan promised response within six hours. What were people doing?

I stayed in Valdez four days. The time was a nightmarish mix of phone calls, press interviews (several at 4:00 A.M. so East Coast viewers could watch "live" news), press conferences, and meetings that hopscotched through the days, starting—and ending—early in the morning. It was a time of overwhelming responsibility and little sleep, little food, and no change of clothes or shower. I once pounced on a toothbrush left lying on a sink counter at Stan Stephens's crew quarters, only to learn later that five others had used the same brush.

The press latched onto me ("Dr. Ott") before I even left the airport for town. They stuffed cameras and fuzzy microphones that looked like fat caterpillars into my unwashed face. My camera etiquette was terrible: I spoke to the cameramen instead of the camera and shouted over the din of helicopters and planes. Take two. Take three.

Finally, I broke away and slipped outside to think. Dazed and overwhelmed, I found solace in the massive mountain peaks, sparkling white against the blue sky. A thought flooded my mind: *I know enough to make a difference. Do I care enough to commit my life to this?* I sensed there would be no short-term fixes for what had happened. I felt a warm wash of love for the Sound and Cordova. I saw how my life had stacked up to put me in this place with this knowledge at this time of need. I was infused with a quiet knowing that I was not alone. With the mountains as my witness, I pledged my commitment. In a deafening roar, the silence shattered and the sounds of disaster response flooded back. I returned to chaos.

Exxon Shipping held its first public briefing at 6:00 P.M. on the evening of the spill. As I listened to reporters ask questions of Exxon Shipping president Frank Iarossi and Exxon scientist Al Maki, it suddenly dawned on me that the press knew nothing—except what Exxon was telling them—about the effects of oil in a cold-water marine ecosystem or the effects of dispersants on sea life. When Maki started explaining how dispersants, the "miracle cure," would get rid of oil, I sprang to my feet to interrupt their volley of questions.

"My name is Riki Ott. I have a master's and a doctorate in marine pollution. I am a fisherman from Cordova." The press all turned toward me. I learned later that the crowd of fishermen gathered around the radio at the union hall in Cordova cheered. "Dr. Maki, you and I were both at the International Oil Spill Conference in Texas last month where the use of dispersants was widely debated by experts. There are trade-offs with dispersant use. Dispersants force the oil down into the water column, where it is toxic to fish. Fishermen are concerned that dispersants could harm the herring that are just coming back to spawn."

I sank back into my seat, listening to reporters question Maki about the harmful effects of dispersants—and to the sonorous organ music coming from the Good Friday mass in a nearby room. I thought, "Organ music, like in *The Godfather* just before the killing began."

Transcripts of internal telephone conversations, recorded at the Alyeska emergency center in Anchorage, captured the oilmen's desperate situation. Alyeska president George Nelson said, "We do have a first-class mess on our hands." Alyeska's cleanup barge, a central piece of its response plan, had been laid up for repairs with its boom and equipment offloaded. Since it was January, the critical response equipment had become buried under snow. But, even buried, the equipment on hand was nowhere near enough to contain and clean up what had spilled. Nelson said, [Dispersants are] the only real hope we've got. There's no way on God's green earth we can pick up 240,000 barrels [of oil]."

But even dispersants were not much of a hope: there was not enough of the product available in Alaska, or worldwide, to treat a spill of this size in the short time window required for effective on-the-water application. In-situ burning, which involves setting the slick on fire to remove most of the oil from the water, was scrapped initially because of the danger it presented to tanker and crew.

Lack of response plans and preparation led to deceptive public relations to bolster corporate image. The small stockpile of boom at the tanker terminal was finally deployed, but it proved to be of poor quality and fell apart. Cordova fisherman Michelle Hahn O'Leary later told Congress, "The boom's only function was for show and tell. . . ." Nonetheless, Alyeska's engineering manager, Bill Howitt, told Alyeska's president, "It behooves us to have everything flapping in the breeze whether it's catching oil or not!"

Thick black smoke from a test burn—well away from the tanker—sickened villagers in Tatitlek, but no medical help was sent; buckets of dispersant doused on the spreading slick like water on a wildfire drenched the tanker crew and spill responders and did nothing to break up the slick, yet oilmen pressed for dispersant use; an emulsion of oily water was lightered (off-loaded) from the stricken tanker and reported only as oil, creating the illusion that less oil spilled; and on and on. I ran ragged trying to dam streams of misinformation, yet every hour there were more and more and more stories to address. I was shocked at how easily Exxon manipulated the truth—and the media.

Saturday Exxon Shipping's Frank Iarossi announced the tanker had spilled

10.8 million gallons, but that was only the low-end estimate. Others, myself included, had heard the figure 38 million gallons as the high-end estimate. When challenged about Exxon's self-reported estimate, Iarossi threw the media off the trail by volunteering that alcohol may have been involved. I watched the media switch tracks to the sexier story as smoothly as a freight train. Eleven million gallons was good enough for the media—it set a new national record—but it wasn't good enough for me. I vowed to resolve this, not knowing it would take ten years.

Sunday night the storm hit.

During the night, howling winds pushed the main slick forty miles into the Sound. Fishermen radioed that the eastern beaches of Naked, Peak, and Story Islands had been hit so hard that oil plastered shoreline spruces up to forty feet. The storm whipped oil and seawater into a mousse, a sticky custard-like emulsion impervious to burning and dispersants. Spray froze on the deck of the *Exxon Valdez* and the wind pivoted the impaled tanker twelve degrees on the reef into the wind, like a weathervane. The storm tore away the boom around the tanker and drove cleanup crews scurrying to sheltered bays. Fierce winds shook Stan Stephens's bunkhouse, where the fishermen's team from Cordova was now staying.

Gut-wrenching news of the wave of black death riding through the Sound with the storm left our team in emotional shambles. This was too much with too little sleep or food and too many decisions to make. Jack Lamb and Rick Steiner flew out to the oil-soaked beaches, walked shorelines littered with dead and dying sea otters and birds, and returned choked with emotion. They had asked me to go, but I have no stomach for open-casket funerals. We no longer had any expectations that the oil spill could be contained or cleaned up. "When there's nothing you can do," said David Grimes, "you're freed from limitations. You can go for it."

This attitude emboldened us. We called our own press conference and eight of us spoke about what was at stake to a room packed with reporters. Much later, at midnight, we crashed a top-level planning meeting with Exxon, the Coast Guard, and state officials—red-eyed, unwashed, wearing wrinkled jeans and shirts we had slept in for four days. Before the Coast Guard Rear Admiral or Exxon's Frank Iarossi and their minions in crisp uniforms and suits reacted, we spread out nautical charts on the table and took turns talking about tides, currents, hatcheries, and key stretches of beach important to wildlife. We explained our need for defensive booming of sensitive areas. As we spoke, I watched boundaries of propriety dissolve. We left the meeting with a promise from Frank Iarossi to bank CDFU—"up to a million dollars"—scribbled on the back of his business card.

Meanwhile, in Cordova, fishermen had waited four long days and nights for Alyeska to tell them what to do to respond to the spill. For a community of doers, the act of doing nothing in a crisis was unfathomable, irresponsible, and hugely frustrating. People could do nothing for only so long. At midnight, while we were meeting in Valdez with top-level indecision-makers, fishermen in Cordova took action. They fueled fifteen boats, loaded the decks with boom purchased by the state, and headed across the Sound to defend the salmon hatchery in Sawmill Bay in the path of the approaching slick.

This volunteer action eventually sparked Exxon's huge cleanup. But, as Jack Lamb would later testify in Congress, "Exxon said they did everything the fishermen asked them to do. The real problem is that's all they did. . . . We are fishermen, not oil-spill recovery experts. No initiative was taken on their part."

However, Exxon exercised plenty of initiative with public relations. As the spill cleanup and public relations were handed off from Alyeska to Exxon, George Nelson warned Exxon media tactician Don Cornett, "This is going to be a public relations nightmare." Cornett responded, "Do you know how I feel? Do you remember when Patton looked out over the battlefield and said, 'God, help me. I do love it so'? . . . When they were going to invade Europe, . . . [Patton] said, 'God wouldn't let this happen and not make me be in on it.' That's the way I feel."

Exxon's "General Patton" was about to invade Cordova.

The Pressure Cooker: Cordova

On the afternoon of March 28, Jack Lamb and I and some others flew to Cordova to attend the town meeting. We found the community engulfed in chaos. It was Cordova's darkest hour. The shock of the spill had worn off. People despaired openly in the streets. People knew this spill threatened the entire town because everyone was linked like a big daisy chain to commercial fishing and the Sound. Fish bucks drove the economy and, without fish, there would be no bucks.

Nearly 2,000 angry, adrenaline-charged people showed up at the high school gym for the town meeting. The crowd hissed at the sweeping promises Exxon's Don Cornett flung to appease us. "You have had some good luck and you don't realize it. You don't have the *Glacier Bay*, you have Exxon and we do business straight. . . . We will consider whatever it takes to make you whole. . . . If your nets don't fill up, that we can take care of. If you show that your motel goes out of business, that we can take care of. . . . If you can show that you have a loss as a result of this spill, we will compensate it. . . ." Cornett also promised Exxon would clean each rock with a toothbrush, if necessary.

Cordovans listened, unbelieving. Many sitting in the gym remembered when oilmen had visited the town during the pre-pipeline days and had promised there would be no big spills. And if there were, the oilmen could quickly and efficiently clean them up. Now it was painfully obvious neither statement was true. The oilmen couldn't even begin to comprehend what we had lost. Motels and fishing businesses! What about our lifestyle? The Natives' subsistence foods? Our beautiful Sound?

The next day, I found the CDFU office had transformed in my five-day absence into a madhouse. There were five phone lines, four desks, and a dozen volunteers at any given time, all operating out of the tiny office. Volunteers found and acquired boom—industrial heavy-weather boom, not Alyeska's "mill pond" boom, as the fishermen called it. They hired and dispatched boats to the cleanup; coordinated efforts with the hatcheries; took donations; screened calls from hundreds of attorneys and "miracle cure" beach-cleaning-product salesmen; made overflights; dealt with constant calls from media around the world; talked with thousands of people who called just to help; met with the state, NOAA scientists, the Coast Guard, environmental groups, and other fishing organizations; and, most importantly, coordinated with the new CDFU office in Valdez. CDFU's phone lines were constantly jammed because the entire community's phone network was overloaded.

CDFU had broad community support. The union hall outside the office became a gathering place to catch up on the news. Bakery-store owners brought trays of doughnuts in the morning, and bread and cold cuts at noon. In the evening, families brought entire roast turkeys, trays of lasagna, pots of spaghetti, and home-baked cookies. Children decorated the walls with whimsical creatures in colorful collages and crude crayon drawings of the Sound they loved. Preschoolers offered finger paintings of "helping hands." Donated dog kennels for the wildlife rescue efforts, temporary stockpiles of boom, and boxes of absorbent pads were stacked from floor to ceiling.

Theo Matthews, president of United Fishermen of Alaska and a survivor of the *Glacier Bay* oil spill, had joined us in Valdez to help with strategy. "You know," he had said, "if this oil spill gets out of Prince William Sound, it's comin' straight to Cook Inlet."

Now in Cordova, Theo took one look at the CDFU office with its over-whelming noise and energy level and pulled me out into the street. "Look, there are enough people getting equipment and boats organized. I want you to find somewhere quiet, sit down, and use your brain and your computer. We need someone to think up ideas for the politicians in D.C. so we're ready when they start working on spill legislation." Theo realized fishermen could use the spill as political leverage to push for safeguards that we had lost or had not been able to pass into law because of the powerful oil industry lobby. When he saw I had a quiet place to stay and work in town, he went home. "Call me any time of the day or night, darlin.' Good luck!"

For three weeks, I pulled fifteen- to eighteen-hour days researching and writing; talking with press, scientists, and attorneys; and attending daily CDFU board meetings to deal with issues of shoreline cleanup, media logistics, state and federal legislation, damage claims, and lawsuits. It was like cramming for final exams at the university, only the stakes were higher. Congressmen and U.S. Senators who were aloof and distant to the UFA delegation during our February visit called repeatedly for information.

In mid-April, CDFU sent Michelle Hahn O'Leary and me to Washington, D.C. to testify. The homework Theo Matthews had me do paid off. I spoke to politicians with a headful of figures and a fistful of documents, while Michelle addressed the failed spill response. Our work helped frame legislation for the Oil Pollution Act of 1990.

Michelle and I raced back to Cordova just in time to celebrate Sound Love Day with our community. Huge brightly colored murals made by elemen-tary schoolchildren decorated the high school gym. One of the town's favorite musicians, folksinger and songwriter John McCutcheon, came cross-country to help shift the sadness and grief. We wore red hearts on our sleeves and cele-brated our love with spontaneous song, statements, silence, prayers, and poems. Buoyed by the atmosphere of trust and sharing, one small child told the crowd of 2,000, "Boat captains should drink milk." Sound Love Day was a psycho-logical turning point for the community. It was a powerful emotional pickup of affirmation and commitment to each other and the Sound. Memories of this day would help townspeople endure what lay ahead.

Sound Love Day drew people from around the world. Jonathan Wills, a reporter with the *Shetland Times* in Scotland, came to write a story compar-ing operations at the Alyeska terminal with its sister terminal at Sullom

Voe, half a world away, also owned primarily by BP. Amazed by Alyeska's lack of spill response preparation and by the government's lack of control over oil industry operations, Jonathan crossed the line between correspondent and participant. He shared his wealth of information with CDFU and others. According to Jonathan, people in Shetland—sheep ranchers and farmers in rural communities not much bigger than Cordova—had demanded and been given a significant role in oversight. Shetlanders had wielded this power to gain significant improvements in tanker and terminal operations. We seized Jonathan's information like drowning victims seize life rings.

Danny arrived shortly after Sound Love Day. Unable to reach me on March 24, he had turned on the television—and there I was. Brokenhearted by oiled images of the Sound and with no stomach for politics, he had delayed his return. While Danny readied our boat and gear for fishing, I bounced across the country, testifying at congressional hearings, attending meetings, and dealing with the crush of media during the preseason time we normally spent together. At the Copper River Fishermen's Co-op, folks referred to O.C. Inc. as "Big 'C'" and "Nonexistent 'O.'" Danny assured me, "If I didn't think you were making a difference, I wouldn't let you get away with all this!"

"Should we work the cleanup?" It was a question I felt obligated to ask Danny. Some fishermen had already made a season's income before the salmon fishing had even started. To my enormous relief, he replied flatly, "*Ambergris* is a fishing boat, not an oil spill cleanup boat."

For us, it was not a hard decision to make or to live with, but about one-third of the fleet worked on the cleanup. The spill had closed the herring fisheries in the Sound and would certainly impact the salmon fisheries. Lawyers advised people to "mitigate their damages" by taking cleanup contracts. Many fishermen reasoned they needed the work to pay home mortgages, boat and permit loans, living expenses, and other bills.

Exxon's contracts were extremely lucrative, but the cleanup program had started out badly. After the successful community-driven effort to protect Sawmill Bay, Exxon assumed full control of the cleanup. The required contracts for fishermen had initially banned personal cameras on the cleanup, boats from transporting press, and contractors from even talking to media. Most townspeople suspected Exxon's cleanup was a public relations effort, not an honest attempt to clean up oil. Part of this was driven by people who had gone to work the cleanup with good intentions, but who had returned sickened and with firsthand stories of the charade. After all, Tom Copeland and his crew on the *Janice N* collected more oil in one day with five-gallon buckets than Exxon with its fancy skimmers.

The ensuing moral debate over whether or not to accept Exxon's money for cleanup work eroded social solidarity. Families argued about it. Friendships shattered over it. The debate even spilled into CDFU meetings, where the board was bitterly divided over whether to ask Exxon for compensation for hundreds of extra hours for meetings that consumed our lives. Charges of favoritism and bribery were rampant as people vied for the lucrative spill contracts. Many believed that Exxon purposefully created divisiveness within the community by selective hire practices and by inequitable pay for similar services to prevent a concerted effort from forming against it. Exxon's money spill shattered what little sanity there was left in town. The weight of it crushed our civil society.

Exxon's pay of $16.69 per hour with overtime also drew Cordova's labor force like moths to a flame. The mass exodus to the Sound crippled the ability of the government and business community to function effectively. Employers were forced to raise wages, pay large amounts of overtime, shut down certain operations, or even close their doors. Processors lost about one-third of their workforce. "Our people . . . are starting to get restless as they see people around, even friends, who have already made a whole season's wages while our crew is just getting by," said one processor. "I can't compete with Exxon wages," grumbled a bar owner who lost two of his four employees. "It's a pit—I have to work sixteen hours a day, because I can't get help," said another employer who lost three of his four workers to the spill. "Our employees need three weeks' prior training. We can't just pick new people up off the street," said a fuel distributor who lost two of his six workers.

Those remaining in town carried the burden for all. There were thousands of decisions and hundreds of hours of volunteer work to hold the community and fishing fleet together. We moved from one crisis to another, hour after hour, day after day. Tempers strained; tensions were overwrought; people argued and fought; children were fearful and confused. The emotional havoc rippled from individuals to families to businesses until the entire town was overwhelmed by trauma. John Crowley, Director of the Mental Health and Alcohol Clinic in Cordova, reported a fivefold increase in the number of patients. Overworked mental health clinic staff couldn't even begin to plug the dike of fear, confusion, anger, and grief that spilled out when conflicts, domestic violence, and drinking skyrocketed. No one knew that these ripples of social chaos would outlast the cleanup by decades.

In early May, my parents came to visit, as planned. Danny, kindhearted and generous with his time, was distraught. He loved my parents, but had no free time to spare. I assured him they were fully prepared to entertain themselves. They had hesitated to come after the spill, but I said, "The birds are still coming, so why shouldn't you?" They volunteered at the CDFU office and filled me in daily on cleanup stories. When I asked how they came by such detailed information, Dad said, "I make a general announcement at the little café in the bookstore—'We are Riki Ott's parents'—and all sorts of people come to talk with us!" Once they flew on the mail plane to the Native Village of Chenega. When the plane entered the spill zone and flew on and on over blackened beaches, the enormity of the destruction sunk in and my mother started to cry. The Native man sitting next to her quietly held her hand. "That made me cry even more," said Mom, "when I saw his home was surrounded by oil." They also attended the first annual Shorebird Festival, an event that the U.S. Forest Service and determined townspeople hosted in spite of the spill—and shared what I had missed.

Coinciding with my parents' visit, Congressman George Miller (D-CA) held a series of field hearings in the Sound. CDFU sent Jack Lamb, Ken Adams, and me to Valdez to testify. My parents flew with us. Before I testified, my father whispered, "Remember, in a public forum like this, never ask a question if you don't know the answer."

A panel of oilmen testified after us. Silver-haired, silver-tongued Theo Polasek, the vice president of Alyeska operations, defended its contingency plan, testifying that it "accurately portrayed what would happen in the case of a 200,000-barrel spill." This was the same contingency plan that ADEC commissioner Denny Kelso had referred to earlier as "the biggest piece of American maritime fiction since Moby-Dick."

My father, watching Polasek intently, nudged me. He mocked an imaginary long nose like Pinocchio. "He's lying! Pink ears!" Listening to my father, I realized I still had a lot to learn.

The Fishing Season from Hell

Most of what I remember about the 1989 fishing season, Cordova's hundredth, is that I survived it—and the kitten made us laugh. I was physically exhausted, mentally numbed, and emotionally drained before the first king salmon returned in search of their birth streams. In my desperate state, I had instinctively reached for what I most needed, something capable of unconditional love. Danny named the small tabby kitten Tsunami for her habit of surging toward us in a tidal wave of playfulness whenever we cut the boat engine.

Danny let me use fishing time to recharge my inner battery. I slept off my mental haze, snuggled with the kitten, while Danny fished. Sometimes I helped pick a set. When we returned to town, I was somewhat refreshed for the awaiting crush of meetings and media. At the Copper River Fishermen's Co-op, no one got much sleep for about a month because fishermen stood in for cannery crew and helped process fish, while tendermen did their own unloading.

During closures, the CDFU board had its hands full dealing with the cleanup or, rather, The Money Spill, as we called it, because it was clear to us that it was more charade than "cleanup." CDFU sent Michelle Hahn O'Leary and I out to see the operations. Instead of being impressed with the array of boats, booms, and orange-suited workers, we were dismayed. The sticky cold oil smeared with wipes, resisted the cold-water flush, and yielded only grudgingly to slide down the beach when blasted with pressurized hot water. Clouds of muddy oil sunk and easily escaped the offshore boom. Each flood tide recoated beaches with shiny black oil like fresh paint. But the real danger I saw was the hot-water wash itself. It cooked clams, mussels, and other intertidal animals that had survived the spill and destroyed sea plants and animals that supported the entire coastal ecosystem.

Government scientists, Exxon, and the U.S. Coast Guard were all aware of the environmental havoc caused by the steam cleaning. At an oil spill conference in Seattle, I was stunned to hear Coast Guard Vice Admiral Clyde Robbins, the person ultimately responsible for approving the steam cleaning and overseeing the cleanup, ask, "How much damage do you want to do to a beach to save it? I don't want people to say about me that I killed Alaska trying to save it." Yet the damage continued because the cleanup was politically unstoppable. It made Exxon look good. Even an Exxon official admitted, "The actual recovery of oil and the money spent became secondary to its public image aspects."

The damage wasn't just to the beaches. I saw no respirators to protect workers' lungs from the same oily mist that coated their rain gear and that was generated daily by the pressure washing. People continued to work after removing their (supposedly) protective rain gear jackets in the hot sun. Workers with oily hands ate sack lunches and smoked cigarettes. Once I saw what was going on, the phone calls I had received from cleanup workers with persistent coughs, sore throats, red eyes, headaches, and skin rashes suddenly made sense.

I didn't find out until ten years later that 6,722 respiratory claims, representing roughly two-thirds of the frontline cleanup crews, were reported to Exxon medical doctors in 1989, but Exxon had failed to report these illnesses to federal and state health officials.

When the Sound opened for fishing in mid-June, we stayed on the Flats along with most of the gillnet fleet. The decision nearly cost us our lives but, at the time, this option seemed better than fishing in the Sound around oil or with the volatile stressed-out seiners, trying to catch a season's worth of fish in a tiny unoiled fraction of the formerly open-but-oiled space.

The Sound's fisheries became a political football. Exxon wanted as many areas opened as possible to lend credence to its public relations campaign and legal defense that the spill caused minimal disruptions and harm. Fishermen were also told that they had to fish in the Sound to qualify for a claim, which turned out not to be true. As the summer progressed without incident of contaminated fish, the state, under relentless pressure from Exxon, opened more fishing districts in late July. Two days after the announcement, all areas in the Sound were closed due to oil contamination of seven boats and gear.

Fishermen, already under considerable stress, were absolutely furious and demanded an emergency meeting with state officials. In voices shaking with pent-up anger and frustration, many shouted it would be better to "shut the whole thing down and give us some direction," than to wait for short openers with the potential for harvesting contaminated fish. The state resumed its conservative approach and allowed limited fishing, but tensions never eased and the season was anything but "normal" as Senator Stevens and Exxon had predicted it would be.

In the midst of the oiled gear debacle, we had our own misadventure on the Flats. We were fishing hard on a late summer pop of reds and we took a chance, crossing Pete Dahl bar on an ebbing tide. Suddenly, a rogue breaker reared up in the glassy calm channel and smashed into the *Ambergris*. It shattered glass windows, smothered the engine, and nearly ripped off our cabin— all in the space of about three seconds. The *Ambergris* yawed drunkenly in the surf until the heavy water load drained out the deck scuppers and was pumped from the engine compartment. Donning survival suits, we motored slowly back to town. The kitten, wet but warm against my chest, began to purr. Danny eyed her. "We're not out of this mess yet!"

We took our time with boat repairs, trying to regain our nerve. Old-timer

Fred Lange came by to watch one day. He cautioned, "First, don't ever tell your parents. They don't need to know." He added, "Second, you think you've learned a lesson from this. But you haven't. You'll be right back out doing the same thing again." Fred was mostly right. Tsunami was the only one who learned anything and refused to go back out fishing.

During the time ashore, I became fully engaged in the dispersant debate, which had moved from the water to the beaches with the oil. Along with many others, including state officials, I reminded Exxon and the Coast Guard of the voluntary ban on dispersant use on beaches to no avail. Labels on chemical drums stating "toxic to fish" and safety information warning to keep the product out of watercourses were ignored. Strenuous objections from fishermen and Native landowners, among others, finally halted application of the kerosene-like Corexit 9580 a year later; however, a concerted EPA–Exxon partnership fast-tracked use of Exxon's experimental product, Inipol EAP22.

According to Exxon, Inipol was nothing more than fertilizer to enhance growth of naturally occurring oil-eating bacteria, but the product contained the same human health hazard and similar safety warnings as some of the dispersants. It acted like a solvent, dissolving oil off rocks. Before long, Inipol workers were sending me reports of workers with skin rashes, blisters, headaches, and nausea—even urine blackened with dead red blood cells. Some reports were backed up by medical records. Eventually, a beach crew from Seldovia, another oiled coastal community, was hospitalized after washing an Inipol-treated beach. That drew the attention of local government, but to no end: the insanity of using this product continued, despite intense opposition from the public, myself included.

The end of the fishing season coincided with the controversial closure of the beach cleanup operations in mid-September. I didn't join Danny to fish for silvers. Our relationship hung by the slimmest of threads. I carried around a disc-sized picture of him with the floppies for my laptop and he kept a picture of me on the locker shelf.

A few days before Exxon's much-publicized departure, Cordova bookstore owner Kelley Weaverling, Stan Stephens, and I organized a protest of the cleanup and general treatment by the pipeline owners. The evening before the event, about a dozen boats from Cordova rafted up in Jack Bay. The low clouds and dense fog created a cozy atmosphere. I hopped from boat to boat, sampling the different cuisine and lending a hand at the "rock party," where friends stuffed oily pebbles from "treated" beaches into six hundred bags, one for each member of Congress. For the first time since the spill, I felt calm.

Everyone was focused. Our old sense of camaraderie was back. I finally felt that we were going to be all right. Our spirit was still intact.

"Riki," a soft voice floated down from somewhere on top of a cabin. I found Ross Anderson, a journalist for the *Seattle Times*, sitting out of the way, quietly observing activities. "I've covered this spill all summer, but this is the first time I understand what it is you have lost." I wondered, *Could he help a nation understand?*

On September 9, our medley of fishing boats, small cruise ships, sailboats, and kayaks paraded in front of the terminal in Port Valdez under the dark brooding hull of the supertanker *Northern Lion*, loading oil. Fishermen strung up banners, made from sheets donated by the Reluctant Fisherman and painted with supplies donated by Seaman's Hardware. "GIVE US BACK ALASKA! NO MORE OIL LIES." "PLAN FOR THE FUTURE!" A big red circle with a slash for 'NO' "INDUSTRIAL SELF-MONITORING." Above our idling engines, we heard the chants of protestors on shore. The protest was a constructive release of pent-up energy that recharged our spirits for what lay ahead.

Community Chaos—Lives in Transition

Prince William Sound fishermen estimated their losses for the 1989 fishing season at over $50 million. Every fishery in the Sound for salmon, herring, halibut, sablefish, crab, and shrimp had been either partially or fully closed because of the spill. Nearly half of the estimated loss was damage to salmon prices from market fears of "tainted" or contaminated fish. The spill's shadow cast a pall on all Alaska salmon, pushing down prices throughout the state, including for Copper River fish. With the flow of fish bucks down to a trickle, the town's economy seized like an engine without oil. A $50 million loss to the fishermen became, roughly, a $200 million loss to the town when fish bucks stopped trading hands. Everyone felt the crunch.

Cordova was not the only community to suffer a crippling blow to its economy. The swath of economic devastation from the spill swept through Prince William Sound, Kodiak, and parts of the Kenai and Alaska Peninsulas, affecting twenty-two communities and about half of the region's 65,000 people. Spill losses from lost fish harvest and lost income in fisheries-dependent businesses exceeded spill gains from cleanup work by a three-to-one margin across the oiled region.

Danny and I felt lucky. We had money to spare after our permit and boat payments, no home payment, no kids, and few needs. The O'Tooles and many others in town weren't so lucky. The O'Tooles had closed on their seine permit based on Exxon's promises that fishermen would be fairly compensated. The value of the highly lucrative Area E salmon seine and herring seine permits had dropped by $100,000 after the spill. People's confidence in the future of the seafood industry was badly shaken. Exxon's promise of fair compensation was years away from the need to make annual payments.

When I finally caught up with Linden, we didn't exchange the usual fun fishing stories. We shared worries. "We made our first permit payment—just barely," Linden said. "Sam worked in that mess on the Sound until fishing started. And we fished to the very end of the season. We couldn't take the kids with us." Her eyes reddened with tears. "I didn't want to risk them getting in oil. They were so traumatized when we both left them to fish. They wanted to come. They didn't understand. One of us has always been with them. . . ." Her voice trailed off.

She agonized over $100,000 of lost permit equity and whether future fisheries would support their huge debt. "We'll just be fishing for the bank if the permit equity keeps dropping. Those baby salmon and herring were born into an oil spill! That can't be good. What do you think is going to happen to the fisheries?"

It was a question often asked of me in town. People stopped me in the bank, post office, grocery story, and on the street. Their voices choked with worry. *Riki, what is going to happen to us?* The answer become almost rote, but I felt deep empathy afresh for each inquisitor. I would find myself taking a deep breath and saying as evenly as possible: "I think it's going to get worse before it gets better." It hurt to see hope die in people's eyes.

Yet, there was something far greater than money that all of us lost. The spill with its long sticky tendrils of worries left emotional scars on everyone it touched. Clinically diagnosed post-traumatic stress disorder and general anxiety disorder were rampant. All of the oiled communities grappled with huge increases in the load of mental health cases as a direct result of the spill and cleanup.

In private, people told counselors they were having difficulty coping: their lives were disrupted on a daily basis, their quality time with family and friends had dwindled. Many had intrusive dreams and gnawing worries over an uncertain future, and almost all reported feeling a loss of control over their own lives. Social workers and police, among others, dealt with domestic violence, substance abuse, children suffering from separation anxiety, and bitter arguments among family members, friends, and coworkers.

All around the affected communities, people watched the systems they had previously trusted to ensure their safety and protect their communities crumble under the weight of corporate pressure—leaving their sense of security shattered. Even the self-confidence of the most trusting among us stumbled. The long summer of frantically cleaning beaches instead of fishing or otherwise going about normal activities prolonged and intensified the trauma. Untended emotional wounds festered, deepened, and spilled over into the community. As one community leader stated, "You can deal with the dead salmon and the dead otters, but you can't deal with damage being done to the social fabric of this community."

At first, I didn't see how the mental health crisis affected me personally. I was still caught up in too-much-to-do. I did some soul-searching and opted out of the citizens' advisory council formed by Alyeska and CDFU in June. I suspected Alyeska's motive in forming the council was to convince Congress that mandatory citizen oversight of the terminal and tankers, being drafted as part of the oil spill legislation, was not necessary. To me, Alyeska's bid for control of the process was transparent: Alyeska forbade its council members to sue the oil companies or to lobby legislators or Congress.

Alyeska was not just bullying citizens. In response to increased congressional scrutiny over the initial failed spill response, the "pipeline people" had entrenched on their turf. When state and federal regulators took steps to curb air and water pollution at the terminal, Alyeska engaged in bitter legal battles and banned Dan Lawn, the state inspector who was critical of Alyeska operations, from site visits. Discouraged employees sought out Chuck Hamel and others to fix the problems. During the summer, readers of national newspapers like the *Wall Street Journal* learned how Alyeska falsified water quality tests, ignored malfunctioning vapor incinerators, and pulled a suite of other tricks to maximize profits at the expense of Port Valdez air and water quality.

I decided to cast my lot with the Oil Reform Alliance (ORA or "aura"), a grassroots coalition of environmentalists and fishermen that CDFU had initiated as a backup plan to Alyeska's advisory group. A richly diverse cross-section of Alaskans, scientists, and government regulators, including Dr. Ihor Lysyj and Dan Lawn, attended the first ORA membership meeting in late September to discuss strengthening state laws regulating the oil industry. Inspired by the upbeat attitudes and collective knowledge, I offered to serve on the new ORA board.

When I returned to Cordova, the steep letdown from the emotional high of the conference triggered what I can say only in hindsight was my own personal mental health crisis. I didn't understand what was happening and could only explode in anger or tears or laughter in response to violent and unpredictable swings of emotions. In an effort to save our relationship and my sanity, Danny booked a spontaneous trip to Hawaii. Within forty-eight hours, we were floating off some white sand beaches on the Big Island. I felt great weights peeling off my shoulders like layers off an onion. I had reached the end of my emotional limits and I was seeing beyond the edge of my sanity. The gentle land and clear water teeming with colorful sea life were a calming balm that chased away dark shadows of grief and betrayal, while coaxing my inner self to regain control of my mental tiller. I was able to pull back to safety.

Returning home refreshed, I leaped right back into the fray, but this time with a commitment to join Danny for telemark skiing in Colorado in January. After Danny left to visit his family and friends in New Mexico, I spent a month on the East Coast with Jeannie Buller, speaking at universities, research stations, and Congress about the spill and cleanup. Jeannie had run the CDFU office in Valdez. It had been a pressure cooker of responsibility in a hostile work environment with daily conflicts with Exxon and its shadow, the Coast Guard, over cleanup operations. Strong-minded, even-tempered Jeannie had stood her ground on issue after issue all summer long. Even though we carried memories of the spill with us and talked about it every day, the trip was a therapeutic break away from the extraordinary stresses haunting Cordova.

We returned to find CDFU and the state embroiled in an intense fight to block a legal motion by Exxon and Alyeska to keep secret all scientific evidence gathered for lawsuits stemming from the spill. Fishermen protested vehemently because, in part, we used pre- and postharvest information to gauge the strength of the next season's salmon returns. This was just the beginning of Exxon's legal tricks to reduce its corporate liability and prevent the truth about the spill's damaging effects from reaching the public.

The Litany of Woe

Within days of the spill, Cordova had been inundated with lawyers. They were everywhere—in bars, restaurants and stores, on the streets, at CDFU, in city offices. In passing, they sought eye contact, questing, hungry. They smelled money. On one occasion, I nearly ran right into one as I rushed headlong into a building. My mind took in the white hair, pinstriped suit, red carnation, white spats, and polished shoes—Melvin Belli, the flamboyant California personal injury lawyer! Wordlessly, I ducked around him.

But there was no ducking the onslaught for long. By midsummer, the fishermen's claims process had reached a zenith of confusion. It had been dubbed "The Litany of Woe," because of the hassles, headaches, pitfalls and reams of dreaded paperwork. Part of the problem was the claims process itself. Exxon's forms initially required fishermen to waive all rights to claims for future losses from reduced harvests due to the spill and to get prior written approval from Exxon before talking to the press. After an uproar from fishermen, the claims form was changed.

There was also a problem with Exxon's loss formula, which was uncovered by Patience Andersen Faulkner, an Aleut by birth and paralegal by training, who ran the plaintiffs' claims office. According to Exxon's formula, nobody's claim exceeded $30,000; most fishermen were owed nothing; and some even ended up owing Exxon money. Once Patience reported the "error"—which could have cost fishermen millions of dollars in "disappeared" losses—it was fixed.

By fall, nearly everyone in town was involved in at least one lawsuit and often more, if people owned multiple permits, damaged land or businesses, or were subsistence users. But it wasn't just us. Fisheries had been closed in Cook Inlet, Kodiak, and even along the Alaska Peninsula. Thousands of fishermen from Bristol Bay and Southeast Alaska had filed claims for diminished prices from market fears of tainted fish. Danny and I were one among over 20,000 plaintiffs from every state in the union. There were over 32,000 claims, spread among nearly sixty direct action lawsuits and over one hundred class action lawsuits, filed in either federal or state court. Someone would have to bring order to the chaos.

That task was assumed, for the most part, by federal district Judge Russel Holland, because most of the cases wound up in his court. It was shared with Judge Brian Shortell for cases files in Alaska Superior Court. Certain that the federal court would be more sympathetic to industry's position, Exxon and Alyeska worked to transfer the bulk of the state cases to federal court over objections from our many lawyers.

As cases shifted to federal court, all of the plaintiffs' lawyers started to fight for the lead position in Judge Holland's courtroom. "They all knew there wasn't room at the top for everyone," explained Anchorage lawyer Dave Oesting. He said, "The lawyers all looked like a bunch of monkeys in the woods when the leopard's hunting." Oesting observed that the judge was not amused by all of the almost comical posturing. According to Oesting, lawyers from west of the Mississippi treated those east of that river as a conceited bunch of academics; East Coast lawyers acted like West Coast lawyers were uncultured and not learned; and all of the Outside lawyers discounted Alaska lawyers as a backwoods bunch of yokels.

The entire heap of lawyers fought to a draw. They presented the judge with a consensus document for organizing the case by shared management. Holland flatly rejected the eight-headed monster, causing "a shock wave of panic through the Outside lawyers," according to Oesting. No one paid any attention when Oesting wrote a memo to the judge. After all, Oesting was an Alaskan—what could he know?

Oesting had known enough to file one of the first class action lawsuits in federal court after the spill. Oesting also knew that "historically in large tort cases with an onslaught of lawyers, those who wound up on top were generally appointed by the court to their positions." So Oesting presented Judge Holland with a proposal that allowed the judge to choose the leaders of the plaintiff team by soliciting, then reviewing, two-page statements submitted by interested parties. The judge accepted the proposal. Seventeen lawyers applied for the lead counsel position, including Oesting.

In December, Judge Holland announced his decision: Dave Oesting and Jerry Cohen would colead the plaintiffs' team. It was an unlikely alliance. Oesting worked for the Seattle-based firm Davis Wright Tremaine, a bigtime, blue chip corporate defense firm. Cohen was a legendary figure in the class action antitrust bar. He was with the Washington, D.C.-based Cohen, Milstein, Hausfeld & Toll. Cohen had helped win the biggest cases against corporations, such as the case against Union Carbide for the chemical disaster in Bhopal, India. The alliance worked because each recognized and respected the other's talents and each wanted the same thing—to hold Exxon accountable for damages and to punish the corporate behavior that led to the spill.

CHAPTER FIVE

VIRTUAL REALITY
1990

In January, I met Danny in Granby, Colorado, with my sister and brother-in-law. The idea was to get away from it all, enjoy the powdery slopes, sunny days, and friendship—and indeed they did lift the spill's shadow, but my head and heart were still in the Sound.

Within a couple of weeks I returned to meet with the Oil Reform Alliance board to strategize on oil spill bills for the upcoming legislative session. We needed a lobbyist—someone to go to Juneau during the legislative session from January to May to spearhead our effort, but we were handicapped by our slender budget. Suddenly, I heard myself volunteering for the job. The fact that I knew absolutely nothing about political lobbying, or that I would be up against some of the highest paid lobbyists in the state, didn't dawn on me until a couple weeks later when I arrived in Juneau.

Oiled Beaches, Oiled Lives

In February, as daylight hours began to stretch and winter storms began to get some distance between them, people in Cordova began to ask, "What happened to the oil over the winter?" The state had conducted a walk-a-thon the previous fall after Exxon and the media departed. It had meticulously documented oil condition on beaches from Prince William Sound to the Alaska Peninsula. The 1,000-plus pages of maps and data served as a starting point for the 1990 surveys. Cordova's new mayor Bobby Van Brocklin, CDFU's Jack Lamb, and others set out on the Coast Guard cutter *Sweetbrier* with one of the state–federal–Exxon teams for a survey.

They returned with bittersweet news. Winter storms had scoured cliff faces and heaped gooey oil, mixed with seaweed and driftwood, in storm berms above the high-tide line. Protected beaches, sheltered from surf, looked largely unchanged. Exposed beaches, which had been heavily oiled, looked dramatically improved, their surfaces polished almost clean by pounding waves and tumbling rocks. Remaining surface oil was tarry or had hardened into asphalt-like mats. Despite the appearance, oiled gravel beaches felt different under-foot, like walking on a soggy lumpy futon.

The weird footing betrayed the subsurface oil. ADEC monitor Dave Conner observed, "You can turn over a rock and see the oil start dripping down." Digging down five to ten inches exposed oil-saturated gravels. The oil was a still free-flowing liquid, and it smelled quite fresh. The widespread buried oil lay below the reach of cleanup crews—at least ones using surface washing techniques.

Spring cleanup plans began to hatch like a clutch of full-term goose eggs. Exxon planned to focus on surface oil—aesthetics—starting in May. Exxon had ignored subsurface oil during its own spring surveys, but people wanted the oil gone, not just beaches that looked clean. Jack Lamb and other community members participated in lengthy "discussions" with state, federal, and Exxon officials to hammer out site selection, priorities, and timing. Townspeople pressed to start the cleanup in March when daylight hours lengthened and fishermen were free to harvest oil instead of salmon. Finally, the City of Cordova developed its own cleanup plan, starting in March, to collect oiled popweed and oiled beach debris. It turned out the oil had its own plan.

By mid-March, spring sunshine and high tides mobilized the buried oil. Heavy sheen bled off oiled beaches. ADEC monitor Dave Conner reported, "Boy, it was bad. . . . There's still a lot of oil on those beaches." No one could stem the hemorrhaging. The unstable condition of the beaches was the subject of numerous meetings as fishermen and state officials planned how to harvest fish not "adulterated by oil." Protocols for emergency restrictions, inspection programs, and boat-cleaning stations were revamped from the 1989 season.

The entire community was still engulfed in the crisis mode, haunted by an unshakeable worry that the oil in the Sound would cause lingering problems for wildlife and our way of life. We were caught in the disaster's aftermath like a stick caught in a powerful current. There were endless meetings, decisions, recruitment for new boards, and required safety or HAZWOPER (hazard-ous waste operator) trainings for spill response—a year after the fact. There were beach cleanups, a city budget to balance in the face of unknown revenues from fishing, and a slim window of opportunity through legislation to reduce risk of future spills and chronic pollution from the Alyeska terminal. People peppered state legislators and congressional delegates with calls, letters, testi-mony, and commentary to advocate double hulls for tankers, citizen oversight of oil industry operations, and improved contingency plans for spill response.

Meanwhile, I was at the other end of the stick, in Juneau, trying to make sure the people's will became written into law.

An Exercise in Democracy

In early February, I set up the Oil Reform Alliance office in a small room in the United Fishermen of Alaska office across the street from the five-story capital building in Juneau. I had a one-member staff, Marna Schwartz, a bright premed student with no experience lobbying, and a phone bank network, organized by a volunteer in Homer. The idea was that Marna and I would track and research the "spill bills," draft position papers, testify at hearings, and keep the spill communities and statewide activists informed and involved through the phone bank network.

Marna and I got off to a rough start. No one paid any attention to us. Money talked and we had none. We were trying to ante into a poker game for high rollers without any chips. There were bar deals, bedroom deals, vote-trading deals, fast talk, double-talk, and lots of downright lies, which, when spoken from the lips of high-salaried oil lobbyists, were taken as gospel until proven otherwise. Most legislators were quick to dismiss what we had to say because it ran counter to the established oil lobby, back in force after its disappearing act last spring after the spill. We reconnoitered.

Our first break came during a House Resources Committee hearing on a bill that raised the stakes substantially for spilling oil. While the pipeline owners could easily afford the increased proof of financial responsibility that the bill required, many of the smaller shippers argued that they would be put out of business by the increased insurance premiums. In the packed room, I testified that almost all of the shippers, big and little, were self-insured. I explained, "The increased cost of doing business would amount to a nickel for a clean piece of paper to write an adjusted insurance policy." I tossed a clean sheet of paper on the table to emphasize my point.

When the next witness, high-paid oil lobbyist Ray Gillespie, argued the familiar "we-can't-afford-this" refrain, I slumped disgustedly in my chair. Despondently, I shook my head slightly when committee cochair, Representative Cliff Davidson from Kodiak, asked questions that I considered off track. I nodded slightly when I thought he was on the right track.

Davidson's questions started getting more pointed. I looked up and we made eye contact. Davidson was following my cues! Straightening up, I nodded or shook more vigorously until the chairman pinned Gillespie. Flushing crimson, the lobbyist admitted that the "higher" insurance premiums would only cost a nickel for another sheet of paper!

The hearing adjourned abruptly as pandemonium broke out. I dashed out to escape the ruckus and nearly collided with Representative Davidson, who had charged out another door to intercept me. Grabbing my arm, he pulled me across the hall into his office, slamming the door shut behind him. His staff stared wide-eyed as he towed me across the room and into his private office, pitching me into a deep easy chair. Then he roared in my face, "*Don't you ever do that to me again! I need to know which questions to ask before the hearing! And I need to know the answers!*"

Not yet fully comprehending the brutality of oil politics, I just listened as he explained how to brief him in the future. Then he sauntered out nonchalantly to check the hallway and, finding it still clogged with oil lobbyists, came back and let me out his ground-floor window to the street, so no one would see me leaving his office. That's when I got it.

After this incident, Marna and I learned just about every window and door exit—fire, back, side, and basement—in the capital. We found legislators eager to listen to us in private, in the security of inner offices. Most were uncomfortable about being seen by the omnipresent oil lobbyists while talking with us, but they were hungry for the solid research and critical analyses that we provided. We slowly built a reputation of honesty and truth. This seemed to be something new in Juneau.

One day assistant Attorney General Joe Geldhof stopped by the UFA office. He was laughing so hard he was crying. He collapsed in a chair and finally recovered enough to tell us about his lunch with Norman Gorsuch, a prominent oil industry lobbyist. According to Joe, when my name came up, Gorsuch had pounded his forehead with his fist and bellowed, "Riki Ott! Riki Ott! She's giving us *such* a hard time!"

Puzzled, Joe had persisted, "Come on, Norman. You outnumber her thirty-to-one and some of your lobbyists are earning six figures. She's a volunteer sleeping on people's floors and couches. What do you mean, 'She's giving *you* a hard time'?"

In response, Gorsuch had roared, "But she keeps bringing in the facts!"

Joe guffawed as he recalled the moment. "They don't know what to *do* with you! They can't buy you; they can't sleep with you. They don't know how to *get* to you. Go get 'em!"

"Getting them" required support from hundreds of concerned people who dedicated time from busy lives to exercise their democratic right to voice their convictions. These voices united to form a powerful groundswell that convinced legislators that Marna and I were to be taken seriously. Yet, the political process was rigged to advantage those who could afford a physical presence in Juneau. Controversial bills were assigned to multiple work sessions where only people present and invited by committee chairs could testify. The tipping point for the remote voices from oiled communities came when legislators invited Marna and I to participate in these closed meetings—along with the high-paid oil lobbyists. As Stan Stephens later remarked, "Exxon probably has to have five extra lawyers and twenty extra staff just to keep up with [Riki]."

Slick Operators

Unbeknownst to me, the TAPS oil companies hit upon a way to try to undermine my efforts as part of their solution to a much larger problem. For the TAPS owners and Alyeska, the perfect storm of bad publicity formed early in the legislative session. "Alaska's Pitted Pipeline," shrieked the title in a special report to the state's largest newspaper. According to the story, "The trans-Alaska pipeline, one of the biggest engineering feats of the petroleum age, is under fierce attack by an elemental force of nature. . . . The nine billion dollar oil-delivery system is pitted with rust in hundreds of locations, and the repair bill could run into the billions of dollars. Alyeska . . . vows the pipeline system is sound. . . . But the company stops short of assuring there is no chance of a rupture."

As story upon story unfolded, it became obvious that regulators had once again relied on oilmen's promises—and the oilmen had failed to deliver. The glaring deficiencies were caused by aggressive cost-cutting measures instigated by major owners BP, ARCO, and Exxon. Yet, pipeline operations had netted $42 billion in after-tax profit for its owners from 1969 through 1987. This amounted to over $6 million a day in net profit—or four times the long-run rate of return on the New York Stock Exchange before taxes. It was later determined that hidden or off-book profits amounted to another estimated one million dollars a day.

As further evidence that the pipeline owners could well afford to take better care of their cash cow, Scottish Eye, an investigative TV and film producer, released an in-depth story by Jonathan Wills that compared BP's operations in

Alaska to Europe's largest oil terminal, Sullom Voe. *Slick Operators* exposed BP's double standards and the lower standard in Alaska that had resulted in the failed initial spill response. Incensed that BP and the other pipeline owners treated Alaska like an underdeveloped nation, people began to demand change.

With state and federal regulators, reporters, and private citizens prying into Alyeska's business after years of neglect, the pipeline owners developed a siege mentality. The choices to fix this bout of bad publicity were to either fix the pipeline—or find who was leaking information and stem the flow. They chose the latter.

The pipeline owners mostly attributed the public airing of their dirty laundry to Chuck Hamel and his "Alyeska Mafia . . . a loose coalition of activists and dissidents coalesced around Hamel," who made continuous public claims of wrongdoing. It disturbed the owners that Hamel's information was "accurate and could only have been supplied by one or more persons within Alyeska and/or the TAPS owner organizations." Who was leaking confidential company documents to Hamel?

Jim Hermiller, a BP oilman and Alyeska's new president, authorized an investigation to find the source of the leaks. His order set loose professional spies working for Wackenhut, a private security and investigation firm that is a primary contractor to the U.S. government—and Alyeska. These hounds of hell descended upon Chuck Hamel, me, Dan Lawn, and Stan Stephens, among others.

Meanwhile, Exxon launched an aggressive public relations campaign to quiet "rumors" of extensive damage from its spill. The extent of injury to wildlife was a secret closely guarded by federal lawyers negotiating with Exxon over damages. Exxon charged into the information void created by the federal gag order, spewing ads and glossy brochures. Exxon's position was one of "mostly good news." Fish and wildlife are returning to previously oiled areas. "Intertidal plants and animals are surviving. . . . Herring and salmon fishing stocks are expected to be healthy and productive."

However, alarming bits and pieces of information dribbled out. During congressional hearings, NOAA scientists testified that oil trapped under the surface of beaches contained toxic hydrocarbons that normally evaporated quickly. Alaska's Commissioner of Fish and Game told Congress, "In the intertidal portion of salmon streams where we would normally find tens of thousands of eggs or juvenile forms, our biologists have been unable to find even a single egg, alevin or fry." State official Gregg Erickson complained, "Exxon contends that because wildlife can be seen cavorting in Prince William

Sound, and because there are salmon in streams, everything is hunky-dory in Prince William Sound. We don't think that's the case."

As part of its campaign, Exxon unleashed three "distinguished" British scientists in Juneau after flying them around the Sound for two weeks in April—presumably to watch wildlife "cavort" on beaches. The public relations trio visited with individual legislators to share their "field observations." I constantly bumped into them in the halls of the capitol. Speaking in clipped accents, the scientists assured people that, "All is not lost. It's okay. The illness is over." They reminded people that a fair proportion of fish eggs develop abnormally anyway. Why, they even had trouble finding oil on the beaches.

Exxon's public relations strategist, Otto Harrison, would later report that Exxon had found the American people were more likely to believe information if it was delivered with a British accent because accents were thought to add scientific credibility.

"The public in Alaska and elsewhere desperately wants to know the straight story about what everybody's scientists are learning about the spill," ADFG's Gregg Erickson told Congress. Yet people's questions went unanswered for three more years until the spill science became public.

In early May near the end of the now frenetically paced legislative session, the oil lobbyists pulled every trick in the book to block the spill bills. One with a wide crocodile smile presented me with a copy of the Cordova Times. "Hermiller Given Keys to City," pronounced a bold headline. According to the article, CDFU and the City of Cordova had reached a "turning point" in their relationship with Alyeska and that turning point was the new president Jim Hermiller. Mayor Van Brocklin and CDFU proclaimed, "The bottom line is that we believe Alaskans can do business with Jim Hermiller. Working together we can protect the Sound and allow both fishermen and the oil industry to exist in Alaska for years to come."

This 800-pound gorilla was now an honorary member of the City and CDFU. I was stunned. I was on the CDFU board, yet no one had mentioned this to me during our weekly meetings. Feeling disgusted and betrayed, I faxed a letter to CDFU, informing the board that Alyeska lobbyists were trying to gut the spill bills and that I felt Hermiller should be partially hanged, then drawn and quartered for this effort.

I lost interest in the session and flew home before it ended to meet with CDFU. It turned out that three days before issuing the Proclamation, CDFU had signed a contract with Alyeska to provide services for local boat call-out in the event of another spill. Fishermen with contracts would be paid to keep their boats in a state of readiness for spill response. Within a month, CDFU would be openly praising Alyeska for its rough trial spill drills, despite the "many rough spots and several holes."

I was a world apart from the rest of the CDFU board in my experiences with the oil industry leaders. I battled the evil Mr. Hyde, while CDFU dealt with the charming Dr. Jekyll. Hurt by the board's actions and heavyhearted, I resigned. I consoled myself by committing to find other ways to help protect and restore the Sound.

Despite my early departure, when the dust finally settled in Juneau, Governor Cowper signed seven spill bills into law. These new laws firmly established government and citizen oversight roles, set up criminal penalties for spilling oil, and strengthened the state's ability to enforce contingency plans, among other things.

The biggest victory for the people was a law that created oil spill response performance criteria. It had passed over intense objections from the oil industry. The new law required shippers with large tankers to plan to contain, control, and clean up an "*Exxon Valdez*-size spill" of 300,000 barrels (12.6 million gallons) and to have the cleanup equipment within the region within seventy-two hours. Further, it mandated that all crude oil tankers and barges must *demonstrate* their stated ability to have on-site, within seventy-two hours, equipment to clean up a "realistic maximum discharge."

Once again Alaska had—on paper—the highest and most specific oil spill response and cleanup standards in the United States. The questions now were: Would Alaska repeat history and gut these standards? Or would the State actually implement and enforce its new laws?

Fishing and Spill Fallout

A lot of things in town weren't making a whole lot of sense; it wasn't just CDFU. Two sociologists had selected Cordova for a long-term case study of disaster trauma. They tried to explain to the community what we were facing, but the researchers were too emotionally distant and the academic gulf was too broad. In long southern drawls that stretched back to their home states of Alabama and Mississippi, they warned, "The negative impacts of the *Exxon Valdez* oil spill go beyond the direct destruction of ecosystem resources in Prince William Sound." The negative social impacts, they said, reflected "high levels of social disruption and post-traumatic stress disorder."

We lived what the sociologists studied. The town's feeling of self-confidence was gone. There was so much uncertainty about the extent of damage to the Sound, the oiled beaches, the upcoming salmon season, and the private litigation that the ambiguity itself was a major source of stress. And there was so much arguing! Danny and I argued on our boat nearly nonstop until one day in late June.

We were fishing for reds on the Flats. Gentle swells tossed sunlight into our faces as we stood together, picking glistening strong fish from our net—and arguing over where to make our next set. I felt an upwelling of deep anger that started in my stomach and surged up my spine into my head, blacking out all reason. It was as if a violent electrical thunderstorm went off in my brain. Coursing with intense energy and afraid of what I might do to Danny, I leaped around the reel to physically separate us. Then for no apparent reason, I grabbed the gaff and stood pounding the boat railing with the wooden handle.

The rhythmic thumping discharged the energy. The squall in my brain passed. I found myself looking at the sunny calm sea. I looked at Danny quietly picking fish. I kept lightly drumming the boat railing with the gaff handle as I thought about what had just happened. Then I had an insight.

"Danny! It's the spill! Somehow, the fallout from last year is making us argue. . . ." I reached, ". . . like carry-over stress or something." He thought for a moment, then agreed. That realization created a truce in our personal war.

Elsewhere in town, personal wars became public problems. Incidences of domestic violence escalated along with drinking and other substance abuse. This social turbulence seemed to be an external mirror of the anger, frustration, and angst that tormented many townspeople.

One stark example of the pervasive, caustic stress generated by Exxon's spill started when councilwoman Connie Taylor served a complaint against Mayor Van Brocklin and two councilmen for alleged violations of Alaska's Open Meetings Act. It was well known that Taylor had a close working relationship with Exxon and had made substantial financial gains from the spill. To make matters worse, she had shared sensitive legal information on the city's losses from the spill with Exxon. People were furious. Anger channeled into a recall drive. One fisherman cruised town in his pickup truck with garbage cans painted in bold letters, "CAN CONNIE!" The whole acrimonious ruckus boiled over into the next year, dragging everyone with it.

It wasn't just Cordova that was having problems. The Valdez Counseling Center reported people in the Sound were still experiencing high levels of stress from the spill. Center Director Robert Donald told the *Valdez Vanguard* that most people didn't connect the spill with the mushrooming problems in their lives. He said, "People do not walk into the counseling center and say, 'I'm stressed and suffering problems because of the oil spill.' They are saying, 'My marriage is in trouble, I'm depressed, my finances are a mess.'" Donald observed, "People didn't have time to think about the stress last summer. We tend to deny, to push, stress out of our mind. We procrastinate and our defense mechanisms tell us to deal with it later." It seemed "later" had caught up with us.

In late July when the summer sockeye run tapered off, Danny and I took a break. Hatchery pink salmon were pouring into the Sound in all-time record numbers, but we were still looking for excuses not to fish in the Sound. The price had dropped precipitously, mostly due to collapse of the Asian economy, the primary market for Alaska salmon. Returns of wild pink salmon were extremely weak with a significant chunk, 28 percent, of anticipated fish missing from oiled streams in the southwest district. To protect the wild stocks, commercial fishing was restricted to terminal harvest areas near hatcheries. Gear conflicts had skyrocketed as mismatched seiners and gillnetters competed for too many fish in too small an area. It was like a high stakes game of musical chairs. We opted to sit out and take our vacation in Cordova.

One sunny day, Linden stopped by the Co-op to find me. "The kids are in the car. We're going up to the Reservoir. We want you to come. I've got snacks!"

"How come you're not fishing?"

"It's crazy over there. We can't take the kids. It breaks their hearts. Mine too to see how the fishery has changed. So I'm taking a break to spend time with them. Let's go!"

Soon our party was headed up the steep, loose cobble trail to the Reservoir. Malani and Makena dashed along, zigzagging from salmonberry bush to blueberry bush with Sparkle in hot pursuit.

"What's that new group you're with?" asked Linden.

"It's a bunch of scientists—a technical advisory group to monitor Alyeska's ballast water discharge. You know, EPA and the state tightened up the standards in Alyeska's new wastewater discharge permit. Now they want independent scientists to review Alyeska's technical reports. It's what the fishermen wanted before they got the RCAC," I said, referring to the Regional Citizens Advisory Committee, formed by Alyeska.

"You don't think the RCAC can do that?" Linden asked.

"I actually *hope* the RCAC can do it, someday. It's just a little too early to tell how effective that group is going to be. Right now, they can't lobby or speak with media, but there are some very determined people on that board. The rules could change, if they get written into federal legislation," I said, referring to the pending Oil Pollution Act.

Linden mused, "A lot of people don't trust the oil industry anymore."

"Why should we? The spin Exxon is putting on the salmon return is all about whitewashing effects of the spill."

Townspeople knew the bonanza of hatchery pink salmon in the Sound was the result of almost two decades of careful planning and work. This bonanza masked the poor return of wild fish to oiled streams.

Just then the kids came running down the trail, berry buckets bouncing. "Look! We picked enough for a pie," Makena announced, his lips and chin stained with red and blue juice.

"It looks like you've eaten enough for two pies," Linden countered. The kids shrieked and went charging back up the trail.

"The fish are really small, too," Linden said. "They slip through the seine mesh."

"Uh-oh. I'll bet these fish grew up in oiled bays last year. Exposure to oil can stunt growth." We stared worriedly at each other. "Well, we'll know more in '92 and '93."

That was the general consensus in town. Unlike Exxon, fishermen knew better than to breathe an "all clear" until we knew whether young fish that survived their oil bath during the spill could produce offspring. We had to wait for the answer—until '92 for the even-year genetic stock of fish and '93 for the odd-year fish.

Our conversation slowed as we picked our way up a steep rocky section. "The media needs facts before then!" Linden said, breathing in short gasps. "Something other than Exxon's stories about record numbers of herring or pink salmon."

"It's got to be simple," I said. "The media missed the difference between wild and hatchery fish, and they couldn't figure out that record numbers of herring happened because of simple math."

"Last year's fish that we didn't harvest plus this year's fish," said Linden. She suddenly yelled, "*Malani! Makena!* Don't get so far off the trail! I need to be able to see you!"

"But there aren't any more berries!" The protests came from thick alders just south of the trail. The alders jostled as the kids made their way back.

"We're almost to the meadows," I told them. "Did your mom tell you about the ponds? You guys get to pick the perfect one for swimming." Eyes wide, the kids shot off up the trail again.

"Exxon's spin is totally confusing people who live Outside," I said. "My sister called to ask what the heck is going on. She said if she's confused, so is everyone else." I shook my head.

"Humph," said Linden. "Too bad the media doesn't talk to bankers. We were lucky: we made our permit payment." With a hint of irony, she added, "I hear that the old *Exxon Valdez* is shipping oil again—in the Mediterranean."

"$30 million in repairs, a new name, and a new route!" I said.

"I don't care what Exxon calls it. The *SeaRiver Mediterranean* or whatever," Linden said dismissively. "I just hope I never see it in Prince William Sound again!" Then she headed off to catch up with the kids.

We reached the top of the trail where the alders abruptly gave way to open muskeg meadows. The town's reservoir lay tucked behind foothills that rose up to the snowfields on Mt. Eccles. Across from the Heney Range lay Orca Inlet, a split pea green color. Beyond, far to the west of Hawkins Island, the Sound shimmered. On the broad stretch of spongy open muskeg meadows between the mountains and sea, the children dashed from one jeweled pond to another.

"Too cold! Too small!" they yelled. "Too muddy! Too deep! Oooooooooh! Just right!" We walked over and settled on a lump of higher ground to watch the kids play. I raised my water bottle. "Here's to a world of new adventures with young hikers!" We clunked our bottles together, laughing. "Are you ready for Malani to start kindergarten?"

"No!" Linden looked stricken. "The plan was to fish in the summer so I could stay home to homeschool them. But I have to work. . . ." Her voice trailed off. We watched the kids. Twenty years later, Linden would still claim this as her biggest hurt from the spill; that it stole her precious time with her young children. She was not alone in this loss.

When Malani started kindergarten in late August, Danny and I ventured over to the Sound for silvers. We didn't see any oil, but we also didn't see the Dawn Patrol loon. The Sound felt empty with its loss.

We heard plenty of arguing over the radio about "how clean is clean?" Earlier in the summer, Exxon had denied public access to citizen groups monitoring the beach cleanup. Then, according to ADEC, Exxon had taken on a "quasi-official, sub-governmental status. . . . [It made] recommendations about the effectiveness and the desirability of treatment techniques; it . . . [offered] comment on the health of fisheries, the recovery of the environment, the ability of people to use the areas. . . ." Over ADEC's objections, Exxon's assessments had become part of the official administrative record, "alongside, in equal standing, to those of the [federal] government."

Citizens were allowed to inspect beaches in August as part of survey crew teams. People were shocked by the condition of the beaches. "It's like the Watergate of Prince William Sound," said Eric Olsen of Seward. "All the PR that Exxon and the state put out saying it's all clean, but it's covered up." Others described how liquid oil pooled under gravel beds and oozed to the surface, compacting into hard rubbery-like substrate—the soggy lumpy futon feeling reported in spring. Moisture beaded on surfaces of oil-stained rocks. Oil bled off beaches, forming sheens along the shorelines. Lynda Hyce from Whittier concluded, "There are two ways of saying it. You can say the spill is 90 percent cleaned up, or you can say 100 percent of the beaches are still oiled. It is the same thing." A Coast Guard admiral promised to continue the cleanup in 1991.

Exxon's parting shot in mid-September was a full-page ad in state newspapers. "Sound Progress," the ad declared. "Scientists report that those areas of Prince William Sound and the Gulf of Alaska affected by the 1989 oil spill are healing rapidly, following two full seasons of cleanup efforts coupled with last year's strong winter storms." The ad claimed, "Bird and wildlife populations are abundant. The water is pure. Shoreline life is thriving in previously oiled water and sediments. Commercial fishing in the area has returned to normal. In fact, this year's catches are setting impressive records." I felt sickened that this nonsense went unchallenged by government scientists who were still under secrecy orders.

One day in late September as the emotionally jagged fishing season wound down, Danny and I anchored the *Ambergris* in Bay of Isles to wait out a fierce fall storm. I drew the first shift for one-hour anchor watches. I sat, mesmerized by the taut anchor line as it vibrated and flung off beads of water. All of our troubles receded. Suddenly an image popped into my head of Alaska's state flag with a different fishery on each of the eight stars—an Alaska fish flag. One hour slid by as I sketched contentedly, then another three hours as winds buffeted our boat.

Danny awoke to find himself littered with paper drawings. "What are you doing?" he asked. I had a plan—but it had to wait until we finished fishing.

Funny Phones and Fall Adventures

Once back in Cordova, I used my line drawings as patterns, cutting and piec-
ing together bits of calico fabric. Then, using skills my mother had patiently
taught me as a child, I appliquéd the colorful calico creatures onto pillows,
bibs, and the Alaska Fish Flag. Danny took one look at the product and said
simply, "You could sell these." That was the plan.

But it was about more than making money. Working with the colors and
images restored a sense of calm. Hungry for this inner peace, I called a girlfriend
in Seattle. "Yosh" now owned the dog I had left for "one summer" when I first
went to Alaska. She was just crazy enough to go for yet another idea of mine.
Together, we launched a fiber art business, Hot Yotts, a blend of our last names.
This became something of an obsession as well as a successful cottage industry.

Years later, I read that art is a form of therapy. In the words of Jungian
analyst and storyteller Clarissa Pinkola Estés, "the craft of the hands (is) the
making of something, and that something is soul. . . . Art is important for it
commemorates the seasons of the soul, or a special or tragic event in the soul's
journey." I didn't realize it at the time, but the art marked the beginning of my
journey of healing deep emotional wounds from the spill.

When the fishing season ended, the meeting season began—and the arguing continued. Fishermen packed meetings to argue over an allocation plan
to avoid repeating the summer's horrendous fish wars. People argued over
fall and spring cleanup plans; ways to improve port and terminal operations;
and ways to improve vessel traffic systems in the Sound. People argued with
attorneys and each other. It was endless. I avoided most of the meetings, not
knowing that the two sociologists from Alabama and Mississippi were counting "avoidance behavior" as an indication of lingering spill trauma.

I busied myself with closing on my first home, designing patterns for Hot
Yotts, and planning a trip to Europe. I wanted to see oil industry operations
firsthand in Norway and Scotland. Norway relied solely on mechanical cleanup
of oil spills: the country had banned chemical dispersants. At the Sullom Voe
tanker terminal in Scotland, citizens played a significant advisory role in daily
industry operations. The new Oil Pollution Act, signed into law by President
George H. W. Bush, mandated similar oversight in Prince William Sound
and Cook Inlet.

The Oil Pollution Act of 1990 (OPA 90) had passed over fierce industry
objections. The tragic oil spill off Huntington Beach, California, earlier in

February had helped generate strong public pressure to drive the bill into law. OPA 90 required double hulls on oil tankers serving U.S. ports by 2015, and it stipulated a phase-in period. 2015 was forty-two years after Interior Secretary Rodger Morton's pre-TAPS promise to Cordova fishermen and the American people. Nonetheless, this sea change in attitude by the United States affected tankers worldwide.

Besides other big-ticket items, OPA 90 also included a shot of housekeeping provisions that tightened up manning standards and licensing requirements to reduce crew fatigue and human error. For example, under OPA 90 it was no longer possible to obtain a captain's license to operate a ship for a person whose driver's license had been revoked for driving a car while intoxicated, as in the case of Captain Joe Hazelwood.

As described in the *Anchorage Daily News*, the law contained "several measures of comfort and solace" for Alaskans, including a first ever comprehensive review and audit of the entire pipeline system in light of the corrosion claims; two citizens' advisory councils; an oil spill research center in Cordova; increased radar coverage in the Sound; and a navigation light on Bligh Reef.

True, there had been compromises. But for the most part, OPA 90 read like a birthday wish list of the people. Only time would tell whether the tough new standards would survive the political whims of different presidential administrations and congresses to be actually funded, implemented, and enforced as the national public expected.

Chuck Hamel and I spoke often. During one call, he filled me in on Alyeska's misdeeds during the fishing season. "Alyeska really butted heads with the EPA and state this summer! The EPA warned Valdez people that their cancer risk was 100 times higher than the acceptable risk level used by the EPA. That got Stan Stephens's attention. You know, that terminal emits 450 tons of benzene a year and I've got the documents to prove it!"

"What?" I interjected. "Alyeska is permitted for 40 tons a year. They promised 'virtually zero VOCs' (volatile organic carbons) would be released. Benzene is a carcinogen!"

"Right, but now they're saying, 'We're at 400 tons a year and we can't go down to 40 tons.'" He chuckled. "Get this: The EPA issued Alyeska a Notice of Violation of the Clean Air Act. Alyeska responded by slowing the flow of oil through the pipeline to reduce vapor emissions."

"Oh, I heard about that. Judge Holland intervened and issued a restraining order against the EPA. His order blocked enforcement of the Clean Air Act!"

"How backward is that?" asked Chuck. "Then Alyeska agreed to "work in good faith" with the regulators—but only after the EPA agreed, in writing, not to prosecute. The arrogance of these people! Then, Alyeska tried to amend the Clean Air Act to suit its needs.

"Didn't Alyeska just release a study of tanker loading emissions?" I asked.

"Have you seen it? Alyeska reported minimal benzene emissions and health risk to Valdez residents. Stan Stephens is so upset that he joined the Regional Citizens Advisory Committee! He wants the RCAC to review the air quality study like what you do with the technical advisory group on the ballast water studies—find where Alyeska lied with statistics."

During another call, Chuck shared exciting news. "Congressman George Miller is interested in my documents! Seems that TAPS tanker spill in his backyard in Huntington made him want to look into Alyeska's business a little more closely."

"That's great news, Chuck!"

"There's more. This environmental law firm, Ecolit, is very interested in Alyeska. I've been spending some time with the director, Dr. Wayne Jenkins. I just can't understand why Muffin has a fit every time this guy comes to visit. The dog just keeps barking and he won't quit. I have to shut him in the basement."

Unlike Muffin, Chuck never suspected "Ecolit" or "Dr. Jenkins" of foul play, not even when his trash or mail was periodically stolen from his home.

The telephone in my new home began acting very strangely. It sounded like a bowl of Rice Krispies with freshly poured milk. Sometimes it went off into a long, sizzling static attack, followed by a disconnection. Chuck said it was tapped. We assumed it was Alyeska. "The bastards!" said Chuck. "Why don't they pick on somebody their own size?"

Not knowing what to do, I decided to ignore this new development. I reasoned I wasn't doing anything illegal—Alyeska was. I warned friends and other people who called that I suspected my phone was tapped. In return for this courtesy, they thought I was crazy or paranoid.

My father, however, took a very dim view of this situation. Once during a particularly loud series of pops and crackles, he said, "Excuse me." Then he roared into the phone, *"Listen you sons-of-bitches! You people work for some of the richest companies in the world! Can't you at least get some decent equipment so you don't have to interrupt our conversations?!"* Lowering his voice, he said, "Now, where were we?"

My father continued to badger the suspected spooks on the line right up until the line mysteriously cleared months later, after my return from Europe.

Defense Tactics

Meanwhile, the lawsuits against Exxon for private damages were taking form. On the same day in December, Judge Holland denied class certification in federal court, while Judge Brian Shortell certified a class of cannery workers and, two months later, four additional classes in state court. This made no sense to me. The judges had read the same case law. How could one decide to consolidate claims into classes and one not?

Law allows for class action when a large number of people suffer similar injuries in a similar way. Our lawyers sought a class action because it cut expenses, it was more efficient, and it was the fairest way to compensate all the injured individuals. In a class action, individual claims are pooled into classes of similar claims. Our lawyers asked for certification of seven classes: commercial fishermen, Alaska Natives, local governments, property owners, area businesses, cannery workers, and recreational users. Exxon and Alyeska vigorously opposed class consolidation, because they wanted to reduce the total number of claims, which could only be done by shooting down individual claims like skeets—one at a time.

To further complicate things, Judge Holland also ordered plaintiffs to exhaust all remedies for economic compensation under the Trans-Alaska Pipeline Liability (TAPL, "tap-el") Fund before they could pursue any claims in federal court. As Rick Steiner put it, this ruling was "a bad omen" for plaintiffs. Congress had done away with this fund just five months earlier when it passed the Oil Pollution Act, but the new law did not grandfather in claims from the 1989 spill. Cordovans were distraught. Many phoned their lawyers and each other. I went to visit Linden.

"What a mess!" she declared as she put a teakettle on the stove. "It's pretty clear now whose side Judge Holland is on, isn't it? I'll bet those oil companies are celebrating—and I'll bet they're not drinking tea, either! What kind do you want?" I could count on Linden to make me laugh. "Tell me about the TAPL Fund," she said as I made my tea selection.

"We just talked about that at the UFA board meeting. Judge Holland made the Cook Inlet fishermen who were oiled by the *Glacier Bay* spill go through that fund, too. About half of the 800 claims settled for $30,000 to $50,000 apiece. Then, it got tricky. The fund administrators offered the remaining litigants more money—between $50,000 to $80,000 apiece. Another three hundred claims settled. So now, there're only one hundred claims still in court."

"So Judge Holland probably thinks that fund works because it reduced the number of cases in his court." She poured tea water, thinking. "But can't he see that's not going to work for us? The *Glacier Bay* spill only closed salmon fisheries in Cook Inlet for two days! That can't add up to a whole lot of money—not like our claims!"

I nodded. "There's $86 million in the TAPL Fund. The *Glacier Bay* claims didn't even come close to that. The *Exxon Valdez* claims are going to be billions of dollars."

"So," Linden reasoned, "that means no one is going to have their claims fully paid through the TAPL Fund. And I can't think of one fisherman who would be happy with some token fraction of his claim. That means everyone is still going to file claims in court. Judge Holland accomplishes nothing—and we get no money until this sorts itself out."

Sam pulled up in the driveway with the kids. We exchanged glances that said the conversation was over. The kids burst through the door. "Riki! Riki!"

"What have you got, Malani?"

"A violin!" Her face shone. "I'm taking lessons with Ms. Cunningham."

"I've got a slingshot!" said Makena.

"And his grandpa is a pacifist," Linden added.

Behind the scenes, a legal war raged with tactics more precise than slingshots. According to Dave Oesting, "Exxon's lawyers are wizards at conducting a masterfully engineered, procedural war to confuse, consolidate, delay, draw out, and exhaust the plaintiff constituency."

Oesting and Jerry Cohen organized lawyers representing over fifty law firms into teams and committees. The team tasked with proving Exxon's oil caused damages had intended to rely heavily on government spill science to make its case. Public access to this information was critical: no science, no case. This team engaged in battle immediately with Exxon as Exxon fought to keep government science secret as part of a pending settlement for damages to wildlife and public lands.

The discovery committee and the law committee also became fully engaged immediately, fighting Exxon over admissible evidence. The discovery process is contentious by nature, but according to Oesting, Exxon made it extremely so by using disputes as a tactical weapon to cause delays and increase expenses.

Instead of producing all documents likely to lead to admissible evidence, Exxon withheld over 12,000 documents as "privileged." This forced Oesting and his teams to evaluate and challenge each listing, document by document. Our lawyers only had time to challenge 3,000 documents, most of which Exxon had to produce. Four lawyers were kept busy, full-time, fighting the "war of motions," as Oesting called it, for five years right up to and through the trial.

Judge Holland's decision to go through the TAPL Fund also gave our lawyers fits. According to Oesting, the fund was "controlled by a bunch of silver-spooned, silk-stocking eastern lawyers who were aligned with the oil industry and who never believed that a spill would happen in the first place." Our attorneys knew, as many claimants had surmised, that the process would not reduce the number of claims. Jerry Cohen predicted, "Instead of putting money into people's hands, this [process] could delay that for three or four years." Also, conveniently for the oil industry, punitive damages were not recognized under the TAPL Fund. Judge Holland's order diverted our attorneys on a wild-goose chase for two years.

I called Linden two days before her family planned to leave to visit relatives over the holidays.

"You haven't heard?" she asked in a voice that raised goose bumps on my arms and legs. "There was a fire on the *Blue Note* last night. Sam's down pulling what's left out of the harbor."

"Oh, Linden! *No!* What happened? Was anyone hurt?"

"No one was hurt. It was a faulty wire on the cabin heater, we think."

"How awful! What are you going to do?"

"We're going to have Christmas with Sam's family," she said grimly. "After that, I don't know. We don't have money for a new boat."

CHAPTER SIX

TRICKS OF THE TRADE

In early January, Cordova made statewide news for squabbling. The Open Meetings Act lawsuit initiated by councilwoman Taylor against the mayor and two councilmen erupted into a community affair when the city council intervened, voting to pay attorney fees and expenses for the city and the sued parties. Threat of mounting legal fees and increasingly bitter debates sapped townspeople's energy. Even the successful campaign to recall Taylor, the first in anyone's memory, failed to stem the money hemorrhaging from the city's budget or the incessant ill-tempered bickering.

What we all failed to recognize at the time was that our community was still reeling from enormous economic and emotional upheaval from the spill like shock waves after an earthquake. The fighting was an outward manifestation of this trauma. Despite the record-breaking harvest of the 44 million salmon, the harvest value was about half of what it might have been worth without the spill. This was according to economists hired by our lawyers and our own Mayor Bobby Van Brocklin, who understood numbers, the fishing industry, and the difference between oil tainting perceptions and the Asian economic collapse. The loss of 30 million fish bucks rippled through the community, creating budget shortfalls in everything from city coffers to processors, the aquaculture corporation, hotels, restaurants, bars, and shops.

Facing an economic slump, city leaders called its citizens together to discuss ways to diversify the local economy. Linden and I were among some 100 people who listened to the city's plans to stimulate the economy. Afterward, we debriefed over tea at my home.

"The city sure has some grandiose plans," Linden said. "The cruise ships might work, but I can't see a deepwater port happening without a huge fight, especially if it's going to be used to export timber. Fishermen aren't going to like that."

I liked her practical attitude. She was never one to wallow in a problem—or shrink from it. She could clearly see and state an issue, usually from multiple perspectives. Then she would explore various solutions, while considering the impacts of each on the community. This way, we could also figure out what really might work to resolve an issue.

I nodded. "And, the town is going to argue over completion of the Copper River Highway—just like it always has."

The history of "the Road" dated back to the late 1930s when the Copper River & Northwest Railroad closed after the once rich copper veins upriver were mined out. The plan to turn the railroad bed into an overland road to Cordova faltered and died, a victim of World War II and the 1964 earthquake. State roadmaps showed Cordova with a skinny red line extending 50 miles out of town, then stopping far short of any other red lines. This remained a sore point in town. Those in favor of completion saw economic opportunity and a way out of town; those opposed saw completion as a way into town for hordes of people driving RVs and bringing fishing poles.

"Hmmm," she said, sipping tea once again. "What are we going to do? We need to find something that we all can agree on—and soon."

"I don't know—yet. For now, I'm going to Juneau to help draft regulations for the new spill laws, otherwise I'll have just wasted my time last year. That new oil spill response law left a lot for interpretation."

The previous year in Juneau I had learned that once a law passes, the agency that the new law governs writes the regulations that interpret how the law is carried out and enforced. In other words, it's like having one set of people design the concept for a new game and then letting the players write the rules. Both the process of rule-making (drafting and passing laws) and regulation negotiation (writing codes for how new laws will be implemented) are open to the public and heavily influenced by corporate lobbyists and other special interest groups. Rules for new laws can reverse or weaken legislative intent during the process of writing regulations.

I explained, "There's some slippery wording like 'realistic maximum discharge.' That means the whole tanker-load to fishermen, but only an *Exxon Valdez*-size' spill to oilmen. I think that's only 30 percent of what spilled."

"How are you coming with that?"

"I found out the state did a secret investigation on it." Linden's eyes widened. "The state hired independent surveyors to look at Exxon's math. But no one will say any more. They are playing it like an ace up their sleeve in the civil lawsuit over environmental damages."

Linden groaned. "Secrets! Lawsuits! I'm sick of it all."

Most people in town felt this way. It was considered responsible behavior to make amends for injury so all involved could move on with their own lives. By stalling and working to reduce its own liability, Exxon was holding thousands of people's lives hostage.

"Have you filed all your paperwork for the TAPL Fund claim?" she asked. "That's due March 25, you know. You'll be in Juneau."

"Danny's going to take care of it. He's the permit holder now; I'm crew. We transferred so I could do politics and sew pillows and stuff for the fall fairs."

"I'm looking forward to that," said Linden, smiling. "Sharing a booth at fairs will be fun. I'll make more earrings this winter—that and find someone to lease our seine permit." Her face saddened. "I won't be fishing this summer. I'm taking classes to be a kindergarten teacher."

We sipped tea as the winter wind rocked the house. The spill had pushed us down different paths and into different lives than we had once imagined. I wondered how it would all unfold.

Finally I said, "Well, you like working with young kids. And that means there'll be time for hikes with your kids in the summer." She brightened and we gave each other a high five. The promise of fun would pull us through an emotionally wearing winter.

Ballast Watergate and Bankruptcies

I arrived in Juneau to find a different playing field. The newly elected governor, Walter Hickel, was elected as a third-party candidate who had entered the race late, campaigned only in the Anchorage area where half of the state's population resided, and won with less than 40 percent of the vote. A bumper sticker proclaimed: "Pot got more votes than Hickel," referring to a failed referendum to keep marijuana legal. Nonetheless, pot lost and Hickel was governor.

Hickel picked up the reins of power essentially where he had dropped them twenty-one years ago when he had left the governor's office for a two-year stint as Nixon's Secretary of the Interior. He pointedly admitted that he was trying to tilt the balance of power from the legislature to the executive branch. His blustery, "can-do" attitude strongly appealed to those who favored development of Alaska's rich resources—his constituency base.

Hickel chose oilmen and foresters for his resource cabinet and proposed to cut the state's operating budget across the board, while pumping millions into the state budget for his pet development projects. He was adamant about giving Alaskans and tourists access to Prince William Sound. Hickel spoke of roads into Whittier and Cordova, and lodges, small boat harbors, and deep-water ports to "improve" the Sound, all built with money from a prospective oil spill settlement for damages to wildlife and public lands. Governor Hickel made settlement one of his top priorities. Legislators were offended, even alienated. An uneasy alliance formed between the public and the legislators to fight the arrogant administration.

While negotiations continued behind the scenes, Chuck Hamel let fly one of his "missiles." He informed the EPA—for the second time—that TAPS tanker operators were disposing toxic and hazardous wastes through the Alyeska marine terminal in Port Valdez. This time he also released documents, showing the EPA had confirmed, then dismissed, his 1985 claims after a three-year investigation. As reported in the *Boston Globe* and the *Wall Street Journal*, TAPS tanker operators admitted that it was "common practice" to transfer tank washings, slops, oily sludges, and other hazardous materials to northbound TAPS tankers, a practice the shippers had adamantly denied in 1985. The shippers now claimed this was not illegal. In addition, Chuck's documents revealed that TAPS tankers were also hauling waste from other tankers and transferring waste from shore refineries, a clandestine practice known as "back-flushing."

Harold Green, chief of water permits with the EPA, told the *Boston Globe*, "I'm finding out about practices I did not know about." Green said, "Deliberately stopping a supertanker and putting the washings into its ballast—there's no way the permit authorizes that kind of discharge."

The Alaska legislature announced it would convene oversight hearings into the matter. Instead of supplying information to help me prepare to testify, Chuck became understandably distracted by his multimillion-dollar North Slope property dispute against Exxon. He told me to "follow the money."

I thought long and hard. The year before the spill, the State of Alaska had designated Port Valdez as a toxic impaired waterway from chronic oil pollution. There had to be a connection between the chronic pollution in Port Valdez and the ballast water dumping practices. What would be the motive to haul oily wastes thousands of miles to Alaska for dumping? *Follow the money.* Shippers must have to pay to dispose of their wastes elsewhere, I reasoned. Where? Shipyards. Who regulates shipyards? The Coast Guard.

After calling the Coast Guard Marine Safety Office in Juneau, I spoke to every large shipyard operator on the West Coast and in Hawaii. I was told in every instance that lightering (transferring) tank cleanings and slops between TAPS tankers was a common practice to bypass ship repair yard disposal fees that could amount to several hundred thousand dollars for a TAPS trader. I was stymied. I thought MARPOL, an international maritime law, regulated handling and discharge of oily ballast to minimize pollution at sea. I decided to visit the Coast Guard office.

In reading the thick book of MARPOL regulations, I found no rule that required tankers to dispose of wastes at the shipyard where the tanker was serviced. This loophole allowed tanker operators to transfer and transport wastes, including hazardous oily sludges, to the cheapest disposal site on the West Coast—the Alyeska terminal. Apparently, Port Valdez had become an industrial dumping ground for the West Coast tanker fleet. I dubbed the practice, "Ballast Watergate."

Senator Curt Menard championed the oversight hearings. He said, "We certainly don't want to be in a situation ten years from now where we have a toxic waste dump in Valdez and people are asking why no one did something about it."

I was invited to participate as a panelist at the hearings. This time, I knew to prep legislators with information, questions, and answers. As staffers wagered on whether I was in over my head, Chuck Hamel came through and sent me critical documents before the first of many hearings, which raged on for six weeks. Ultimately, the hearings were productive. The legislature appropriated $175,000 to ADEC to contract independent environmental monitoring of Port Valdez. The EPA and the Coast Guard started their own investigations into TAPS tanker practices.

Meanwhile, in early March when I called Danny to ask how he was doing with our TAPL Fund claim, he had shocking news. "We might have nowhere to sell our fish this year. The Co-op filed for bankruptcy. So did Chugach Alaska Corporation. Both of its processors in town might close."

"What? This has to be because of the spill."

"The spill started it, at least for the Co-op. We didn't have enough volume in '89 because guys worked the cleanup. That drove up operating costs. The processors are all saying they paid too much for fish last season. A record number of buyers drove up the price. The market bought cheaper farmed fish. Now there's a huge inventory of canned wild pinks. Banks aren't loaning money. They say there's going to be a huge drop in pink prices."

"Danny, those Chugach canneries process half of the fish in town!"

"Yeah. We've got all these fish and no market. There's talk of new products and markets, but that's going to take awhile. PWSAC is worried about buyers for its fish. It asked the state to approve foreign floaters [floating processors]. The shore-based processors don't want the competition." He sighed. "The town is pretty wigged out."

"God, everything is falling to pieces. I don't know if I should be there or here."

"There's nothing you could do here to help and people think you're doing a good job there. So stay. But you are missing some good skiing!" I also missed his smile and lighthearted companionship.

Assigning Value to Spill Losses

In the midst of the Ballast Watergate hearings, Governor Hickel and the U.S. Justice Department announced a global settlement of all government criminal and civil claims against Exxon for spill damages.

The fact that the spill settlement had fallen on Hickel's watch was a fluke of fate. A year earlier, Rick Steiner had innocently stumbled upon the George H. W. Bush administration's first secret plea bargain with Exxon. A visionary thinker, Rick had hit upon an idea for using Exxon's penalties and fines from spilling oil to thwart another impending disaster. The looming disaster was that Alaska Native corporations, aided by a federal tax loophole, had started to clear-cut Native people's ancestral lands in the Sound. The loophole allowed Alaska Native corporations to devalue their timber assets that could not be harvested profitably, and then sell the losses to profitable corporations like Purina, Nestlé, and Kellogg. The corporations that bought the losses would then deduct them from their profits to reduce the amount owed in federal taxes. In other words, the loophole was a tax evasion scam.

Rick understood the intertwined relationship between the coastal temperate rainforest and the sea. Many species injured by the spill spend part of their lives in the forest adjoining the sea. For example, some sea ducks rear their young in tree cavities, diminutive marbled murrelets nest in thick moss draped on tree branches, and shy river otters den in root tangles. Trees also nurture young salmon by keeping stream water cool for eggs and fry, stabilizing banks from erosion, and providing needle litter to nourish insects and invertebrates— the food for young fish. Rick reasoned that clear-cutting activities would delay the Sound's ability to recover from the oil spill.

His idea was eloquently simple: Why not use money Exxon was going to have to pay in civil and criminal fines to protect the forest as a step toward

restoring the Sound from the spill? By putting private land into conservation easements, critical habitat could be protected without diminishing the
Native people's ability to create other economic opportunities from their land
or taking away their land base—the critical link to their subsistence culture.

When Rick proposed his idea to Exxon Shipping, he learned of the federal
government's pending settlement with Exxon, which largely ignored Alaska.
Rick immediately shared his "privileged" information with the state and our
lawyers, among others. When the *Wall Street Journal* splashed details of the
proposed sweetheart deal across its front pages, the deal imploded. A year had
passed.

By March 1991, community support for Rick's idea reached an almost feverish pitch, which I followed anxiously in the *Cordova Times*. Eyak Corporation
was starting to clear-cut its forests around Lake Elsner, prime sockeye and coho
spawning and rearing habitat on the Copper River Delta. People penned their
frustration in a volley of letters to the editor, protesting the loss of prime sockeye habitat near popular hiking and berry-picking trails for what amounted to
corporate tax evasion. The Native community split over the destruction to its
lands versus income. Some tried unsuccessfully to stop the logging and unseat
the corporate board. Eyak Corporation entrenched in its legal right to cut the
trees and was deaf to economic and emotional appeals.

The second settlement was announced in the middle of this uproar. It
included a criminal fine of $100 million to be split between the state and
federal governments and a civil settlement of $900 million for environmental
damages. An additional $100 million could be claimed between September
2002 to September 2006 under a "reopener" clause for any "unanticipated
injury" or lingering harm. The agreement included a thirty-day public
comment period. The public reaction was not what the governor expected.

Most legislators were shocked by the notion that the oil spill had damaged
the Sound. A year earlier, many had turned a deaf ear to my pleas for stronger
spill prevention and response measures. Some, callously, had told me flat-
out that their constituents had made money from the cleanup and that it
had boosted the entire state's income. In the absence of any counterevidence,
most had believed Exxon's story of minimal harm and rapid environmental
recovery. Yet now leaked estimates from a secret federal economic study put
the range of natural resource damages from *three to eight billion dollars*. This
was based on "contingent valuation" that used surveys of Americans to set the
cost of a sea otter, a bald eagle, a marbled murrelet, and so on, to society.

The proposed $900 million settlement was three times lower than the minimum estimate from the federal survey. When inflation, tax breaks, and the proposed ten-year payout period were factored in, the civil fine amounted to $500 million—or ten percent of Exxon's annual earnings in 1990. Even Exxon chairman Lawrence Rawl scoffed at the amount, claiming that it would "not have a significant effect on our earnings. . . . We're talking about stretching a bill out over ten years. It will not curtail any of our plans."

The proposed settlement was also a bargain for Alyeska. It released Alyeska completely from criminal and civil charges because, according to Alaska's attorney general, Exxon did not want to settle its own liability only to find itself liable through its shared ownership of Alyeska. Yet people believed that Alyeska and its seven owners should be held accountable for the failed initial cleanup.

While I lobbied hard against the settlement in Juneau, people in communities throughout the oiled region also fought the deal—and demanded to see the secret spill science. "Please don't ask us to trust you," Cordova Mayor Van Brocklin told a panel of visiting legislators. "We've lost our ability to trust."

With everyone clamoring to see the publicly funded spill science, the federal government relented. On April 8, it released an eighteen-page summary of injury. The summary showed that the oil spill took a much greater toll on wildlife, shorelines, tidal zones, and the valuable herring and salmon fisheries than previously suspected. The death toll included up to 580,000 murres, 5,500 sea otters, 500 eagles, 200 harbor seals, twenty-four missing orcas, and on and on. But even worse, the report indicated the *killing did not stop in 1989* for salmon, herring, sea otters, and a number of other species. The federal government's report sent shock waves through Cordova.

Nine days later, Exxon unveiled twenty corporate-sponsored studies and unleashed a media blitz to counter the government's information. Exxon's propaganda claimed that Prince William Sound was well on its way to recovery: "The water is clean, fish are abundant and safe to eat, and wildlife is likewise abundant and thriving, and the beaches have been effectively cleaned."

The huge disparity in the scientific findings was a harbinger of things to come. But, before people could get too worked up about that, Judge Russel Holland threw the settlement out of his court on April 24, saying that the $100 million criminal fine was too low. Holland's move shocked many people, including myself, who had assumed that the judge would accept the settlement as it favored Exxon.

In the midst of this debacle, the deadline for TAPL Fund claims passed. In Cordova, Patience Andersen Faulkner operated one of the few fishermen's claims offices left in Alaska after our lawyers' mass exodus to their own home offices throughout the United States. Once a week, Patience joined a teleconference with all the lawyers to discuss strategy and stay current with issues. That was how she learned that our lawyers were planning to ask for a million dollars a permit for claims filed under the TAPL Fund.

"So I asked some simple questions," Patience said, "and caused a nice debate for an hour on the phone. 'Does this cover one year? Does this cover crew? How about the vessel?' I had to educate our attorneys that the seine permits were worth a fortune, and the vessels were worth a fortune, and the seiners that had a history of making money—well, in one year, a million dollars might come close to it, but it might not." The lawyers agreed to ask for two million dollars a permit. "Fine with me," said Patience. "Now let's talk about crew." After more "education," the lawyers agreed to ask for $100,000 for each crewmember.

Our lawyers filed over $50 billion worth of claims against a $100 million fund. This infuriated Judge Holland. He would find another way to reduce the number of claims in his court.

Meanwhile, the job that I originally came to Juneau to do—monitor the process of drafting regulations for new oil spill prevention and response law— hit a speed bump. I had participated in some of the early ADEC working group sessions on the regulations, but I quickly found I had zero tolerance for oil industry shenanigans, bureaucratic mumbo jumbo, and lots of meetings. Luckily, staff with the now federally sanctioned Prince William Sound Regional Citizens Advisory Council stepped in to fill the void. Then, inexplicably, the ADEC delayed public release of the draft regulations until after the legislative session adjourned.

When I learned that the ADEC Deputy Commissioner, an oilman, had secretly provided Alyeska with a draft of the regulations prior to its release for public review, I realized the reason for the delay: Alyeska had objected to the draft document. Citing abuse of discretion by ADEC and improper influence by the oil industry, I helped spearhead an effort to file a complaint with the State Ombudsman's office. This triggered an official investigation that dragged into summer, along with the public review of the draft regulations.

Ongoing Spill Trauma

In early May I left the legislative session in Juneau and reported to Anchorage for my deposition with Exxon and Alyeska in the private damages lawsuit. The deposition process for the plaintiffs' lawsuit was in full swing with literally thousands of people—fishermen, Natives, business owners, government and city employees, scientists, oilmen, tanker crews, and others—giving their sworn testimony. The plaintiffs' lawyers had listed me as an "expert witness," which meant that I had to document everything I might address at the trial. I brought over twenty cardboard file boxes of papers, including phone logs, documentation of air and water quality problems in Port Valdez, correspondences with politicians and regulators, and drafts of legislation. It had taken me a week just to find, organize, and pack the material.

Sitting in a small room with an attorney at my side and facing half a dozen dark-suited and grim-faced oil lawyers, I sensed immediately that their game was intimidation. After a spiel about the importance of telling the truth, Alyeska's lead lawyer asked me how I would like to be addressed. "Anything but 'Honey,'" I retorted. The oil attorneys burst out laughing and the opportunity for intimidation vaporized. For an entire week I answered question after question about my doings during and after the spill, the Oil Reform Alliance, and my four year relationship with Chuck Hamel, whom they mistakenly thought was bankrolling my work.

After my deposition, I joined Danny and the gillnet fleet for fishing reds and kings on the Copper River Flats. During closures, I caught up with the O'Toole family. One night as we cleaned up after a salmon barbeque, I asked Linden if she went to the city council meeting on the budget. She rolled her eyes. "The library meeting room was packed."

"So I've heard. With a nice calm crowd, too, I bet," I said sarcastically.

"People are so upset! The city wants to raise taxes to make up for the lost raw fish tax and the Connie Taylor lawsuit. People don't want higher taxes, but they want the city to provide all of the counseling services that Governor Hickel cut. . . ." She shook her head and looked at me over a sink full of soapy dishes.

Linden was happy and optimistic by nature. I knew things had to be very serious for her to be this upset. She was also extremely sensitive to the feelings and emotions of others, much more so than me. She usually reflected the town's mood like a thermometer takes someone's temperature.

"There's just no confidence in the future," she said.

"I can feel it. People need a good fishing season in the Sound to set things right."

"Do you think we'll get that? We're supposed to get another good return on pinks, but the price forecast is pretty bad. A lot of fish could add up to a whole lot of nothing if we don't get a decent price."

I shook my head as I dried dishes. "We'll find out soon enough on the fishing."

"What's going on with our lawsuit? I've heard that people's claims are being dropped."

"It's Judge Holland. He ruled that our lawsuit was a maritime tort. He decided all of our claims—business claims, property claims, fishing and subsistence claims, everything—fit under maritime law since all losses came from a spill at sea. So he roped us all together under one law.

"Then he decided that all claims have to pass something called the *Robins Dry Dock* rule. Dave Oesting says that if a claim can't prove physical injury to person or property, that claim will get thrown out. Oesting says, 'No touch, no foul.'"

Linden stared at me wide-eyed. "Can Judge Holland do that?! Exxon promised to make us whole five days after the spill! Exxon promised the Chamber of Commerce it would acknowledge our business claims! Exxon agreed that Cordova was unique—that all of our businesses were linked to commercial fishing. . . ."

She thought a minute as I finished putting away the dishes. We sat down at the table with some tea. Finally she said, "So Exxon stood in our gym and lied to us."

"Pretty much, but that's not all. You've heard Judge Holland ruled that boat and permit devaluations don't count unless the boat or permit is sold?"

Linden nodded glumly. "The bank is ignoring the devaluations too! We still have to make payments on the full value even though our permit is worth about half of what we paid for it two years ago."

"You and the whole seine fleet. What are you going to do?"

"We've leased a boat. Sam is going to fish. I don't know yet what I'm going to do. The kindergarten teacher jobs in Cordova are filled. We don't want to move. This town has lost thirty families already. A lot of people are just barely hanging on. I can't even think about it any more." She shook her head. "Let's have some ice cream. Isn't your family visiting soon?" Linden called the kids inside as I dished out ice cream. We began to plan some activities for my visitors.

My family was still in Cordova in late July when a shipload of Soviets visited Cordova as part of Russia's celebration of its 250-year anniversary of "discovering" Alaska. Hundreds of volunteers coordinated efforts to feed 3,000 people during three days of community picnics and potlucks. Bands blared on the streets. The Natives and Russians shared a ceremony honoring their ancestors at Nuchek, once the site of a thriving Native community and Russian mission. In return, the spontaneous and generous Russians gave Cordova its first taste of opera. Thirty-one members from a troupe sponsored by the Leningrad Department of Culture and State Theater performed in the high school gym, a double feature of *Juno and Avos* and *Jesus Christ Superstar* to thunderous applause and standing ovations. The town was reminded of the performance for weeks afterward by the brilliant red hair shades of girls who copied the coiffures of the lead actresses.

My father, full of energy and not one to miss any fun, stood with nearly the entire community on the dock at midnight as the Russians set sail amid fireworks and streamers. In the din of well-wishing and waving, I sensed this was about more than a reunion with our past. It was about soul retrieval—and that was something that, according to the southern sociologists—we desperately needed. Earlier in the summer, those sociologists had bridged the academic divide. They reached out to their study subjects and warned that a community could lose its soul through selfishness, greed, fighting, quarreling, and lack of forgiveness. People were shocked as they heard the scientists explain that until everyone quit asking, "What's in it for me?" and started working for the greater good, spill trauma would linger and healing would be postponed. They had warned if Cordova's soul died, there would be massive outmigration. Worse yet, there would be no revival possible.

Standing on the dock with my father, I sensed a deep hunger for working together—and a deep happiness that resulted from collective acts. Cordova's soul had not yet died. There was still hope of recovery. But that slim hope was about to be sorely tested.

After the departure of my family and the Russians, Danny and I eased back into the summer routine. While Danny prepped the *Ambergris* for fishing silvers, I used the analysis from the Regional Citizen's Advisory Council to write comments to the state on the proposed tanker contingency plans. Using timely press releases, the RCAC had garnered more influence and political leverage than the TAPS owners had anticipated.

Further, while still hiring its own technical staff, the RCAC had teamed up with the technical advisory group that I was on to design environmental monitoring studies of Alyeska's ballast water treatment plant. These studies were critical as both federal and state Ballast Watergate investigations had confirmed Chuck Hamel's allegations. Further, investigators had found that TAPS tankers were discharging dirty ballast intermittently along the entire West Coast between Panama and Alaska with the oily water monitoring equipment required by international law turned off! Undeterred by paltry fines of $10,000 that amounted to less than 5 percent of what the shippers had saved by disposing the wastes at Alyeska instead of a shipyard, the TAPS owners proposed to legalize transfer of many of the oily wastes to its treatment plant.

In the midst of this, I received a strange late-night phone call from Chuck Hamel. Instead of his usual bravado and candor, he was angry and afraid. He wailed, "I've been had, snookered, fucked, screwed, blued, and tattooed!" He ranted about spies, parabolic microphones, pen registers, body wires, phone taps, impostors, Ecolit, and Wackenhut. He claimed that he had been ten days without sleep. He was very worried about the safety of his wife, his sources—and now this new group of whistleblower spies, dubbed "Chuckie's Angels." "This country is coming apart at the seams!" he bemoaned.

During the disjointed conversation, I gathered that Chuck's superstar law firm, Ecolit, was a front created by Alyeska's security firm, Wackenhut, to trick Chuck into revealing the names of his sources—the company insiders who were divulging information on Alyeska's wrongdoing. Naming names would jeopardize jobs and maybe put people's lives at risk. Trying to think of something to calm him down, it dawned on me: "Chuck! That's why Muffin barked at Jenkins! The guy's body wire must have made a noise your dog could hear." Chuck stopped short in his tirade and burst out laughing.

When we hung up, I stared out my lone office window. I thought of my bout the previous year with my strangely acting phone. Suddenly I was terrified by the full impact of Chuck's revelations. "Real spies in my life?" I wondered. "This is only supposed to happen in Hollywood movies." Images of *Silkwood* sent me straight to bed, where I lay, fully clothed, with the sheets pulled over my head, waiting for Danny to come home. I fell asleep. Sometime later I jerked awake, hearing sounds in the kitchen. The spies! I heard the freezer open, a cupboard, then the silverware drawer. . . . Danny was getting a bowl of ice cream.

I shot downstairs and spilled the story, matching Chuck's hysteria. Danny listened, frozen, and wide-eyed. Finally, he tipped back in his chair and announced to imaginary electronic "bugs" in each corner of the house, "I don't know her! I've never seen her before! I'm just having some ice cream. I'm leaving soon!" Danny, as usual, was supportive of my work even with this bizarre new twist.

A few days later on August 7, Congressman George Miller subpoenaed all the players involved in Alyeska's sting across the country from Florida to California to Alaska at the same time so that no one could legally destroy any documents. A congressional oversight hearing was scheduled for early November. The media scrambled for stories.

Economic Disaster

Danny left to go fishing in the Sound. Two weeks later, he returned with horror stories of "lost fish." He said no one—not the oldest fishermen, the biologists, or the Native people with their oral history stretching back thousands of years—could ever remember a time when the salmon behaved so strangely. Instead of returning directly to their natal streams or hatcheries to darken and spawn over a six-to-eight-week period, the pink salmon had milled for weeks in deep water in the middle of the Sound in areas closed to fishing. Danny said, "The fishermen think the fish imprinted on oil as eggs in 1989. Now there's less oil and the fish are lost. The guys joke that the hatcheries should spill some oil to bring the fish on home."

Danny described how the fish—dark green, ripe, and ready to spawn—had surged en masse into the nearshore areas in near record numbers and completely overwhelmed the fleet. Tendermen put fishermen on catch limits so that everyone would get some income, but tenders filled quickly and could no longer buy fish. Millions of dead and dying fish filled bays and hatchery harvest areas as still more millions of dark fish swarmed in from the deep. Danny said, "The jumping fish sounded like heavy rain." Fishermen were furious at seeing the Sound inundated with wasted fish. Danny, disgusted, left to fish silvers on the Flats while the pink drama played itself out.

Thirty-seven million fish in less than two weeks was a disaster. "We can't do six weeks of work in ten days," said one beleaguered processor. The canneries were plugged with fish and shorthanded because crews had left earlier for lack of work. To further complicate things, the pinks were all about 25 percent smaller than normal. They jammed cannery machines made to process larger fish. Then the canneries quit buying because the fish quality deteriorated rapidly. The state gave belated permission to foreign processors to bring in their floaters, but no one was interested in poor quality pinks.

With no saleable markets, Governor Hickel concocted a scheme with Exxon to have the corporation pay to can three million pounds of surplus hatchery pink salmon in Cordova and Kodiak and distribute the food in the former Soviet Union "to celebrate the victory of democracy." Exxon turned the whole disaster into a big public relations campaign. It circulated videotapes to thousands of Alaskans, claiming that the second highest "pink harvest" on record proved the Sound had nearly recovered from the spill. Meanwhile, tenders quietly carried away another six million pounds of surplus hatchery fish and dumped them out at sea—the Humpy Dump.

PINK SALMON AND HERRING LIVES AND RELATIONSHIPS

Wild Pink Salmon

Prince William Sound has about 800 to 1,000 streams where wild pink salmon start and finish their lives. Pink salmon used to ascend these coastal forest streams to spawn. However, the 1964 earthquake uplifted land in the Sound and made many streams too steep for salmon to ascend. Pink salmon adapted by becoming "intertidal spawners," which means they spawn on beaches where a freshwater stream meets the sea.

The fish spawn in "redds" or nests dug in the stream gravel from July through mid-September. They die within seven to ten days after spawning. Depending on the water temperature in the fall, the bright orange eggs hatch in October or November. The "alevins"—larval salmon with big yolk sac bellies—work their way deeper into the streambed for the winter. They emerge as "fry" in about six months with their yolk sac absorbed or "buttoned up." The skinny, hungry fry salmon "out-migrate" or drift to the sea from late March through mid-June or so. The young fish, now called "juveniles," spend the summer in nearshore nursery areas, feeding and growing rapidly. Many fall prey to other fish and seabirds. By August or September, surviving fish, now adults, move outside the Sound and feed in the open ocean of the North Pacific until they return to spawn a year later.

Wild pink salmon are extremely vulnerable during their early life stages to oil spills, particularly spills that contaminate beaches and coastal waters.

Hatchery Pink Salmon

Prince William Sound hatchery pink salmon go through the same life stages as wild pink salmon, but hatchery pinks spend their early life stages at one of five hatcheries in the Sound. Eggs and alevins incubate in controlled laboratory conditions. Fry out-migrate to saltwater net pens, where they are held and fed until the spring bloom of microscopic sea plants, or "phytoplankton," peaks. The juveniles are released into this rich food source to increase the odds of their survival. Once released, the juveniles spend the summer feeding and growing in nearshore bays with their wild counterparts. In fall, the fish, now adults, move outside the Sound and swim in the open ocean of the North Pacific until they return to spawn to the hatcheries where they were released a year later. Since the fish are not held in captivity their entire lives, this form of fish farming is called "salmon ranching."

Like wild pink salmon, hatchery pinks are extremely vulnerable to oil spills during their early life stages. However, hatchery fish are reared in controlled conditions until they out-migrate. This protects eggs, embryos, and fry—the vulnerable early stages—from oil exposure. Oil spills are thus less likely to have the same devastating effects on hatchery pink salmon that they do on wild pink salmon.

Pacific Herring

In Prince William Sound, adult herring arrive at their natal beaches—the beaches where they were born—in late March. When water temperatures warm to about 40 degrees F, they spawn in shallow bays near shore and along beaches, blanketing sea plants, the seafloor, and beaches with their sticky, milky-white eggs. Many eggs are lost to seabirds, fish, invertebrates, and pounding by waves. Surviving eggs hatch in two to three weeks and release tiny yolk-sac larvae to drift in the water column.

Herring larvae absorb their yolk sacs within days, and the weak swimmers must learn to feed on passively drifting microscopic sea plants, or "phytoplankton." During their extended, three-month larval drift, many herring are lost to tiny drifting animals, or "zooplankon," or to currents that carry them out to sea.

Survivors are swept into shallow bays, where they can safely metamorphose to juveniles in late July or August. Chances of survival greatly improve after the first critical winter, a four-month period of semi-fasting.

Juvenile herring spend the next two to three years in the protected "nursery" bays, feeding and growing. They join the adult fish as four-year-olds and for the rest of their adult lives, six to eight years, they return to shallow water every spring to spawn and they move to deeper offshore water to overwinter. Unlike pink salmon, herring do not die after they spawn.

Like pink salmon, Pacific herring are also very vulnerable during their early life stages to oil spills, especially spills that contaminate beaches and coastal seas. They are also vulnerable when they return to coastal areas to spawn. Herring migrate to the surface at night to gulp air to fill their air bladders. They also break the water surface to escape predators. These behaviors, which were not recognized in 1989, also make herring vulnerable to oil spills.

Source: Riki Ott, *Sound Truth and Corporate Myth$* (Cordova, Alaska: Dragonfly Sisters Press, 2005); Prince William Sound Science Center Pacific Herring Research Program.

The ruinous fishing season wreaked havoc in the community. Only two of the town's five processing plants survived the oil spill and the 1991 season— North Pacific Processors and Ocean Beauty Seafoods, both based in Seattle. When Chugach Corporation closed its Orca Point plant, Prince William Sound lost its largest and oldest pink salmon cannery in operation since the 1880s. The town lost its only locally owned plant—and the one that had put Copper River salmon on the map—when the Copper River Fishermen's Cooperative closed: the bank called the loan due and there was no money to pay it. The Aquaculture Association dipped into its contingency funds to make up an $8 million shortfall—nearly 80 percent of its budget. Most seiners were lucky if they made 10 to 15 percent of their normal season. Few could make their boat payments. The O'Tooles were not among them.

"What are you going to do?" I asked Linden one brilliant fall day in mid-October. We were sitting on the picnic table halfway up the ski hill, soaking up sun that looked warmer than it felt. Malani was in school. Makena was in the woods nearby, stalking spruce grouse with his slingshot.

"That's exactly what my girlfriends asked me in Anchorage!"

This didn't surprise me. Alaska is a state full of doers; it wasn't only Cordova. When someone faced a life crisis, friends would rally in support.

Linden said, "The interest on the loan is increasing at $34.68 per day! Oh my God! It hit me: *I* need to do something. At Sheep Mountain, I lived on $34 per day." She did a quick mental calculation. "Actually, less. I lived on $2,000 a year." Worry carved lines in her face and stole the sparkle from her eyes. "I'm training to be a real estate agent." She sounded determined.

"A real estate agent?" I stared anxiously at her. "Isn't that a high-stress, aggressive job? That doesn't seem like you."

"Cordova doesn't have a real estate agent, but it has plenty of kindergarten teachers," she said practically.

We mulled this new future in silence as a flock of about 100 sandhill cranes flew across Orca Inlet, then overhead, as they made their way south. High-pitched "*pe-e-eps*" of newly fledged young birds punctuated the deeper rusty-door-hinge calls of the adults. I thought about what it would be like trying to support a young family with growing needs when so much was uncertain—except a mountain of debt. I admired her drive and attitude.

Finally I said, "There's going to be a lot of changes. There are a lot of desperate people."

"The whole town!" she said. "Governor Hickel turned down the city's request for disaster relief. What's up with that?" She switched with ease from her personal worries to those of the larger community.

"Politics, I think. The city never supported Hickel's pet project."

"The Road?! That would be political suicide for the city to support."

I nodded. "The U.S. Army Corp of Engineers shut the state down."

The Army Corps had charged the state with 147 violations of the Clean Water Act. Hickel had cut loose bulldozers to ram the Copper River Highway through the wilderness like he had done twenty-three years earlier with the haul road to the North Slope. But times and laws had changed.

Linden said, "That's one bad idea off the table. But what's happening with the settlement money? I wonder if some of it will go toward Rick's land easement idea."

The governor had snuck the second civil settlement for environmental damages past the legislature and the people by waiting for the legislature to adjourn. The new settlement was nearly identical to the earlier one. It just shifted $100 million from a criminal fine to "criminal restitution" and split it between the state and federals. The civil settlement released $90 million a year for ten years and established the *Exxon Valdez* Oil Spill (EVOS) Trustee

Council, which was in charge of funds and restoration projects. Under the settlement terms, restoration meant scientific studies, capital construction projects, and habitat acquisition—Rick's idea but with a subtle twist of buying rather than leasing land, which would create enormous problems later. The choice of projects was up to the politically appointed Trustee Council, which reflected the will of the state and federal administrations.

"There're a lot of people who want that to happen," I said. "People say the logging on the Delta looks like Nagasaki after the atomic bomb fell."

"The new city council and mayor have some ideas for bringing in new money—or at least plugging some drains, like settling the Connie Taylor lawsuit."

"That'd be good," I said. "What do you think about Kelley Weaverling's idea to annex lands to increase tax revenue?"

"You mean *Mayor* Kelley Weaverling?"

We grinned at each other. The bookstore owner had become the highest-ranking Green Party official in the nation.

"It's going to be a huge fight," she said.

"Well, I think it's fair. The area is too small, really, to have only some of us paying for services that we all use."

"But we need something we can all agree on." She sighed.

Unbeknownst to us, the southern sociologists had tallied their initial survey results and found that commercial fishermen and Alaska Natives—the two subgroups with closest ties to the environment—were still experiencing extraordinarily high levels of stress. The levels were similar to the post-traumatic adjustment in rape victims, people who had lost family, and combat veterans. Sociologists consider these to be among the highest levels of stress experienced by humans. The stress fueled the fighting.

"Well," I said, groping for something positive, "maybe the governor's Salmon Strategy Task Force will help pull fishermen together to work on marketing strategy."

Suddenly, there was a shout from the forest downhill of our sunny perch. *"I got one! Mom!! Riki! I got a spruce grouse!"* Makena came rocketing out of the woods, holding a grouse by its neck in one hand and his slingshot in the other.

"That's not his first," said Linden in low voice. As he rushed up, beaming, she said, "Well, my son, it looks like you'll be helping cook dinner tonight."

"You can clean it, Makena?" I asked, admiring the mottled browns and golden flecks in the feathers. "You're only five."

"Almost six," he said, and off he ran down the mountain, towing us in his wake.

Lawyers, Laws, and Legal Entanglements

On Makena's sixth birthday in early November, I was in Washington, D.C., for the congressional oversight hearing on Alyeska's covert surveillance operation. I had promised to call and bring back stories about spies. Chuck and Kathy Hamel invited me to stay in their comfortable four-story townhouse in Alexandria along with their lawyer, a woman named Billie Garde. Unlike the phony lawyer-spy Wayne "Jenkins" (a.k.a. Wayne Black), Billie was real.

In contrast to Chuck's animated style, Billie exuded calm. She was a large woman, yet she moved with serene grace, practically floating around the house. Dark ringlets of shoulder-length hair framed porcelain skin and alert black eyes. Amid constantly ringing phones, she quietly filled me in on her background. Her expertise and passion were whistleblower protection. She had carved out a career protecting nuclear regulatory whistleblowers, establishing case law in the process.

In July, the winds of fate had blown Alyeska's sting operation into her lap with a phone call from an anonymous lawyer, representing an anonymous former federal agent. "This was all very mysterious," recalled Billie.

At a meeting in Miami, Billie met Rafael "Gus" Castillo—a former federal agent and Wackenhut spy. Castillo suspected Wayne Black of foul play during the Hamel investigation. Castillo had contacted five women operatives on the case and found they also believed Wackenhut had violated state law and constitutional privacy and liberty rights of the targets. Billie had advised Castillo that he needed to talk with Congressman George Miller. She had worked through Miller's office with the nuclear regulatory whistleblowers. Miller was the House Interior Committee chair, one of the nation's most powerful environmental policy positions, and he had been a target of Alyeska's sting. The depositions of Castillo and the "Chuckie's Angels"—the five women spies—had led to the congressional subpoenas and hearing.

Wackenhut and Alyeska had fought the congressional investigation. Alyeska had mounted a huge public relations smokescreen in Alaska, portraying the oil company owners and itself as victims of Chuck Hamel, an "extortionist" who kept "stealing" documents from inside its company, thus endangering national security. The oil companies and Wackenhut had refused to provide the House Interior Committee with "privileged" documents, the work product of its attorneys. This conveniently included most of the critical information. Following a flurry of legal maneuverings and more subpoenas, they finally had flooded the committee staff with thousands of papers one month before the hearing in a desperate hope that key papers would be overlooked.

Oil company allies pulled one more trick on the first day of the three-day hearing. With the Republican minority outnumbering the Democratic majority, Alaska's congressman Don Young voted to hold the proceedings in executive session. We all had to leave! Behind doors closed to public scrutiny, Wackenhut's spies asserted their Fifth Amendment rights.

During the next two days, the Democratic majority was there in force and the sweeping extent of Alyeska's operation became evident. The investigation of Congressman Miller was much more than "a single trip to the public library," as Mr. Wackenhut had claimed in his opening remarks. There was plenty to tell Danny and Linden.

During a break, I called Danny from a pay phone in the marbled hallway. "Alyeska is in deep," I said. "One of the exhibits was a legal analysis on how to investigate a congressman! It showed how to set up George Miller for indictment and avoid legal pitfalls."

"The first thing on the list should have been not to get caught," Danny remarked dryly.

"No kidding! You should see the diagrams of the phone tap networks. The first one shows three connected circles with "Hamel" in between me and "Miller." The final one shows Chuck in the center of this web of informants—the Attorney General of Alaska, the whistleblower Robert Scott who gave Chuck the documents that proved Alyeska's incinerators were polluting the air, . . ."

". . . and got him fired," Danny pointed out.

"Right. There's actually a memo that says, 'get rid of [Alyeska employee Robert] Scott—based on demerits.'

"And get this: there's a memo from Alyeska's head of security Pat Wellington to superspy Wayne Black about *me*. Wellington wrote, 'This gal is a real pain in the ass! She is very active in our state legislature. We think she is receiving inside info—Pat.'"

"I agree with them," said Danny.

"What?"

"You are a pain in the ass!"

"Oh, very funny. Hang on a minute." Gus Castillo was rapping on the glass door of the phone booth. He showed me a business card.

In a thick Cuban accent he asked, "You know dis person? He's tellin' your whole life story on da' phone." Gus jerked his thumb toward another phone booth.

I glanced at the card. "It's okay, Gus. That's the *Boston Globe* reporter." He wandered off satisfied. I spoke back into the phone. "Danny! Now the spies are spying for us!"

"You better call Linden. The kids want spy stories and she has something to tell you."

We hung up and I called Linden. I rattled on about James Bond-type spy toys—parabolic microphones, pen registers, alligator clips, body wires—stolen trash, and illegally gained telephone records, credit records, and financial information. Finally, I thought to ask about Makena's birthday.

"We gave Makena a B-B gun—and a gun safety course. I'm going to take it with him."

"A gun!" I was shocked.

"It's Alaska! Boys here have guns. He's already killed a squirrel. First shot."

"Oh, man! And skinned it and cooked it, I suppose?"

"Yes." Maternal pride swelled her voice. "He's not even in kindergarten yet!"

I thought quickly about my childhood. "Well, my parents always supported my interests. I can do the same. Uh-oh. Kathy Hamel is waving at me. They must be starting up again."

"We want to hear all about it!" Linden said.

In the hearing aftermath, federal, Virginia, and Florida law enforcement officials started their own investigations to determine whether any laws protecting the privacy of citizens were violated. The State of Alaska refused to investigate the matter any further, despite evidence that this most recent investigation was an extension of similar past practices of Alyeska. Meanwhile, a handful of Alyeska quality control inspectors who had watched the November hearing very closely contacted Chuck Hamel because they were concerned about safety issues at the marine terminal in Valdez—and they were now convinced that Alyeska did not care. These employees would open Pandora's box.

That fall Linden and I crisscrossed the state, peddling pillows, bibs, and earrings at high-end craft fairs from Juneau to Fairbanks. To my total

amazement, I grossed more from the fairs than from fishing—and we had
fun, which built some resistance against the enormous stresses haunting
Cordova.

Meanwhile, the city tried in vain to self-arrest its economic freefall. In a
stunning reversal of a previous rulings, the judge in the Connie Taylor lawsuit
decided the case was not "frivolous" after all and the city had to pay Taylor's
attorneys' fees and costs. But people had no more money to give. Fishermen
tried to carve out niches in the steep wall of farmed fish flooding the market.
Uncertain of what lay ahead, the community braced itself for more hardship.
The city manager observed, "Lifestyles were being shaken to their roots."

To make matters worse, developments in the *Exxon Valdez* litigation
spooked everyone. In November, in state court, Judge Shortell set an April
1993 trial date for both compensatory and punitive damages. According to
Dave Oesting, "that panicked Exxon and Exxon's lawyers started removing
everything they could to federal court." Judge Holland had found handholds
in Exxon's arguments. He decided one of the issues filed by some direct action
plaintiffs, an environmental group called Trustees for Public Justice, had raised
a federal question. The group maintained that Exxon was reckless because the
Exxon Valdez was a single-hull tanker, which was more likely to spill oil than
a double-hull tanker. Judge Holland decided that this claim was a "collateral
attack" on *Chevron v. Hammond*, despite the fact that the state had lost this
case over a decade ago.

The environmental group was a small part of a large consolidated class
action, which linked the bulk of our claims into one multistrand rope. By
pulling on the weakest strand, Judge Holland tugged us all into federal
court. Holland would later dismiss the complaints of the maverick faction
on summary judgment, after, as Oesting said, "we all got lodged in federal
court."

While Exxon focused on removing the consolidated class action to federal
court, Alyeska did the same to the direct action plaintiffs. To help ensure that
the direct action cases would stay in federal court, Exxon sued the Airport
Depot Diner, a small café near the Cordova airport. Exxon linked the Airport
Depot Diner with other direct action business plaintiffs, then the business class action, until eventually, according to Oesting, "the whole plaintiff
constituency, Natives, everyone, were defendants in the *Airport Depot Diner*
case." Judge Holland stayed the action as a legal strategy that allowed him to
retain jurisdiction of all the cases.

Our lawyers appealed Judge Holland's rulings in both the *Trustee for Public*

Justice and the *Airport Depot Diner* cases to the Ninth Circuit Court, but by the end of 1991, most people in Cordova realized that we were not "lucky to have Exxon," as Don Cornett had told the crowd at Cordova high school gym five nights after the tanker had grounded. Instead of compensation for "reasonable claims" as Exxon had promised, we found ourselves facing a protracted court battle to protect even our most basic oil spill claims.

CHAPTER SEVEN

WHEN RIGHT
MAKES MIGHT

1992

In January, Cordova made statewide news—again—for squabbling. Desperate for economic development, the city council reversed its decision to stay neutral on the Copper River Highway issue and voted to support construction despite emotional opposition. Shortly thereafter, the governor's Copper River Highway Task Force held its first meeting in Cordova. Guaranteed a good show, the Alaska media flocked into the lion's den of resistance to the governor's pet project. With TV cameras rolling, Attorney General Charlie Cole announced to a standing-room-only crowd, packed into the elementary school cafeteria, "The Governor wants to build this road. Therefore, we will only be taking testimony on how to build it."

I couldn't believe my ears: The Attorney General of Alaska was trying to limit freedom of speech. But I needn't have worried. It was Cordova. After the jeers and catcalls quieted, townspeople proceeded to speak their minds. People in the rest of the state learned that, despite the desires of a fanatical governor, this issue was still quite controversial in the community that would be most impacted by the project.

Governor Hickel shut down his "task farce," as it came to be called, after its disastrous first and last meeting in Cordova. But governor and city council continued to endorse the highway project as part of a budding regional economic development plan to promote tourism. The city council decided that Cordova needed a road to the Interior and a deep-water port for its economic salvation. People divided over whether the infrastructure was needed to promote our scenic value and fisheries or whether it would encourage offshore oil development, coal mining, and clear-cut logging on the resource-rich Copper River Delta.

Cordova was facing a looming budget crisis just midway through its fiscal year. The city was reeling from a bill of over a million dollars for the Taylor lawsuit—20 percent of its budget, mounting expenses from an antiquated accounting system to deal with complex oil spill billing, and gaping budget holes from drastic cuts in state spending for municipal assistance. The city government abruptly tightened its fiscal belt. It started a four-day workweek for the first time in anyone's memory. It laid off three of its five policemen, trimmed museum and library hours, slashed over 13 percent from all departments, and stopped purchasing supplies. The library started an Adopt-a-Book program. City employees cleaned bathrooms and vacuumed floors when janitorial services were cut.

The town's financial troubles landed in a heap on kitchen tables around town.

Kitchen Table Talk

"All this talk of higher fees for garbage collection! Higher fees for harbor use! Hikes in property taxes! Hikes in sales taxes! Where do they think this money is going to come from?" asked Linden after dinner one night. "Seiners are broke and gillnetters can't support this town. The cost of living here is already among the highest in the state." In fact, she pointed out, it was nearly twice as expensive to live in Cordova as it was to live in Seattle.

Businesses were closing because they couldn't pay back taxes. The Odiak Child Development Center had closed because parents owed back payments. Even some of the bars were in financial trouble, because people had cut spending on nonessential items. There was no extra money in town.

She looked at me. "We have something to ask you." Raising her voice, she called Sam, who had been reading a book to the kids. They piled into the kitchen. "Rick Steiner's partner, Claudia, was the godmother of our children, but she moved to Juneau. The kids are old enough now to understand that a godmother would take care of them if something happens to us. We took a family vote. We all want you to be our godmother."

The immensity of the request hit me as I looked into the smiling, expectant faces of the kids. I had decided not to have my own children, yet here was a gift membership to my favorite family in town. My chest flooded with a warm feeling that stole my voice. All I could do was nod. Looking up, I saw my friends wipe away tears.

"Let's have some ice cream!" said Makena.

"Makena!" said Sam. "I just told you if you tried a little harder to read we could have ice cream!"

"Wait. I have an idea," I said. I pulled my dinner ticket—three cartons of ice cream—from the freezer and set them in front of Makena, who was standing eye level with the table.

"What kind are they?" he asked.

"You tell me."

A lightbulb went on over his head. He stared intently at the containers. "Van-ill-a. *Vanilla!* Cho-co-late. *Chocolate!* Cho-co-late ch-ip. *Chocolate chip!*" We all cheered.

"So much for *Green Eggs and Ham*," I said.

Makena dug into his bowl of ice cream with gusto. "Tell us a story!"

"How about more spy stories?" asked Malani.

"How about whistleblower stories?" I countered. The kids stared at me. "Okay, remember I had my phone tapped?" They nodded. "Well, the reason Alyeska tapped my phone was to find out who was telling us about the air and water pollution at the tanker port. Alyeska fired those people for telling the truth. But it turns out, that's illegal. A company can't fire a person for blowing the whistle—for reporting pollution or safety problems."

The kids struggled with the concept. "Like a tattletale?" asked Malani.

"Sort of, but whistleblowers help protect people like you and me. See, they report problems first to their company. But if their company doesn't fix the problems, they report the problems to people outside the company to get help. Right now at Alyeska, whistleblowers are saying the big oil pipeline might leak because of corrosion—well, rust." I caught myself, remembering the age of my audience. "You know how rust eats metal on cars and trucks around here. If the metal pipeline leaks, what will happen?"

"An oil spill!" shouted the kids.

"Right. That's why I'm working with whistleblowers. So we don't have another oil spill."

"Time for bed," said Sam as the kids finished their ice cream.

"What do you call a person who is fired by a company for reporting environmental problems?" I asked.

"*A whistler!*" crowed Makena, puffing out his chest.

"Close enough, Makena," I said as the kids shot out of the kitchen.

Sam hugged me. "Not every godmother can tell 'whistler' stories." He trailed the kids.

"So that's what I've been reading about in the paper?" Linden asked. "All those people getting fired at Alyeska?"

"'All those people' happen to be top-notch quality-control inspectors.

Alyeska hired them from all over the country after the spill to prove the oil companies were serious about fixing their problems. Instead the inspectors validated the problems—major problems from years of cost-cutting. Chuck Hamel says he gets boxes of documents nearly every day. He says corrosion is rampant up and down the pipeline. He says he has reports of hundreds of "weeping wires" that drip insulation, substandard repairs, faulty welding—it goes on and on. The inspectors are warning of 'massive breakdown' of the pipeline."

"People are still bringing Chuck documents after what happened with Wackenhut?"

"He says Alyeska whistleblowers are coming out of the woodwork."

"But why would they do that?" Linden asked, puzzled. "They just get fired."

"Yeah, but that's illegal. Alyeska is going to have to hire them back. Billie Garde is working with Chuck. She's helping the whistleblowers file complaints with the Labor Department. And Congress is interested in the condition of the pipeline now after the Wackenhut sting. I think these problems on the pipeline have been brewing for awhile, but now the whistleblowers have cover—an attorney to protect their jobs and Congress to fix the problems."

"That still doesn't explain why anyone would choose martyrdom."

"I've been reading reports on whistleblowers."

What I had learned about whistleblowers, I admired. Conscientious employees are the front line of defense in protecting public health, worker safety, and the environment. They are the first to know when a company or government agency is not adhering to laws designed to protect people and the environment. Whistleblowers are people who adhere to a "universal truth," judging issues as right or wrong, black or white, with no shades of gray. Then, they courageously act on their convictions without regard to consequences to themselves, which usually involves job loss at a minimum.

Linden stared at me. "You've been reading about whistleblowers? Why?"

"It's about fixing the problems at Alyeska. Whistleblowers know where the critical problems are. So by helping to protect whistleblowers, I can help fix the problems at Alyeska."

"So you'll have more 'whistler' stories for the kids," Linden concluded.

Many more, as it would turn out.

My work with whistleblowers began to affect my personal life. "Do you remember when you said you could 'fix the problems at Alyeska' over the winter—as in 'one' winter?" Danny asked one night over dinner.

"Yeah, well, there turned out to be more problems than I thought, but we are on the verge of fixing one of the original ones."

"Ballast Watergate?"

I nodded. "Dan Lawn found the missing link between Ballast Watergate and the water pollution at the terminal. Tankers were supposed to offload only ballast water and keep oily sludge onboard. Crude oil was supposed to be loaded on top of the sludge and waste oil. But instead of allowing the sludge and waste oil to separate from the ballast water—which takes time and time is money—Alyeska has been pumping everything ashore. Oily sludges weren't monitored at the terminal since they were never supposed to come ashore. So the sludge and heavy oil had been going right through the treatment plant and winding up in the bottom of Port Valdez, just like the fishermen suspected."

"And for figuring this out, Dan Lawn lost his job," said Danny.

"Well, Dan lost his job because he's actually been doing his job—and his supervisors don't want to hear about safety and environmental problems at the tanker terminal."

Readers of the *Anchorage Daily News* had followed Lawn's story for years. Charged with inspecting terminal and tanker operations, Lawn had documented everything from lack of spill response preparation to noncompliance with air and water quality permits to illegal tanker discharges, despite repeated harassment by the state and pipeline people. When the state cut his job, he had filed the first of several lawsuits to get his job back. I had worked with Lawn closely ever since my political debut at the now-distant EPA hearing, and I admired his tenacity and morals.

"When does it all end?" he asked softly.

I heard the quiet plea in his voice. "Just one more spring in the legislature," I said. "I want to work on a whistleblower protection bill."

"One winter," was all he said of the four years that had slid by while I had learned of more problems than I resolved.

It was April before I returned to Cordova.

Spill Entanglements

During my lobby tenure, diligent efforts by whistleblowers, citizen advisory groups, and fishermen forced government regulators to demand change at Alyeska. Survey forms were revised to require reporting of unauthorized ballast water; testing and sampling programs were designed to catch those who still smuggled hazardous waste north in ballast water; and load-on-top became a standard practice—finally, fourteen years after the first oil had been pumped from the terminal. Pipeline owners chafed under the rising citizen influence over its operations, but some of the shippers began to work with the new system. The *Boston Globe* reported, "Exxon Shipping Company quietly issued orders to its tanker captains and engineers to change their procedures for discharging oil-contaminated ballast water into the treatment plant at Valdez." The flow of hazardous wastes north along the West Coast reversed. Water quality in Port Valdez would slowly improve.

Further herculean efforts, largely spearheaded by the Regional Citizens Advisory Council, slowly forced the oil industry to prove up on its pre-spill promise to make ". . . operations at Port Valdez and in Prince William Sound the safest in the world." People from oiled communities wanted a response planning standard of a full tanker load; the industry argued that 30 percent of a tanker load was more "realistic." The state compromised at 60 percent. Unhappy with the state's decision, the oil industry tried unsuccessfully to outflank resolute Alaskans by promoting weaker federal regulations under the Oil Pollution Act.

The oil industry also tried to win back lost ground by fulfilling the planning standards with spill response equipment based on "nameplate capacity" rather than on actual performance standards. But spill survivors well remembered the "mill-pond" boom and other malfunctioning equipment from the failed initial response in 1989. People were not about to be fooled again by cheap equipment that couldn't perform as designed.

Further, the owner companies tried unsuccessfully to foist responsibility for the costly spill response equipment onto their service contractors and, failing that, to wiggle completely out of preparation for beach cleanup either inside or outside the Sound. But people refused to tolerate this nonsense. The *Exxon Valdez* spill had oiled thousands of miles of beaches outside of Prince William Sound.

Encouraged by so many people investing time to keep the oil industry honest, I focused on marginalized issues. I managed to uncork more genies than I stuffed back into bottles. While researching the history of whistle-blower protection in Alaska, I found the state only provided minimal protection for public employees. The State Ombudsman told me protection for private employees had been stripped from the original legislation by a large private employer—the oil industry. With the help of Billie Garde and the Government Accountability Project, I drafted a whistleblower protection bill.

I found a committee to champion our bill and lined up people to testify at our first hearing, but the hearing was canceled at the last minute and never rescheduled. Apparently, the oil lobby was still paying attention to this issue.

Another genie escaped from this bottle. After I spoke at a whistleblower conference in Washington, D.C., a man in the audience asked if I knew about the workers with respiratory problems and other illnesses, stemming from Exxon's cleanup. He insisted that people had filed toxic tort lawsuits against Exxon and VECO, Exxon's primary cleanup contactor, and that the cleanup work had left others disabled or dead. The stranger asked point-blank, "What are you going to do about it?" I saw Chuck Hamel, sitting in the audience, perk up. This genie followed me home to Cordova.

The sick worker story broke in the Sunday *Boston Globe* in mid-April. I was home, helping Danny prepare for our first wild kelp harvest. The investigative reporter suggested the handful of toxic torts "may be the tip of a legal iceberg." He wrote of chemical poisoning of thousands of workers by exposure to crude oil and toxic cleanup products. I read with horror the workers' complaints: severely diminished lung capacity, dizziness, skin rashes, headaches, and neurological disorders. It struck me that the illnesses were hauntingly similar to those predicted from overexposure to crude oil and Exxon's chemical products used on the spill. A number of sick workers had sought treatment at the Environmental Health Clinic in Dallas. The head of the clinic, Dr. William Rea, told the *Boston Globe*, "This is extremely serious. People need to wake up." Instead, after a spurt of national stories, the well ran dry as the lawsuits dragged on. The issue would land in my lap again, with a vengeance, nine years later.

In April I returned to Cordova to join Danny for our new venture to harvest herring-roe-on-kelp. We anchored the *Ambergris* along with fifty other boats in shallow water off Boulder Bay near Tatitlek. Danny and a friend donned scuba gear, then jumped into the clear water. They swam off, trailing long mesh bags to harvest the spawn-covered kelp.

While waiting for their return, I soaked up the bright sun and watched raucous gulls gorge on kelp on beaches white with herring spawn. Offshore, sea lions and humpback whales fed on herring. The sheer energy of it all was intoxicating. I felt alive. I understood now why the herring pounders and divers spoke of this time with such glowing fondness. Where else on the planet could you spend a month with close friends in such incredible beauty right when the Sound is coming alive—and call it "work"?

The divers repeatedly surfaced with mesh bags filled with kelp, which I dumped onto a sorting table. I held the rubbery, white-speckled leaves up to the sun for inspection and cut out patches of dirt. I layered clean kelp in boxes for delivery to the tenders.

I couldn't resist trying a bit of our raw product, which Asians considered a delicacy. I examined a small piece before popping it in my mouth. It looked like a reverse Oreo cookie. Thick layers of tiny white eggs sandwiched dark green kelp. I chewed it. The eggs burst like little salty flavor bubbles and the kelp had the texture of a tough pickle. I decided the high price must be for the texture sensation: it tasted like a mouthful of chewy rubber.

We grossed over $2,000 for our catch, which was a small fraction of the $17 million harvest for the spring herring fisheries. Who knew that herring would practically vanish from the Sound within a year, or that the herring fisheries would still be closed indefinitely at the time of writing this book—sixteen years later?

The town mentally switched gears for the upcoming salmon season. Biologists predicted a strong return of hatchery pink salmon, but earlier in March, Chugach Alaska Corporation had dismantled its big Orca Point plant and left it gutted and vacant. This had rocked the town to its core. "Selling that equipment was like cutting off the right arm of this community," declared Chugach shareholder Sylvia Lange. "We lost our biggest processor—and all local ownership of our major processors." The bankrupt Copper River Fishermen's Cooperative managed to sell its plant and assets to Seattle-based Norquest Seafoods at a loss of over a million dollars. Still, people worried there were not enough markets or processing capacity to handle a massive fish return. Even Governor Hickel commented, "We don't need another disaster like last year."

The city borrowed money from the bank for payroll expenses. Well aware of the town's dire straits, voters passed four bonds for immediate infrastructure needs, including a new landfill and repairing a leaky sewer line. The governor provided matching money, noting that Cordova was one of only three communities in the state to provide funds for requested capital grants. As the salmon season began, the town prayed for the best and prepared for the worst.

Sound Defense and TAPS Offense

By mid-July, "the worst" looked imminent. Danny was fishing reds in the Sound. He reported no sign of pink salmon.

I stopped by Linden's real estate office one Friday afternoon to see if she had any news from Sam, who was fishing their permit with a leased boat.

"Nothing . . . yet." I admired her tenacity for hanging on to hope. "I saved this to show you." She handed me a folded paper from her desk drawer. It was a copy of a handwritten letter from eight-year-old Malani to the governor. In unmistakable child's scrawl, it read, "Dear Governor Hickel, Here is $5 to buy trees in Prince William Sound. I saved my allowance. My mom sells rile estate. My dad is a fisherman. My brother wants to be one. Trees help salmon grow." She had signed her name big like John Hancock.

With a mixture of pride and awe, I said, "The kids talked with Rick Steiner."

She nodded. "That bill was such a big deal here this spring. Most people in town want the spill money to buy trees. People are sick about the clear-cutting."

"It was a big deal in all the oiled regions. People in Kodiak and Cook Inlet don't like the clear-cutting either. People wanted 80 percent of that $50 million criminal fine for conservation easements. But, no!" I shook my head and handed the note back to Linden.

"Governor Hickel vetoed it," said Linden sadly. "Even the kids were sad. Rick Steiner is so mad about it, he went straight to Washington, D.C."

"Rick's mad about more than that! Over half of the first $90 million payment from the civil settlement went to reimburse government agencies for cleanup expenses. God knows where the rest went. There's zero public accountability right now of the spending process. Actually, there's zero public accountability on the cleanup too."

"What happened now?"

"Oh, the U.S. Coast Guard and Exxon declared the beach cleanup was 'complete.' There's oil all over out there still, but there's a presidential election in a few months. It seems oiled beaches made for embarrassing campaign issues. So, they're not oiled anymore! They're 'clean'!"

Linden shook her head. "The scale of this is so much more than a spill in the Sound."

Just then, the kids burst through the door, holding remnants of ice cream cones. "We want to go camping!" Linden looked at me with a silent question.

"I can be ready in fifteen minutes."

She laughed. "Well, it'll take us a little longer. We'll pick you up in half an hour!"

Five hours later, we sat by a crackling campfire on the Sheridan River. The glacial stream flowed swift, strong, and silty in its middle tributary. The eastern channel was mostly dry, carpeted with round smooth stones and splashed with patches of soft silty sand and clumps of dwarf river beauty. Our two tents were pinpricks of color in the wide-open river bottom. The solid flanks of the Chugach Range rose into glaciers and snowfields that seemed to run into the clouds. We had spent hours exploring with the kids. We all had pitched in to make jaffles—fancy stuffed grilled cheese sandwiches, cooked with a jaffle iron set in coals. Linden and I built the fire back up as the kids zoomed off to play in the soft long evening light. We settled down to talk.

"What's the news on our lawsuit?" asked Linden.

"Exxon filed two motions to dismiss it. Exxon claims that the steering gear system on the *Exxon Valdez* was faulty and that it failed to respond when the third mate put the helm over to miss Bligh Reef. So the accident is Sperry-Rand's fault, not Exxon's fault or Hazelwood's fault."

Linden gave the fire a poke in disgust. "How can they sleep at night?"

"I don't know about Exxon, but I don't think our lawyers are sleeping at night. Oesting says, 'If there was any doubt that Hazelwood was pie-eyed drunk, a person should just listen to that little squib of the transmissions from Hazelwood to the Coast Guard station after *Exxon Valdez* ran aground.' He says this is just another 'wild scheme' to dodge paying us."

"Well, it sounds lame. Hopefully, the judge won't buy it. What about the other one?"

"Oesting says the other one is more serious. Exxon claims that the state settled its punitive damages claims as part of the civil settlement."

"What does the state have to do with us?" asked Linden, shifting around so she could keep an eye on the children.

"That's what I asked Oesting. He says Exxon is arguing that the state was acting *parens patria* or like a parent on behalf of all its citizens when it settled its punitive damage claims as part of environmental damages. Exxon claims the matter is over and done with."

"That's *nuts.*" She sounded more flabbergasted than mad.

"That's what Judge Holland thought. 'No dice,' as Oesting says. But Exxon appealed it."

"Where does that leave us?"

A gentle breeze swirled the campfire smoke. We adjusted our position. "The case still goes forward to trial, but I guess the Ninth Circuit could throw a big monkey wrench into the works whenever it makes a decision."

"The more I learn about the legal system, the less impressed I am," declared Linden. "It's just a game for lawyers. Do you think the *Glacier Bay* case will help us?"

A year earlier, a young Minnesota lawyer with Fagre & Benson had won a stunning $51 million victory. The average payout was $400,000—five times as much as received by the fishermen who had settled under the TAPL Fund.

"At least it set some precedent in court."

As it turned out, the *Glacier Bay* win was a pivotal point in our lawsuit. Our attorneys had closely watched the case development and trial. The young Minnesota lawyer, Brian O'Neill, and his team had run right through one of the first major roadblocks in their path—the TAPL Fund. Federal law required the ship insurer to pay the deductible, up to $14 million, first, before any claimants could be paid. The insurance company had simply refused to do so. O'Neill and his team changed the law, with help from Senator Stevens, *retroactive to the Glacier Bay spill*. Then a month before the trial, O'Neill and his team had worked feverishly to revamp their arguments when three mock juries had returned verdicts of little or no damages to the fishermen. They had won when it mattered, in front of the real jury, in Judge Russel Holland's court.

Fagre & Benson was one of the eighty-four law firms with claims in the *Exxon Valdez* case. With the *Glacier Bay* win under his belt, O'Neill had joined the team working on the *Exxon Valdez* case. It was the break Dave Oesting had been looking for. Oesting knew his damages team "wasn't worth a shit." He had fired the entire lot and put O'Neill in charge of pulling together a team that would gather, consolidate, and distill information on 32,000 claims into winning oral arguments. It was a job that O'Neill had eagerly accepted.

I pushed a few pieces of wood between the orange coals and burning logs as Linden broke more sticks. We watched some bald eagles cruise the river bottom. The sun hovered near the top of Hinchinbrook Island.

"What time is it?" she asked.

"Ten-ish."

"I love summer. We can give the kids a bit longer. Looks like they're building a house with driftwood. Any news on the whistleblowers?"

"God, what a snarl. Congress—well, George Miller's committee—finished its report on the Wackenhut sting. The report's full of incriminating evidence. And it pretty much concludes that Alyeska and Wackenhut broke laws."

"What are you going to do?"

"Sue."

Linden sat bolt upright. "Are you nuts?! Those are some of the richest oil companies in the world! Why? What will that accomplish?" She sounded worried.

I expected this reaction from my gentle-natured friend. "Look, I'm in good company with Chuck Hamel, Stan Stephens, and Dan Lawn. There are a few others, but I know and trust those three. Billie Garde is Chuck's attorney; Doug Bailey—the former Attorney General of Alaska—is representing us. We decided we had to sue, otherwise we would send a message to the oil companies that they can get away with this crap. We don't ever want to go through this again."

After Linden mulled this a minute, I added, "The whistleblowers are going to sue, too, if the U.S. Labor Department rules against them. Billie Garde says it will—the government nearly always rules against whistleblowers. Some of the stuff they've been predicting from faulty wiring has already happened. A worker at the terminal was nearly electrocuted and the big remote gate valves are malfunctioning. If one of them swings closed for no reason, the pipeline could burst like a too-full water balloon."

"This is all so big! How are things ever going to improve?" I could hear the distress in her voice.

"With citizen oversight. The Regional Citizens' Advisory Council just nailed Alyeska on air quality at the tanker terminal."

Alyeska's study had completely missed the main source of the benzene emissions, the loading tankers. Alyeska had released tracers into an air stream that was located up on the hill away from tankers and that blew out to sea rather than toward town. The RCAC scientists had recalculated Alyeska's numbers and declared the terminal was the major source of air pollution in Port Valdez.

"So what's going to come of that?" she asked.

"A big fight, no doubt, but Stan Stephens is pretty determined. The RCAC is pushing the EPA to require vapor recovery at the terminal like they have in California and Louisiana."

"It sounds like we need an RCAC for the pipeline," Linden observed.

Suddenly, there was a chorus of high-pitched yips and yowls from the woods along the far riverbank as the lengthening shadows brought out the night hunters. The kids came running to the campfire.

"We need a dog," said Makena, worrying about the distant howls in the forest. Sparkle had died.

"We've been looking at Australian shepherds," Linden said.

"Can I hunt with them?" asked Makena.

"Not tonight! Are you two sure you want to sleep in your own tent?" she asked.

The kids eyed the six feet of space between our tents as if it was a mile. They nodded.

"All right. To bed! We'll stay up a bit longer."

We sat by the fire until the sounds from their tent fell silent and were eclipsed by the sounds from the twilight night.

Downward Economic Spiral

August came up nearly empty for pink salmon.

It was the worst season in fourteen years. Only 25 percent of the predicted hatchery fish run returned—and even less of the wild fish. This was about one-fifth of the volume of each of the previous two years' harvest. Everyone was dazed. "Where was the season? Where were the fish?" asked the local manager of one processing plant.

There was nothing left to do but pick up the pieces.

Sea Land Services sent its empty forty-foot container vans out on barges. Normally the company sent over 600 vans of canned salmon out of Cordova. But in 1992, they sent fewer than 100. Some seasonal cannery workers had to borrow money to pay for plane tickets home. With less than half its budget secured through fish sales, the Aquaculture Corporation scrambled to cut costs and sought a loan deferral from the state. Banks sponsored workshops on managing money for hard times. The city council even suggested ways for fishermen to pay their debts.

The city cast about desperately for other ways to fill its empty coffers. All of its choices sparked controversy. The battle over annexation reached epic proportions and pitted the community against itself. The Copper River Highway project remained trussed up in court. The state settled with Alyeska for oil spill damages. The deepwater port project received a $6 million earmark from the state's $32 million settlement. This further divided the community. No one believed it was for tourism or for oil spill response—not with the state conducting a feasibility study for extracting coal, oil, and timber on the Delta. Clear-cut logging by the Native corporations had triggered injunctions, lawsuits, moratoriums, protests, and off-again-on-again land deals as different factions struggled for control.

Fishermen and townspeople looked to scientists for explanations of the disastrous return, but the government scientists were still silent. Pink salmon returns were also lower than predicted in oiled regions of Kodiak and Cook Inlet, while the unoiled fisheries in Southeast Alaska had strong returns. People wondered whether oil had damaged the parents of the missing fish and whether the oiled fish had been unable to produce offspring. Unbeknownst to worried townspeople, federal scientists were wondering this very same thing and had already started experiments to find answers.

Exxon may also have wondered. But instead of looking for answers, the corporation produced a skillfully crafted video that painted a rosy picture of the Sound, well on its way to recovery, and sent it to educators and policy-makers.

Defending Livelihoods and Values

Meanwhile, during the fall board meeting of United Fishermen of Alaska, I took the lead on another pressing issue. In September, the state announced proposed "revisions" to the state's water quality standards. The revisions gutted the state's high standards and even went so far as to challenge basic prem-ises of the Clean Water Act. Besides proposing to allow industries to dump dioxin, arsenic, oily particulates, and other hazardous pollutants into the water at concentrations *3,000 to 10,000 times higher than the EPA standards*, the state also proposed to allow conversion of any "waterbody"—such as a lake or river—into an industrial "treatment works" for mine tailings disposal.

To legalize these actions, Hickel's minions proposed to reduce public protection by drastically lowering the cancer risk level based, in part, on a seafood consumption rate of five pounds per person per year. Many Alaskans ate this much seafood in a week! Even the national average was fifteen pounds per person per year. An irate public barraged the state from all quarters with thousands of comments opposing the proposed changes.

From the rubble of the first public comment period emerged a new water quality standards advisory "task farce," formed by Governor Hickel, and a counterforce—a new statewide public interest group called the Alaska Clean Water Alliance, based in Haines. I served as the fishermen's delegate to both boards for three years. I didn't know at the time that this experience would open a door of possibilities for defining "progress" as something other than economic development and that it would link my work to a new global vision, birthed at the Earth Summit in Rio.

Cross-country skiing alone in the peaceful stillness of late December, I mulled my options. A month earlier, everyone had a scare when the fully loaded tanker, *Kenai*, had lost rudder control and narrowly avoided Middle Rock in Valdez Narrows. The Regional Citizens Advisory Council had thoroughly investigated the incident, proving the citizens had become a political counterforce to Alyeska and the TAPS oil shippers. However, the RCAC was restricted to tanker and terminal oversight. I thought the timing was right to brief a new presidential administration on the status of the rest of the trans-Alaska pipeline system and what could be done improve it. Dan Lawn and Stan Stephens thought so too.

Alyeska was on the verge of firing another whistleblower. Quality-control manager Richard Green had supervised the other fired senior inspectors. When Green suffered the same harassment and intimidation tactics that he had witnessed used against the others, he crossed over into Chuck Hamel's camp. Green was the proverbial last straw. Congressman John Dingell announced his intentions to conduct oversight hearings into the whistleblowers' concerns that the safety of the trans-Alaska pipeline system had been compromised by Alyeska's actions.

Dan, Stan, and I made plans to visit Washington, D.C., in February.

Dave Oesting also mulled his options at year-end. Oesting had watched Brian O'Neill's work closely, because Oesting had serious problems. As he said, "I had to have somebody do all the legal, technical, strategic planning and implementation, and get it all staffed, and I needed somebody to present the evidence in the courtroom. I knew I couldn't do both." Up until O'Neill became chair of the Damages Committee, Oesting didn't have "even a glimmer on the horizon" of who among his team might be able to argue the *Exxon Valdez* case in Judge Holland's court. Oesting liked O'Neill's style. They were both defense lawyers. But, unlike Oesting, O'Neill had an affable courtroom manner—and he had proven jury appeal. So Oesting met with O'Neill in private and asked him to try the case. It was an offer O'Neill couldn't refuse.

CHAPTER EIGHT
AS BAD AS IT GETS
1993

On January 4, the tanker *Braer* grounded on the rocks off the Shetland Islands in Scotland and lost its entire cargo—twenty-five million gallons—of light crude oil over the next ten days of hurricane-force winds. Dan Lawn, Rick Steiner, Stan Stephens, and other Alaskans flew over to help our friend Jonathan Wills and residents of his fishing community cope with their disaster.

I was at a retreat on the Washington coast with my fiber art partner Yosh. We were designing our first commissioned piece, a twelve-foot-long wall hanging called "Arctic: The Last Refuge." Our work transforming my simple sketches of wildlife into bright swatches of calico prints was deeply relaxing. But the long arm of bad news found me, and I spent many long hours on the pay phone outside, recounting names and phone numbers of scientists who could help. The cold emptiness I felt was from more than the winter wind buffeting the lonely phone booth. It was from seeing another time when black oil floated on deep blue seas.

Upon returning to Cordova, I noticed it wasn't just me who felt haunted by the *Braer* disaster. The spill freshened memories and emotional pain. It sensitized people just before the first public presentation of the oil spill science. This was just the start of the roller-coaster ride in a year that would prove nearly as emotionally challenging for many as 1989.

Just before I left for the EVOS Trustee Council symposium in Anchorage, ADFG herring biologist Evelyn Brown stopped me at the post office. "Riki, remember what you told us at the Fish and Game office just after the spill? That the spill was possibly as much as thirty-eight million gallons?"

I nodded. Evelyn recounted how, at a meeting of spill scientists in Anchorage, she had asked Exxon's lead scientist Al Maki point-blank, "Where did this figure thirty-eight million gallons come from?" Her blue eyes widened. "Riki, *he laughed.* He said thirty-eight million gallons was always the high-end estimate for the spill and eleven million gallons was the low-end estimate! He didn't say, 'What are you talking about?' Or any other numbers like 'forty-two' or 'twenty-seven.' He knew immediately what I was talking about *and he laughed.*"

Al Maki subsequently denied all knowledge of this to the press at the symposium. Frustrated, I called assistant attorney general Craig Tillery to plead, once again, that it was important for people to know the truth. A year later, Tillery would quietly release the entire record of the state's investigation to the Alaska Resource Library and Information Services in Anchorage.

Sound Truth

Alaskans from oiled communities flocked in droves to the oil spill symposium. So did Exxon scientists who had declined to participate in the conference, claiming that their papers were not yet ready to present. Exxon scientists aggressively courted the media and Exxon public relations specialists videotaped every session of the three-day symposium, giving an air of siege to the event.

Sitting up front in one session and taking notes, I noticed a couple dozen friends from Cordova and other communities, standing all clumped together at the back. I sensed their discomfort in a room full of scientists and media. In a sudden shock of connection, I felt their wild, dark fear of the future and intense love of the Sound. I felt their desperate need to understand what was happening to our environment, to our lives. I swallowed a lump of frustrated anger and forced myself to focus on the unemotional—dispassionate—droning—scientific presentations.

Slowly the mystery of what was happening in the Sound revealed itself in charts, graphs, and slides. A picture began to emerge of lingering harm to beaches, birds, mammals, and fish like a puzzle revealing its design when key pieces are assembled. The trouble seemed to center around oiled beaches. In study after study, the killing did not stop in 1989.

Scientists reported that oil trapped under thick mats of mussels did not break down as expected in 1989, but was still poisonous four years after the spill. Mussels soaked up the highly toxic oil like sponges and passed it on, poisoning wildlife that ate them. Local stocks of shellfish eaters like harlequin ducks, black oystercatchers, and young sea otters had crashed in oiled areas of the Sound. Even wildlife that only occasionally snacked on mussels, like river otters and pigeon guillemots, were not doing well on oiled beaches relative to those that lived on unoiled beaches.

Scientists reported herring and pink salmon that spawned on beaches and grew to adults in bays were also having problems. Almost all of the herring eggs spawned in 1989 along oiled beaches in the Sound had died, and a high portion of the oiled wild pink salmon eggs had died as well. Slides of pink salmon larvae from oiled streams showed tiny bodies twisted and hideously deformed. Ominously, a progressively higher portion of salmon eggs in oiled streams died each year through 1992, causing scientists to scramble for answers. Oil stunted growth of young wild and hatchery pink salmon in oiled nursery bays. These effects all added up to fewer adult wild pink salmon than anticipated by state biologists despite the two years of record hatchery returns.

I thought the new information linked the spill to the 1992 wild and hatchery pink salmon collapse. It was possible that juvenile pink salmon in 1989 had been damaged by their oil bath and were unable to produce offspring, resulting in the collapse. Cordova fishermen drew similar conclusions and asked simple questions: Had oil damaged pink salmon's ability to reproduce or survive? How many generations might be affected? These questions hung unanswered in a room thick with apprehension.

Scientists did not know as much about the early lives of herring—what happened between eggs and adults—but they warned that if oil had similar devastating effects on these young fish, the consequences for the Sound would be disastrous. Herring are a "cornerstone species," one explained, a species that holds the entire ecosystem together. A crash in the herring population could delay recovery from spill losses of birds and mammals that fed on these schooling fish. I turned to look at my friends. Unspoken worry deeply etched their faces. We all knew that the herring born into the spill were supposed to return as adults this year. Now we wondered if they would.

I stared at my pages of notes. The findings pointed to lingering damage from oil—something scientists had said in 1989 would not happen. The studies contradicted what I had been taught in my field of study: Oil does not cause long-term harm. The findings were also at odds with the glowing predictions of record returns of hatchery pink salmon and herring for the upcoming season—134,000 tons of herring and a pink return triple that of the previous year's prediction. Years later, I would learn that the mathematical models used for predictions did not take into account any possible impacts from oil like higher death rates. In other words, predictions based on these models were practically worthless.

I started to think of this new reality presented by the scientists as "Sound

Truth." It was as if the Sound was trying to tell us something, yet no one could fully understand it. At the time, it did not occur to me that what I had been taught might be wrong, because it was a function of what scientists knew at the time and time had moved on. The old knowledge could be bowled over like tenpins by more sophisticated science that allowed greater understanding of complex systems.

Back in Cordova, I debriefed with Linden early one evening while Malani practiced on her violin in the other room. Linden finally said, "Well, I hope the scientists are wrong and the predictions are right. This town needs a good fishing season. *We* need one. We're so far in debt! We only made $800 last season on a $20,000 permit payment. Another bad season might tip a lot of people into bankruptcy, including us!"

"You know, some economists at the conference estimated spill losses at $17 million to $86 million. . . ."

"That can't be right!" With a head for numbers and finances, Linden made some quick calculations. "That's only 20 percent—or less!—of what we counted on before the spill."

"I think they left out the missing fish and lost value on fishing boats and permits."

"Those economists should come talk with my banker! We owe money on something those economists aren't even counting! How are people ever going to be made whole if all the losses don't count?" Linden's frustration with the situation was mirrored by many in town.

I shook my head. "I think Bobby Van Brocklin has some better numbers." Our former mayor was one of the key witnesses in the *Exxon Valdez* case. He had spent the past four years documenting and charting how the spill affected salmon markets and Cordova's economy.

"I hope our lawyers listen to him and not just the fancy PhD economists."

I broached another worry with my friend. "I found out Exxon is presenting its spill studies in April in Atlanta."

"Uh-oh. That sounds like a media setup," she said referring to the home of CNN.

"Yeah. Big-time. The conference is called ASTM for 'American Society of Testing and Materials.' I put together a team of us—our mayor Kelley, Lisa Rotterman, Dune Lankard, Rick Steiner. We can cover all the bases: effects of the spill on community, subsistence users, fishermen, wildlife, and policy. Our lawyers are sending us. We're calling ourselves the 'Alaska Squad of Truth and Morality'—ASTM!"

When Linden stopped laughing, she said, "Exxon is not going to know what hit them!"

Malani came into the kitchen, holding her violin. "What's so funny?"

"Oh, Riki and Rick and some others are going to a big meeting of Exxon scientists to make sure the media understands what's happening in the Sound," Linden explained.

"You'll have stories!" said Malani.

"Yes, I will. Hey, you're sounding pretty good on that violin, Malani!"

"Fiddle," she corrected me.

"Fiddle? I thought it was a violin."

"I'm playing bluegrass with dad. So it's a fiddle. When I play classical music, it's a violin." She beamed at me.

"Oh." I knew so little about music. When learning to write in first grade, I couldn't remember all the letters in my long given name, so I had tucked a small note with my name spelled out, F-r-e-d-e-r-i-c-k-a, into my sleeve. One day, when the class stood up to sing, the note had fallen out. The teacher found it and embarrassed me in front of everyone. With imperfect kid-logic, I had refused to sing ever since and had listened to very little music growing up. But this wall of resistance was crumbling in my desire to support my goddaughter.

"We're going to play at Folk Festival in Juneau!" Malani announced excitedly. Linden smiled.

"Then we'll all have stories to share," I said.

Corporate Myths

A few weeks later in Atlanta, Kelley stopped me at the registration tables. "Hey, Ottster! Did you notice all the police?" He was smartly dressed in a three-piece suit. His beard was trimmed and his wavy black hair was pulled back in a neat ponytail.

"Yeah." I looked around the room where at least a dozen armed cops stood near the walls. "What's up with that?"

"Well, I asked them, 'Isn't it unusual to have police at a scientific convention?' They said they were off-duty police, hired by Exxon. They said, 'We're expecting trouble from Alaska.'" I stared at Kelley. Relishing the moment, he said, "So I introduced myself as the mayor of Cordova, Alaska! They were very surprised. One asked, 'Do you know Riki Ott?' I said, 'My good friend

is over there registering.' They asked if you were going to shoot off anything.
I said, 'The only thing she'll shoot off is her mouth.' They said they protect
First Amendment rights." Kelley's black eyes sparkled. "This is going to be
fun."

All members of the Truth Squad took part in the "fun." In a room jam-
packed with mostly national press, government officials, and oilmen, Exxon
scientists claimed *Exxon Valdez* oil was merely a "blip" on the background level
of oil already in the Sound before the spill. The oil had come from a seep, they
claimed, a tear in the earth's skin that oozed its black blood, 150 miles to the
east of the Sound on the Copper River Delta. Nonsense, Rick Steiner said.
How could Exxon confuse low amounts of oil that had collected in deep sediments through eons of time with fresh toxic oil, concentrated on beaches, that
was killing fish and wildlife?

But Exxon scientists claimed they found few effects from the spill and the
Sound was recovering rapidly. As part of their proof, they boldly claimed sea
otters were "thriving" in oiled areas and producing more pups than in unoiled
areas. Dr. Lisa Rotterman stated coolly that pup production or having babies
was one thing, but the young pups were dying in oiled areas, not "thriving."

When Exxon scientists spoke of wild foods being "safe" for subsistence
users, Eyak Native activist Dune challenged them with a Native perspective
of "safe" foods, which did not include items collected from oiled beaches, no
matter what scientists in white lab coats said.

When Exxon scientists spoke of communities recovering, Kelley painted a
grim economic picture of post-spill life in town.

And when Exxon scientists claimed the record salmon returns in '90 and
'91 indicated a healthy fishery, I challenged them with evidence of the emerging link between the spill and the 1992 salmon collapse.

Then, 5,000 miles away, the Sound shouted her truth. The record herring
return failed.

Hotel staff brought me faxes, pages and pages of faxes, from the Fish and
Game office in Cordova. The Truth Squad pored over the information in my
room: 120,000 tons of fish had simply vanished. Of the 20,000 tons of fish that
did return, about one-third were covered with white spots and quarter-sized
raw lesions, oozing pus. Instead of swimming in tight synchronized schools,
the fish were lethargic and tipped at crazy angles. When cut open, female fish
were found to be absorbing their egg masses, a last-ditch strategy for survival.
State biologists determined that an unprecedented viral disease outbreak had
decimated the stocks, but the cause of the outbreak was unknown, pending

testing. State managers canceled the multimillion-dollar fisheries. We could well imagine the frantic despair of fishermen and townspeople.

When Exxon claimed oil had no effects on early life stages of herring and they anticipated no long-term effects from the spill, I described what was happening in the Sound and asked whether the herring collapse might be related to the spill. "Absolutely not!" snapped the Exxon scientist, and my floor microphone was turned off so I could not respond.

I knew the devil was in the details of Exxon's studies, buried in the methods and statistical design, and not the conclusions. For my doctorate, I had minored in this tricky technical area that divides good science from bad science and valid conclusions from public relations. The only way to find the deception was to read the studies carefully, so I went to Exxon's pressroom to retrieve copies of the papers.

Two burly police blocked the doorway. They told me I couldn't go into the room, because my name was on "a list." Disarmed by my solution, which was to have one of them go into the room and bring out a packet for me, one of the police asked, "What did you do to deserve this treatment from Exxon?" So, for twenty minutes, I told stories about the *Exxon Valdez* oil spill and its devastating effects on Cordova. After that, police disappeared from doorways whenever the Truth Squad challenged Exxon presenters.

By the last day, I couldn't contain myself when Hans Jahns, a retired German geologist, stated in an arrogant, condescending manner that he had "a theorem that oil could not be both bioavailable and long-lasting." I announced I, too, had a theorem. I posited, "The more direct and greater one's funding from Exxon, the more likely one is to conclude that everything is fine in Prince William Sound." The audience erupted. The police were nowhere in sight. The Exxon moderator pounded on the podium for order, shouting, "Courtesy rules the day!" to which I retorted, "Too bad it's not the truth."

In the end, the national media left for the most part disgusted by Exxon's blatant distortion of truth or "corporate myths," as I dubbed it. Some even told me they tore up their Exxon credit cards after the conference. Others came to Alaska to search out the facts for themselves. Even Exxon's hired police realized the deception. As the Truth Squad gathered to bid each other farewell, the police encircled us in an informal, curious manner. I overheard one say, "I've never seen such a large corporation afraid of such a small group of people."

On the long flights home, I was filled with a sense of foreboding. What the Truth Squad had witnessed in Atlanta was the opening volley of a well-financed campaign to whitewash the spill's damage. Exxon had plenty of incentive with potentially billions of dollars at stake in the *Exxon Valdez* case. The odds for countering such a campaign didn't look good. Government scientists were not trained or paid to aggressively advocate their findings in public. Also, politics trumps science. Government scientists could change their tune, depending on political whims of administrations. That left the media, which could be misled into believing things that were not true, and a handful of citizen scientists. I felt like an ant trying to change the course of elephants. "What can I do," I wondered, "to help people understand the full impacts of the oil spill on our lives and the Sound?"

Fuel on the Fire

There wasn't any time to strategize, because when I returned to Cordova in late April, the town was in an uproar. The failed herring fishery had frayed emotions to the breaking point. Fear, anger, worry, and depression galloped wildly across the town's emotional landscape like the four horsemen of the apocalypse.

A week later, community leader Bobby Van Brocklin took his life.

People were stunned. Bobby had left a note saying that he had felt the stress from dealing with Exxon and the financial stress were too much to deal with alone. His brother tried to explain that Bobby was a "troubled man in a troubled town in troubled times." Yet people became angry. Almost everyone in town had suffered spill-induced business losses. Why had Bobby thought his troubles were more unbearable than anyone else's pain? It was true, people reasoned, that Bobby had been in the forefront of many issues as mayor, and he had been a scapegoat for Connie Taylor's misguided wrath, but still people agonized: How could he have done this? We needed the security of knowing that we were all in this mess together. His death left a gaping hole that sucked bits of each of us away with him. "It's hard not to be angry at our friend," Michelle O'Leary wrote in a letter to the *Cordova Times*. "But we must forgive him because he was one of us and we need to forgive ourselves."

At Bobby's service, the tightly packed church was thick with grief and remorse. One word, unspoken during the service, hung in the air like a dark storm cloud: Exxon. After the service, the storm burst and person after person told a visiting reporter from the *Anchorage Daily News* how the spill had affected Bobby's life and ours. In people's minds, there was no separating the death, the grief, the spill, and the town.

Although no one realized it at the time, Bobby's death was a turning point for the community. His suicide forced people to realize that life was an option and that, by not choosing his path, the rest of us chose to live ours. Now, committed to living, those who had been emotionally adrift since the spill started to regain control of our lives. With this mental shift, collective action was possible.

The community had little time to process Bobby's death, because sockeye began pouring into the unoiled Copper River in record numbers. The fish were eagerly scooped up by fishermen anxious to pay bills and loans. With fish bucks flowing into town and people busy working, some of the pain and emotional tension from Bobby's death eased.

In late May, another issue stoked the fire of community emotions. Fishermen and townspeople packed into the Mt. Eccles grade school cafeteria to voice opinions on restoration projects to visiting members of EVOS Trustee Council. The groundswell clearly favored studies to determine what was wrong with herring and pink salmon, and habitat acquisition to protect salmon streams.

Yet just days later, the Trustees selectively axed studies on herring, pink salmon, harlequin ducks, and juvenile sea otters—all species that showed lingering harm from the spill. Politicians also swiftly stripped funding for ADFG's popular magazine, *Alaska's Wildlife*, after state biologists dedicated a special issue in January to a compelling summary of oil spill damages. To frustrated townspeople, it seemed the Trustees and state politicians were determined to pretend there were no problems in the Sound.

Persevering through the town's emotional roller-coaster ride, the city council managed to settle on a budget despite what the city manager called "the most confusing budget process . . . ever. . . ." Contributing to the confusion were looming shortfalls from lack of fish revenues, lawsuits and endless demands from newly annexed residents, and no support from Governor Hickel, who vetoed all state-sponsored projects to Cordova. Some speculated the governor's move was retaliation for the town's lack of support for the Copper River Highway. There was simply no way to make ends meet without raising taxes beyond what residents could be expected to pay. The council was forced to adopt a plan that raided the city's savings to subsidize its spending. "A day of accounting will come," the city manager warned. Everyone grimly adjusted to modest price hikes in basic services and prayed the pink salmon would return in record numbers like the Copper River reds.

They didn't.

The early return of hatchery pinks was very weak. Seventeen seiners, about 12 percent of the fleet, left to fish in southeast Alaska. One person observed, Cordova "is becoming a summer fishing camp. There're families who grew up here . . . [moving] away. I resent it." Fear and worry escalated over the poor pink return, dangerously overpressuring the community for the fourth time in as many months.

I was home, waiting for Linden and the kids to return on the ferry with their new puppy. A production crew of women, whom I had trained to cut, piece, and prepare our designs for sewing, kept a constant stream of unfinished product flowing to me or Yosh to appliqué. The sewing was usually soothing, but I was anxious for Linden's news on fishing.

Danny's reports were disheartening: 10 percent of predicted returns of hatchery pinks, dismal returns of wild salmon, and seiners spending more money on fuel and groceries than they were earning. But what really frightened the fleet was the lifeless condition of the Sound. Gone were the porpoises; the minke, humpback, and killer whales; the birds. Gone were even the tiny plant and animal plankton, the rich living broth that nurtured sea life and formed the foundation of food webs. The seawater was see-through clear.

Finally, the phone rang. "We've just had the 'Ferry Ride from Hell,'" Makena announced as if he was introducing the Queen of England.

"The what? Makena! Put your mother on the phone!"

Linden, laughing, took the phone. "That's what I've been calling it!"

"I can tell. What happened?"

"It was so rough coming across the Sound! Everyone on the deck was either lying down or throwing up. Even our puppy was seasick! Then, when we finally came around Salmo Point into flat water, the wind pushed the ferry onto a sandbar! We had to wait six hours for the tide to lift the boat. I don't think I'll be interested in eating for a week!"

"So now's not a good time to come over?" I was disappointed.

"Of course it's a good time! That's why we called. Cassie is so cute! She's a tricolor Australian shepherd. The kids want to play down by the lake. I just want to sit and not move."

"I'm on my way!" In spring before fishing, the O'Tooles had purchased lakefront property with a three-bedroom log cabin. They had outgrown their small, loft-bedroom rental and had decided to spend their scarce dollars on mortgage instead of rent. The kids spent long hours on makeshift rafts or in a canoe exploring the water's edge.

The fuzzy gray puppy was irresistible. She had one blue and one brown eye, and splashes of tan and white markings. She bounced, tripped, and rolled down the steep hill with the kids to the lakeshore. We sat on the small deck in the sun and watched them.

When I asked about fishing, Linden shook her head. "Something's really wrong with the Sound. There's nothing there, but Kodiak and Southeast are catching record numbers of pink salmon. People are just not handling this well, especially after that dumb article in the paper about Picou's work."

Earlier in spring, Exxon had sued one of the southern sociologists, Steve Picou, in federal court in Alabama to obtain access to the confidential names of hundreds of townspeople who had participated in his surveys about the emotional toll of the spill. Most were also plaintiffs in the *Exxon Valdez* case. People were worried that Exxon would use their interviews to try to diminish their damage claims or to weaken our whole case against Exxon. Many, including Bobby Van Brocklin, had called Picou, begging him to keep their names a secret as he had personally promised. Picou, backed by his university, had fought Exxon in court over confidentiality and won, but the *Anchorage Daily News* had sensationalized the story with a headline that proclaimed, "Exxon wins look at spill stress data."

"But that article was wrong!" I said. "Exxon only won access to the published data, not people's names. Picou flew here himself to explain what happened."

"I know. Everybody knows. But that story really upset people. It's like being told a friend died. You go through all the grief. Then you find out they didn't die. Well, you're happy, but you still went through all that agony."

"Everyone just seems to be way overreacting. Maybe that's why people are so stressed about logging."

Hostilities over logging had reached a feverish pitch when the governor announced plans to use money from oil spill fines to build an access road for a deepwater port, instead of protecting trees. Some people in the community felt logging jobs might replace fishing jobs jeopardized by the spill. Those against logging perceived the access road would facilitate clear-cutting. They didn't want oil spill money used for something that would further divide the community.

"We saw the first clear-cut from the ferry!" Linden exclaimed.

"Yeah, I'm really worried the town is going to explode. I even called the Attorney General to ask for help. I told him people here are talking guns to stop the logging." Linden's eyes grew wide. "We're taking boats across the inlet to do a healing ceremony with Chief Marie. I'm hoping it'll help people vent some energy."

A few days later, about sixty people in seine boats charged across Orca Inlet to the logging camp. We brought press to focus attention on the habitat acquisition proposal, pending before the EVOS Trustee Council. Chief Marie Smith Jones, the last Eyak fullblood, led a prayer of healing, then we threw fireweed, a symbol of rebirth, on the water.

Within days, mostly out-of-town loggers retaliated by driving their trucks, loaded with logs and festooned with banners, down Main Street to City Hall. They met a counterprotest of townspeople and fishermen. People in the two battle lines just stood and screamed at each other. My heart ached.

July wore on with only a trickle of pink salmon in the Sound. With tensions still high, people learned that Alyeska had agreed to pay $98 million to settle its damages in the *Exxon Valdez* case. A surge of alarm ran through the community: $98 million wasn't nearly enough compensation! Was that the best our attorneys could do? "That's not going to keep me in Coca Cola for a year," quipped Patience Andersen Faulkner, referring to her share after dividing the settlement among thousands of plaintiffs.

Our attorneys flooded into coastal communities to explain the settlement's primary advantage. As in the *Glacier Bay* case, mock juries had found average people were confused by lawsuits against both Alyeska and the pipeline owner that had spilled oil. Juries were likely to decide upon a smaller punitive award against Exxon, because people perceived Exxon was part of Alyeska. It didn't matter that Alyeska and Exxon were separate entities; that each entity had made separate decisions that contributed to the spill and failed response; and that each entity should be punished for its decisions. These perceptions counted—and they counted against us.

Standing, listening, in the packed Elks' Lodge where it was so quiet that you could hear people breathe, I was skeptical. One of the attorneys pulled me aside before I could speak. He whispered that the performance by the Truth Squad at the Atlanta conference had so impressed BP and ARCO attorneys with the weaknesses in Exxon's "science" that they had convinced the four minor owners in the consortium to settle out of court without Exxon knowing. "This settlement is in our best interest," he insisted. "We need your support." The attorneys managed to quell all protests.

But in August, the community's patience snapped.

The Blockade

I was home alone when seiner Jim Gray called. His deep voice crackled over the phone line. "I'm here in Chenega Bay with the seine fleet. A hundred of us just had a meeting. There's no fish. The Sound is a dead zone. We're sick of Exxon's press releases that 'everything's better than ever' in the Sound.

"We've gotta do something to focus attention on the problems here. We decided to escort the next Exxon tanker into Port Valdez, but we need some help. Can you find out when the next Exxon tanker is due in, make us banners, and call the press, but otherwise stay out of it? The guys think you're pretty well known. We want people to know we're *all* upset."

"You got it," I told him.

The next Exxon tanker was due in two days. Word of the seiners' plan spread quickly in town. CDFU and PWSAC sent a flurry of press releases nationwide. Banner crews wielded foot-wide rollers, painting nine-foot-high slogans on long strips of donated Tyvek. NO PINKS 1992 & 1993. NO HERRING 1993. PRINCE WILLIAM SOUND IS A DEAD ZONE. DEAD EGGS, MUTANT FRY, SICK ADULTS. COMPENSATION NOT BANKRUPTCY! Gillnetters organized boats to transport press, townspeople, food, and banners to the seiners.

In the wee hours of Friday morning on August 20, the seine fleet battled through a fierce early fall storm, and everyone converged in Valdez Narrows as planned. Everyone, that is, except the Exxon tanker, which was "delayed" in the Gulf of Alaska, according to the Coast Guard. The storm laid down, but another Exxon tanker became inexplicably delayed in the gulf. Then another, and another, TAPS tanker stalled in the gulf. Kelley Weaverling and I anxiously monitored events relayed by VHF radio to the CDFU office.

Under advisement that the fishing fleet was targeting Exxon, BP decided to bring in one of its chartered tankers. As the tanker loomed ever larger on the horizon, the media urged protest leaders to form a blockade just so they could take pictures. A blockade tentatively formed. . . .

Then something happened as the boats lined up side by side, stretching across the Narrows and beaming their deck lights in defiance and desperation at the oncoming tanker. The fleet became more than 100 individual boats. They became a single empowered presence.

Hovering overhead in a helicopter, the Coast Guard sensed the change and ordered the fleet to disband—to no avail. Jim Gray sensed the change and radioed the Coast Guard, "Captain, I have lost control of my fleet." BP oilmen, overhead in another helicopter, sensed the change and radioed the tanker captain. Stan Stephens, on his tour boat with 100 passengers, saw the changing shape of the tanker profile as it started *to turn around.* His passengers erupted in a spontaneous cheer. Stan cried.

The fleet held firm for three days. In all, seven tankers stalled in the gulf to wait out the "political storm," as an Alyeska spokesperson put it. Governor Hickel and a dozen cabinet members flew into Cordova for an emergency town meeting, then on to Valdez. Interior Secretary Bruce Babbitt detoured from Anchorage to Valdez to meet with protest leaders. Exxon maintained that the spill had absolutely nothing to do with the failed fish runs, and it refused to meet with fishermen. Babbitt told the press, "I think it's outrageous that an American corporation with the size and sophistication of Exxon Company doesn't have the will to come and sit down and talk with a bunch of fishermen."

Rick Steiner and David Grimes, in Valdez during the meetings, called to tell me that the feeling of solidarity among the fishermen was intense. One overheard Governor Hickel say, "If I was a fisherman, I'd probably go out there." The meetings were tense, but productive. Political leaders promised to fund "ecosystem studies" to determine the cause of the Sound's ailments. They promised that state banks would grant emergency relief from overdue loans on boats and permits. They promised that fishermen would not be fined for disobeying Coast Guard orders to disband. BP and ARCO oilmen promised to work with fishermen to expedite TAPL Fund claims, stalled by Exxon's legal maneuvering. Finally satisfied, the seine fleet peaceably disbanded the blockade.

Two days later Interior Secretary Babbitt attended his first EVOS Trustee Council meeting. He came armed with the results of Rick Steiner's lobbying efforts—the newly released report from the General Accounting Office. The GAO found the Bush and Hickel Trustees had spent over $200 million in the first two years on virtually everything except restoration. President Clinton's mandate to his new federal Trustees was to stop the money hemorrhage by redirecting funds to land conservation and science as people wished. Under Babbitt's lead, the EVOS Trustee Council allocated $5 million to design and start up comprehensive ecosystem-wide studies to figure out what was wrong with the Sound. Nothing on this scale had ever been tried before—and it would lead to a new understanding that oil is much more toxic to life than previously thought.

Community Unity: On a Roll

That fall, the mood in town shifted. The seiners brought back to town with them what crewmember Torie Baker called "the energy of the blockade." Torie, a lanky, good-natured redhead had been part of the blockade from its inception in Chenega. She said, "The energy and clarity of that civil disobedience had the same kind of energy and clarity that fishermen hadn't seen in the Sound or the fisheries since the beginning of the hatchery movement." The energy of the blockade pervaded town, carrying with it a boldness and momentum that propelled people into action. The infusion of self-confidence and solidarity heartened townspeople, who turned to face a dismal economic situation with gutsy determination.

The community was broke. The fishing season was the least profitable on record. Seiners grossed just 60 percent of the disastrous 1992 season and less than 10 percent of the 1987–1988 pre-spill average. Entire extended fishing families were destitute and facing bankruptcy. With loans pressing and urgent, fishermen presented their plight to bankers, but bankers refused to deliver on the governor's pledge of financial relief through debt deferment. Bankers claimed they couldn't afford any more excuses.

The abrupt and extreme losses to permit value threatened to topple a huge chunk of the state's business. According to Ed Crane with the Commercial Fishing and Agriculture Bank (CFAB), lenders and brokers viewed permits as investment devices rather than simply a ticket to fish and, in doing so, they had artificially inflated permit prices. This created a "mob mentality," dangerously overcapitalizing the state's commercial fishing business. Lenders scrambled to arrange mortgages on homes and other assets to secure fishing business loans. CFAB was structured as a cooperative and it had already reduced fisheries capitalization across the board before the spill.

To make matters worse, after the blockade Exxon filed an injunction to block the $98 million Alyeska settlement. This dashed hopes of some financial relief for cash-strapped families. Family savings were exhausted to pay bills and buy groceries, and second mortgages were taken out on homes to pay boat and permit loans.

Despite the financial hardships, more than sixty fishermen, Natives, and local scientists volunteered to design a study to determine the cause of the Sound's ailing fisheries. This odd mix of talents and training met several times a week throughout the fall to share what they knew about pink salmon and herring ecology. Ecology is the combination of factors such as chemistry,

temperature, sea condition, currents, weather patterns, and numbers of predators and prey that influence how many young salmon and herring survive. By
sharing what they knew, the group identified gaps in knowledge. This way,
they learned what questions needed to be asked to determine whether the
oil spill had harmed salmon and herring, as many suspected. These gaps in
knowledge and questions became the focus of the first ecosystem study, the
Sound Ecosystem Assessment (SEA) Program.

The high level of trust, motivation, passion, and history carried the diverse
group through long evenings of talking and listening and through strong
undercurrents of tension from the various factions. Torie described the process
as "brutal. We had to reconcile all these different vocabularies, all these different perspectives, all these different interests. It was tough, very, very tough."
She said, "There was a lot of vocabulary swapping. Most of us didn't run
around talking about 'testable hypotheses,' but we had to figure out how to
translate that very human, very simple question—'What is wrong with Prince
William Sound?'—into testable hypotheses."

Fueled by optimism and constructive criticism from an independent peer
review process, the local group fine-tuned the SEA Program to launch in spring.
Although no one understood it at the time, the process of working together for a
common goal began to stitch peoples' lives together again, re-forming community. Three years later, sociologist Steve Picou would validate that the group
process of problem-solving was a way to heal social splintering after disasters.

I spent most of that fall traveling to craft fairs on my own, as Linden could no
longer afford the time away from her young family, and to Washington, D.C.,
for TAPS issues. In December, I returned home just before Malani's elementary school Christmas concert. Linden invited me over to help make cookies.
I ran up the snow-packed steps into her house and nearly into the arms of a
bushy spruce tree, sparkling with lights and ornaments.

"Whoa! Nice tree!" Cassie came bouncing over, her whole body wagging
a greeting.

"It's a new family tradition! Our other house was too small for a big tree.
We're going to have a family outing every year to find the perfect tree." We
hugged each other.

"How's Makena liking first grade?" I washed my hands and donned an
apron.

"He's not." Linden rolled her eyes. "I'm not liking it either. The house is so
empty."

"Jeez, what are you going to do when they go to college? What are we making?"

"Oh, please! That's years away. Gingerbread people. The kids want to make sugar cookies when school gets out." She passed me a bowl of butter and eggs to cream. "Makena has a new friend, Zak, so that helps with school. You'd like Zak's mom, Lisa Marie."

"Really? What does she do?"

"She fished in Southeast and she's into politics—she's running the Legislative Information Office. She actually moved here a year before the spill. She ran the childcare service where we took our kids. Now she's the founding president of the new Cordova Family Resource Center."

The new center planned to tackle the spike in domestic violence and substance abuse, among other issues—it sounded like a perfect job for Lisa Marie, based on Linden's description. I measured molasses, Linden worked the flour mixture, and we talked about all the new projects in town.

It turned out the Native Village of Eyak was planning an annual Sobriety Celebration, complete with Native dance groups and artists.

"You don't drink anyway," teased Linden, "so you can celebrate sobriety." We combined the contents of the two bowls, then I plopped globs of dough onto four wax paper sheets. Linden wrapped them and put them in the refrigerator. I poured tea water. We moved into the living room to visit while the dough chilled enough to roll.

"The SEA Program, too," she said, referring to the ecosystem study that resulted from the fishermen's blockade. "There were a lot of people working together on that. That's what I liked. Did you go to any of the workshops?"

"The peer review one. It's a good program, but it's going to take years to produce results. Meanwhile, Exxon is roaring around now to scientific conferences all over the country, telling press that the Sound has recovered."

"Is that what happened in Texas?"

"Yeah, Rick Steiner and David Grimes and I did all we could to counter them, but there were only three of us and lots of them. It's like Hitler's Big Lie: 'If you tell a lie big enough and keep repeating it, people will eventually come to believe it.' The press is already confused." I slumped wearily on the couch.

"Did I tell you I ran into one of my former professors who was working for Exxon?"

"What happened?" Linden asked.

"Well, basically, I asked, 'How could you?' and he said he knew he was ethical and he figured Exxon needed ethical scientists. He found out later that Exxon had editing rights and he couldn't talk about how things were edited. He's not working for them anymore, but that doesn't stop Exxon from using his name and 'his' paper."

"When is that going to get out—that Exxon's studies are full of holes?" asked Linden.

"Oh, Greenpeace is funding me to write a paper about it for the fifth memorial next year," I answered. "We'll see how far that gets. But there is something else—the pipeline!"

When a handful of us had briefed the Clinton administration on pipeline issues, it turned out we knew more than the federal regulators about the real problems on the pipeline. They were thoroughly embarrassed and promised to make up for lost time.

"Congressman John Dingell held a hearing on TAPS issues this summer. Alyeska does this huge makeover right before the hearing. The president and security chief get fired—well, okay. They take 'early retirement.'" I rolled my eyes at Linden.

"I hope the president gave back the keys to the city before he left," she remarked.

"Oh, very funny. The whistleblower lawsuits get settled the night before the hearing and the whistleblowers are supposedly put on a rehire list. Meanwhile, Chuck is scrambling to raise money to get the whistleblowers back to Congress to testify. I start an 'Adopt-A-Whistleblower Program' during the Arctic Refuge trip this summer. My sister and her husband bought one plane ticket. So did I."

Linden was shaking her head in dismay or horror, I couldn't tell which, but I was on a roll.

"In July Dingell opens his hearing with a classic statement: 'Gentlemen,'— yeah, right, I'm thinking—'this hearing is déjà vu all over again.' In 1976, he says, his committee held a hearing on the pipeline quality control system and learned of a total collapse of Alyeska's inspection system. Now, here we are again, he says. The only improvement he's seen is that in the mid-seventies, inspectors received death threats and bullet holes in their truck windshields. Now, the inspectors are only being threatened with broken arms! 'Small progress indeed,' he says!"

"Oh my God!" said Linden. "I can't believe you're in the middle of this."

"Yeah, well, neither can I! Do you think we could start rolling dough?" Suddenly, I had a lot of energy to burn.

Linden fetched one package of dough as I cleared the kitchen table. I laid into the rolling pin and continued my story.

"So the whistleblowers testify about so many serious problems that they've lost track of many of them! And they talk about a leadership culture of intimidation and harassment. They warn disaster is imminent. Nonsense, says the new Alyeska president. Yes, the problems denied by the past president exist, but we're taking care of them, he says. Dingell calls this 'somewhat disingenuous' because some of the problems were identified in 1988 and no corrective action has been taken. Dingell's committee orders up an audit of the pipeline."

"That's thin enough!" said Linden. She stopped me from rolling and we cut out little dough figures, arranged them on a cookie sheet, and stuck them in the oven. Then she broke out another batch of dough for me to roll.

"So the audit confirms the whistleblowers' stories—or at least all of the issues that the auditors had time to check out, because they couldn't get to all the issues in three months. Especially with Alyeska still trying to cover up this mess. There was a classic 'File Stuffing Incident,' where technicians actually made up safety plans and other documents that didn't exist and stuffed them into folders so the feds could find them." Linden just stared at me.

"I'm not kidding," I said. "So now there are more whistleblowers and more lawsuits. In November Dingell reconvenes his hearing to decide what to do about the pipeline. Meanwhile, just before the hearing, ABC News does a live interview with the original whistleblower Glen Plumlee and the interviewer hands Plumlee an ARCO blacklist with the names of the original five whistleblowers and a big scrawl at the top of the page: 'Former Alyeska inspectors—do not touch.'"

"So Alyeska thinks they can get away with this?" Linden asked as we traded shapes and cut more cookies.

"Alyeska just has to outlast the Clinton administration and hope the next president and Congress don't look too closely. The head of BLM testified that Alyeska has 'an adversarial attitude that bred contempt for the concerns of the public interest.' He said the only reason we haven't had a catastrophe is because there are a handful of people doing their best to keep everything sort of glued together. He says, 'It's just a matter of time before their luck runs out.'"

"You'd think our government would pay closer attention to what Alyeska is doing," Linden said in her practical tone. "That's 25 percent of our domestic oil going through that pipeline every day. Talk about a threat to national security!" I pulled the batch from the oven and set them to cool, while Linden grabbed another pack of dough. "One more after this," she announced.

"This is going fast," I said, grabbing the rolling pin.

"So what is happening now?"

"It's up to Alyeska to fix the problems. The new president says they will." I looked at Linden.

"Do you think they will?" she asked.

"Of course not! So Dan and Stan and I hatched a plan after the court hearing on Alyeska's spy operation that started four days after the second TAPS hearing."

"Jeez, no wonder you've been away so much this fall," she said.

"Chuck's invasion of privacy case winds up in Judge Stanley Sporkin's court. It turns out Sporkin is a people's judge. He loves big corporate corruption cases. So picture this: Dad and I walk into the courtroom—"

"Your father went to the hearing?"

"Oh, he wasn't about to miss it! There were two tables of attorneys. Chuck had two women: Billie Garde and Mona Lyons, the country's two leading lawyers in whistleblower protection cases. And the defense had seventeen attorneys, all men. One is the former U.S. Attorney General representing Wackenhut! Another is the former president of the Washington, D.C., bar representing Alyeska, BP, and ARCO. Dad's like, 'Whoooeeee! Look at that!' Hey, I think those cookies are done. They smell good."

We changed out the cookies in the oven and Linden took out the last pack of dough. "Most of the good stuff happened before we got there though. The oil companies tried repeatedly to move the case out of Judge Sporkin's court. That really pissed off Sporkin. Then they made a run at getting the names of Chuck's sources when Sporkin went on vacation. The stand-in judge nearly let them have the names, too. Billie managed to stall until Sporkin returned. That pissed Sporkin off even more when he learned what had happened.

"Then, Billie and Mona get this Notre Dame University law professor who was the primary author of RICO. You know, the Mafia law? The Racketeer Influenced and Corrupt Organizations Act? Well, this professor is listing examples of cases that fit under RICO: the Chicago Mafia, the New York Mafia . . . Alyeska!"

"*Oh my God*," said Linden.

"Yeah, I guess that really shocked the defense into silence. Hah! About time someone called them what they are." I rolled with gusto. "So it starts to look bad for the defense and the next thing you know: Mr. Superspy Wayne Black says—under oath—that the conversations he recorded between himself and Chuck were illegal but it was an accident. He had no idea,"—I gestured innocently—"his Dictaphone was turned on, despite that fact that he had to physically hold the button to activate the machine."

"How can they get away with lying like that?" Linden was exasperated. We cut the last round of shapes and stuck the sheet in the oven. "So the Guilty—the electronic guys, the spies—are pleading the Fifth like crazy and lying under oath. Meanwhile, there are intense settlement talks behind the scenes. Our Alaska spy case gets linked with Chuck's case, because the oil companies don't want to go through this again. It's too big a risk of actually getting caught. We figure we might as well settle, because dragging these guys into court certainly didn't change their behavior. And Chuck needed the money. He's hurtin' after years of fighting the oil companies. So, we settle and—boom!—it's over on Solstice."

"How much did you get?"

"Well, I'm not supposed to say as a condition of the settlement, but I will tell you it was worth one good gillnet season before the spill." I watched her reaction closely.

She did a quick mental calculation. "That's not much for all that hassle!"

"No." I was relieved. "I hope other people see it that way, too. And here's what I'm going to do with it. I'm giving Danny half because I really couldn't have put the time into all this without him doing the lion's share of work in our fishing business."

"That's overly generous."

"Wait, there's more." I took a deep breath. "Then he's going to buy out my share of our boat and permit for the same price. I'm going to quit fishing. Dan, Stan, and I are each putting up half of our settlement to start a new group, a citizen oversight group of the TAPS like an RCAC for the pipeline. I'm going to start doing this work full-time."

Linden took the last batch of cookies out of the oven in silence. Finally, she said, "Sam and I decided to sell our seine permit, too, if we can." She was crying. "We didn't make our permit payment for the second year in a row. We're trying to avoid bankruptcy. Sam is going to crew for people."

This, I knew, was a real blow to their dreams. Still, I couldn't muster up anything but "Oh, Linden!"

"That's not all. You know, Judge Holland set a trial date of May 2, 1994?"

I nodded.

"Our attorneys picked me to be one of the three witnesses for Prince William Sound fishermen," she said. "Listening to your stories. . . ." Her voice trailed off. "What have I got myself into?" she asked softly.

We stared at each other. I can't remember admiring my gentle, well-meaning friend more than I did right then. I held up a warm gingerbread man. "This is Exxon." I bit off its head. "Let's go kick ass!"

Linden grabbed a cookie and snapped off its head. "You're on!"

We leaped up and hugged each other, crying and laughing as only women can.

PART THREE
COURAGE
1994–1999

"Out beyond the field of right-doing and wrong-doing,
there is a field. I'll meet you there."

JELALUDDIN RUMI

CHAPTER NINE

DECISIONS
1994

On January 2, the inbound tanker *Overseas Ohio* hit a submerged iceberg near Bligh Reef. The ice ripped a twenty-foot-long hole in the tanker's single hull, puncturing a segregated ballast tank. Coast Guard crew inspecting the tanker said, "The whole thing was crumpled like a piece of paper." The only thing spilled was clean ballast—seawater—but it could easily have been oil. Within two weeks, TAPS shippers instituted a voluntary system of "ice scouts," escort vessels for inbound tankers in conditions of poor visibility or darkness when ice was within a mile of shipping lanes. The RCAC started a study to help tankers predict and avoid heavy ice.

Other things could not be so easily fixed. Danny and I spent three weeks in Belize. It was our first time alone since the spill. We had spent six years as a couple, but had been too caught up in nearly separate lives to deal with thorny issues that had been bothering each of us for some time. We sifted through our troubles under the warm tropical sun and on moonlit beaches. The crux of it was my political involvement, which I saw as a civic responsibility and Danny saw as inevitable after getting to know my father. The problem was more my inability or unwillingness to balance my full-throttle politics and our relationship. We decided to live as housemates, sharing connected but less intimate lives. My home was 900 square feet, palatial compared to the living space on the *Ambergris*. We could make it work, at least for a while.

Derailed

We returned to Cordova in late January on the heels of a town meeting that the *Cordova Times* described as "therapy for residents." The editor of the paper noted, "Local council members have crawled into 1994 with nothing more to look forward to than a capricious oil spill settlement, a new city manager, and what is expected to be a pittance from state lawmakers." With no economic relief in sight, I wondered, "How could everyone be so high after a town meeting?" I went to the O'Tooles' for dinner to catch up on the news. There were two new faces at the table.

I sensed immediately why Linden liked Lisa Marie: She was upbeat and had a friendly, easygoing manner—and she liked to laugh as much as Linden. Her dark hair waved and curled around dark eyes that crinkled into slits when she laughed or smiled. Her young son Zak shared her clear pale skin, but his blond mop framed striking green eyes that also disappeared into slits when he smiled. Makena took Zak into his room to show Zak his collection of bones, skulls, and skins.

"That's Cassie's favorite room," noted Sam as the dog bounced after the boys. "Makena's been dragging squirrel skins around, teaching her to hunt."

"Malani," said Linden, "Riki hasn't heard your new song." I looked quizzically at Malani.

"I wrote my first song! I'm going to play it for the Family Resource Center fund-raiser and at Folk Festival! I'll sing it for you." Malani rushed off to her room to practice.

I looked at Linden. "What happened? Did I blink? How come she looks so much older suddenly?"

Linden laughed. "She's going to be ten in May! The music is really helping her self-confidence." Malani was one of the youngest singer-songwriters in the state.

"This moose roast needs a little longer," Lisa Marie decided. "I shot him this fall. We're going to be eating moose all winter! It sure helps with the grocery bills."

"You shot it?" I asked, impressed. Lisa Marie looked like she could hold down an evening in a New York disco. I tried to imagine her out moose hunting. "Jeez, what else did I miss?" I asked. "The town seems to be in a good mood."

Apparently one reason for that was the new mayor, Margy Johnson, who wanted build up the town's spirit and businesses, despite a controversial election. Margy had decided to run for mayor against the popular incumbent Kelley Weaverling. A long-time Cordova resident and co-owner of the Reluctant Fisherman, she had a solid support base in town—and with the oil industry. People expected a close race. On the day of the election, Alyeska had called a surprise spill drill that drew seventy of Kelley's voter base out of town before the voting booths opened and kept them out past closing of the polls. Margy had won by one vote.

"Margy's headed in the right direction," observed Lisa Marie, sipping a glass of wine.

The mayor and city council had worked up an economic development plan, the first in nearly twenty years. They planned a series of town meetings to gather ideas on projects and priorities.

"There were a lot of positive ideas at that town meeting," said Linden. "People want to better market what we've got here: fish and scenery. There were ideas to reduce the cost of our fish to make them more competitive. Tourism was a popular idea. People suggested ways to spruce up the town's image. And people really want to work together. That's what I liked."

Lisa Marie added, "A lot of people liked that. That's why everyone's in a good mood. It's a good thing, too, because this town usually gets really stressed out right before the fishing season opens in spring. In all the other places I've worked, the high stress point is right before Christmas. That's when problems like domestic violence and drinking peak. But in this town, it's April before the herring season starts."

"The moose is done!" proclaimed Sam. "Let's eat!"

The town derailed two months ahead of schedule in February.

It started with calls from national media for stories for the upcoming fifth year memorial of the oil spill. Callers stirred the cauldron of simmering unrest, tensions, and stress left over from the spill. Mayor Margy suggested a parade to "bury the blues. Cordova doesn't need to be known as 'The Depressed City,'" she said. "It's been five years. . . . It's time to move on."

Tempers flared. People perceived that Margy could afford to move on, but most others could not. Fisherman Rich Septien called the burial idea "bogus." In a letter to the *Cordova Times*, he wrote, "To forgive Exxon without justice being served can be equated to someone raping and killing your mother, then telling you, just forgive them and go on with your life—while the perpetrator is still at large. . . . The Sound did not just die—the Sound was murdered by negligence." With fishermen threatening to crash the parade with burning effigies of Exxon CEO Lee Raymond hanging from cranes in the back of pickup trucks, the mayor canceled the event.

Then a week before the memorial, tragedy struck. A drunk driver killed a Cordova mother and her young daughter and critically injured the popular judo coach, who were all in Anchorage for the state championship tournament. A fresh wave of grief engulfed the town.

Judge Holland picked this emotionally prickly time to deny thousands of people's claims worth potentially billions of dollars. He dismissed claims of out-of-area fishermen, tendermen, fish processors, cannery workers, seafood wholesalers, area businesses, and municipalities. He tossed out Native claims for cultural damage and fishermen's claims for loss of quality of life. The only surviving claims were those to commercial fishermen for lost economic opportunity, landowners for property damage, and Alaska Natives for economic losses to subsistence harvest. "No touch, no foul," as Oesting had said. Oesting appealed the rulings, and some dismissed claims were later reinstated, but the town was emotionally wasted.

Knowing well that his decision would devastate thousands of people, the judge wrote "a further word of explanation . . . for non-lawyers who will review this ruling." It was as if the judge wanted people to forgive him for making a hurtful decision that he felt the law bound him to do. He wrote, "There is no question but that the *Exxon Valdez* grounding impacted, in one fashion or another, far more people than will ever recover anything in these proceedings. There is an understandable public perception that if one suffers harm, which is perceived to be a result of the conduct of another, the harmed person should be compensated. That perception does not always square up with the . . . case law under which the court must operate. . . . Legal liability does not always extend to all of the foreseeable consequences of an accident."

My take on the whole matter was: Bullshit. These companies shouldn't be allowed to transport hazardous substances, if they are not going to be held fully accountable for any mess. People expected a legal system to dispense justice, not just what the law allowed. Besides, it all boiled down to an interpretation of the law: State judge Brian Shortell had reviewed the same law, for the same event, the same spiller, and the same injury claims. Shortell had allowed all the claims to go forward. It seemed to me, and many others in town, that Judge Holland allowed his personal sympathies to bias his interpretation of the law and excuse Exxon from fulfilling its promise to make thousands of people whole. This did not bode well for the federal trial, starting in two months. I had no idea the pretrial was already raging behind the scenes.

On the fifth memorial, my parents joined me in Anchorage for the Alaska Conservation Foundation's annual award ceremony. The conservation community was recognizing Rick Steiner and me for our work on the oil spill. Dan Lawn planned to release a report he and Chuck Hamel had sponsored to document the pipeline owners' voluminous promises made in trade for operating permits.

An hour before the gala event I noticed I had forgotten to pack a nice set of clothes. My yelps of alarm brought my parents running. They took off shopping, while I worked on final edits for my report, "Sound Truth." During my talk, I tried to explain how Exxon had manipulated its spill studies. As I had suspected in Atlanta, Exxon scientists had used a variety of statistical tricks that weakened their study design so they literally could not detect effects from the spill. The trouble was, my report was too technical. Standing before the crowd in stylish, smartly fitting new clothes and shoes, I could see people didn't get it. There was a communication barrier as solid as a wall. I realized that in all my years of academic training, I had never learned how to speak science to nonscientists.

In celebrating afterward with friends and my parents, my father consoled, "You've chosen a tough path. But you understand this stuff. You just need to think more about your audience." I resolved to try again.

For my father and I, the trip was special for reasons not evident to our friends. It was my mother's last trip before Alzheimer's clouded her mind and confined her to the familiar landscape of her Wisconsin home. We were still in Anchorage when Cordova's judo teams swept the state championships in their best tournament ever—without one of their star players or their beloved coach.

Less than one-third of the anticipated herring returned to the Sound. The fish were infected by the same nasty virus as the previous spring. With stocks down to less than what was needed to sustain the wildlife population in the Sound, the state canceled the fisheries. The EVOS Trustee Council, now reflecting the wishes of two Democratic administrations, started up two more ecosystem studies to understand the effects of large-scale upsets, one from oil spills and another from natural cyclic shifts in ocean temperature.

Knowing results from these studies were half a decade away, people turned their attention to more immediate concerns—the Copper River fishery and the *Exxon Valdez* trials. Half of the people in town and the town itself had a direct stake in the litigation.

Phase I: Negligent or Reckless?

The federal trial was divided into four distinct parts. In Phase I, the jury would decide whether Exxon was reckless, or merely negligent, in the acts leading to the spill. A finding of reckless behavior would entitle plaintiffs to punitive damages; the amount would be determined in Phase III of the trial. In Phase II, the jury would determine the amount of compensatory damages to be paid to fishermen for herring and salmon losses, and in Phase IV, a different jury would determine compensatory damages for other fisheries, property owners, aquaculture associations, and other claims not covered in Phase II.

Phase I had ended June 3 and the jury was locked behind closed doors, deliberating the evidence. Linden would be leaving soon for Anchorage. She was one of three fishermen witnesses from the Prince William Sound fisheries, who had been handpicked by our legal team to testify during Phase II about fishermen's losses. She was carrying the hopes and dreams of all Area E fishermen on her shoulders. It was a huge and weighty burden.

"How are you holding up?" I asked Linden. I had dropped by my friend's new "rile estate" office on Main Street, a small building that she had spruced up with wood siding, blue and purple trim, shutters, and flowers in baskets and beds. She looked frazzled. Deep worry lines etched her forehead and her eyes were tired.

"Come on. Let's go sit in the sun." The hexagonal picnic table in the midst of salmonberry bushes and fireweed was my favorite part of her office. I dragged her outside and we plopped down at the table.

"I've been prepping for this trial for weeks," Linden declared. "I've spent hours digging through boxes for paperwork to back up our losses. Bank statements, fish tickets, bills. It's a nightmare. The only fun part has been looking for photos of our family fishing. I found some great pictures of the kids—little chubby Makena kissing a salmon, Malani asleep on the net stack. It brought back such good memories." She brightened at the thought. "Then, I was told we couldn't show those photos in court!"

"What?"

"Nope," said Linden. "Exxon argued that the photos show quality of life, not economic losses, and Judge Holland dismissed quality of life claims. We can't even hint about family fishing because it might 'prejudice the jury.' That's what Oesting said. It might make them more sympathetic so they might award us more money for economic losses."

"What do you mean, 'Exxon argued'?"

"Oh, there's a whole sideshow going on behind the scenes. Exxon and our attorneys argue over what evidence is presented in court—"

"Wait!" I struggled with this concept. "Do you mean it's not all of the evidence?"

"No, not even close," said Linden. "Oesting has been arguing with Exxon attorneys for months about what can be presented in court, since way before our trial even started." I stared at Linden. She explained, "If Exxon concedes a point, then all the evidence for that point doesn't get presented."

"Who makes these decisions?" I demanded to know.

"Judge Holland and a court-appointed Master. Holland decided Captain Hazelwood's conduct violated Exxon's ban against alcohol use, so he excluded all the evidence about Hazelwood's drinking history and alcohol abuse. That's why our attorneys couldn't present evidence that Hazelwood had a DUI conviction or that his driver's license was revoked at the time of the spill! Hazelwood lied under oath when he said he hadn't had a drink since the spill, according to Oesting. Oesting said the flight attendants saw him drinking heavily on a flight Outside a few days after the spill, but our attorneys couldn't talk about it in court."

Linden had been carrying this information a long time. She seemed relieved to dump it on me. Suddenly, things were beginning to make sense.

"So that's why our attorneys never talked about Hazelwood's DUI. I mean, everybody knew about it. It was in the paper."

"Everyone except the jury," Linden reminded me.

"I'll bet that's what happened to Rick Steiner, Ross Mullins, and me," I said. "We were all supposed to testify in Phase I. I'll bet Exxon conceded all those promises it made about making Prince William Sound the safest port in the world, and double-hull tankers, and all that. So we didn't get to talk about it."

Linden's eyes glinted. "I heard that you and Rick were each traded out for two of Exxon's lead witnesses."

I snapped out of my musing and stared at her. "How is a jury ever supposed to make sense of all this if they never get to hear 'the whole truth and nothing but the truth'?" I asked, quoting part of the oath taken in court. "It's like they're looking at a puzzle and they're supposed to say what they see, but the key pieces are missing!"

"I know," said Linden, "but that's what's going on. It seems Brian O'Neill is doing a good job arguing our case even if he does have one arm tied behind his back."

We fell silent, each lost in our own thoughts, basking in the warm glow of our friendship and the sun.

Jury deliberations lasted one week. Normally, the public is not privy to what happens inside a jury room, but in September after the trial was over, six of the jurors agreed to press interviews in spite of Judge Holland's objections. Confused by contradictory testimony from expert witnesses and stacks of boxes of documents, they simply decided that the experts canceled themselves out. They had to rely on their own common sense. They set up two easels and argued the case all over again with one juror acting as attorney for each side, while the others sifted through the boxes for proof for their "lawyers."

In Hazelwood's case, the jurors eventually threw out all the testimony on alcohol and decided that a person did not have to be drunk to be reckless. They made a list of mistakes the captain had made and wound up with three they could not excuse.

1. Hazelwood had violated the Coast Guard's rule that he couldn't drink within four hours of going on duty.
2. Hazelwood had left the bridge during a critical part of the voyage.
3. Hazelwood had assigned an unqualified third mate to the ship's controls.

They all agreed these actions were negligent, but were they reckless?

What cinched the matter was something they found on their own, digging through the boxes. They found the tanker's computerized log and noticed that the load-program-up button had been pushed: The ship was accelerating to sea speed as it struck Bligh Reef. The captain had told the Coast Guard that he was slowing down to "wend his way" through the ice. Everyone makes mistakes, the jurors concluded, but they don't make four in a row. That made Hazelwood reckless.

But was Exxon reckless? Exxon Shipping Company's president Frank Iarossi had called Hazelwood "the most closely scrutinized individual in our company." But the jury could find no evidence of this—not a single document in the boxes in their room. Still, they had discounted Hazelwood's alcohol problems: How could they not discount the company's lack of monitoring for those same problems?

The jurors knew that when the captain had returned from alcohol rehabilitation treatment in 1985, Iarossi could have assigned him to shore duty, but Iarossi had testified that the company felt that might make Exxon liable for discrimination. This testimony convinced the jurors that Iarossi was aware of the risk, but had made a conscious choice to assign the captain to sea duty.

What finally decided them was Jury Instruction Number 33: "The reckless act or omission of a managerial officer or employee of a corporation in the course and scope of the performance of his duties is held in law to be the reckless act or omission of a corporation." There had been testimony that Hazelwood was a managerial employee for Exxon. That made Exxon reckless, too.

Their job in Phase I was over.

When Judge Holland read the verdict before a packed courtroom on Monday, June 13, fishermen, attorneys' spouses, and others leaped to their feet, cheering and applauding. "Knock it off!" snapped the judge, restoring order to his court. Brian O'Neill didn't move when the judge read the verdict, but tears of joy and relief flooded his face. Outside the courtroom, O'Neill told reporters, "We want to change Exxon. We want to make the Exxons of the world aware that they are responsible in the same way that you and I are responsible."

News of the verdict spread immediately to Cordova. "I talked to fifty people by 11:00 A.M.," said Patience Andersen Faulkner. "They are dancing . . . in the streets." Townspeople's confidence in our jury of peers rose. The verdict opened hearts to hope that maybe we would come out of this all right, after all.

Phase II: Compensatory Damages

The Copper River spring fishery was pretty much over and fishermen were waiting anxiously for pink salmon to show up in the Sound when the federal jury reconvened to hear arguments over compensatory damages.

Linden called me from Anchorage. "You should see what's going on over here, Riki! This is like David and Goliath! Exxon rented the three top floors of the Captain Cook Hotel for its trial office. Our trial office has used furniture, folding chairs, and big banquet tables. Oesting says it has some 'damn nice computers' though."

She related how Oesting had taught our trial team to speak Alaskan. He had set up a whole vocabulary of terms, places, names, and locations. He then imposed a stiff penalty system for mispronunciations. It cost $50 if you used "millions," not "billions." (Oesting paid that fine twice himself. Getting people to think in billions was not easy.) "Valdez" rhymes with "sleaze." That was $20. Oesting said those Easterners could not get "salmon" right. They kept pronouncing the "L." SaL-mon. There was thousands of dollars in the penalty pot, but according to Oesting, "Those sons-of-bitches speak Alaskan in the courtroom!" I had always admired Oesting's ability to think of such minute but important details.

"You should see the courthouse!" Linden said, getting serious again. "Exxon serves tea and coffee to reporters, and they use real silver pots and china cups with little silver spoons. It's such a show.

"The trial room looks like a music-recording studio. It's got all this high-tech electronic stuff. The judge and lawyers have their own monitors, and there's a huge television screen near the jury box. Everything is on CDs. God, there must be millions of pages of evidence. Our lawyers pull up what they want with a bar code reader, just like at the grocery store. They use light pens to draw on the screen. I didn't even know those things existed! I feel so intimidated!"

At the time, the federal *Exxon Valdez* case was the largest one tried electronically, a paperless case. It revolutionized courtroom technology. A much more sophisticated version was used later in the O. J. Simpson trial.

It turned out that Linden never testified. None of the Prince William Sound fishers did. Brian O'Neill decided their testimony was not necessary after the Kodiak fishermen witnesses captured the jury's hearts with their stories. Linden felt relieved, Robbie Maxwell felt betrayed, and R. J. Kopchak and the rest of the town were furious. People felt it was important for the world to hear our story. There was no bringing closure to something left untold.

Yet there was plenty else left untold. Before the Phase II trial had started on summer solstice, Judge Holland had excluded more evidence. He ruled out over half of the dramatic photos of the spill and cleanup by *National Geographic* photographer Natalie Fobes. The jury was supposed to focus on facts. Perceptions weren't facts; emotions weren't facts. He ruled out chunks of testimony related to noncommercial species. Judge Holland was not a scientist. He did not understand that salmon and herring were part of a larger ecosystem, an intricate interwoven web of life. Touch any strand and the whole is affected like touching a spiderweb. Take fish out of the context of the whole and one could not understand all the harm to fish. With each exclusion, the jury lost critical information.

The Phase II trial lasted for what seemed like an eternity, but was really only three weeks. Both sides presented legions of expert witnesses who were, for the most part, extremely dry and tedious and ever attentive to minute details that only excited academics. The jurors chewed gum and sucked hard candy to stay awake. All the testimony conflicted. It was Sound Truth versus Corporate Myths, but instead of debunking the legitimacy of Exxon's studies, our lawyers focused on presenting the evidence of harm. Exxon's bought "science" paid off. The jurors were completely confused by the conflicting testimony.

Ross Mullins watched the hearings closely. He was disgusted. He told me, "I used to think scientists had a lot of integrity until I began to see Exxon's scientists presenting studies that were diametrically opposed to those done by the common property users and the government. It just boggled my mind."

What upset Ross even more was the focus on short-term harm. The cause of the fish collapses was not yet fully understood by scientists—and would not be for another five years for salmon or twelve years for herring. Absent scientific evidence, our attorneys had to rely on economic experts to prove damages through declines in fish prices and marketability. Ross worried that any compensatory damages would be inadequate, because they wouldn't cover future harm to the fisheries. His worries would prove valid.

When Phase II mercifully ended, the jurors were locked in the jury room with an enormous stack of document boxes and twenty-six questions to answer. The questions involved eighty-eight calculations specific to five species of salmon, four salmon fisheries, four herring fisheries, and four fishing areas over a seven-year period. Several jurors were overwhelmed and outraged. One asked, "How are just average people supposed to figure out what these PhDs can't even agree on?" Others started digging into the document boxes.

Eventually, they all split up into committees to work on different issues. Fish permit devaluation was easy. Judge Holland had instructed them to only determine the lost value of permits that sold after the spill. Lost harvest value was more difficult. They decided to use the state's Fish and Game harvest reports and calculate the lost values themselves. A couple jurors had experience with accounting, so this became a matter of tedious number crunching. This worked through 1993, but the ADFG reports did not yet exist for 1994 and 1995. The jury instructions said they were to base decisions on a preponderance of evidence. So, they tossed out future losses because of lack of evidence.

Losses due to price declines were the toughest to determine. They weighed the fishermen's evidence of "oil taint" and market effects against Exxon's arguments of a farm-fish glut and worldwide drops in salmon price. Confused, they returned to the trusted ADFG reports, which showed that the salmon returns were very cyclic with years of good returns and poor returns. How could they blame Exxon for that? They felt comfortable with awarding damages for price declines only in 1989.

Jury deliberations spanned five long weeks, longer than the actual trial. Finally, jurors tallied all the damages. It amounted to $287 million, about one-third of what the fishermen wanted and about three times what Exxon had presented as "fair." They were satisfied with their number.

Their job in Phase II was done.

When Judge Holland read the verdict on August 11, the courtroom was very quiet. Fishermen were stunned. Later, outside the courtroom, one fisherman, who had fished Upper Cook Inlet for forty years, fought back tears as he said, "It makes me sick to my stomach. We are talking about thousands of fishermen whose livelihoods are completely different."

People in Cordova had a similar reaction: $287 million would not go far when split among thousands of claims. One fisherman summed up the discontent, "I'm really disappointed by the figures. It doesn't come close to what my losses are. Why have we wasted all this time for $9,000 after attorney's fees and taxes? Exxon got a real good deal on this. It places a large emphasis on having a large punitive damage, in order that some restitution can be accomplished." People's faith in the jury was shaken.

But it wasn't the jury's fault. When presented with only a portion of the truth, the jury had come up with only a portion of the desired compensation. The legal system was not operating in a way that could make injured parties "whole." It was rigged to minimize financial harm to corporations.

The legal system also proved inadequate to compensate subsistence claims. During Phase II of the trial, Exxon had settled with the Alaska Native class of 3,500 people for $20 million for economic damages to subsistence foods. This amounted to just over $15 a day per person for one year. It wasn't even close to compensating people for losses.

Oesting explained these damages were calculated strictly on "a buck a duck" basis, an accounting system that assigned a monetary value for snails, limpets, bidarki (chiton), mussels, fish, birds, and other wildlife consumed as wild foods, based strictly on what such foods would have cost in a grocery store. Yet the acts of harvesting and sharing wild foods forge bonds between Native people and the land, and among the generations, that create a culture. Subsistence-harvested wild food carries a cultural value that far exceeds its "grocery-store" price. Yet this intrinsic value is ignored in a legal system that only tallies physical losses—only part of the whole.

The only hope was that the punitive award would make up some of the real losses incurred by fishermen and Natives. Everyone now set their sights on Phase III: How much punitive damage should Captain Hazelwood and Exxon pay for their reckless behavior?

Phase III: Punitive Damages

The pretrial arguments over evidence lasted longer than the actual trial. Judge Holland excluded evidence of two Exxon oil spills and an Exxon tanker grounding in 1988 through 1990 even though this showed a pattern of negligent conduct like Hazelwood's history of alcohol abuse. The judge excluded evidence that Exxon could pay $1 billion a year for ten years without incurring a "material affect" on its business; he excluded evidence of Exxon's indemnity agreements, showing a punitive award would be partially covered by others; he allowed Exxon to show its "extraordinary effort" on the cleanup. These orders served to bias the jury against a large punitive award.

One large cloud of uncertainty hung over the federal court proceeding: Was the Ninth Circuit going to remand the direct action cases to state court? No one had a crystal ball. With jurisdiction of the direct action cases in legal limbo, Judge Holland decided to proceed with Phase III and try all the cases for punitive damages in his court under a mandatory punitive action class.

Phase III of the trial started on August 25 and lasted only four days. On the second day of the trial, jurors visited three beaches in Prince William Sound at their request. They were given shovels and a set of furiously negotiated jury instructions over what they would hear about each beach. But what affected the jurors the most was what they didn't hear. Most were familiar with Alaska's wild beaches. They expected to see some wildlife, but there were no gulls chattering, no black oystercatchers sounding their shrill warning from the rocks, no general bird busyness. Just quiet. There weren't even any sea otters mewing and whistling in the nearshore water. There was only the sound of their boots and shovels crunching on the cobble beaches. They found oil. That wasn't hard. They could judge for themselves the effectiveness of Exxon's cleanup.

After closing arguments, Judge Holland read the voluminous jury instructions. At Exxon's request and over Oesting's objections, the instructions went well beyond the standards set by the Supreme Court. Among other things, the judge imposed an additional threshold, instructing the jury to award punitive damages only if they found Exxon's behavior to be sufficiently reprehensible as well as reckless. He told them they should consider Exxon's post-spill remedial actions as mitigating factors to atone for its spill. Like his pretrial orders, these instructions also served to bias the jury against a large punitive award.

For the last time, the jury convened behind locked doors. This time, there was basically no guidance other than each individual's own moral compass. Two of the jurors expressed problems with awarding *any* punitive damages, despite saying they could do so during the now-distant jury selection process. The rest of the jurors started by talking about what would be fair for Captain Hazelwood. Eventually all the jurors joined in the discussion.

They settled on $4,989. Alaska was the forty-ninth state and the spill happened in 1989. They threw in another $11 for eleven jurors. (One had been dismissed during Phase II for stress-related health problems.) They agreed upon $5,000.

Punitive damages against Exxon were a whole different matter. Exxon's $5 billion net annual profits and $20 billion asset value stuck in their minds from Brian O'Neill's arguments. Exxon's stock value had increased since the spill. What would it take to punish a corporation that could spend $3.5 billion in fines, penalties, and cleanup with no apparent financial harm?

A paper poll showed opinions ranging from $0 to $20 billion. Emotions ran hot and tempers flared as each argued their number. One breakthrough occurred when a juror with one of the two $0 votes, realized that she was supposed to be speaking for society, as the jury instructions stated, not herself. That left Rita Wilson as the lone holdout for $0 punitive damages. It was slow, stressful, frustrating, tough work. The jurors had become friends during the months of the trial. Now friendships strained as each tried to convince Wilson of the need for punitive damages.

On the fifth day of deliberations, the jurors sent a note to the judge, saying they had reached "an impasse." Judge Holland told them to keep trying. Wilson left early the next day. The jurors sent another note saying, "Rita Wilson is emotionally unable to deliberate." They asked the judge to remove her from the jury. Judge Holland called Wilson into his office and there, with one lawyer from each side as witness, he asked if she would like to be excused. She said no, but within an hour of being back in the jury room cauldron, she sent a note to the judge, asking to be excused. This time the judge said no.

As time crawled by, the numbers on paper polls gradually grew closer together. Those who favored a high award realized that the wildlife deaths and the emotional trauma caused by the spill couldn't count, as stated in their jury instructions. They adjusted down. Those at the low end realized the money Exxon had spent on the cleanup had nicked the company's profits in 1989 but, since then, Exxon's average annual net profits had rebounded. They adjusted up.

Finally, the numbers on the paper poll were all the same: $5 billion. It was

Friday, September 16. The jury had been sequestered for over two weeks. They had no idea that they had just awarded the largest punitive damage award in history. They just knew their job was done.

There was no containing the spontaneous celebration that erupted in Judge Holland's court when he read the verdict. On the courthouse steps, an Exxon attorney leaned over to O'Neill, who was holding his three-year-old son, and whispered, "He'll be in college before you get any of that money." This ruthless attitude reflected the true nature of the same beast that had stood in Cordova's high school gym and promised to make us whole. Within half an hour of the announcement, Exxon's stock shot up by $1.50, signaling Wall Street's relief. Analysts had feared an award of $15 billion.

People in Cordova were ecstatic. The news came on the heels of a $34,000,000 pink salmon season—the hatchery fish had rebounded—and a strong silver season. The town felt optimistic. Mayor Margy said, "It is my fond hope we can use this to put a closure to a sorry episode of our history and let us get on with the business of being a community again."

But Exxon chairman Lee Raymond quickly dashed any hopes of payment and closure. He vowed to "use every legal means available to overturn this unjust verdict."

Life Goes On

To celebrate the court victory, Linden and I took the kids on one of our favorite fall hikes. The flood tide pushed late run pinks and silvers up Hartney Creek. The Forest Service trail loosely followed the creek, crossing smaller streams and open muskeg meadows as it climbed steadily to the base of the Heney Range. In the forest, the trail was springy underfoot, woven with roots of spruce, hemlock, and a carpet of berry bushes, ferns, and shrubs. The shoulder-high devil's club sported bright red berry clusters and their prickly leaves glowed golden like reflected sunlight, brightening the forest floor. Overhead, families of ravens called to each other. Broods of young had fledged and were learning to master the aerial tricks and adept maneuvers of their parents. The commotion and calls reminded me of a group-driving lesson for teenagers. The cries and splashes of gulls feeding on salmon drifted up from the creek.

The kids and dog ran just ahead of us, picking late blueberries like the bears that had left purple-stained piles of poop along the trail. "I thought bears would eat more fish now," Linden remarked, skirting one large pile.

"They must snack on berries as they walk down to the stream," I noted. The evidence was hard to miss.

"I'm just glad there's so much for them to eat so they leave us alone!"

"Well, that's our operating theory anyway," I said. "Let's stick with it, otherwise we'd miss some nice hikes. Plus, we're making quite a racket—or at least your kids are! Oh, jeez, they found a salmon on the trail. Someone dropped their dinner."

Linden shouted, "Makena! Malani! Don't let Cassie eat that! Or roll in it!" The pack ran on down the trail. We stepped over the salmon, noting to our relief that it had been there awhile. "It makes me nervous when they're still floppin' fresh," Linden said.

We stepped down the log staircase that half-spiraled around a large hemlock as the trail dropped over a small cliff. We paused on the small viewing platform, watching the feeding frenzy in the creek. "Hey, I heard you guys sold your permit!"

"We found a buyer at $47,000," she said with a heavy sigh.

"$47,000?! So you owe like a quarter million in debt?" I asked, horrified.

"We were lucky to even find a buyer."

"Some luck," I said, as we continued on. "How's the 'rile' estate going?"

"I've sold some houses. And I have listings. Sam's going to get a real estate license too."

"Sam? I can't see him selling real estate." I struggled with the mental image of her gentle, easygoing husband in a pushy, aggressive job. "I guess he is a people person. . . ."

"Fishermen who can't find other jobs to support their fishing business are moving," Linden said. "Banks aren't loaning money to fishermen. The state is, but the state is taking fishing permits as security! And it's taking paid-off boats and homes to secure devalued permits.

"This is a financial train wreck," she declared. "We need healthy fisheries. What's the story on herring?"

"Salmon are easier to study than herring," I said. "The SEA Program has focused on pink salmon, so far, to get some kinks ironed out of the studies. They start work on herring next year. But the answers are still years away—in all the ecosystem studies," I reminded her.

"The city can't wait years," she said decisively. "The city's settlement with Exxon isn't going to go far and neither will the city's ideas for economic growth. The city just keeps getting crossways with people."

"You mean like having Princess Tours and Chugach Alaska Corporation pay for the city's economic development director?" I asked. "That was quite a move. Fishermen definitely don't want our harbor turned into a theme park. Did you see in the paper where Dennis McGuire protested bringing 'busloads, trainloads, and boatloads of gawking, picture-snapping humanity to a working harbor to buy T-shirts'?"

We laughed at the jarring image as we walked from the trail onto the long split tree-trunk bridge spanning Hartney Creek. The children and dog were already racing back and forth along the gravel shore, following groups of salmon on their final journey upriver. We sat down midway across the bridge, took off our packs, and dangled our legs over the clear shallow stream.

We watched the migrating fish. Some powered through riffles, tails flapping furiously. Some rested, noses pointed upstream in eddies formed by fallen logs. Others courted or fought, pursuing each other across the river bottom. For a while we simply gazed, absorbed by the river of life moving steadily upstream, the pungent odor of moldering carcasses on the gravel bar, and the sounds of splashing and barking.

Finally, Linden said, "People seem to like the idea of ecotourism. We need to do something. Our economy is in a nosedive."

"Ecotourism is compatible with commercial fishing," I said. "It's not like oil and gas development or clear-cut logging or coal mining or mega-cruise ships," I pointed out as much to myself as to Linden.

"So what can we do to support that?" asked Linden.

"It would be nice to work for something instead of just against things all the time," I sighed, thinking about the political battles to block pending oil and gas lease sale proposals and the deepwater port and road. A yearlong moratorium had temporarily stayed the clear-cut logging.

"You started the Alaska Forum! The paper called you guys, 'the Doberman of watchdog groups.' That's for something—it's for preventing an oil spill on the pipeline! I'm for that!" Linden said.

I smiled in appreciation at my friend. "Well, citizen oversight is working in the Sound. It's making sure those spill response plans actually work. That *Eastern Lion* oil spill at the terminal this spring—people were all over it with boats, skimmers, and booms within a day. The RCAC made Alyeska put in vapor recovery controls at the terminal. And they're monitoring ballast water at the terminal—no more Ballast Watergate."

"That's all great news," exclaimed Linden.

"Yeah, but it's like day and night with the tankers and the pipeline. The same companies operate both, but they just keep jerking us around on the pipeline. Alyeska even did its own audit and found things were way worse than the feds claimed!" Linden stared at me. "So now Alyeska is treating the problems like this public relations thing and making promises to 'address' all the thousands of audit items by the end of next year—"

"Can they?" asked Linden.

"No way! It took twenty years to get in this mess. It's not going to get undone in two. There's a stream of whistleblowers coming out of Alyeska, reporting 'paper fixes' instead of real fixes. Billie Garde is writing a nice fat letter to Congress and Stan Stephens about this." Her letter documented complaints of ten Alyeska whistleblowers and the status of five ongoing federal or congressional investigations.

Stan was president of both the Alaska Forum and the RCAC. He felt the Oil Pollution Act should have authorized citizens' oversight of the entire pipeline, not just the terminal and tankers.

"I hope Congress listens," said Linden.

She pulled cookies and apples from her pack. "Malani! Makena!" She waved the package of cookies in the air. The kids shouted and came running as I pulled dog biscuits from my pack. Linden laughed. "You spoil her!"

"Not any more than you spoil me!"

The running feet set the log bridge to bouncing like a trampoline. We grabbed the rolling apples and water bottles as the kids and dog came charging down the bridge.

Thirty days after the jury verdict was announced, Exxon and Hazelwood filed twelve voluminous posttrial motions asking Judge Holland to retry the case, reduce the compensatory award, or throw out the punitive award. One legal brief alone was more than 150 pages long. These motions were just the tip of a legal iceberg that would stall case closure for over fourteen years.

Exxon's legal action devastated people who had hoped for a quick closure. People found it difficult to move on when large chunks of our lives had been put on "pause" by Exxon's actions. Although I kept myself busy, I felt something was missing from my life. The idea of working for something was inviting and intriguing.

Earlier in the summer, while the federal jury had deliberated lost dollars, I had rafted the Copper River with family and friends. The wild river stitched together wide-open space with rainforest, canyons, and snowfed streams. We had stopped to snack or camp on gravel bars festooned with dwarf river beauty and tracked by claws and cloven hoofs. We foraged for wild foods and stayed up long into bright nights, lit by the glow of campfires, lively folk music, and camaraderie. Like the big river, our thoughts had flowed big and broad. How could we diversify the region's economy without spoiling this living landscape? The pressure to open up the region to large-scale extraction industries was relentless. The series of town meetings had pointed in good directions and, I felt, to a need to continue the public process to guide the city's choices on specific projects. We needed to pick stepping-stones to our future.

This was heavy on my mind when I left town in the midst of the fall economic maelstrom to visit my parents in Wisconsin. While there, I met my father's friend, Greg Septon, a board member of the Dutch-based Artists for Nature Foundation. He explained that the artists chose little-known areas of the world where globally significant resources, such as migratory corridors or wetlands, were threatened by development. The group brought their top-notch international artists to the target area for two weeks. Then, with the artwork and a book on the project, the group arranged for a tour to advocate nature conservation as an essential element of sustainable development. Greg said the group was considering the Arctic National Wildlife Refuge as its first target in North America. He asked what I thought.

My answer surprised Greg as much as me. "Nah. But the Copper River Delta would make a great site!"

By the time I left Wisconsin, Greg and I had hatched a plan to bring artists to the Delta the very next year. It would be part of a bigger, community-driven effort to find practical solutions for achieving a sustainable economy and maintaining a healthy ecosystem. This was exactly the vision expressed during the town meetings. I would work through the Alaska Clean Water Alliance. ACWA executive director Gershon Cohen had a seat on the President's Council on Sustainable Development. He was itching to try a sustainable development project in Alaska. The Alaska Forum had hired a consultant to research and write up a report summarizing the whistleblowers' concerns and congressional findings. For the time being, I would devote my energy to creating a project for something—in Cordova.

CHAPTER TEN

STEPPING-STONES

For some, the next four years spun into a blur of activities to rebuild our community. It wasn't as simple as pounding hammer to nails, and the progress was harder to see than new homes replacing the old. Instead of carpenters, we were more like netmenders, mending the torn web of our civil society by stitching lives back together into relationships. It was slow work. Events transpired to rip anew the social fabric even as we repaired it, yet those who first pulled themselves out from the spill wreckage reached to help others and, slowly, our town began to heal. We were an unlikely looking bunch of healers—just ordinary people who carried heavy burdens of financial debt and emotional pain. Among our ranks was the first generation of children who grew up in the long dark shadow of the spill.

Defense and Offense

The new year had barely begun when I set about trying to raise funds to bring a team of international artists to the Copper River Delta. I raised nothing except people's curiosity about the work of Artists for Nature Foundation. The town was broke. Still hoping I could raise the needed $50,000 once fishing started, I invited a foundation scoping team to visit in early May. After their visit, I switched to defense.

The oil and gas lease sale was still pending on the Copper River Delta. Almost everyone opposed it. Yet the state had twice determined that it was in the state's best interest to proceed with the lease sale although, the state officials admitted, future oil development in this area "would have localized impacts that might be significant." The people and town itself could not afford any more "localized impacts" from oil spills—and we said so in some 253 pages of comments, asking the state to withdraw the sale.

While the state considered what to do about the lease sale, the Alaska Department of Fish and Game closed the spring herring fishery. Another disease outbreak of unknown origin had further decimated the population. Townspeople grieved the loss. "I'm depressed we're not going to have a fishery," ten-year fishery veteran Thea Thomas said. "Each spring I look forward to getting together with a group of people I have a partnership with, and going out on the Sound. It makes me sad that we're not going to do that [again] this year." The owner of Orca Oil figured the herring fishery provided about 10 percent of his yearly business. Hotels and bars sat empty.

In March, the logging moratorium expired. Last-minute efforts to extend the moratorium to key parcels failed, and two sections of critical habitat in Orca Narrows were traded out of a previous deal for protection "in perpetuity." Rick Steiner said, "The whole idea was to protect large, intact ecosystems. This is like cutting a hole in the Mona Lisa." Negotiations for protection doggedly continued under intense pressure from out-of-town logging companies to work. Meanwhile, the debate over the deepwater port and access road, each critical components of the logging plan, sharply divided the town and the Native community. When a Native corporation gave land to the city for the access road right-of-way, some shareholders sued.

Under this cloud of gloom and fighting, townspeople turned to face what Mayor Margy called "a financial siege." With the city treasury nearly empty, municipal buildings "held together with glue and baling wire," the fisheries in decline, and the community opposed to or split right down the middle on nearly every issue, someone asked the mayor how she could sleep at night. She replied, "I sleep like a newborn babe. Every two hours I wake up and cry." Ultimately, the city's budget and services were reduced, and sales and property taxes were raised, although no one knew where the money would come from to pay the taxes.

In the midst of the contentious budget process, the commissioner of Alaska's Department of Natural Resources visited to meet with town leaders over the oil lease sale. He was met by protestors who presented him with a petition signed by half of the adult population in town. Quietly, the commissioner told me, "Whatever decision I have to make, it will be harder when I have to put Cordova's faces, asking me to withdraw the sale, in the front of my mind." But the state was determined to press ahead. When the state tried to limit the city's authority to influence decisions on development activities in our fishing grounds, the city and fishermen sued.

When fishing season opened to a strong return of reds and kings, I pounded on doors of just about every business in town, pitching soft (eco-) tourism and showing an art book from a past Artists for Nature project. I explained, "We could have a book like this on Cordova!" People, businesses, and the U.S. Forest Service pitched in with cash and pledges of lodging, fish, groceries, boat and plane charters, and more. I borrowed $10,000 to reach the goal and in early July, the artists arrived from England, Scotland, Russia, Spain, South Africa, the Netherlands, New Zealand, and the Lower 48.

Their two-week visit was pure magic. The town wrapped its arms around the artists and the artists responded in kind. Sylvia Lange and her family hosted the troupe at the old Morpac Cannery, its net loft hastily converted into an "Art Loft." Countless locals volunteered countless hours to take artists out by car, plane, boat, bicycle, kayak, or foot. The artists quickly adapted to the rhythm of place, venturing far afield on sunny days and sculpting, painting, or carving in the art loft during drizzle or downpour. Some artists frequented canneries, loading docks, net-mending haunts, and homes and camps where Native people sewed skins, prepared traditional foods, and celebrated their culture. I helped orchestrate the details. I felt like a camp director.

Seventy-seven-year-old Dutchman Piet Klasse commented appreciatively to me, "This is the best organized event since D-Day!"

"He should know," quipped Seattle sculptor Tony Angell. "He was there!"

The day before they left town, the artists invited the town to an art show. Over 400 people came, fresh out of canneries, fishing boats, church, home, or hikes. Watercolors hung from clothesline or were tacked to cardboard boxes. Woodcuts and wood engravings lay on tables where artists demonstrated their skills. Clay sculptures captured images to set in stone. The artists' message hung in the air like the scent of flowers in spring: If the Delta and fisheries were not protected, "It'll be gone tomorrow," as New Zealand artist David Barker intoned. Awed and thrilled, townspeople wanted to know: What's next? The promise of another artist visit, a documentary video, and an international art tour was a ray of hope for a new industry, one that was compatible with our fisheries.

Some time after the artists left, Linden and I gathered the kids, Cassie and her six wriggly round puppies, and our ready-packed box of jaffle-making supplies, and we headed out "the Road" to our favorite picnic spot at the Sheridan River. The river rearranged its bed each winter, leaving a fresh new layer of smooth cobbles, soft sand, and driftwood. We searched for the perfect spot, not too far from the car this time, because the six-week-old puppies had enough trouble just keeping up with their bouncing mother. We picked a broad swath of sand, littered with wood. After we gathered sticks and root tangles, Linden and I sat to watch Malani, Makena, and Zak play with the puppies.

"Where's Lisa Marie?" I asked.

"Planning her wedding!" she announced happily. "September's coming up."

Unlike many places Outside, September was a popular month for weddings in Cordova. It was after the fishing season was over, but before the summer work crews left town.

"Tell me about the artists' visit!" she said. "You must have a million stories. They were such a fun group!"

"Oh, I could fill a book! They gave me so many panics about bears," I recounted, "So one of the Russian artists, Victor Bahktin, is out on Montague Island. He sees this lovely scene with harbor seals sunning on rocks in the surf. He sets up his easel and paints for five hours. When he packs up to leave and turns around, he sees huge brown bear tracks right behind him! He sees where the bear came out of the woods, wandered down the beach, saw him, wandered over, sat down to watch him paint, got bored, and wandered off."

"He's so lucky!" Linden gasped when she stopped laughing.

"Victor didn't think so. He never saw the bear! But that got the artists to thinking about bears as something other than models. So the Canadian couple, Pat and Rosemarie Keough, is out photographing artists in the field. They find the stream where the other Russian artist, Vadim Gorbativ, is supposed to be. They see his pack and art supplies, but no Vadim. They think immediately: Bear! So they start to shout—and Vadim nearly fell out of the tree he had climbed to do a close-up study on lichen."

Linden guffawed. "They had some really nice pieces on flowers and plants."

"That's because I finally had to say, 'No more eagles!' Every night I reviewed their work. The first few days it was heavy on eagles. So I asked for plants and some diversity!"

"You told them what to do?" Linden asked.

"Well, general categories. We wanted them to cover as much as possible. That was the whole point of the scoping team in May to select a team of artists who could portray landscapes, wildlife, people, and plants. Plus get a blend of different mediums," I explained. A different group of artists would be coming back in two years to cover the bird migration. And the following year I was planning to host workshops on sustainable development to give people ideas for what might be possible other than clear-cut logging, huge cruise ships, or oil drilling.

Squeals and sharp barks distracted us. The kids had set the puppies up in the roots of an overturned tree. Cassie stood on the tree trunk and barked as the puppies disentangled themselves and crawled to her. The kids ran along the slippery bare trunk and spotted, but some puppies tumbled into the soft sand.

"Have you found homes for them all?" I asked.

"All except the black-and-white male, the one the kids call Buckshot. You want him?"

"No thank you. I have an Only Cat. Hey, how was Malani's music camp?"

"Belle Mickelson is a saint," Linden declared.

Our friend had organized a 4-H Music Camp for kids. Belle loves bluegrass music and wanted to share it with her son, Mike, who is a year older than Malani, and other kids in town. She had wanted to start up the camp years earlier, but the oil spill had consumed her considerable energies. One of her achievements was an oil spill curriculum for grade and high school children.

"Malani loved it. And she's really good with the fiddle. We're going to start the O'Toole Family Band," Linden announced with a flair.

"Hooray!" I shouted. "Great idea!"

"I'm doing it for two reasons," Linden said suddenly serious. "Sam and I have been arguing a lot. He just hasn't been himself since the spill—after we lost the boat and permit. I think he's depressed, but he won't see anybody about it." She paused. "I'm hoping the band pulls our family back together."

"That goddamn spill!" I muttered. "It's split apart so many families!"

"I know," said Linden. "We're trying not to be one of them."

We watched the kids and puppies. Suddenly, Linden was laughing again.

"I'm going to miss those puppies! We're only going to have this one litter. It was too hard on Cassie. We had to lock her in the closet with the puppies when Makena went squirrel hunting. She wanted to go with him so badly. Let's fix some jaffles before the puppies come over here and get sand in everything!"

The People's Will

In fall, Mayor Margy remarked, "If I were to state the greatest achievement in the last two years, I would choose the change in attitude in Cordova." It was unmistakable: People had started to work together again, at least on some issues. Results were tangible.

Hundreds of people in the community reached consensus on a fair distribution of damage awards stemming from the *Exxon Valdez* case. This was no small matter. In spring, the lawyers had drafted a very rough Damage Matrix with allocations for each class, area, and type such as specific fishery or landowner. Every single plaintiff had to agree on his or her individual claim. The task was enormous—and stressful. Ross Mullins was one of hundreds who participated in dozens of fishermen's class meetings throughout the year.

Ross described the initial meetings as "explosive." He said, "Every fisherman likes to think he's the greatest and can do better than anyone else. It was hard to get rid of that testosterone factor."

Even the area allocation, rough-cut by lawyers, raised red flags. Ross said, "Everyone perceived that the basic division of the pie wasn't really fair to Prince William Sound fishermen. We were the only area with all the ongoing problems." Even though the spill science had not yet confirmed the link between lingering harm and the spill, thousands of fishermen throughout the oiled region believed the Sound's ongoing problems stemmed from the spill. Ross said, "We were able to negotiate an additional share, 'The Prince William Sound 89 Fund,' in the interest of overall fairness."

By late fall, the Damage Matrix was largely complete. Common sense and an innate sense of fairness had prevailed. Numbers were crunched, individuals assigned their share, and plaintiffs were in agreement. Ross explained, "Every individual had a number by their names just like a telephone directory. The number shows, for every dollar that comes through the door in the end, what their percentage of that dollar is." The Damage Matrix became, according to Ross, "the great equalizer."

In mid-December, after another round of craft fairs and before the Christmas frenzy, Linden called me for dinner with Lisa Marie. I had missed her "Girls' Gourmet" birthday party, an extravagant affair of six courses, all cooked by Lisa Marie and friends. They were chopping vegetables around the table when I arrived. The dogs bounced over, barking excitedly.

"You still have Bubby?" I asked. "It looks like his leg is healed." Bubby had spent most of the summer in a splint after breaking a leg in a run-in with a car. "Where are the kids?"

"Malani's at a music lesson. Makena and Zak are at judo practice." Linden passed me a knife and cutting board. "We've decided to keep Bubby. He's turned into the family clown. He makes us laugh and he's good company for Cassie."

I smiled. "What are we making? Something smells good."

"Rosemary olive bread," said Lisa Marie. "And some deer stew to go with it—way different from the menu last week! Hey, we have a question for you.

Can you explain the SEA Program to nonscientists? The whole town is excited about it."

I thought about the Sound Ecosystem Assessment Program as I looked at my two artist friends and the pile of vegetables. "The sea is like a big soup but instead of carrots, potatoes, and onions floating around, it's little plants and animals called plankton. Fish like cod, walleye pollock, and halibut eat copepods. . . ." I grabbed a carrot. "They come in sizes." I chopped the carrot into big and small bits. "The predators prefer the large copepods because they're easier to catch and they don't have to eat as many to fill up." I popped a large carrot bit into my mouth and chomped away. "If there are only small copepods, predators switch to eating young salmon and herring—more calories for the effort to catch them."

Lisa Marie stared at me, her knife frozen mid-chop. "That's why people are excited?"

"Well, eventually this information will improve the models used to predict fish returns so we'll have better management, more accurate predictions, and hopefully more fish," I explained.

"Ahhhh," said Lisa Marie as she continued chopping potatoes.

"What determines whether there are large or small copepods?" asked Linden.

"The temperature of the soup," I said. "Oceanographic conditions. That's what the scientists are looking at next. That and herring—they're still a mystery."

"I think people are excited because they're working together on something positive," said Linden, as she grabbed a big bowl for the chopped vegetables.

"There's something to that," said Lisa Marie.

She dumped a plate of deer chunks into a cast-iron skillet. The meat sizzled in the hot oil, adding a touch of game to the bread smell. As she browned the meat, she explained, "Steve Picou is starting a study next year with the RCAC people. They're looking at different ways to reduce stress and speed up trauma recovery after a disaster. One of the things he's interested in is whether working together helps heal."

She shook her head. The litigation keeps stirring things up. It's always something, it seems. Now it's the Rita Wilson thing."

Linden and I both groaned. "Rita Wilson!" we chorused.

In late January, Judge Holland had denied every single one of Exxon's posttrial motions. Fishermen were heartened by the sea change in the judge's attitude toward Exxon. The judge defended the jury's decisions, writing, "The court respects the 'collective wisdom of the jury' and accepts its findings." People had

1. In fishing tradition, Danny and I celebrate our first big season in 1988, the year before the spill. 2. Danny minds the net during his turn as skipper. 3. Father and daughter share a story at a family reunion (Pt. Reyes, CA, 2006). 4. "It's like fishing in Switzerland!"–Fred Ott. (*Ambergris* in Prince William Sound, 1988.)

Growing up in Cordova, the O'Toole family–Sam, Linden, Makena, and Malani–share adventures with Riki. The spill cost priceless quality family time. The photos of the kids on the family seiner, *Blue Note*, were banned in court because they showed non-economic losses.

1. The "Dancing Lady and the Bear" on Mt. Eccles grace Cordova and its working harbor. 2. *Ambergris* makes a delivery of red salmon to a tender. 3. Jumpers (leaping pink salmon) promise a good catch as a seiner purses its net. 4. Gillnetting herring before stocks collapsed and fisheries closed indefinitely after the spill.

The *Exxon Valdez* hit Bligh Reef in Prince William Sound, spilling 11 to 38 million gallons of crude oil in America's deadliest spill. The killing did not stop in 1989. Wildlife has not fully recovered and many cleanup workers still suffer lingering harm from oil exposure.

Rick Steiner (left) and exhausted workers (below left) display the futility of cleanup. Over 3,200 miles of beaches were oiled, according to federal scientists.

DAVID JANKA

ROBERT CORNELLIER

DAVID JANKA

ROBERT CORNELLIER

BRIAN O'DONOUGHUE

1. The stain remains: Ross Mullins, Zak Jacobs, and Riki find buried *Exxon Valdez* oil on northern Knight Island in 2007, Smith Island in 2006 (inset), and 2. Knight Island in 2003. 3. Patience Andersen Faulkner drums for community healing, 2007. 4. Fishermen protest "cleanup" ending in 1989. *Facing page:* 1. Fishermen blockade Valdez Narrows in August 1993. 2. Ross Mullins watches as coffin representing over 6,000 deceased plaintiffs and lost hopes and dreams sinks during blockade reenactment in 2006. 3. Mike Webber and Shame Pole, 2007. 4. Citizen-driven improvements: tractor tugs with ability to push/pull 360 degrees and disabled tanker towing. 5. Cleanup workers received adequate training and protective gear one year too late, after 6,722 respiratory illnesses were reported in 1989.

1. Chuck Hamel, 2007. 2. Dan Lawn and Trans-Alaska Pipeline, 2007. 3. Lisa Marie and Zak Jacobs, 2008. 4. Brian O'Neill (holding son) speaks with media after jury finds Exxon reckless, 1994. 5. Stan Stephens, 2006. 6. Riki, Zak, and pre-law students wait on the sidewalk outside the Supreme Court the night before final arguments.

hoped this meant the case would be over quickly. But when the judge stood firm, Exxon had turned from attacking the jury decisions to attacking the jurors themselves, in particular, Rita Wilson, who had become emotionally unhinged by the whole experience and had tried to commit suicide.

In June, Judge Holland had granted Exxon an evidentiary hearing in response to its charges of juror misconduct. He had decided there was no reason for a new trial. But Exxon persisted. In September, Exxon resurrected issues the judge had dismissed, and Exxon demanded a new trial based on jury coercion and intimidation. This time, Exxon argued that one of the court security officers, Don Warrick, had tried to influence the trial by offering a bullet from his gun to a juror to try to intimidate Rita Wilson when the jury was deadlocked over the amount of punitive damages. Judge Holland would eventually rule there were no grounds for a new trial and call "Exxon's melodrama . . . an extraordinary and exaggerated account of the events." However, two years later, Exxon would resurrect these same issues again.

I said, "Rita Wilson, the bullet thing, Exxon's appeals—Dave Oesting says it's all part of Exxon's strategy not to pay us. Exxon can afford to have its lawyers run us in circles. It's paying off. Oesting says Exxon is saving $684,000 in interest every day just by stalling entry of the $5 billion jury award as 'final judgment.'"

Linden sighed. "So that's why the fishermen in other fisheries settled for next to nothing? Just so we could all start collecting the interest?"

The Phase IV trial, slated to be tried with a different jury, involved claims for fisheries other than salmon and herring such as crab, shrimp, oysters, halibut, black cod, and pollock, as well as claims from aquaculture associations and landowners whose property was directly oiled. The Phase IV cases had claimed over $50 million in losses, but had settled for $3.5 million in trade for a fair stake in the punitive award.

"Yep, and that's what all the hustle is about to finish the Damage Matrix and figure out offsets. The way Exxon figured offsets, some fishermen owe Exxon money! This all has to be figured out before we can collect interest." Linden just shook her head.

Dave Oesting had waged a furious battle with Exxon over offsets. Offsets were primarily payments already made to people through the Exxon Claims Program for fishermen, the Alyeska settlement, and the TAPL Fund, and were to be deducted from any damage payment. Exxon, however, claimed it was entitled to other adjustments, which would negate the jury award of $287 million for compensatory damages and leave plaintiffs owing Exxon money.

Judge Holland accused Exxon of "superficial logic" and called its arguments a "massive assault on the jury determinations." He rejected most of Exxon's arguments, concluding, "It is specious of Exxon to argue that it conferred a benefit on commercial fishermen by spilling oil."

However, Exxon had managed to get more claims dismissed. Judge Holland refused to allow 130 fishermen who had signed damage waiver forms with Exxon in 1989 to share in the jury award. Fishermen who had signed these forms had not had lawyers at the time and were unaware that they were giving up claims against Exxon. They had believed Exxon's promise to make people whole. Further, when the Ninth Circuit Court of Appeals finally decided on jurisdiction of the direct action cases and ordered Judge Holland to remand the cases to state court, Exxon had resurrected the old *Airport Depot Diner* case to argue the claims should stay in Holland's court. The judge agreed. Then he had dismissed most of the claims under *Robins Dry Dock* as he had done in his earlier rulings!

"Well, I can tell you that these legal shenanigans are causing a lot of stress among the people who were 'offset,'" Lisa Marie observed. She had added vegetables, spices, and stock to the browned meat, while quietly listening to our conversation. She joined us at the table.

"Let's talk about something happy," said Linden.

"Christmas!" said Lisa Marie. "We're having a cookie-making party at my house this weekend and we need lots of little kids to make a really big mess!"

"How about a big kid who's really good at making a big mess?" I asked, referring to myself.

Mirrors of Our Soul

The headline story of the very first *Cordova Times* of the New Year announced, "Community Education Program Set for 1996." And there it was, right in black-and-white—SPILL TRAUMA—not to be ignored or denied, but to be dealt with. It was like a giant sticky spider web that had ensnared us all.

The program was designed to recognize social ills caused by the spill, break old patterns, and find ways to cope or heal at the individual level. Some elements of the program were based on trauma mitigation research from other human-made disasters such as Three-Mile Island, Love Canal, and Times Beach. Other elements were new like the "Peer Listening Training" and using the Native Talking Circle to heal spill trauma.

I did not join the public workshops at the end of January. I convinced myself instead that my grant-writing and general political busyness was a good outlet for my spill trauma. It wasn't, but I played out the pretense for another three years until finally the dark shadows grew too big to ignore, like towering black thunderclouds before a storm.

For those who went, the Talking Circle opened a deep well of grief and loss. In keeping with Native tradition, it released emotional pain through drumming, dance, ceremony, and circle upon circle of compassionate talking, listening, and healing. Facilitators and counselors worked with separate circles of men and women in recognition of their different needs. One ceremony, held on the shore of Orca Inlet, honored and released spirits of animals trapped by sudden death. Throughout the two-day workshop, the Northern Lights Native Dancers swirled and stomped, releasing stuck energy and lifting hearts, minds, and spirits of participants.

The Peer Listening Training, following the workshops, began to prepare volunteers to help community members cope with mental health effects from the spill. Steve Picou anticipated a need for trained peers during his summer educational series on technological disasters and mental health. Picou and his colleague Duane Gill taught deep communication and listening skills, and support skills for dealing with grief and loss transmuted into anger, depression, substance abuse, and other issues. After the full training series, Peer Listeners were ready, like volunteer firemen, to help people in crisis over spill trauma. The trick was: people had to know enough to ask for help and many, like myself, just buried the grief like land mines and kept on going.

In the midst of heavy coverage of spill trauma by the local news, the state canceled the spring herring fishery for lack of fish. The Department of Fish and Game warned that the future did not look good for the 1997 herring season either. Shortly after this, fireworks erupted in the *Exxon Valdez* case.

Greed—Plain and Simple

In February, Dave Oesting submitted the "Plan of Allocation" or Damage Matrix to Judge Holland for preliminary approval. He did so with great anticipation that it would flush out a nefarious plot by seven Seattle processors. In a desperate attempt to hide what they had done, the seven processors sued Oesting and lawyers representing the other processors. The lawsuits wound up in Judge Holland's lap. Judge Holland realized something was up. He consolidated the lawsuits with the allocation proceeding.

On March 18, the seven processors came to court and claimed nearly 15 percent, or $745 million, of the punitive award. The paper trail revealed that Exxon had paid the "Seattle Seven" a total of $76 million to settle damage claims in exchange for the processors' share of the punitive damage award. The processors also had agreed to be Exxon's front to assist it in recovering punitive damages with Exxon footing the processors' bill for attorney fees and expenses.

When the full extent of the secret deal was revealed, Judge Holland angrily declared the action bordered on outright illegal conduct, or "fraud on the court," as Oesting gleefully put it. The judge expressed shock and outrage, saying "Exxon has acted as a Jekyll and Hyde, behaving laudably in public and deplorably in private." Judge Holland concluded, "Public policy will not allow Exxon to use a secret deal to undercut the jury system, the court's numerous orders upholding the punitive verdict, and society's goal in punishing Exxon's recklessness. . . . The court will not countenance Exxon's astonishing ruse and allow it to manipulate the jury and negate its verdict." He tossed the Seattle Seven out of his court. Exxon appealed the court's decision through the seafood processors.

Judge Holland then turned to resolve the only other complex objection to the Damage Matrix from the "Fortier Group" after their attorney Sam Fortier. Oesting had been waging war with six Native corporations ever since they had opted not to be part of the allocation plan. Instead, the six corporations had decided to take their chances in state court, where they hoped to receive a high compensatory award, and then demand a higher share of the punitive award than their peers would have allocated. Oesting described this as "greed, plain and simple."

During the Damage Matrix discussions, Oesting had reserved 3 percent off the top as a placeholder for the six Native corporations because he knew, someday, they would have a share of the punitive damages. Sure enough, the six corporations bombed in state court. After the jury verdict, Oesting managed to get three of the six corporations to agree to an allocation of 2.46 percent off the top of the punitive award. The other three corporations—the Fortier Group—held out for a much higher percentage.

Judge Holland found Oesting had acted in the "best interests of the class as a whole" by *not* allowing one group to "thwart a result that might be in the best interests of the class." Further, he found the Fortier Group was "benefiting from the 'peace' that the [other] plaintiffs have bought" by including all injured persons in the punitive damage award, not just those with viable legal claims. The judge concluded, "Public policy favors equitable allocations. . . ." He ruled that Oesting's allocation of punitive damages to the Fortier Group was "fair, adequate, and reasonable. . . ."

Judge Holland approved the Plan of Allocation and the Phase IV settlement on the same day. Oesting was ecstatic. He immediately filed a motion requesting final judgment on the jury verdict for punitive damages. Exxon managed to stall several more months with legal bickering.

Dreaming the Future

Meanwhile, during the winter while CDFU kept pressure on the state and oil companies to block lease sales on the Copper River Delta and to fulfill paper promises in spill response planning, I focused on logging. Huge patches of denuded hillsides marred Orca Narrows. On Montague Island, steep sections of formerly forested land wept plumes of sediment into fertile fish spawning and rearing streams. Raids on "pumpkins"—choice old-growth Sitka spruce in streamside buffers—left the thin margin of trees protecting stream habitat vulnerable to wind damage. Eyak Corporation had even turned down an offer by the EVOS Trustee Council for twice the appraised value for its land. While corporate ads promised stewardship, the state reported harm to fish and wildlife from forestry practices, similar to what had happened in the Pacific Northwest.

For the March oil spill memorial, I planned the first public workshop on sustainable development. Organizing that workshop was an act of pure desperation. I knew nothing about building consensus or how to bring people together to work for, instead of against, something. I had been in the thick of every fray in town and was perceived as being either part of the problem or part of the solution, depending on the person. And as for "sustainable development," there were no community-driven models in Alaska, but there were scattered projects in some small towns in western states. In hopes of replicating these early success stories, I found a small group of funders interested in supporting this effort.

Working through others, I asked six community leaders who had fought bitterly over development issues to sign an invitation to attend the workshop. The invite, published as a half-page ad in the *Cordova Times*, drew sixty curious townspeople to the workshop. Participants grew hopeful as speakers shared their offer to stop fighting and start bridging environmental and economic concerns. Twenty people, including many leaders with diverse interests, volunteered to serve as a steering committee to continue the work of consensus-building, problem-solving, and identifying viable economic options. People left hopeful that the town was "coming together."

I left feeling weighed down by everyone's expectations. The project's success rode on whether steering committee members could work together at the next meeting without a neutral facilitator. This seemed highly unlikely. Then one night I had a dream. In it, Linden and I hiked through an old-growth coastal rainforest. We stopped to watch Natives drum and dance, and we listened to seals barking on the beach. On the return hike, I literally walked into the future and, when I tried to return to the forest and past, I couldn't. It was all gone—the forest, the Natives, and the seals.

The dream haunted my waking thoughts. One day I spilled it, like a glass of water across the table, onto the lap of Aleut Native leader Ilarion Merculieff. "Larry" was the former Commissioner of the Alaska Department of Commerce and Economic Development during the oil spill. He was widely recognized as a gifted facilitator, especially in polarized and cross-cultural situations. He was coming to Cordova to guide the Family Resource Center's weekend conference on healthy living as a proactive approach to healthy families. Larry explained over the telephone that Natives believe in four types of dreams. What I had, he said, "was the most powerful dream—a vision from your inner self to guide your footsteps in the outer world." The dream continued to gnaw at me until I finally wrote it down and submitted it to the local paper. Then it vanished from my thoughts.

Larry greeted me the following week with a question: "What did you do?" The weekly paper was out and he had heard people talking about the dream. I explained how it had kept pestering me until I let it go. He said knowingly, "Then it had more work to do." I could not imagine what he meant.

The dream triggered cascading events. Other Native people also recognized the dream as a vision. Some invited me to an outing on the Delta. Over a driftwood fire, they shared their concerns with the contrived choice of either selling their ancestral lands to "save" the trees or retaining land ownership and being forced to clear-cut. They wanted other options. Rick Steiner's idea of purchasing land easements to save trees have been "simplified" by the federal and state governments to purchasing their land outright, which they calmly explained was cultural genocide. I pledged to find a path we could walk together. That path was through the sustainable community project, which would eventually incorporate as a nonprofit organization with a founding board of four Native leaders.

The dream also opened the floodgates on a six-week torrent of letters in the paper over effects of clear-cut logging on wildlife and fish. The letters washed over the first rocky meeting of the steering committee, filling hearts with commitment to end the fighting. It was our only common ground at first, but it was enough. The letters flowed right up to the May workshop on sustainable forestry, bringing townspeople who wanted to find solutions to divisive logging issues.

After the workshop, the CEO of Eyak Corporation appealed to the steering committee to help him put a better business plan on the table—and the logging on the Delta stopped. It seemed the workshop, with its positive approach and honest economics, might have been the final straw after years of efforts by many people, numerous lawsuits, a collapse in the pulp market, and no market for trees with rotten cores as many of the large old-growth "pumpkins" had.

A year later, three Native corporations would sell major parcels of ancestral lands, totaling nearly 200,000 acres in Prince William Sound, including Orca Inlet, to the EVOS Trustee Council—and the logging in the Sound would stop.

Rocky Road to Healing

"Thank God!" Linden pronounced. I had stopped by her office to visit on a rainy day. "Those workshops turned out a lot better than I expected. Everyone was focused on options and solutions. I'm telling you: the power of healing lies in working together." She chuckled. "Picou's articles might have helped. Did you plan that?"

"No, I did not!" I said. "But talk about good timing to have Picou's articles about working together to heal trauma come out just when everyone was coming unglued over the logging."

Steve Picou's articles on technological disasters and mental health had flowed right along with the logging letters. Contributors, some of the nation's leading disaster trauma experts, explained that floods, fires, earthquakes, and other acts of God affected people differently in the long run than disasters caused by humans such as dam failures, nuclear and chemical accidents, and oil spills or "acts of us" as they would later be called. Sociologists explained that natural disasters brought people together in crisis, while human-made disasters tore communities apart.

Lawsuits, a hallmark feature of "acts of us" where there was someone at fault, stalled recovery because they were daily reminders of the trauma. The sociologists wrote of coping strategies to handle the prolonged stress from litigation and fighting in general. They identified Cordova as a classic "corrosive community," polarized by intense fighting over issues. Picou counseled, "Drawing together to create . . . positive outcomes will help people heal."

Picou's articles flowed through a summer of good salmon returns, brightened first by top prices paid for Copper River reds and kings as West Coast restaurants and grocery stores competed for "First Fish," then marred by low prices for pinks and silvers due to a world market glut from farmed salmon. Townspeople realized times had changed. The flush upbeat 1980s had been good to the fishing town. Then fortunes had shifted. First the spill, then the Japanese market collapse, then the flood of farmed salmon had all crippled Alaska's fishing industry. Cordova's economy was particularly hard-hit with the salmon and herring population collapses. Facing another winter lean on cash and heavy on debt, fishermen bent to the task of creating markets where there had been only demand and townspeople cast about for ways to grow the economy.

As the season wound down, Judge Holland entered final judgment of the jury award in the *Exxon Valdez* case on September 24. Interest began to accumulate on the $5 billion punitive award at a government-fixed rate of 5.9 percent or $295 million per year.

Linden and I set out on "the Road" with the kids and dogs to celebrate. When we reached the Pipeline Loops trailhead, Makena announced he and Malani were going to "hunt" mushrooms. "Just keep up with us!" said Linden to their backs as they shot off up the trail.

"I don't think that will be a problem," I said. We wound through the forest, walking on boards covered with "no-skid" herring seine webbing. We admired the soft sounds of small streams flowing in mossy shallow channels.

"Hey, those banners look great!" I said. "They really spruce up Main Street." As part of a city-sponsored beautification project, Linden had organized a banner project where artists submitted designs and the four top choices were made into banners. The banners hung from the city's new lampposts along with baskets of bright flowers.

"Thanks! We're trying to make the town more attractive to visitors and pretty for us! Have you seen Fleming Spit?" The Cordova Sporting Club had shored up the muddy beach to provide better access for anglers to the small hatchery-enhanced king and silver returns. With the city's help, they had also put in a restroom facility and a fish cleaning station.

"Yep, that certainly ought to bring in more sport fishermen. I'm still hoping to bring in ecotourists."

Linden skipped down the trail with her hands in the air. "A pretty town! More tourists! Beautiful art to advertise our special place! This is what we need to help turn things around."

"Let's hope!" I said. "Did you see the list of delinquent taxpayers this spring? It's like half the town!"

We emerged from the forest into open rolling muskeg meadows laced with ponds large enough for the Forest Service to stock with fish. We detoured to the edge of the first pond to look over the dark waters at the looming peaks dusted with early snow. "These highbush cranberries could use a good frost," I mused of the bushes at the pond's edge as the kids came rushing up.

Makena's sweatshirt pouch bulged with mushrooms. Eagerly he pulled some out to show his mother. "See, these white ones are Angel Wings, and these are Hedgehogs," he said, turning one over so she could see the hedgehog-like prickles underneath the cap.

"Makena, my son, my Only Son," Linden intoned. "Are you sure these are edible?"

"Yes, Mom!" he said, grinning. "I've been reading books." They shot off again.

We resumed our hike in the open meadow that abutted the forested slopes of the Chugach Range. "I'll check on those mushrooms," I offered.

"There's more good news from the Sound, too." I ticked off improvements. "There's a new vessel tracking system that can track tankers out beyond Hinchenbrook Entrance. There are new weather buoys so exact conditions are known all the way to Middleton Island. There's a vapor recovery system on two loading berths—finally. And we're getting new tractor tugs like they use in Scotland and Norway because, it turns out, the conventional tugs can't do diddley-squat to control these big supertankers that the pipeline owners promised would not be used in the Sound in the first place."

"Yes, yes, yes!" said Linden. "What about on the pipeline?"

"No, no, no!" I said. "At least, not anything really meaningful. Richard

Fineberg documented the whole sorry state of affairs for the Alaska Forum. It's in our new report, *Pipeline in Peril.*

"Basically, Alyeska worked to fix the easy problems first, but most of the high-priority problems, the expensive ones to fix, they're still not fixed. Alyeska is still harassing whistleblowers despite lip service to the contrary. It's writing off the legal costs as a business expense. There you have it," I concluded with a flourish, "an aging pipeline and no political will to fix it."

Linden sighed. "Alyeska just ignores you guys, because there's no law that says it has to listen like with the RCAC."

"Yep, pretty much," I agreed. "It's not like the oil companies can't afford to fix their pipeline."

We were hiking up a long open meadow to a narrow bridge. The mountains rose abruptly at the far end, creating a breathtaking vista. "This part always wants to make me sing, 'The hills are alive with the sound of music,'" I said.

Linden took a moment to revel in the scene before switching topics. "Hey, how long do you think before Exxon pays us?"

"Oesting says five years."

"How does Exxon get away with that?" she asked.

"I don't know, but let's not let it ruin a perfect day."

At an informational meeting a month or so later, the regional Native corporation, Chugach Alaska, unveiled its Carbon Mountain Project. This was a grandiose plan for developing 8,000-acres of its 73,000-acre inholding on the eastern side of the Copper River Delta in the heart of prized red and king salmon habitat. Road access and exemptions from environmental assessments were guaranteed under federal law. The corporation planned to harvest timber, mine coal, and provide access to develop oilfields, all tied to the Cordova deep-water port and access road, partially funded by oil spill monies.

With fresh battle lines drawn, townspeople quietly girded for war over different visions of "progress." Most people wanted to diversify the economy in ways that grew a self-reliant community with healthy fisheries and Native cultures. A huge majority had said so in town meetings. Community leaders on the steering committee were working toward this end. With fresh urgency, I redoubled my efforts to fund-raise for the second artists' visit and more public workshops on sustainable development.

CHAPTER ELEVEN

GAINING GROUND

Naked Pursuit of Profits

"What *is* going on?" Linden asked. "Why is Exxon trying to bring the *Exxon Valdez* back into the Sound? Don't they get it? It's like letting a child molester back in the neighborhood! And why are BP and ARCO suddenly being so generous? Computers for the high school, support for the Chamber, tours on the North Slope for city leaders—what do they want?"

It was late January in 1997 and I had slogged over to her office to visit during a slushy snowstorm. Snowplows rumbled in the streets. Intermittently, sheets of wet snow cascaded off the roof, making a loud "*whump!*" when they hit the ground. I brushed sticky snow off my clothing. The dogs settled back down when they realized we were not going for a walk.

"It's all a plot to make me crazy," I joked, plopping into a chair. "You know Exxon renamed that tanker the *SeaRiver Mediterranean.*"

"Paint's cheap. It'll always be the *Exxon Valdez* in Alaska."

"Yeah, well, apparently it's not so cheap to operate a Jones Act vessel in a foreign trade. Exxon wanted a federal subsidy—$2.5 million a year—to operate the *Exxon Valdez* in the Middle East trade. That was to pay for a U.S. crew required under the Jones Act since Exxon couldn't hire cheaper foreign crews."

"Why should taxpayers subsidize Exxon's profits after it trashed our lives and the Sound?"

"Right, Exxon didn't get the subsidy, but it didn't give up either. Last year, it filed two lawsuits. One claims the Oil Pollution Act is unconstitutional, because it singled out the *Exxon Valdez.*"

Linden summarily dismissed that. "The law bans any tanker that spills more than a million gallons from shipping oil in the Sound!" Judge Holland would later agree.

"The other lawsuit is kind of curious though," I said. "Exxon claims the Oil Pollution Act is an 'unconstitutional taking' of property. Oesting says that's a Fifth Amendment right guaranteed to people."

"Then how can Exxon claim it?" asked Linden.

"I don't know. I have to look into it. Usually after I talk with Oesting, I have more questions than answers." I rolled my eyes. "Lawyers!"

"Well, what about BP and ARCO?" asked Linden.

"I think they're doing a full-court press to open the Delta for oil lease sales. It just seems all so transparent to me," I sighed. "BP puts on a good show on the North Slope for our city leaders—little things like drip pans under vehicles and stuff. Meanwhile, a BP contractor is caught illegally dumping hazardous drilling waste back into wellheads, all to save the cost of legally disposing of the stuff." Working through the Alaska Forum, whistleblowers had reported this activity, which eventually led to federal investigations and criminal fines.

"And, of course," I added, "pipeline repairs are w-a-y behind schedule. BP and the other major owners focused on the little stuff first and left the big, expensive fixes for last." I shook my head. "You just can't trust these oil companies. It's all about money all the time." A "whump!" of snow hit the ground as if to emphasize my point.

"Tort reform is back," said Linden.

"I saw that in the paper."

The previous year, the state legislature had passed a tort reform bill over concerted objections from people and communities throughout the oiled region. The oil industry's heavy hand was evident in the bill. It artificially capped jury awards, initially retroactive to the *Exxon Valdez* case. It limited liability for environmental damage to $300,000 or 10,000 times less than the range of damage for the *Exxon Valdez* spill. And it protected wrongdoers with immunity from misconduct.

"Governor Knowles vetoed it last year, but now there is a veto-proof majority," Linden said. "It'll be a slam-dunk this year." She had worked hard to defeat the bill last year.

"What are you going to do?"

She sighed. "Fishermen are working on language to add that says the bill does not affect the *Exxon Valdez* case or 'any other federal admiralty action now or in the future.'"

"Politicians are so shortsighted!" I said disgustedly. "Obviously if a law doesn't work for one set of injured people, who have to get an exemption from it to protect their rights, it's not going to work for others either."

I mulled for a minute while Linden broke out some cookies. "You know, there's something really wrong here. We're going through the same thing with the Coastal Zone Management Program. People and communities around the state support that program, but the legislature is trying to repeal it."

"Is that the law the fishermen are using to make the oil companies plan for spill response on the Delta?" Linden asked.

I nodded. "And the same one the city and fishermen are using to protest the oil lease sale on the Delta."

The law allowed rural communities to have a say in development activities in their backyard. Cordova has one of the earliest coastal plans in Alaska.

"Why would the state legislature repeal that?" asked Linden. "Because it gives the people too much power," she said, answering her own question.

"But that's what's wrong! This is supposed to be government of, for, and by The People!" I said, waving a shortbread biscuit in the air. "The oil companies talk about 'environmentally sound development,' but then they lobby to weaken or repeal laws that hold them to their promises. Then, when something goes wrong, they say they are within the law. Something needs to change."

Linden shook her head. "How do you keep sane?"

"Your family, for one." We smiled at each other as a snowplow rumbled down the street, rattling the windows. "I'm not swimming in debt, for another," I said quietly.

"*Thank God* we were able to sell our seine permit!" said Linden. "I never thought I'd feel that way, but we were lucky to get out when we did. They're only worth $30,000 now and no one is buying!"

Since the Asian economic collapse, farmed salmon, initially from Norway and Chile, had steadily captured a growing share of world markets. Farmed salmon now made up 42 percent of the world's production of 3.3 billion pounds and were shoving more wild Alaska salmon from shelves every year.

"So the real estate . . ." I left the question unfinished, but Linden picked it up.

"Yes, the real estate will bail us out of debt—before Malani goes to college. But I feel sorry for everyone who is stuck with the debt from those pricey permits! Some of the highliners own two seine permits for salmon and herring." She looked horrified at the thought. "I talked with Rhonda Platt . . ."

"John Platt's wife?" I knew John from the Co-op days. He was a local boy, quietly understated, but an aggressive fearless fisherman. He had advanced rapidly, using his gillnet earnings to leverage a salmon seine permit and then his combined fisheries' earnings to leverage a herring seine permit. "He's kind of quiet," I said.

"Rhonda's not!" Linden laughed, then grew serious. "Their debt is tearing that family apart. They've got those three boys. The oldest is Makena's age. . . ." Her voice trailed off.

I realized suddenly that I worked now more with businessmen, policymakers, and government people than fishermen. I was still on the board of United Fishermen of Alaska, but wouldn't be for much longer as the sustainable future work had peaked my interest. Most of the grants I had written to support the sustainable future work had materialized, putting me at the helm of a quarter-million-dollar project.

Finally, I said, "I don't know what to do, other than what I'm doing. I feel like Rome is burning, but instead of helping put out the fire, I'm sketching plans to rebuild it!"

"You need to keep doing that!" said Linden. "People wallowing in debt don't have time to work on rebuilding the community. They're fighting for survival. But we need to think about the future." Indeed, a lot of people were happy the artists were coming back and people liked the idea of tourism.

"Speaking of artists," said Linden, "I bought sound equipment for our family band. Malani has a really nice voice, but no one can hear it because Sam is such a strong singer. Microphones make a huge difference. She's the lead singer for some of the songs she wrote. You should hear her."

"I'd like to. Call me when you practice. Where are the kids, anyway? School's out."

"Malani's got a music lesson and Makena is in Anchorage with Zak and Lisa Marie at a judo tournament." Her eyes sparkled mischievously. "When I talked with Makena this morning, he asked what morning sickness was!"

"Where would he hear about that?"

"From Lisa Marie talking with Glenn. She's pregnant!" said Linden triumphantly.

We began to plan a surprise baby shower for our friend as the winter storm blew on.

Whose Vision?

A disappointing herring season, the first in three years, came and went. Managers had allowed the fishery based on hydro-acoustic surveys that indicated a slight surplus of fish, but when the herring showed up, they were mostly small and immature with low egg counts. In comparison, herring from Sitka, an unoiled fishery, were fat with an average of two to five times more mature egg roe than the young Sound fish. One fisherman called the harvest "a fiasco." I thought of John Platt and his family with no way to pay off a staggering debt. Five years later, John would break his quiet and reach out for help.

Meanwhile, during the short herring harvest, part of the sustainable community steering committee and the editor of the *Cordova Times* flew up the Copper River to meet our neighbors. We were six in all, enough to fill a Beaver, the work plane of the Alaska bush.

During the winter, the steering committee had decided to hire consultants to figure out how we could do more with what we have in terms of fishery, forestry, and tourism, and they wanted to involve the upriver communities in the study. People reasoned that since salmon swim upstream, it only made sense to protect upriver habitat, too, by creating economies compatible with sustaining healthy fish populations. North of the Chugach Mountains, Native corporations were clear-cutting right to the riverbanks. During an earlier reconnaissance trip, I had met with many area leaders—public land and resource managers, Native corporations, college administrators, and engaged citizens. Their work seamed together the small communities into a functioning whole. They had wanted to learn more about the sustainable community work and had committed to a public meeting.

As the Beaver droned north, we each twisted in our seats to look out windows. Between Cordova and the upriver towns was wilderness, huge and humbling. Bluish-white glaciers poured from towering mountains into rivers and ice fields. Granite on bare ridges was deeply furrowed by ice like a newly turned farmer's field. The coastal rainforest that blanketed steep slopes and valleys gradually gave way to sparse open taiga in rumpled flatland. Muddy brown rivers snaked through it all, flowing from different valleys to form the Copper.

The scale of it all is staggering. The basin of rivers, ice, and mountains drain nearly 28,000 square miles or an area slightly larger than West Virginia. One ice field is the size of Rhode Island. Of the resident 5,000 people, half live in Cordova, while the others are scattered in some twenty unincorporated towns, some only loose collections of buildings.

During the next several months, I made the "commute" to the upper watershed many times with donors, consultants, and Cordova steering committee members. I never tired of the trip. At the crux of all the land use and resource use conflicts was the issue of value. The rural watershed had what some wanted to exploit: vast forests, spectacular scenery, wild rivers, subsurface oil and coal, and rich populations of fish and game. In the face of large-scale development pressure, it made sense for people to work together to grow their towns and future in ways that people valued, ways that balanced economic needs with human needs to sustain cultures, local livelihoods, and the living ecosystems that supported it all.

In Cordova, the sustainable community effort, now dubbed "The Copper River Watershed Project," had earned broad support with its emphasis on open process and consensus. As Linden once pointed out to me, after I regaled her with stories of meetings and workshops, "You've missed the most important part of what you're doing. A year ago, you were all fighting!" At one workshop, as we considered impacts from small to large cruise ships like trying on different shoe sizes, thirteen-year-old Malani observed brightly, "I get it, Mom! This is like adult problem-solving!" It was. In the supportive atmosphere, creative ideas flourished. Another person commented, "I want to see diversification, but I want to make sure we have brakes and can control the speed of . . . [development]." The Watershed Project steadily charted a plan of action supported by the people in Cordova and upriver, but often at odds with developers and the city.

On a sunny September afternoon, I sat outside on my deck, pouring over the budget for the Watershed Project with Kristin Smith. "Who?" my father had asked. He was closely following my work. I explained Kristin had recently moved to Cordova and been hired by the steering committee to conduct a quality of life survey or Wealth Index. We had added this fourth component of our study to identify and protect what made Cordova special in the eyes of residents. The idea was to protect what people valued—the reasons people lived in Cordova—as we sought to diversify the economy. "She has a master's in public policy from Harvard," I told my father. "Where do you find these people in Cordova?" he wanted to know. "Under rocks?!"

Once again, I was feeling overwhelmed. It wasn't just the budget. Earlier in the year, the director of Artists for Nature Foundation had called from the Netherlands to discuss the book and artwork. "English is not my native language," he said. "Can you write this book?" I had thought: Why not? It would be more fun to write than a PhD dissertation, and the University of Washington Press had already agreed to publish it. Then, he asked if I could "curate" the art show tour in North America, which, I learned, meant contacting dozens of museums, organizing the tour, shipping thousands of dollars' worth of art from place to place, and making sure each piece was accounted for. That wasn't so much fun, but I figured I could do anything once.

So book-writing, fund-raising, and curating had piled on top of organizing workshops and meetings, and managing Kristin and three other high-powered consultants, whom I had hired to do the forestry, fishing, and tourism research. But the final straw was that the Watershed Project needed to open an official office. After incubating with its sponsor organization for three years, the baby was ready to fledge as its own nonprofit. I had done office hours once, briefly, and once was enough.

Kristin's voice snapped me out of my woes. "Isn't this exciting? I've always wanted to be the director of a nonprofit organization!"

I stared at Kristin, than shoved all the papers across the table to her. "Kristin," I announced, "my kingdom is yours."

With that act, we committed to a power transfer that took eight months to consummate. Once again, I had no idea what I would do, but I sensed that in order for the Watershed Project to grow, it needed an office on Main Street with a full-time director—and I knew I was not the person for that job. However, my job wasn't quite over.

I had organized a public workshop in Glennallen for the consultants to share their research findings and for upriver residents to decide if they wanted to formally participate in a watershed organization. The night before the meeting I had another power dream. In it, I was in a fierce sword fight with a much larger opponent. When my opponent raised its sword to deliver the fatal blow, I put down my sword and shield and radiated love. My opponent melted in a dark puddle at my feet. The next morning just as I awoke, the words "Love—Patience—Tolerance" flashed again and again across my mind like a roll of ticker tape. This time I knew it was a vision, but I didn't know what it meant.

In Glennallen later that morning, I sought out our facilitator, Larry Merculieff, before the meeting. He listened to the dream, then turned in silence and disappeared into his hotel room. He emerged minutes before we were to begin, smelling strongly of white sage, which is used by indigenous healers to purify intent and ground purpose.

The fifteen minutes allocated for introduction of the watershed project turned into 105 minutes of hostile questioning from people I didn't know. Deflecting blows of "hidden agendas" and being "a front for the U.N. sustainable development movement" reminded me of the sword fight. I put down my sword of cutting words and my shield of logic. I answered questions with love, patience, and tolerance. When the questions became repetitive, Larry called a ten-minute break before proceeding with the meeting agenda.

He approached me and quietly asked, "Did you know what you were doing?" My shell-shocked silence was his answer. "You did everything right," he assured me. "You never got defensive. Now this is going to take off."

He was right. People listened with rapt attention to the consultants who had targeted their research to address regional needs and concerns. Two consultants spoke in dollars-and-cents terms of value-added forestry and fishery products and niche marketing to create stability in industries and communities during changing times. One spoke of ways to grow a tourism industry that would fit with the scale of the communities. Kristin explained that noneconomic "indicators" were quality-of-life measures such as household use of subsistence foods or percentage of locally owned commercial fishing permits. She described how they contribute to making our communities exceptional places to live. Monitoring these indicators would allow communities to regularly take stock of their growth and assets. In the end, despite the rocky beginning, people agreed to form the Copper River Watershed Project so residents could continue to work together.

In December, after what turned out to be my last statewide round of craft fairs, I organized the founding meeting of the Watershed Project. The steering committee had built a blueprint of possibilities into the leading sustainable community project in Alaska. Already results were tangible. The Watershed Project's tourism research had led the city, Chamber of Commerce, and U.S. Forest Service to link efforts in one inclusive public planning process unthinkable two years ago. Now, finally, I felt I could let go and trust in the founding members' committed leadership to carry the research into reality. I still had to finish the art book and tour, but the bulk of my work was done.

I turned to other pressing matters. In a letter to Governor Knowles, I asked the state to request that TAPS oil shippers indicate in writing their plans for continuously shipping oil without disruption as they phased in double-hull tankers. The *Exxon Valdez* incident earlier in the year had tipped me off that shippers were looking for ways to dodge the double-hull tanker requirements in the Oil Pollution Act. Returning the relatively young *Exxon Valdez* to service would have allowed Exxon to keep shipping oil in that single-hull tanker for several more years.

The problem was that 78 percent of TAPS oil was being carried in eighteen vessels, scheduled for phaseout by 1999. ARCO and BP had announced plans to build new double-hull tankers to meet replacement deadlines mandated in federal law. Exxon was silent.

In mid-December, SeaRiver (Exxon Shipping) and Chevron announced they were not replacing four older single-hull tankers. They were "reconfiguring" them. The shippers had found a legal loophole in the Oil Pollution Act big enough to drive a supertanker through. The paper exercise involved nothing more than remeasuring oil tanks, with a little fudging, and designating some as ballast tanks. This put the tankers into a different category of the law that extended their shelf life five more years. In response to public outrage, Congress acted quickly to close the loophole, but not before several more single-hull tankers were reconfigured to continue legally shipping oil in the Sound past the year designated for their replacement.

Two Steps Backward, One Step Forward

"We're going b-a-c-k-w-a-r-d!" Linden declared, opening her arms to the bright blue sky and the snow-covered mountain. Her ski poles dangled from her wrists. We were knee-deep in fresh powder, breaking trail up the ski hill on our new snowshoes. The ski club opened the lift—Sun Valley's first chair lift—on weekends and one afternoon midweek, but the slopes were always open to those with good lungs and a sense of adventure. Many people packed telemark skis or snowboards for downhill runs, but Linden and I were "extreme snowshoers." The dogs huffed and puffed up the hill in our track, occasionally flopping in the powder to roll happily.

"Now why would Judge Holland reopen the whole Rita Wilson mess?" Her voice drifted over her shoulder back to me. It was 1998, and at the judge's request, the Ninth Circuit Court of Appeals had remanded the *Exxon Valdez* case back to his district court in Anchorage.

"It wasn't Judge Holland," I puffed. "It was Exxon. Three years ago Judge Holland ruled Exxon had no grounds for a new trial over the bullet incident. Then a U.S. Marshal spotted Don Warrick's name in the newspaper. Warrick was the security officer."

She stepped aside and I moved ahead to break trail.

"So, the Marshal Service conducts its own investigation. Warrick flunks a seven-hour lie detector test. He confesses the bullet incident had happened. The U.S. Marshal forces Warrick to resign. The guy dies of a heart attack. But the story lives on."

I spoke in spurts as the grade steepened.

"A year passes. The U.S. Marshal starts a new investigation . . . on improper use of firearms by court security personnel. . . . The federal lawyers go to Exxon for more information on Warrick. . . . That tips off Exxon that this

whole thing really happened. . . . Exxon demands a new trial based on 'extraordinary newly discovered documents.' . . ."

I paused for breath. "I swear, you couldn't have written a more twisted
script."

"This is bizarre," Linden declared.

"Oesting had a few other words for it." I pushed on. "Oesting says he
has a 'stack of investigative reports and crap knee-deep from the Marshall's
Service—and no witness. Warrick's not around to refute his wild-ass testimony.' But Rita Wilson is."

We crested a ridge and stopped briefly to look at the view.

"Oh no!" Linden said. "That poor woman is crazy. Who knows what she'll
say?"

We mulled our fate in silence as we watched a pair of eagles fly across the
inlet and spiral up the mountain in an updraft. The dogs rolled and tussled.
The dry snow slid off their silky coats. I maneuvered my snowshoe tips out
from under them and continued uphill.

"We're going backward with the Oil Pollution Act, too."

"Now what?" Linden said to my back.

"The Coast Guard was supposed to automatically increase oil spill response
equipment in the Sound this year—booms and boats and skimmers and barges
and stuff," I huffed in cadence with my pace. "But the oil industry wants to
use dispersants."

"That stuff we fought with Exxon over in 1989?"

"From Day One on," I said. "The Coast Guard opened up the issue for a
national debate. The RCAC is going to oppose it."

The RCAC had conducted a two-year study on dispersants and found no
new information: No dispersants were effective at breaking up sticky North
Slope crude in cold water. Yet the EPA permitted their use by allowing oil
companies to average lab tests on North Slope crude and Louisiana crude.
In other words, the chemicals only worked on paper—and when the test was
rigged. Since dispersants did not work well in Alaska, the RCAC opposed
substituting them for mechanical cleanup equipment.

"That's good! How's the art book coming?"

"I'm having fun writing it!"

"Maybe you could get Makena to think writing is fun."

"Why? What's he doing?"

"He decided to drop out of the fifth grade gifted program. He figured out
that it's more work than regular school."

"He's not stupid! It is more work." I thought a minute as I step-kicked up the slope. "I'll ask him to review the ecology chapter. That's half the manuscript—and he's interested in ecology."

"And a kestrel."

"A what?" I turned to look at Linden.

"He's getting a kestrel to hunt rabbits. He passed all his falconry tests and he has a mentor in Anchorage. We're going to wait until summer."

"Huh. Well, Dad had an owl when he was in college. I'll see if he has any advice for us."

We crested the top of the ski hill and found the picnic table poking out of the snow. We pulled snacks and water from our packs before we sat on them on top of the snowy table. The dogs crowded in for their biscuits, then eyed our cookies. "No mooching!" Linden announced. They backed off a bit.

"We sure live in a pretty place," she said appreciatively. The snowfall had powdered the spruce and hemlock on Hawkins Island. The trees and inlet sparkled in the sun. The distant mountains glowed white against the bright sky. Eagles soared overhead and crisscrossed the sea below us. "I can't believe we've had this all to ourselves for so long. We've been discovered though. Did you see the *Sports Afield*?"

"Cordova—'where people are real and your dog is as welcome as you are,'" I quoted from the article. "I liked the *Alaska Magazine* piece, too."

"The one that called Cordova 'a gem—a classic small town that time forgot?' Oh! No, you liked where it said Cordovans still participate in the 'art of civic debate'!"

"'*Vigorous* civic debate,'" I corrected her. She laughed.

"We've certainly had our share of that again this winter. What do you think is going to happen with the cruise ships?"

Mayor Margy and the city invited big ships without telling residents—despite the fact that we'd established a public process to get opinions and consensus on what type of tourism townspeople wanted for Cordova. I waved my mittens in the air. "People want ecotourism—small ships."

"But the big ones are coming in May. They can't even get in the harbor. They have to shuttle people. Those big ships carry 800 people!"

"There's not much all those people can do in a few hours. The Watershed Project is working with the city on an evaluation survey for all visitors. From everything I've been reading, the surveys should show that big cruise ship passengers spend the least in town compared to the small ships that stay a few days."

"So we'll get our taste of these big ships and then boot them out in a couple years once we build up our ecotourism market?" she asked doubtfully.

"I guess we'll see."

"What do you think of the governor's bike trail idea?"

After settling the Copper River Highway lawsuit from his predecessor's days, Governor Knowles had unilaterally decided to build a "world-class bike trail" instead of a road. The plan was introduced as a done deal. It had received broad support from Anchorage and Fairbanks people who pressed relentlessly for better access to the region's fish and game. The plan had virtually no support from the two small communities at either end of the proposed trail, Cordova and Chitina.

"I like what Kelley Weaverling said: 'The Lewis and Clark Trail is now U.S. superhighway 90.' It's funny, though. People who don't want a road oppose the trail because they think it will become a road. And people who want a road oppose it because they think it won't become a road."

"So that will probably go nowhere, done deal or not," Linden concluded. "The city is talking about raising property tax and keeping the sales tax at 6 percent," she said worriedly. "Fish prices are staying low. Where is the revenue?"

"I just hope it's not from logging and mining on the Delta. Chugach Alaska Corporation found over 100 salmon streams in that little section of road it wants to build to Carbon Mountain."

Linden looked horrified. "That fishery is supporting the town! They can't mess with those streams!"

"Oh, they could. The Native corporations are guaranteed access to their inholdings, you know—environmental laws be damned. That's causing quite a bit more 'vigorous civic debate.'"

We fell silent. The dogs pricked up their ears at the sea lions grunting and belching in the inlet far below. "It is pretty," I said.

"We've got to keep it that way, because that's what's going to bring in dollars—drop-dead gorgeous," said Linden. We took one last look around before heading down the mountain.

Two months later in mid-April, the herring fisheries in the Sound opened, but the fish were mere shadows of their former glory. They were mostly young and small—and scarce. This would be the last herring fishery in the Sound for the indefinite future. At the time of writing this book, there was still no sign of recovery.

Defying the Odds

"What are you going to do now?" Linden asked.

In late April, melting snow made mountain hikes treacherous. Avalanches rumbled like freight trains as snow lost its grip on steep slopes. Meltwater flowed freely under the shrinking snowpack, making happy gurgling and gushing sounds. On more than one occasion, I had to dig myself out of a "spruce trap," where boughs bent by snow suddenly released with my weight, dropping me to the base of the tree and filling the hole with snow. I switched to mountain biking and pedaled by Linden's office after a ride.

"That's what I came over to tell you!" I had mailed the completed manuscript for the art book a few days earlier. The art show was booked for three years. The founding board of the Watershed Project had hired Kristin Smith as executive director and moved into the back office of Linden's building. The consultants had finished and presented their reports to the community, laying a solid foundation for future work. I had cleared my plate not knowing what would come next, but trusting that something would present itself. That morning, with the dawn, it did. "I'm going to write a book about the oil spill's effects on the Sound!"

"Good idea," Linden said. "But keep it simple so people can understand it." Her words sunk in as I flashed back to the time when I had lost my audience in a maze of statistics and scientific minutiae.

"Did you hear the Copper River Queens are performing for the 'First Fish' visitors and for the first cruise ship?" She grinned in anticipation.

The Queens are a performing troupe of spirited, creative Cordova women decked out as glittery salmon. Top chefs from around the country were gathering in town to share tips about cooking fresh wild Copper River salmon while national media captured the raw excitement and hubbub of a working fishing community on opening day. Meanwhile, CDFU had staked out Cordovans from Seattle to Los Angeles.

"That's perfect. That'll give everyone a real taste of Cordova. This is a real media blitz."

"That's going to raise the price of our sockeye and king salmon!" Linden said gleefully, as she pounded the air with her fists.

Years of dedicated work by fishermen and townspeople had finally paid off. Fishermen were paid record high prices for Copper River kings that summer. The record would be repeatedly broken in following years as the Copper River wild salmon craze would sweep across America each May. Already, the Copper

River fishery was bringing more fish bucks into town than the Sound fisheries, and it was the primary thing keeping Cordova afloat.

In late September, I was back in Washington, D.C., with Dune Lankard and David Grimes to quash a hornets' nest of trouble that had erupted earlier in the summer. As part of the habitat acquisition program, Rick Steiner had asked the EVOS Trustee Council to consider purchasing the subsurface rights to the Carbon Mountain coalfield. Such a purchase would stop the planned clear-cut logging and the access road across the Delta's salmon streams.

In response to Rick's proposal, which the Trustees rejected, Alaska's Senator Frank Murkowski introduced legislation in Congress requiring the Forest Service to grant "an irrevocable and perpetual 500-foot wide easement for . . . non-public roads . . ." The road rider dispensed with environmental safeguards, releasing the corporation from its promises to protect fish and wildlife. It also provided for other roads on the Delta, presumably for oil exploration.

When the corporation positioned to start road construction, Dune organized an "action camp" on the Delta to protect it with nonviolent action, if necessary, against what one young fisherman called, "too much leeway for carelessness." Five activists were arrested after they "arrested" a bridge, locking themselves down to it in protest of the road's thrust across the wetland. The arrest attracted national political attention, stirring opposition to Murkowski's legislation for a private easement.

To elude public debate, Murkowski morphed his legislation into a "rider" on the Interior appropriations bill. A rider is an add-on that automatically passes if the bill passes. President Clinton threatened to veto the entire $13.4 billion spending package if the road rider was not removed. Then, the Asian timber market crashed, erasing the economic value of the Delta's forest, but not its ecological value. Interest mounted in Congress to strike the road rider from the Interior appropriations bill.

Dune, David, and I stayed a week in D.C. With floor votes on the issue pressing, we packed as many "Hill visits" as physically possible into each day, racing from one side of the Capitol to the other as we switched from House to Senate and back again. We burst into office after office and spread out maps on the floor as we shared stories of people and place. We passed out letters of support from fishermen and the Eyak people and gifted copies of the beautiful coffee-table art book from the artists' project, literally hot off the press.

The tide turned. An omnibus National Parks bill was defeated because it contained the same road rider as the spending bill. Alaska's Congressman Don Young screamed at his colleagues, "*What is wrong with you people? You voted in favor of this last week!*" A New York representative responded, "Last week I didn't have people from your state in my office asking me to vote against this." The road rider was pulled from the spending bill.

Meanwhile, the very week we were in Washington, D.C., British Petroleum conducted its second "spill of national significance" drill—300,000 barrels or near the low-end estimate of the *Exxon Valdez* spill. It was play for real. BP flew in equipment from the North Slope, West Coast, and England. Fishing boats, skimmers, floating barges, and Coast Guard support vessels and helicopters staged an on-the-water response near Montague Island, while fifty more boats were trained for response in Seward and Homer and another team worked on support logistics for an extra 5,000 people in Valdez. It was 1989 all over again. The only thing missing was oil.

During the drill, I received frantic requests from the RCAC to call the Coast Guard to protest its decision to give BP blanket permission to use dispersants, including in Zone 3, the shallow nearshore seas teeming with sea life. Further, people were asked to protest the decision by the Unified Command (the Coast Guard, the State of Alaska, and the spiller) to shut the RCAC out of the top-level decision-making process. Our objections fell on deaf ears, but I did learn that the Coast Guard was holding a public hearing in Washington, D.C., on whether dispersants should be included in the federal planning requirements for oil spill response.

Before we flew home, David and I dropped by the Coast Guard hearing. It was packed with oilmen and industry supporters. My comments on human health effects from dispersants used during the *Exxon Valdez* cleanup drew a curious response from the Exxon's Dick Lessard. He claimed to have no knowledge that Corexit dispersants were applied to shorelines in Alaska, and he emphatically denied that the chemicals cause a health problem, except when people get it on their skin. The Coast Guard brushed me aside and quickly moved to other people with comments. David and I exchanged a glance that said there was more to this story.

On the long plane rides home, thoughts of the spill flowed around and around in my mind. I had read the state's investigation into spill volume that was on file at a library in Anchorage. Records clearly showed that eleven million gallons was only Exxon's low-end estimate, not the volume that spilled. State-hired surveyors estimated the volume spilled to be closer to thirty to thirty-five million gallons, or three times what Exxon had reported and much closer to the high-end estimate of thirty-eight million gallons.

I guessed that Exxon's motive for lying about spill volume was to reduce fines since fines are based on volume spilled. Federal and state laws had also passed requiring the oil industry to be prepared to respond to an *Exxon Valdez*–size spill. Since the actual spill was three times larger than reported, this meant oil companies had saved money by not having to purchase and maintain three times more supplies of response equipment. In my mind, the volume mystery was solved.

Then there was the captain and his ill-fated ship. Exxon had appealed Judge Holland's decision banning the old *Exxon Valdez* from the Sound. (Four years later, the Ninth Circuit would uphold the ruling.) Meanwhile in July, Captain Joe Hazelwood was fined $50,000 for negligent discharge of oil and sentenced to 1,000 hours of community service in Alaska. The sentence had bounced back and forth like a tennis ball between the Alaska Appeals Court and the Alaska Superior Court five times before it finally stuck. Charges of drunkenness and misconduct were dismissed. (Hazelwood stalled fulfillment of his sentence for four more years.) These issues were nearing closure.

Other issues were stuck in quicksand. The *Exxon Valdez* case was tangled in a welter of appeals to the Ninth Circuit. A year earlier, Oesting had uncovered another eight processors that had assigned Exxon their punitive damage awards in exchange for cash up front, just like the Seattle Seven. Since none of the eight had filed claims to participate in the punitive damage class, Oesting requested they not be allowed to share the award. Judge Holland agreed. Two processors appealed.

Further, Exxon had appealed the $5 billion punitive portion of the jury verdict to the Ninth Circuit. Among the litany of complaints was an argument that the award was "grossly excessive" relative to the compensatory award. A recent U.S. Supreme Court decision signaled the court was seeking to cap punitive damages, although no "mathematically bright line" had been drawn. The other case had argued for a cap under the due process protection of the Fourteenth Amendment. Punitive damages in our case were less than ten times the compensatory award, according to our lawyers' calculations—within the single-digit ratio favored by the high court. But what I found "excessive" was the corporate use of the Fourteenth Amendment to argue their cases. Those rights were intended for people. I still did not understand how corporations could claim this privilege, and I still felt this was not right.

The Rita Wilson debacle had resulted in another appeal. The former juror had broken down while testifying, creating emotional hell for herself and a field day for Exxon. Judge Holland found her testimony "bizarre and shocking." He decided Wilson's present memories did "not reflect what really happened." He concluded that the security officer's behavior had not prejudiced the jury or influenced their verdict against Exxon. Exxon appealed. We had to wait on the Ninth Circuit for decisions on each of these appeals.

Beyond the legal morass was the spill science. Since 1993 when the spill science first went public, Exxon had challenged all studies that found the oil spill had harmed anything from clams to whales. I suspected Exxon's fuss was a smokescreen to throw people off the trail of lingering harm from its spill. On or before September 1, 2006, the federal or state government could reopen the 1991 civil settlement for natural resource damages and claim up to an additional $100 million for "unanticipated injury." No one had pieced together all the studies of lingering harm into a solid story, which I now realized was critical for people to make a case to reopen the settlement.

All that fall, I bent to my task. I didn't realize what an epic six-year journey this would become.

CHAPTER TWELVE
MOVING ON
1999

No one in Cordova anticipated the three-month nightmare, leading up to the tenth-year memorial of the oil spill. No one.

My telephone started ringing in January—around 6 A.M. every morning—and it didn't stop until mid-March. Press needed background material for their tenth memorial articles. The calls shattered my quiet mornings, reserved for writing. Strangers intruded into the private sanctuary of my home for hours until I walked away from the ringing phone at midday to catch what I could of the brief winter sun. In late afternoons, I was spared by Alaska's time offset. My phone sat silent as the Lower 48 settled into evening.

I decided to allow the calls, intrusion, and chaos into my life because of the commitment I had made ten years earlier. The book could wait; the press would not. Calls from the *Wall Street Journal*, *Los Angeles Times*, *Seattle Post-Intelligencer*, *Houston Chronicle*, *Newsweek*, *People Magazine*, *National Geographic*, the *Boston Globe*, and *USA Today* were sprinkled with calls from dozens of towns across America and from the major television networks—ABC, CBS, NBC, CNN, BBC, and SkyNews, Europe's version of CNN, among others.

The calls were emotionally draining. Each stirred old wounds. They were also extremely frustrating. Many of the reporters had not covered the spill in 1989 and needed to be educated on basic things, like the difference between gillnetting and seining, or what it meant to be a fishing community that was oiled, or what it was, exactly, that we had lost. They expected help planning trips to Cordova. Where would they stay? Who could fly them out to the Sound to see oiled beaches? Who could they interview? Their needs had to be meshed with the reality of Alaska winter. It's dark in January. There's snow on the beaches. There's howling winter storms. No one would fly to the beaches in January.

Overwhelmed, I called other Cordovans who had played leadership roles in 1989 and found they also were being bombarded by the media. In response, Sylvia Lange invited a small group to her home at Cannery Row to devise a plan to save our sanity and to deal with the press. After venting our frustrations, there was a moment's silence. Fisherman John Renner mused, "There's 22,000. Where are the other 21,982? Why does it always come down to us?"

The answer lay buried on beaches in the Sound. The wildlife biologists and chemists had traced lingering harm in the Sound's ecosystem directly to residual oil. This translated to economic damages through the fisheries. Sociologists had traced lingering harm in people and Cordova directly to the spill and litigation. Like it or not, Cordova was the media's choice to illustrate ongoing harm from the spill.

We divvied up the tasks. Sylvia, Patience, and Linden would coordinate opportunities for people to share stories with press. CDFU would help with logistics. Others and I would provide background material. For me, this meant spending hundreds of volunteer hours on the phone to frame our overarching story, document our points and concerns, and provide contact information to other key players. But now, even as I worked alone, the feelings of isolation and frustration were gone. We knew we could count on each other. We were no longer drowning in an ocean of spill trauma. We had moved on.

Turbulent Times

Early one afternoon on a rare calm February day, I drove out "the Road" to go snowshoeing on a trail that was only open in the winter. A recent warm front had compacted several layers. The snow had refrozen and formed a hard crust. It would be easy hiking, I figured, on the hard surface, but I had been unable to find Linden. At 17 Mile, I spotted Linden's car pulled over by the side of the road near the woods. I pulled behind her, hopped out, and ran up to her window.

"Are you okay?" She was bundled up, reading a book. "What are you doing?"

She cracked the window, laughing. "Sitting here freezing my ass! Makena is hunting rabbits." She waved south. "He's too young to drive."

I burst out laughing. "Oh, man! He's still got two more years before he can drive!"

"That's a good thing! Hop in. Let's visit for minute." I walked around to the passenger side and climbed in.

"You and Danny got your claim in, right?"

All the salmon fishermen—permit holders, boat owners, and crew—and Native subsistence users affected by the spill had to have filed loss claims by February 1. Those who missed the deadline were forever barred from the *Exxon Valdez* case. These claims were among the first of fifty-one distribution plans approved by Judge Holland.

"Oh, yeah. Danny took care of it years ago. There sure were a lot of people who waited until the last minute though."

"It's called denial! There are a lot of wounded people still in this town. All of this media to remind people of the claims' deadline—'oil spill losses, blah, blah, blah'—it stirred up a lot of ugly memories. Besides that, fishermen hate paperwork. Thank God for Patience!"

Patience had volunteered long hours at the Union Hall on Main Street, helping fishermen fill out their forms. She realized that, for some people, reimbursement for losses would bring case closure, and she was determined to help these people file timely claims. "We're never going to forget," she said, "but we can do that much."

"I heard some people dropped their claims," I said.

Some people had reevaluated their priorities after ten years and decided to embrace a sense of moving forward. Claims were stark reminders of loss, of things past that could never be again. Some people, such as bed-and-breakfast owner Becky Chapek, had voluntarily jettisoned their claims to move on.

"It's not so hard to see why, really," said Linden.

"Did you see the letter Patience wrote to Senator Murkowski? The one asking him to reject the ExxonMobil merger until Exxon pays its spill debt?"

"That merger is one dumb idea," Linden declared. "Exxon is already running the country. Making them bigger will just give them the world."

The federal government had busted John Rockefeller's Standard Oil empire in 1911. Putting just these two pieces back together—Exxon and Mobil—would once again create the largest oil company in the world.

"Do you realize if Exxon was a country, it would rank third in supplying oil right behind Saudi Arabia and Iran?" Linden just shook her head.

"I signed your double-hull tanker petition!" she said. "Looks like a lot of people did."

Pipeline owners had sent yet another proposal to the U.S. Coast Guard to dodge the double-hull tanker mandate in the Oil Pollution Act. This time, the oil companies wanted to retrofit old single-hull tankers with double sides or a double bottom and keep these patchwork jobs in operation beyond the 2015 replacement deadline. The TAPS-trade fleet was already one of the oldest fleets operating in U.S. waters and its single-hull tankers had a disproportionately high number of structural failure problems, according to the Coast Guard. To make further mockery of the law, BP reconverted its old tankers—the *Tonsina*, *Prince William Sound*, and *Kenai*—back into double-bottom ships by patching the holes in the inner cargo holds that had allowed the ships to carry oil for years as single-hull tankers. Cordovans wanted nothing less than new double-hull tankers that had been promised nearly 30 years ago.

"Yeah. These guys are relentless at trying to save themselves a buck," I said, referring to the pipeline owners. "Too bad they don't put the same resources into training crews for spill response that they put into fighting safety laws. Now Alyeska is cutting its spill response workers—oh! Maybe it'll just cut the ones who aren't properly trained for response," I said sarcastically.

The state had conducted two surprise spill drills—one on land and one on water. The state found the majority of supposedly fully trained responders at the Alyeska terminal were not fully trained.

Linden rolled her eyes. "You've been doing this too long."

"We all have!"

"Let's talk about something happy. It's too nice a day. Wasn't that great when Mike and Michelle O'Leary received the Citizen of the Year Award at Iceworm Festival?"

Michelle had served with the RCAC for nearly a decade. Together, the O'Learys had volunteered thousands of hours, dedicating their lives to helping restore the Sound and prevent future spills.

"Yes! I loved how the applause went on and on after the announcement. That had to feel good for them. I liked your family band, too. Malani sounded great. You all did."

"Malani is writing a song for the ten-year oil spill anniversary. She wants to surprise you."

"Oh, wow. She's going to be, what? Fifteen this year?"

"In May. Belle Mickelson handpicked her and Mike and four Anchorage kids from her music camps to form a teenage band. *Bearfoot Bluegrass* they're calling it."

"That's great! Belle is amazing. What a cool town we live in. Well, daylight's burning."

I excused myself and headed off down "the Road," leaving my friend to read her book in the afternoon sun.

Increasing daylight hours in mid- to late February brought throngs of media to Cordova. Many resented the media invasion and the painful memories it evoked. Walking down Main Street one day, I noticed a person peeking down the street from behind a building. Curious, I walked over. "If you don't want to be on 'B Roll,' stay here," he whispered, flagging other innocent pedestrians to his side. I peeked around the building's edge. Sure enough, TV cameras on the far end of Main Street were quietly filming life in Cordova. The cameras missed the real story—the growing crowd hovering behind Seaman's Hardware.

Others, new to town since the spill, watched the show with wonder and tried to understand what so engulfed the community. They hovered at the edge of potluck-cum-discussion circles, organized for the media, and listened as survivors explained that losses to quality of family life, sense of security, and control over one's life were as serious as lost income and grossly devalued fishing permits, yet these losses were not counted or compensated. As Sylvia Lange said bluntly, "We will never be compensated [for our losses]—a check's not going to do it." As the newcomers listened, I saw their understanding, compassion, and respect grow as the survivors painted a living history of shattered lives and a community forever changed by disaster.

Even Cordova's children reflected the continued social upheaval. In an essay competition sponsored by the EVOS Trustee Council, Brian Johannessen, sixteen, wrote, "A decade later we are still trying to fix what was once right." Sean Sjostedt, eleven, penned poetry: "We have all learned lessons/ and have all felt the pain./ Be more responsible/ and this won't happen again."

Seventeen-year-old Laura Honkola, who seined with her father and younger sisters, won first place with her analogy of an oil truck spill in a farming community. She wrote:

"[The farmers] worked harder than ever before to restore what they had once known, but it would never be the same for them. Their soil had been damaged past repair by the oil, and the only thing to do was to stick it out until the soil had rejuvenated by itself. This could mean years of poverty. . . . (T)he corporation was not willing to budge in the least on the subject of compensation for damages, even though the sum of money asked would not have even touched the edges of the corporation's wealth. . . . To this day, [the farmers] remember what happened as if it happened yesterday, and they tell their children of these tales. . . ."

The Tenth Memorial

By March, teams of Cordovans were flying to key events around the country to share stories of lingering harm to the Sound and our community—and to counter Exxon's mantra. "Prince-William-Sound-has-fully-recovered. It's-not-Exxon's-oil-that-is-causing-any-lingering-problems. People-have-been-fully-paid-for-lost-income. The-communities-are-back-to-normal." It was a steady drumbeat like a heavy rain in Cordova. I felt like a chess piece in a high-stakes game.

In Seattle, a small group of spill survivors "captured the flag," as my sister put it, at the International Oil Spill conference. The oil industry had lined up actor Ted Danson as its keynote speaker, but we had managed to get information to Danson's speechwriter before the event. The roomful of oilmen grew very quiet when Danson spoke of ecological damage, financial hardships, and emotional stress. He challenged the oil companies to work to address these issues rather than cover them up.

Instead of rising to the challenge to put people's lives and communities back together, oilmen and state politicians focused on the "night-and-day differences" since the spill. Governor Knowles bragged of having the "toughest oil spill prevention and response laws"; of tankers "escorted by the world's most sophisticated tractor tugs"; of sophisticated radar and weather stations; and of a fleet with "nearly 60 percent" double-hulled or double-bottomed tankers. The governor even praised Alyeska's new vapor recovery system that "reduced harmful pollutants by 90 percent." In part, this oversized helping of praise was to grease the skids for reauthorization of the pipeline permit, now due after 30 years of operation.

What the governor and oilmen failed to mention was that it had taken one huge spill and a lot of concerted effort by people to force the recalcitrant industry and complacent governments to deliver on promises made a quarter of a century earlier. Most of the "improved" technology actually existed and was in use somewhere before the spill, like tractor tugs and advanced radar. Had it been in use as a condition of operation, as originally promised, the Sound likely would have been spared the spill. Further, by ignoring the improvements forced by citizens, the oil industry and governments could—and would—ignore the public's demand for citizen oversight of the entire pipeline during the permit reauthorization process.

The week of the memorial, I was emotionally exhausted from fighting a constant barrage of corporate myths, political boasts, and old trauma, dredged up from dealing nearly nonstop with media. Yet I still had one more big event to go—a live television interview in Anchorage with the governor, lead spill scientists, and Alyeska representatives.

Before I left town, I meditated and prayed for guidance as I snowshoed up the flanks of Mt. Eyak. Alone in the swirling fog on the windswept ridge at 1,300 feet, I closed my eyes and soaked up the wild, raw silence. I opened my eyes to a stunning vision. Mt. Eyak was cloaked in a silver mist with a brilliant white shimmering aura cast around the perimeter. Later, a scientist explained this apparition as "a glory," an event so rare that Buddhist monks believe Nirvana can be instantly achieved by throwing oneself off the ridge into the haloed mist.

This image burned brightly in my mind as Linden, Malani, and I headed to Anchorage. During the midday press conference, Malani sang her oil spill song: "Visions of dying otters, fish and birds/ Filled her mind and their cries she heard./ Oiled bodies and tortured souls,/ Corporate profits had taken their toll." I sat riveted in my chair, pinned by powerful gusts of emotions and floods of tears. Every Cordovan in the audience within my view had the same reaction to her clear young voice and heartsong.

Later that evening at the broadcast station, after an emotionally jagged candlelight vigil, Linden and Malani gave me a pep talk before they were escorted to a soundproof room. Left behind in the recording room, seated in a circle under harsh bright lights, I was unable to concentrate at first. Then, the burning image of the mountain flooded my mind. It pushed out all thought and allowed a laserlike focus on the moment. In the ensuing debate over spill effects, I repeatedly spliced facts and comments onto the interviewers' questions or the others' responses. When the interview wrapped up, the shimmering mountain dissolved. I had no memory of what I had said or done, but I saw by the beaming smiles from Linden and Malani that the interview had tilted in Cordova's favor, despite the odds. The Alaska Press Club would later award the interview first place in its documentary division in 1999.

Meanwhile, back in Cordova, the town had emptied of press, and it sat quiet on the memorial. It was the first nonevent in ten years. As one local told the *Cordova Times*, "That's okay with me."

Reassembly Required

"You're not the only one!" Lisa Marie told me.

Emotionally wasted after the memorial events, I had walked over to her home to lick my wounds and try to pull myself back together. I found her home and presence comforting in a soul-nourishing kind of way. There was always busywork to occupy the hands while we talked about more meaningful things. I pitched in to help fold an avalanche of clean laundry that had buried the couch. Her two-year-old daughter played on the floor with her three-year-old Haitian sister whose adoption papers had gone through during Lisa Marie's pregnancy. Zak was out playing with Makena. The inky black kitten tucked herself out of harm's way up on the bookshelf, while the small black moppish-looking family dog wedged herself in the midst of floor action.

"I'm just worn out." I paused, searching for a better description. "Wrung out. Wasted."

"The memorial was brutal on this town. Did you see the letters in the paper pleading for sanity?"

I shook my head, suddenly realizing I hadn't even had time to read the local paper. Social workers know that a "precipitating crisis" such as the oil spill creates stress and financial hardships, which in turn are a major cause of individual and family problems. Precipitating crises lead to situations where people reach their mental and emotional limits and do something they would not normally do like lash out uncontrollably at others or themselves with abusive behavior. In anticipation of a spike in such activity around the ten-year memorial, the Cordova Family Resource Center had pleaded for full funding from the state. The pleas had fallen on deaf ears.

"Well, the Family Resource Center has been *busy*. I tell you what's going to help this town is getting everyone's mind off the spill. The theater troupe is performing *Oliver* this spring. That should help. About a hundred people and crew are in it!"

"Oh, what fun! How do you know?"

"I play the female lead!"

She stood up, took an armful of folded clothes, and disappeared into the back rooms. I played with the girls and dog until she returned with another basket of washed clothes. She dumped them on the pile, laughing at my face.

"This is more clothes than you own, right? There're five of us! Zak and Glenn should count double." As we began to fold again, she asked, "What are you going to do for yourself?"

"That's what I came to talk about. Something weird happened to me in Anchorage." I described the television interview. Lisa Marie listened quietly, folding clothes. I felt safe talking with her. She was deeply intuitive, open-minded, and able to make sense of most things.

"That sounds like channeling," she said when I finished and looked questioningly at her.

"I'm a scientist! I can't be channeling!"

"Well, you prayed for guidance and you got it. Did you think Guidance would just appear and be normal? You have to be alert. Guidance comes in different forms. It seems like you get a lot of help through dreams."

"I wonder if there's a way to access this help on a regular basis. It all seems so random."

"It's called prayer! Or meditation. You're doing both. Just keep with it and see what happens."

One of the first things that happened was that Danny, who had been living in my home, moved out. He found this new pursuit even more unsettling than the politics. He began dating—and I gained new girlfriends as our friendship continued to evolve.

Meanwhile, I left town to attend a school of esoteric teachings from different spiritual practices around the world. I hoped exploring the human consciousness might lead to better use of the gifts that had blessed my life. I also sought understanding to heal and bring balance to my work. The teachings would have immediate application in unexpected ways.

Two months later, I was in Dallas, Texas, at an Exxon shareholder meeting where things had taken a bizarre turn. Our lawyers had sent Patience and I to attend the Mobil and Exxon meetings on proxies. Our plan was to request that Exxon pay its outstanding oil spill debt to injured people and communities before the proposed merger of oil giants. We had letters from Ann Rockefeller Roberts, the granddaughter of Standard Oil Trust's founder, and another from Cordovans, pleading for payment of spill debts.

Before the meetings began, we upstaged media coverage of the oilmen's events with our "Valdez Victims" press conference and separate protest by the Interfaith Center for Corporate Responsibility. In the hotel parking lot, nuns and clergy crashed a huge helium-filled blimp of the *Exxon Valdez* into an even huger blimp of planet Earth, while Dallas cops looked on and giggled. Hotel security was not amused. They eyed me, but I just watched the protest. Then Patience and I parted ways to attend the separate shareholder meetings.

After the shareholder meeting adjourned and the merger was overwhelmingly approved, I passed out the letters to snowy-haired shareholders, standing just outside the room as instructed by Exxon security. When asked by Exxon security to move outside the hotel, I complied, only to find myself immediately challenged by hotel security. When the guard accompanied me back inside to verify my story, the guard who had asked me to move seemed to have "forgotten" that he gave me permission to stand outside. I felt my stubborn streak kick in and knew that I would continue passing out the letters as long as possible whatever the consequences. Less than ten minutes later, I was hauled off the property in handcuffs by Dallas County cops!

In the jail's holding room with thirty other women all shouting, I tried unsuccessfully to call Linden to let her know where I was, then my family and Yosh—the only numbers I could remember. After reaching no one, I felt a rising panic. I paused to regroup and turned around to find a sea of faces looking at me in a room suddenly grown very quiet.

Finally one woman said, "You're dressed too nice to be in here. What did you do?"

Unsure how to explain things to this audience, I ventured, "Does anyone remember the *Exxon Valdez* oil spill?"

The ladies all started talking to each other at once. I heard bits of half a dozen different conversations. They remembered! Even with all their other troubles, they remembered. I took heart.

When it grew quiet again, the same woman said, "That was a long time ago. What are you doing here now?"

I explained why I was here and what had happened at the meeting. The ladies listened, shaking their heads. They told me that I had fallen for the old bait-and-switch trick: I had been given permission by Exxon security to pass out material inside the hotel, not by hotel security to do so outside the hotel. Exxon security had set me up. The ladies told me it would take my friends awhile to figure out where I was. A small group made room for me on a hard tile bench.

For the next twelve hours, I listened to their stories and shared mine. The ladies were attentive and compassionate toward every individual, whether the story revolved around losing jobs, smoking pot, picking up "dates," or corporate criminals in Alaska. The ladies took me into their protective fold. There was always a shoulder to cry on when anyone, including myself, felt overwhelmed. In return for their kindness, I told stories of Alaskan adventures to give some relief of the circumstances that were their lives, but were only a passing moment in mine.

The day wore on. I finally reached the O'Tooles. *"Mom! It's Riki!"* Malani shouted into the phone.

Apparently my earlier calls had left an automatic recorded message from "an inmate in Dallas County jail." They had pieced together what happened—as did everyone else who received similar messages. I learned later that Linden called the lawyers to get a message through to Patience. My father tried to call Exxon CEO Lee Raymond to protest his daughter's treatment at the shareholder meeting only to find the "bastard has an unlisted phone number!" My sister meditated. Yosh kept my father up to date by calling Linden. And Patience made seventy-five phone calls to release me.

I could only trust in my friends' efforts outside the jailhouse, but inside, I could practice being in the moment. The righteous, aloof attitude of Exxon's shareholders contrasted sharply with the warmth and compassion of the hard-luck ladies. I was witnessing a chasm between the "haves" and "have-nots" that was about more than money. It was about two starkly different societies: one that provided financial wealth for a few at the cost of poverty for many and a plundered planet, and another that was built on compassion and human-scale values and needs. Right there, I resolved to work toward a shift from a corporate, money-driven society to a human rights-based community.

It was after midnight before I was released. I walked out of the jailhouse into the moonlit night—and the arms of Patience.

We returned to Cordova in time to catch the last night of *Oliver.* Word had spread rapidly of our Dallas adventures. In the packed gym, townspeople embraced me as a hero. No one appreciated the captivating, creative performance that evening more than me. It felt wonderful to be home.

"WHAT HAPPENED, OTT?" Oesting roared into my phone the following Monday. After I duly reported the setup in Dallas, Oesting summoned the executive committee of lawyers and announced that they needed "to back the ground troops." Given permission to do so, Oesting hired a Texas lawyer to represent me and personally handled my case for two years as the hotel pressed charges of criminal trespass.

New Directions

In late summer before school started, Linden and I took the kids, dogs, two cars, and a load of wood to Alaganik Slough for a cookout. After hiking on the boardwalks and exploring along the riverbank, we set up camp at a picnic table by a river bend. Malani and Makena built a fire while we moved the cars a short distance away. As we settled down to the serious business of making jaffles, a flock of green-winged teal rocketed around the bend, hell-bent upriver. Makena mimed shooting them. Now that he had a hunting rifle, his interest in his kestrel had waned.

"Is Sam catching his share of fish?" I asked. An unexpected strong return of pinks had flooded the Sound in July.

"Yes!" said Linden. "We've been celebrating!"

"Let's all celebrate!" I said, banging on my mug of hot chocolate. "Okay, everybody: Good news only! I'll start. BP is gobbling up ARCO in the merger, but BP is not interested in drilling for oil on the Delta. Oil lease sale 79 is over!" We all cheered.

"Captain Joe is serving soup at Bean's Café!" said Malani.

Hazelwood would spend the next three summers at the soup kitchen in Anchorage, dishing up meals for the homeless to fulfill his 1,000 hours of community service.

"The Quinn family has an awesome heli-ski operation," Makena added. "They have some real pretty women skiers!"

"Makena!" We all shouted in unison. He just grinned.

In spring, the Quinn family had relocated their heli-operations from Valdez to the old disbanded Orca cannery. They catered to a new brand of tourists, wealthy extreme skiers who sought out Cordova's steep and deep powder slopes in the winter months. The Quinns livened up the town with their clients' antics and adrenaline-rushing stories. They also helped out at the ski hill and volunteered for search and rescue when avalanches buried people.

Linden popped two jaffles out of the irons and handed them to Makena and me. Malani set in two fresh sandwiches and put the iron back in the fire.

"We've seen the last of those big cruise ships," I said, munching away. "Just small ecotour ships from now on!"

Norwegian Cruise Lines had replaced the *Dynasty* with a ship nearly four times as large and way too deep drafted to sail into Orca Inlet. The company had set sail for bigger harbors.

"Aren't you going to speak at some big conference?" Linden asked.

"The Leopold legacy conference! It's to celebrate community-based conservation and the fifty-year anniversary of the publication of *A Sand County Almanac*." I said. "Dad and I are going together."

Through his teaching, writing, and life, Aldo Leopold had created an entire conservation ethic, the movement for wilderness and land preservation, and the roots of wildlife and land management in the United States. He was a lifelong hunter and fisherman.

"Tell your Dad I really liked that book," Makena chimed in.

"Makena, Dad was one of Aldo Leopold's last students! That's partly why I was invited to speak at this conference—to show how the Leopold legacy is passed between generations. The other part is the Watershed Project. It's leading the state in community-based tourism planning."

I took the jaffle irons out of the coals and handed the toasted sandwiches to Linden and Malani. Makena put in two more for himself.

"How's your book coming?" he asked.

"Well, it's getting more complicated. I think I stumbled onto a hornets' nest." The kids exchanged glances and looked back at me expectantly.

"Natalie Phillips with the *Anchorage Daily News* wrote a really good investigative article on sick workers on the spill memorial. I've been following her leads. I think she's on to something. It looks like the cleanup work made thousands of people sick—and Exxon covered it up."

"Riki," Linden said in her practical mother voice. "If Exxon wanted it covered up in 1989, do you think Exxon will want you uncovering it now?" She looked worried; the kids looked excited.

"Well, at least I'm going to call some of the medical doctors and lawyers in the records. It seems like a bunch of sick people will make a stronger case for a bunch of sick animals. I think it's all tied together somehow."

The kids grinned and confided in each other. "There will be stories" was their take on my new research angle. They would be right.

I went to move my car, signaling Malani to come with me. As we walked up to it, I told her to get in the driver's seat. She froze and stared at me.

"Go on!" I encouraged her. "This is your year to learn to drive. We might as well get started."

Malani settled into the seat. Her eyes were huge and glowing. I coached about reverse and the brake through the window. Cassie watched intently, a wise look of knowing on her dog face. Malani pulled up slowly to the picnic table as I walked alongside the car. When Makena saw his sister behind the wheel, he rocketed off the table.

"Mom! I want to learn to drive! I'm as tall as Malani!"

"Oh My God!" said Linden.

I grinned at my friend. "Opens up a whole new world, remember?"

We let each kid drive a car the five miles back to "the Road." It was a milestone picnic.

On Christmas day, half a world away, oil began to wash up on France's southern Brittany coast. Two weeks earlier, the tanker *Erika* had broken in two and sunk, spilling initially at least three million gallons of heavy fuel oil. The French government was poorly prepared for spill response. Local people, armed with putty knives, shovels, and buckets, mobilized to clean beaches and defend fishing and tourism livelihoods.

For us in Cordova, it felt like 1989 all over again. I paid particular attention to news stories of volunteers who complained of respiratory problems, skin rashes, and irritated eyes. Natalie had described the same symptoms with the *Exxon Valdez* cleanup workers.

In the wake of the *Erika*, thousands of French people protested for more protection from spills. Within three months, French oil companies, ship owners, and charter companies signed an agreement to ban single-hull tankers starting in 2008, eleven years earlier than originally planned and seven years ahead of the United States. Ironically, this international movement would eventually seal the change to double-hull tankers in the United States as well.

PART FOUR

NEW BEGINNINGS

2000–2008

---

*"We can't solve the climate crisis until
we solve the democracy crisis."*

AL GORE

CHAPTER THIRTEEN

LEAVING THE OIL AGE
2001–2006

The Set Up

"So you're going for June 2, 2006." Linden posed it matter-of-factly, rather than a question. "That's five years from now."

It was April 2001 and we were headed out "the Road" to Alaganik Slough to check out spring migrants. Our first stop was the kiosk at 10 Mile. En route I explained the latest twist in the saga to reopen the 1991 civil settlement for natural damages from the oil spill: Any party intending to make a claim had to file paperwork ninety days before the September 1, 2006, deadline—or on June 2 of that year.

"And no settlement has ever been reopened before." Again, Linden stated it as a fact.

I explained my motives for reopening the *Exxon Valdez* settlement: It would set legal precedent that low levels of oil can cause long-term harm to the environment. This, in turn, could trigger a chain reaction to tighten up all public policies regulating oil pollution and even to challenge continued oil use.

I explained my plan to meld the work of two nonprofit organizations: the Alaska Forum and the Alaska Community Action on Toxics. My friend Pam Miller, who had commissioned my original Sound Truth report in 1994, had started ACAT to advocate community health and reduce use of toxic chemicals. Pam was interested in helping workers who were sick from the cleanup. ACAT staff had researched spill-related toxic tort cases and effects on humans of oil and chemical products used on the cleanup.

Meanwhile, the Alaska Forum had received a grant to have lead scientists in the ecosystem studies write a "briefing paper" tying together all of their research findings of the past six years. I had read hundreds of technical papers, but there was no overall summary. I figured a line connecting all of the dots would clearly illustrate the unexpected—and unprecedented—finding that oil is more toxic to wildlife than previously thought. I also planned to interview a number of these scientists for my book. Using Linden's idea to "keep it simple," my plan was to tame the science by presenting it as a human story of discovery and to have the technical papers for backup.

"Sort of like *Silent Spring*," I explained to Linden as we turned into the pullout for the kiosk. We left the dogs in the car as we hopped out and scanned the ponds for action.

"Five years," said Linden. "Malani will graduate from college in June 2006! She hasn't even applied to colleges yet. I can't wrap my head around five years."

"Wrap your head around the 'shovelers' at the back of this pond," I said, peering through my binoculars. "This is a good start. Those are my favorite ducks!" The males had emerald green heads and chestnut flanks. Sunlight sparkled off their overlarge, wet bills that resembled shovels.

"What are those little guys over there?" I turned to look. In the pond across the road, a pair of horned grebes courted. As we watched, the pair reared up on their lobed toes and danced madly across the water surface, flaring their golden "horns" or feather tufts in an ancient mating ritual. "Cool!" said Linden as the birds dropped out of sight in the lily pads.

We counted three pairs of swans nesting on top of three different beaver lodges and saw a beaver swimming along with a freshly hewn alder branch in its mouth. After a last look around, we continued out "the Road."

"I've been reading some of the toxic tort cases."

Linden concentrated on dodging potholes in the road. "Is that what you've been doing in Anchorage?"

"Yeah."

I had spent days in the tiny windowless document room in the federal courthouse, reviewing records, and more days in the crowded state courthouse, scrolling through reels of microfiche. I focused on cases that ACAT had flagged as most useful for showing harm to the greater community of spill workers, not just the individuals who had sued.

From the cases, it seemed that exposure to benzene-laden vapors and clouds of crude oil droplets and oily mists had been a near universal experience for workers with skiff and beach jobs. I read about strange illnesses that wouldn't go away during the cleanup—respiratory problems, fatigue, and blazing headaches—and illnesses that developed after the cleanup, including brain fog that clouded the ability to think and concentrate, vicious mood swings, liver and kidney problems, debilitating chemical sensitivities, and increased susceptibility to colds and flu. These were the same complaints that callers had reported over the years.

The *Stubblefield* case was a gold mine of information. Garry Stubblefield had operated cranes on several barges during the 1989 cleanup until he was incapacitated by coughing, wheezing, and shortness of breath. Stubblefield believed his ailments were a direct result of breathing the oily mist, raining onto his cab from the rock-washing operation, and the diesel exhaust from generators. He had sued Exxon for occupational asthma.

His Anchorage lawyer had methodically unearthed Exxon's internal medical records and air quality monitoring data. The air quality records revealed that workers were exposed to levels of oil in the air that exceeded government safety standards. Exxon had successfully argued in court to seal the incriminating evidence to prevent people from finding it, but not before reporter Natalie Phillips had obtained copies for her investigative article. Another copy had been mailed anonymously to me.

"I read the case where Natalie Phillips found 6,722 workers had filed claims for respiratory illnesses. The court records were sealed from the public, but I've got the documents from it sitting on my bookshelf."

I tried to sound nonchalant so as not to alarm Linden. I quickly moved on.

"Anyway, 6,722 claims means two of every three workers who were actually out on the beaches got sick. Remember the 'Valdez Crud'?"

"Yes, Exxon said that was what people had—all the colds and flu that was going around during the cleanup." She stopped suddenly. "Are you saying it's something else?"

"Why would people still be calling me if they had a cold or flu in 1989? It's been eleven years. They shouldn't still sound all wheezy and stuffed up like Darth Vader."

Linden stared at me. "This is giving me a b-a-a-a-d feeling."

Ka-lunk! The car jolted as the right front tire dropped into a pothole.

"Jeez! *That* gave *me* a bad feeling! It went right up my spine. Dodge those suckers!"

"I'm trying!"

We turned down Alaganik Slough at 17 Mile. Linden drove slowly. We all stuck our heads out the windows to smell the sweet pungent cottonwood and willow buds. The dogs snorted and huffed the air.

"That's my favorite smell in the whole world!" I breathed deeply. *"Ummmmmm."*

"It makes me feel like dancing. It's spring!" A minute later, Linden pulled her head back inside. She looked concerned. "So what do you think happened to the workers?"

"The expert witness in the *Stubblefield* case is an occupational medicine doctor, Daniel Teitelbaum. He laid it all out in his deposition. He thinks the pressurized hot water wash created a splash back effect that bounced oil off the rocks and into the air where people breathed it."

"Exxon's worker safety program didn't protect people?"

"Teitelbaum tore Exxon's program apart." Teitlebaum's deposition revealed key reasons Exxon's program had failed. Nowhere near enough respirators for the beach crews. No training of supervisors to recognize the health threat from breathing fine oil particles. No training of workers to recognize that colds and flu could actually be symptoms of chemical poisoning. No reporting to the federal government of the high number of respiratory claims. No follow up of sick workers because Exxon refused to recognize that workers were sick—despite the fact that Exxon had records of thousands of people who got sick.

"How many sick workers are there now? How can they get better?"

"That's what I'm going to Dallas to find out."

"Dallas! I don't know if I can handle another Dallas adventure."

She pulled into a roadside cut and killed the engine. We were at the thinning edge of the spruce-hemlock forest where it gave way to open wetland and sweet-water ponds that changed size, depending on the tide. A strong flood tide would block the freshwater drainage and the ponds would swell, creating prime habitat for ducks and other waterbirds. The dirt road wound through the wetland for another 1.5 miles before it reached the river.

We shouldered our packs and let out the dogs. They shot off down the road after nothing in particular. *"Cassie! Bubby! Come back, you clowns. Stay with us!"* She looked at me.

"Oh, for heaven's sakes. This is all meant to be. Dr. Rea down in Dallas treated some of the cleanup workers. He's an environmental medicine doctor, one of the leaders in his field. I read his books. He specializes in chemical detox, eliminating poisons from the body. So my Dallas case from when I was arrested . . ."

"Oh, yeah! How's that going?"

"It's all connected. The hotel pressed charges. I passed a lie-detector test. The Texas judge scheduled a court hearing. The lawyers bought me a ticket to Dallas for the hearing. Then the hotel dropped the charges at the last minute. So I've got this ticket to Dallas!"

Linden shook her head in disbelief. "Just stay out of jail this time."

"That's exactly what Oesting said!"

We stopped to check out birds in a pond. Wigeons with bold white splashes down their foreheads paddled through grasses. Further out in the lily pads was a mixed flock of pintails and ring-necked ducks. A pair of trumpeter swans honked hoarsely overhead as they swung low to land near a flock of dusky Canada geese at the far edge of the pond.

We started walking again. "So, I've actually talked with some of these sick workers who filed court cases," I said. "There's this really nice grandmother, Phyllis La Joie. She goes by 'Dolly.' She was one of the 'decon' ladies who washed workers' clothes. She had a camera on the cleanup and she put a photo album together for her kids and grandkids. Exxon took the album at her deposition and didn't give it back. I'll bet it's got some incriminating photos. I'm going to try to help her get it back."

Linden was staring at me, her eyes widening in alarm.

"Then there's Ron Smith. He told me he couldn't talk because of a gag order, but he said 'something funny' happened in his case. He told me to review the records. He also said I should check out Dr. Rea's clinic because he thinks Dr. Rea saved his life."

I turned to look at Linden. She had stopped dead in her tracks about ten feet back. Her face was ashen. I ran back to her.

"Riki! Gag orders, stolen photo albums, sick people, sealed records, incriminating evidence sitting on your bookshelf—*Are you nuts?* Alyeska tapped your phone over a lot less last time. They're going to kill you."

"Jeez, calm down! I thought that was only a figure of speech about someone going pale. You actually are!" The dogs came rushing up to see what the fuss was about.

"We have to do something to protect you!"

"Jeez, you and Yosh. That's what she said, too."

"She did? I wish she was here right now so we could talk."

"She's coming up in two weeks for Shorebird Festival."

Linden looked relieved. Color returned to her face. We set off birding again only this time we talked about Malani and her music. Bearfoot Bluegrass was planning to record its first CD during the summer and Linden was just as excited as if the CD was her own.

By August my phone was acting strangely again. We implemented our plan. I put on a nice shirt and vest to look professorial. I brought my research over to the O'Toole's home, where Linden had set up a video camera. For an hour I described the sick worker saga, replete with backup documents. The story had grown. In its literature review, ACAT had found medical studies that linked exposure to oil mist and fine oil particles in humans and animals with a host of maladies, including respiratory damage; central nervous system disorders; liver, kidney, and blood disorders; immune suppression; and endocrine (hormone) disruption.

Also in its literature review, ACAT had found that respiratory problems and skin, blood, and kidney disorders were linked with exposure to an active ingredient in several products used on the cleanup. This included Exxon's dispersant Corexit 9527, Exxon's experimental fertilizer Inipol EAP22, and the household cleaner Simple Green. The active ingredient, 2-butoxyethanol, is a known human health hazard, which the EPA recognizes as a "fetal-toxin." Corexit 9527 and Inipol were sprayed on beaches despite safety warnings to prevent product from entering sewers, low areas, and watercourses. Cleanup workers had used Simple Green by the gallon to wash skiffs, skin, rain gear, and personal clothing.

During the videotaping session, I told stories of workers whom I had contacted and interviewed like Donnie Moeller and Captain Richard Nagel, who had been exposed to Inipol and were horribly sick. Workers who sprayed Inipol had been discharged when they tested positive for blood in the urine, an indication of overexposure. Exxon was apparently aware of the health dangers of Inipol and the dispersants: I had found in the court records a liability waiver that Exxon circulated. The waiver "absolutely and irrevocably" released Exxon from any damages stemming from the spill and cleanup. Further, sometime after the cleanup officially ended in 1992, Exxon had quietly discontinued use of Inipol.

Early into the interview, Makena and a pack of his friends had burst into the home. They had frozen in their tracks when they saw us, questions radiating from their heads. They had stayed to observe the interview. When it was over, the boys leaped up, all talking at once about how my story had reminded them of the film *Erin Brockovich*. Makena gave me a high five as the pack thundered out of the house.

"Humph," said Linden as she packed away the video. "Let's hope this ends like *Erin Brockovich* and not like *Silkwood!*"

I made ten copies of the video and my key documents. Then I mailed packages with cover letters to Erin Brockovich at Masry & Vititoe and the *Los Angeles Times*, among others. I spoke openly of my activities on my suspect phone line, but I never disclosed the targets of my mailings. A week later, I followed up by calling each of the ten targets from different public phones around town to ensure privacy. The *Los Angeles Times* promised an investigative piece. Erin Brockovich herself began to work with ACAT to recruit sick workers for a potential lawsuit.

A month later, the twin towers in New York shattered, along with the nation's sense of security. 9/11 stories filled the news as Americans struggled to understand and adjust our worldview.

Less than two months later, on November 5, the *Los Angeles Times* ran its story, "Exxon Spill's Cleanup Workers Share Years of Crippling Illness." For about two weeks, media called from around the world. One reporter told me, "This would be the biggest story in the news right now if it wasn't for 9/11." Congressional staff inquired about health precautions for the 9/11 workers who were starting to experience the same respiratory symptoms described in the *Los Angeles Times* article. After that, all went quiet again. ACAT and I persisted with our work.

Convergence

"This whole scene is surreal!" I whispered to Linden. "I don't remember high school graduation being a big deal. But now I understand what my parents went through!"

It was late May and I was sitting with Sam and Linden at the high school gym in the section reserved for parents. Linden and Sam had decided that meant godparents, too. They were teary-eyed as they watched their daughter, the class valedictorian, sing a song she had written for this occasion. When the scholarships and schools were announced, Malani's acceptance at Stanford with a hefty four-year scholarship brought down the house. Townspeople knew that loss of fish bucks and Exxon's default on its promise to make people whole had crushed many college dreams for Cordova's generation of spill children. Each dream fulfilled made everyone feel good. This confident young woman had graced the town with her cheerful nature and music from the heart and now she, and many of the other graduates, were poised to leave. It was a bittersweet celebration.

Shortly after the seniors' graduation, I planned to travel once again to Dallas, this time to speak at Rea's twentieth-annual conference on chemical illnesses. During our initial meeting the previous year, we had become mutual fans of each other's work. After listening carefully to my stories of sick people and sick wildlife, he had said, "When you have sick workers and you have sick animals, and they are sick because of the same chemical, then you have the strongest evidence possible that the chemical is causing the problem." His words had guided my research.

The human story had grown again: The federal government was also at fault for what happened during the 1989 cleanup. Exxon's faulty worker safety program had slid through the regulatory bulwark supposedly designed to protect workers. The Alaska Forum and ACAT had hired a summer intern, Annie O'Neill, a medical student from Yale. She had found deep in the thick government (OSHA) regulations a one-sentence exemption for reporting colds and flu as work-related illnesses. Rea confirmed that early symptoms of chemical poisoning by inhalation could mimic cold and flu symptoms. A human body only has a limited number of ways to say it's sick.

The single exemption allowed Exxon to dodge the injury and illness reporting requirements for 6,722 respiratory illness claims. The nonreporting sabotaged federal regulators' efforts to evaluate Exxon's worker safety program and assess worker health care needs. Not knowing thousands of workers were sick, federal officials erroneously concluded there was "no basis for recommending long-term medical surveillance of the health of the workers involved in the cleanup of the oil spill."

We also found out that the federal (OSHA) chemical exposure standards could not deliver on the promise of health protection. The OSHA standard for toxic, carcinogenic crude oil mist was based on purified, nontoxic mineral oil! The OSHA standard for highly toxic crude oil aerosols was based on "nuisance dust." Dust! In his deposition, Dr. Teitelbaum had pointed out that neither of the government-approved surrogates had the immuno-toxic or carcinogenic properties of crude oil mists and particles. In other words, the government safety standards protected workers against exposure to mineral oil and dust—not crude oil mist and aerosols.

We learned the OSHA injury and illness coding system had been designed to protect farm and factory workers from physical injuries in the 1970s when little was known about the symptoms of chemical-induced illnesses. When qualifying illnesses reported by cleanup workers, data coders with no medical training had lumped headaches, dizziness, burning eyes, ear- and nosebleeds, and other classic symptoms of central nervous system damage from inhalation of crude oil and solvents as "undefined illnesses." Medical doctors and worker compensation boards relied on guides that did not rate illnesses and impairments from chemical-induced illnesses. Under such an outdated system, illnesses from the cleanup were misdiagnosed as colds and flu and disregarded by doctors, courts of law, and health care institutions.

Of course, if OSHA could not accurately diagnose, treat, or compensate workers who suffered harm from chemical poisons during one disaster like the oil spill, OSHA would also fail to adequately protect workers from chemical exposure during other disasters like 9/11 as leaders involved with that tragedy had realized.

The human aspects of the oil spill story wound into the wildlife story. Before I left for Dallas, I practiced my "sick wildlife" talk on Linden. By comparison, my "sick worker" talk was relatively straightforward and I felt the audience, some 300 people, including medical doctors, academics, and persons with chemical sensitivities, would have no trouble understanding it. But the briefing paper written by the scientists pointed to a new discovery in the field of oil "ecotoxicology" and I needed to make sense of this to the audience.

We were having a late lunch at the Lighthouse, a specialty bakery and restaurant owned by Lisa Marie and Glenn. The fishermen were out fishing, so it was quiet. The girls played outside where Glenn was cutting alder for the brick oven. Zak was helping his mother clean up and prep for the next day. They drifted in and out of our conversation.

"E-co-tox-i-col-o-gy," Linden counted. "That's seven syllables! Why can't scientists just use simple English if they want people to understand what they've discovered?" Zak guffawed.

"Okay, so toxicology is the science of poisons and their effects on the body. Ecology, you know: it's the study of relationships between animals and their habitat. So eco-toxicology is . . ."

Linden made a stab at it. ". . . the study of effects of pollution on animals and their habitat."

"Bingo! Oil pollution in this case. The ecosystem studies point to a paradigm shift in this field."

"You just lost me!" Lisa Marie hollered from the kitchen.

"Okay, this is like the Holy Grail of science," I explained. "Science isn't absolute. It's based on observations and models to explain relationships. In other words, it's all theories. So when models are found that better match an observation, then science advances. That's a paradigm shift, a new understanding of the world."

"What's an example?" asked Zak, listening quietly as he wiped tables. He had just finished his freshman year of high school.

"Oh. Well, scientists once believed that the world was flat, but all the theories had to shift once Columbus sailed around the world." Zak grunted in agreement.

"So are you saying that the scientists can explain what happened in the Sound? Why the salmon collapsed? Why the herring disappeared?" Linden asked.

Lisa Marie came into the dining room with her cutting board, bowls, two knives, and a pile of vegetables. Zak washed his hands to help his mother chop.

"Yes, but hang on. So in the 1970s, scientists used these lab tests called bioassays to test oil toxicity and set standards for water quality. Seawater with oil dissolved in it was put in beakers. Little sea creatures were added to the beakers. Scientists counted how many lived or died in ninety-six hours. Four days. From this, scientists used models to predict what levels of oil were dangerous for sea life. Other chemicals were tested with bioassays and these studies became the basis for the Clean Water Act."

"That's dumb," said Zak. "Four days is nothing."

I nodded in agreement. "Four-day bioassays aren't good tests for a lot of reasons. They leave out the parts of oil that don't dissolve in seawater—the black stuff we still have on our beaches! The tests use mostly adult animals, not young ones that are more sensitive to pollutants. And there are a lot more subtle measures than death that warn when a chemical is dangerous.

"Anyway, based on bioassays, scientists in the 1970s believed that oil didn't cause long-term harm. They believed it was a quick-acting poison that caused narcosis in high doses."

"The medical doctors ought to understand that," said Lisa Marie. "But I'm not sure I do."

"Remember the dizzy seals in 1989? They were breathing oil vapors and the vapors acted like a narcotic. It knocked the seals out. If a seal can't get to the surface to breathe, it dies."

"Maybe that's what happened to the whales, too," said Linden sadly.

"Most likely," I said. "But we didn't have any whale carcasses like we had seal and sea otter carcasses. Autopsies showed their brains were fried, burned from the oil vapors."

"I just remember the oil-soaked birds and otters. I thought they died of hypothermia," said Lisa Marie.

"I don't remember anything," said Zak. "I was too little."

"This is grossing me out," Linden announced. "And bringing back horrible memories."

"Hold on!" I said. "The new science isn't so graphic.

"Animals died in 1989 because of poison and hypothermia. That was expected based on the models. But scientists expected the killing to stop in

1989 and things to recover. That didn't happen—as we know now. The ecosystem studies were designed to interpret the new observations that oil caused lingering harm. So here comes the paradigm shift."

"Are the ecosystem studies connected to NOAA's new beach surveys that I read about in the paper?" asked Lisa Marie. "Where they found tons of oil still buried on beaches?"

"In a roundabout way," I explained. "The oil buried on the beaches includes P-A-Hs, the polycyclic aromatic hydrocarbons that the cleanup workers breathed. Scientists took a closer look at these PAHs and found that PAHs do not dissolve in seawater. PAHs stick around in the environment and they affect wildlife in very low amounts. PAHs act inside cells to disrupt synthesis and function of proteins, hormones, and even the basic coding of life, DNA."

"Okay, now I'm sure that means something to medical doctors," said Lisa Marie, "but what did you just say?"

I took a breath. "It means low levels of PAHs kill pink salmon and herring eggs. PAHs deform and kill developing salmon and herring embryos. PAHs stunt growth in young pink salmon and other wildlife, because young bodies have to shunt energy to make enzymes to break down the poison instead of use energy to grow. PAHs disrupt the ability of pink salmon and herring to produce viable offspring."

"Viable offspring?" echoed Zak.

"Healthy eggs that survive to become healthy adults. So the pink salmon crashed in 1992 and 1993 because the spill killed a lot of eggs and juveniles, and the ones that survived couldn't produce as many eggs—or the eggs they did produce didn't survive in the oiled streams."

There was a collective, "Oh."

I continued my litany. "Harlequin ducks that eat oil-soaked mussels starved in the winter, because their bodies shunt energy to make enzymes to breakdown the poison instead of using energy from food to survive. River otters starved because PAHs disrupt the synthesis of heme. Without heme for hemoglobin, blood can't carry oxygen and otters can't catch fast-swimming fish."

I paused. All three were staring at me. Chopped vegetables were heaped in bowls.

"So the fishermen were right," Lisa Marie concluded. "Prince William Sound is a 'dead zone' just like what we said during the blockade in 1993."

"I'd say it was a dead zone then, but after that, wildlife slowly started to recover on some beaches, especially ones that were only lightly oiled in 1989. That's why NOAA scientists started the beach survey to find where the oil is and how much is still there. Since oil makes wildlife sick and less likely to survive, it makes sense that fish and birds and animals are going to take longest to recover on the most heavily oiled beaches."

"Why are salmon recovering and not herring?" asked Linden.

"Herring are a good example of ecotoxicology," I explained. "Herring live around eleven years and are the basis of the food web in the Sound. Seals, seabirds, whales, sea lions, halibut, and more, all prefer herring. Herring are nice oily fish that school, so predators can get a lot of calories for a little effort. Since the collapse, the trouble seems to be that predators are eating herring as fast as they're produced. Evelyn Brown calls it a 'predator pit.' There's no buildup of the population. It's stuck at 16,000 to 20,000 tons, barely enough to sustain the ecosystem and no surplus for us to fish. We haven't even begun to replace that 100,000 tons we lost after the spill."

"But why did herring collapse four years after the spill?" Linden asked.

"They didn't. The collapse started with young fish right after the spill. The oil wiped out the 1989 eggs and larvae. But it took four years for the survivors to become adults. So we didn't see this loss until 1993. Neither did the scientists who used an older computer model to predict herring returns. But the Science Center started using hydro-acoustic surveys in 1993 to monitor herring. After a decade of collecting data, the Science Center was able to use its model to see back in time; it's called hindcast. The Science Center confirmed the herring collapse started with young fish in 1989."

Acoustic surveys (1993–2007) and acoustic survey hindcasts (1986–1992)

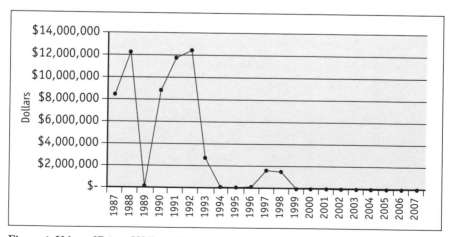

Figure 1. Value of Prince William Sound Herring Harvest, 1987–2007
Source: ADFG Annual Management Report, Prince William Sound, 2006 (www.sf.adfg.state.ak.us/FedAidPDFs/fmr08–30.pdf)

track real population and show the oil spill was a major factor in the herring population collapse. Acoustic surveys show loss of adult fish from 1990 through 1993 when young fish killed by oil failed to show up as adults. The older method of predicting herring, based on a computer model, overestimated the adult population between 1989 and 1992 because this model did not take into account the increased mortality of young fish from the oil spill. When young fish born in 1989 failed to show up as adults in 1993, the computer model simply adjusted for the missing adult fish. The "1993" collapse shown by the computer model is an artifact of this model.

"What about the herring disease outbreaks?" Linden asked.

"Well, that's another problem. Some scientists found that PAHs weaken young herring by suppressing their immune system. So when the sickly young survivors joined the adults in 1993, there was a disease outbreak that wiped out the fish—and it kept rolling through the population for a number of years after that."

"Well, this all makes sense," said Linden. "It fits what we're seeing in the Sound. But how can Exxon say everything is recovered?"

Here was my chance to explain once again how Exxon had manipulated its studies to hide the effects of its oil spill. Since 1994, when I had lost my audience in a statistical wasteland, I had found easier explanations. I proceeded with caution.

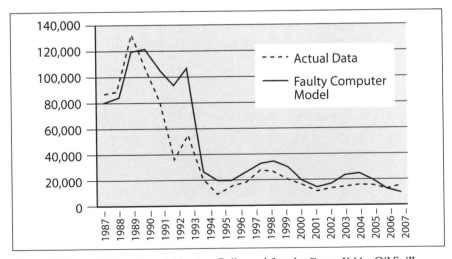

Figure 2. Prince William Sound Herring Collapse After the *Exxon Valdez* Oil Spill
Adapted and updated with permission from Richard Thorne and Gary Thomas, "Herring and the Exxon Valdez Oil Spill: An Investigation into Historical Data Conflicts," International Council for the Exploration of the Sea (ICES) Journal of Marine Science 65 (1): 44–50, 2008.

"Conclusions like 'everything is recovered' are only as strong as the study itself. Studies can be designed to find things or to hide things, like proof of oil effects. I believe Exxon's studies were biased to hide things."

"Can you give us some simple examples?" asked Linden. "Simple."

"Sure. Exxon used averages to hide effects. Exxon took seawater samples to see if the amount of oil dissolved in seawater was high enough to kill sea life."

"That wasn't obvious?" asked Lisa Marie.

"Wait for the abracadabra! Levels were high enough at the surface and immediately under the slick, but not outside the path of the slick and not down deep under the slick. So Exxon took lots of samples from areas where there wasn't any oil. Then, they averaged lots of zeros with a few high numbers and—*Abracadabra!* The average was below the state's water quality standard, so Exxon claimed its studies found no basis for harm from the spill."

"That's so lame," said Zak.

"Yeah, Exxon's trying everything right now to ignore the black stuff on the beaches, the PAHs, and discredit the NOAA study."

"How can Exxon hide all the animals that died on the beaches?" Linden asked.

"Oh, by asking the wrong questions. Like for sea otters, Exxon studied if animals were producing pups on oiled beaches. Well, yes, sea otters were having pups, but the babies weren't surviving. They still aren't on heavily oiled beaches. Exxon didn't look to see if the pups lived. Sea otter pups feed close to shore. Where there's buried oil, they eat oiled shellfish and they die."

The audience looked shocked, disgusted, and intrigued, but not confused. I decided to test another example.

"Exxon played games with pooling data, too. They would count and identify all the animals and sea plants on a square meter of beach. Some animals, like certain species of worms and limpets, are real sensitive to oil, while other species thrive on polluted beaches. So, when Exxon found lots of the sensitive species on clean beaches and lots of the other kind on oiled beaches, they just lumped everything together. Worms and limpets on all beaches! No problem! You can see why pooling data is a statistical no-no."

The audience groaned. "That's like cheating with science!" said Zak.

"There's actually a book called *How to Lie with Statistics*," I said. "Pooling data is a classic example of how to lie with statistics. But here's my favorite trick. Last one, okay? So, beyond the worms and limpets, wildlife on oiled beaches was pretty devastated by the spill, right?

"Wiped out," said Lisa Marie.

"Right. So, here's the trick. If Exxon could find clean beaches with hardly any wildlife to compare to oiled beaches with hardly any wildlife, then by comparison oiled beaches wouldn't look so bad."

"Clean beaches with hardly any animals?" asked Lisa Marie. "Where would that be?"

"Up near the glaciers," I said, "where the water's cold, silty, and not so salty. By choosing glacial beaches for controls, Exxon actually concluded wildlife are thriving on oiled beaches."

"That makes me mad," said Linden, "that Exxon would deceive people like that."

"You?! I've been reading Exxon's junk science for nine years and trying to explain it to the press," I said. "But, no! The press prefers to focus on the controversy rather than the facts."

"You need to talk at the high school," said Zak.

"You need to finish your book!" said Lisa Marie.

"Jeez, I'm working on it! I'm really close to tying together the human story and the wildlife story. Zak, what year do you take marine biology?"

"Junior year."

"Then, I'll be there your junior year. Now, I think I'm ready for those medical doctors!"

Coalition-Building

In fall 2003, I gave a talk on the oil spill legacy to Zak's marine biology class. During the preceding 18 months, I had found the link between sick workers and sick wildlife. The EPA had listed twenty-two PAHs as "persistent, bioaccumulative, and toxic pollutants."

"Persistent" in the sense that PAHs are hard for bacteria to break down so they stick around in the environment as we had seen with the buried oil in the Sound.

"Bioaccumulative," meaning that PAHs are picked up by animals and people and passed through the food web.

"Toxic" in the sense that PAHs make people and animals sickly and less able to survive and thrive.

The EPA based this listing on scientific evidence of PAH effects on animals and the general populace, including children.

The EPA's list also includes lead, dioxin, mercury, DDT, and PCBs. All of these chemicals are known to persist in air, water, soil, and food. They "can build up in the food chain to levels that are harmful to humans and ecosystems," according to the EPA. Further, the EPA stated these pollutants "are associated with a range of adverse human health effects, including the nervous system, reproductive and developmental problems, cancer, and genetic impacts."

The biggest source of PAHs in our environment, I had found to my surprise, is not oil spills: It is burning fossil fuels in our vehicles and coal- and oil-fired power plants. The National Research Council reported that over 90 percent of PAHs in our air, rivers, and coastal seas come from exhaust particles. The PAHs' ultrafine particles are spewed into the air, deposited on land by rain and snow, and carried into rivers and coastal seas by runoff.

Medical doctors linked low levels of PAHs in urban traffic with asthma, depression, and chemical sensitivities. The latter is a new illness in which people's bodies literally become overwhelmed by chemicals present at low levels in our environment. The world becomes toxic and deadly.

The same illnesses were the leading symptoms reported by oil spill cleanup workers by our former intern Annie O'Neill, working independently to complete her master's thesis at Yale, and by another one of our interns in a separate study. Based on O'Neill's thesis, I estimated around 2,500 to 3,000 oil spill workers may be sick from Exxon's cleanup.

Meanwhile, the team of scientists who had written the summary of the spill science prepared an expanded and more technical version for the popular *Science* magazine. Word of the paradigm shift rattled the scientific community, media, and oil industry like a powerful earthquake. All the research added up to show that laws designed to protect public health, workers, and the environment from toxic effects of oil were no longer adequate. Years later, they still need to be updated based on the new science. Further, the evidence pointed to the need to reduce oil use, because even small amounts of PAHs could harm people and wildlife.

The press finally locked on to the $100 million reopener as the drive for Exxon's "slippery science." While the face of the media battles appeared to be over oil on beaches, the heart of it was over continued oil use. Reopening the case would mean acknowledging that oil is more toxic than we thought. It would mean that laws need to be changed to protect public health, workers, and the environment. And, really, it would mean that we need to get off oil, that we need to find an energy source that wouldn't kill us. Reopening the case would affect ExxonMobil's operations and profits, and those of the entire oil industry, worldwide.

After my talk, Zak and another student approached me. "Riki, we want to help."

I looked at the young determined faces and didn't have the heart to turn them down.

On the fifteenth memorial of the spill in March 2004, a group of Alaskans descended on Washington, D.C., to share the *Exxon Valdez* legacy with congressional delegates, government agencies, science institutions, and media. Zak and two other Cordova high school boys explained oil spill effects on wildlife. The boys had finished an independent research project and they were completely at ease discussing their findings with top-level policy-makers.

With the innocence of youth, they posed a simple question that no one could answer: "If you know oil is this toxic, why don't you change the laws to protect *us*?" The policies would be harder to change than the science for reasons that I was just beginning to unravel.

In May, a small group of girlfriends gathered at the O'Toole home to celebrate Linden's birthday and completion of my book manuscript. It was the first salmon opener of the season and Makena's first opener fishing his own boat and permit. Linden was a wreck of worry.

Mid-meal, Makena called. His voice boomed over the phone. "*Mom! This is the best day of my life! I was born to do this!*" Linden beamed. "But, Mom, I ran aground on a sandbar and I have to wait on the tide. I saved a king salmon for you, but it will be tomorrow morning early before I'm home. Don't worry!"

When he hung up, Linden burst into happy tears. "This is the best birthday present! He thought to call his mother!" Makena would miss his high school graduation in two weeks. He would be fishing.

Meanwhile, Yale's environmental law clinic had found several legal angles to pursue reopening the settlement and incorporating the new science into public policies. Yale students also emphasized the need for a constituency to advocate the reopener in the face of unwilling federal and state administrations. With the help of Lisa Marie, whom I had hired as an assistant, we launched a tour through twenty-five states and Washington, D.C., stopping at universities, elementary through high schools, bookstores, and regulatory agencies, and at meetings of citizen organizations, labor unions, and church groups. The plan was to build a constituency by making people aware of the problem in hopes they then would take action.

In November, I gave the first lecture of the six-month book tour at the University of Washington School of Law. My talk inspired Professor Bill

Rodgers and his students to take up where the Yale Law Clinic had left off. They worked to refine the legal arguments to reopen the case, while I made my way around the country.

Six months later in May 2005, sitting in a sunny corner of my home in Cordova, I listened by telephone as University of Washington law students made their case to reopen the *Exxon Valdez* settlement. It made statewide news in Washington and Alaska. This helped alert people to the opportunity, but the political odds were still stacked against reopening the case.

Meanwhile, another issue related to oil use had blossomed in the public consciousness: global climate change. People wanted to transition off oil and coal, which were linked to a warming planet. During my tour, I had seen dozens of backyard, local, and regional efforts across the nation to reduce oil use and develop clean energy. Fourth and fifth graders could explain hands-on biofuel projects. There were high school classes on solar power and converting diesel cars to biodiesel. "Green" building projects at universities minimized heat and water waste and maximized use of recycled nontoxic material. Entire universities campaigned to reduce "carbon footprints" by slashing oil use. California was pressing for tough new limits on greenhouse gas emissions by cars and trucks. Coalitions of states were initiating efforts to cap regional greenhouse gas emissions and reduce greenhouse emissions from power plants.

What I did not see during my tour was any effort by the federal government or the George W. Bush administration to reduce oil use or even to acknowledge the connection between oil use and climate change. The media, however, had linked the administration's reluctance to change our energy future with political influence from oil companies. Under public scrutiny, the oil companies were slowly stepping forward to acknowledge the global risk from oil use. All except one.

In May, *Mother Jones* reported that ExxonMobil had "pumped more than $8 million into more than forty think tanks, media outlets, and consumer, religious, and even civil rights groups that preach skepticism about the oncoming climate catastrophe." People were furious. ExxonMobil was making record profits at the expense of the planet and future generations.

I regrouped to tap into the grassroots movement to reduce oil use and this well of public outrage against ExxonMobil. In fall 2005, I launched a national petition drive through my tour network to ask the federal government to reopen the settlement and hold Exxon accountable. To increase our odds of success, I also helped initiate similar campaigns within the state through the

Oiled Regions of Alaska Foundation, a new community foundation, and, separately, a coalition of environmental groups.

Mission Accomplished

Shifts happen when old habits change. Sometimes small things can trigger big changes. Leaving the Oil Age will take changing oil habits. One key habit to change is the old belief that oil is a benign substance that can safely power our global society's energy future. Scientists and medical doctors who are not blinded by oil-industry dollars know that small amounts of oil derived from human activities and deposited in air, water, and soil are toxic to life on the planet. Oil and coal are not benign substances: The health risks outweigh the benefits of relying on fossil fuels to power our future.

In March 2006, the EVOS Trustee Council listed only nine of twenty-four species of wildlife and habitat originally injured by the spill as "recovered." Pacific herring and pigeon guillemots (seabirds) were still not recovering at all, seventeen years after the spill. Harbor seals and mammal-eating orca whales had not recovered from their spill losses. Overall, the Sound was still experiencing measurable effects from the spill and there is still literally tons of oil buried on the beaches, a potent toxic land mine for decades to come.

In May, public health, labor, business, and environmental groups representing nearly four million Americans petitioned the federal government to reopen the *Exxon Valdez* case and hold Exxon accountable for lingering harm. Dozens of communities, representing the majority of voters in Alaska, asked the State to do the same.

On June 1, the U.S. Justice Department and the State of Alaska announced they would seek $92 million from ExxonMobil to try to remove buried oil from beaches.

Eighty-nine days later, one day short of the September 1 deadline, the governments issued a formal request to reopen the settlement and have ExxonMobil pay for unanticipated injury from its oil spill.

In hindsight, I believe the federal and state administrations made the call for political, rather than scientific, reasons. Under duress of sinking voter confidence and upcoming elections, I think the governments bent to the peoples' wishes. The decentralized approach of the community foundation in mobilizing towns, boroughs, and Native tribes across the state, along with constant pressure from the environmental coalition and interest from millions of Americans, was a winning combination. From the public's perspective, holding Exxon accountable was the politically correct thing to do. ExxonMobil had become the company that everyone loved to hate for its denial of global climate change.

(As of the writing of this book, the federal and state governments have failed to collect the $92 million from ExxonMobil.)

The next day, on September 1, I turned my full attention to another issue that was boiling over. The fishermen of Prince William Sound were fed up with Exxon's stalling on the private damages litigation.

CHAPTER FOURTEEN

A NEW SPECIES
OF TROUBLE
2006–2007

The growing unrest in Cordova was palpable. A large part of the fleet had converged in town for Labor Day weekend, some to spend time with families, others to put away their boats and gear for the winter, still others to resupply for the silver season.

People were fed up with waiting for the Ninth Circuit to make a ruling in the *Exxon Valdez* case. Energy jumped between groups of gathered fishermen like lightning between clouds. People were primed, ready for action. The buzz in town was Bill Black's latest idea: a reenactment of the Valdez Narrows blockade staged in Orca Inlet, because holding up tanker traffic was now out of the question due to 9/11 and Homeland Security.

After peppering the fleet with his idea, Bill asked me to "help" organize the event. At a hastily called meeting, sketchy ideas were shared in a circle of spill survivors, and tossed and reworked until they sprouted into a solid plan. Willing hands set to work with donated sheets, posters, paint, and a coffin, while others bent minds to writing press releases, public notices, and short statements.

Three days later, on a sunny Saturday afternoon, some 200 people gathered at the Fisherman's Memorial in the harbor. Mayor Tim Joyce told the crowd, "We all remember the *Exxon Valdez* oil spill. We all know our punitive damage case is sitting in the Ninth Circuit because of Exxon's appeals. We all know this community and the commercial fishermen have been harmed by the spill and not made whole as Exxon promised seventeen years ago."

As the mayor spoke, the crowd swelled. Finally, over 400 people—fishermen, families, friends, and even curious tourists—filed down the docks to boats. The harbor roared to life as 100 workboat engines fired up.

I stood in the wheelhouse of the *Alaskan Pacific*, a seventy-foot Louisiana-converted Gulf of Mexico mud boat, as we funneled through the harbor entrance. Our emcee boat idled as spaghetti-like lines of gillnetters slowly joined into one long string that stretched from the old Coast Guard dock out into Orca Inlet.

The *Alaskan Pacific* moved slowly in front of the line of rafted boats and cut her engines. Ross Mullins, Patience Andersen Faulkner, myself, young Robert Masolini, and others wove our story of empty promises and injustice into future actions to protect our community and industry. The story was relayed via cell phone to the local radio station and broadcast live to the community. Boat engines revved, horns blared, and cars honked from the dock in applause.

In closure, boats circled the *Alaskan Pacific* as Ross and the crew heaved the coffin overboard. The coffin represented over 6,000 plaintiffs who died before justice was served. It sank amid a shower of fireworks, leaving a wreath and white lilies floating in its wake.

Justice Denied

Earlier in the year in January, a panel of three judges on the Ninth Circuit Court of Appeals heard oral arguments for the second time on the amount of punitive damages in the *Exxon Valdez* case. This was Exxon's lone surviving appeal after seventeen years of legal wrangling. Since 1999, courts had ruled against Exxon's charge of jury tampering in the bullet incident and against Exxon's attempt to bar punitive damages under the Clean Water Act. There would be no new trial and punitive damages would be allowed. Twice, the Ninth Circuit had vacated the entire award and returned it to the district court with an order to reduce it. Twice, Judge Holland had defended the jury award in his court. Judge Holland's final decision—$4.5 billion plus interest—had sat for two years in the lap of the Ninth Circuit Court of Appeals, simply waiting for a hearing.

Cordova fishermen held a candlelight vigil on the courthouse steps in San Francisco the night before the January hearing. The past seven years had been particularly brutal, emotionally, as the courts worried the punitive award like dogs tussling over a stick. Fishermen had watched their claims vanish and be reinstated, and then shrink by 11 percent when the Ninth Circuit decided the Seattle Seven and six other processors were entitled to a share of the award even though Exxon would pocket this money.

The town had taken a roller-coaster ride from its rank among the top ten seaports in the nation before the spill (based on ex-vessel value), to a low

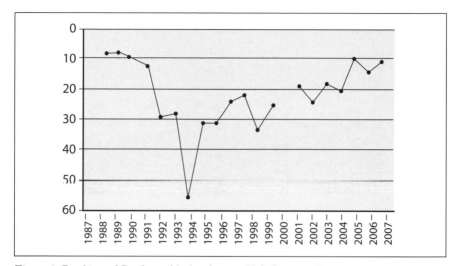

Figure 3. Ranking of Cordova, Alaska, Among U.S. Seaports Based on Value of Commercial Fishery Harvest, 1987–2007

Source: U.S. Department of Commerce, NOAA, National Marine Fisheries Service, "Fisheries of the United States," by value and year, www.st.nmfs.noaa.gov/st1/commercial/landings/lport_yeard.html (accessed July 24, 2008). NOTE: Year 2000 data is intentionally blank. Cordova was not listed in NOAA's rankings that year.

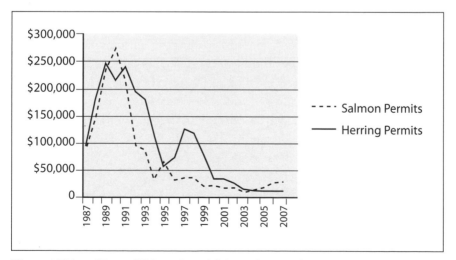

Figure 4. Value of Prince William Sound Salmon Seine and Herring Seine Permits, 1987–2007

Source: ADFG, Alaska Commercial Fisheries Entry Commission, PWS salmon purse seine (www. cfec.state.ak.us/bit/x_s01e.htm); PWS herring roe purse seine (www.cfec.state.ak.us/bit/x_g01e.htm)

of fifty-one in 1993 when the salmon and herring runs collapsed, to back up in the top ten in 2005. Fishermen who had tickets to ride in 1989 had lost hundreds of thousands of dollars in devalued herring and salmon seine permits—their retirement security. Those who bought into the fisheries well after the spill capitalized on seine permits worth under $30,000 or less than 10 percent of the pre-spill values. The pink salmon fishery adjusted for oil spill losses, market changes in Asia, and an influx of farmed fish. Permit prices and fish prices reflected the new reality. The herring fishery remained closed, a source of bitter disappointment for those who reaped no return on their investment.

In their indomitable style, fishermen joked that a highliner used to be a number-one fisherman. Now a highliner was someone whose wife had a job. But in a growing number of cases, money from extra jobs was consumed in the conflagration of growing fisheries debt that exceeded individual shares of the *Exxon Valdez* punitive damage award, even at the full five billion dollars. And the spill had cost so much more than money.

Fishermen John Platt was one of those cases. His once highly prized, herring-seine permit was strangling him financially. When the herring fishery remained closed, year after year, the original debt from John's fishing permits had swelled alarmingly in size as his fisheries' earnings had shrunk. He was forced to cut a deal with Scrooge. He signed over his fishing boat, all of his permits, including ones that were fully paid off, and his entire punitive damage award to the unrelenting State of Alaska to avoid bankruptcy. He lost his wife and sons to Oregon and his home to debt. He wrote letters to newspapers and legislators, pleading his case. He didn't want a handout. He wanted the simple dignity of a job, a home, and a family. He wanted the state to take no more than it had already grabbed. His position was perilous. Any reduction of the punitive award would make bankruptcy inevitable.

Debt was drowning the Maxwell family as well. I learned pieces of Robbie and Cindy's story while working with their son Matt on his sophomore science project, a documentary film on the spill. At fifteen, Matt was already a seasoned fisherman. He gillnetted with his father and dreamed of seining when he turned sixteen, which is the earliest his parents would allow him to fish on other people's boats. He sought to understand the unwelcome guest in his family life—something he had grown up hearing about; something that happened before he was born. The guest had stolen his grandfather's retirement years. It has stolen the opportunity of him fishing as a child on a family seine boat that never was. It had forced his father and mother into a constant spin of worry and work, two or three jobs plus fishing, in a losing battle to make ends meet. It was threatening to gobble their home in town and the family cabin on Hinchinbrook. It had robbed Matt and his older sisters of choices for college.

The town was made up of people who had stories similar to those of John Platt and the Maxwell family. Many business owners also felt the financial strain. The Lighthouse was among the casualties of the high cost of living and lack of fish bucks. After declaring bankruptcy in spring, Lisa Marie and Glenn divorced. Lisa Marie and the girls would leave town in summer, seeking new dreams and the chance to fulfill them in faraway places. Zak, eighteen and on his own, would stay to fish. Many, many other families, or parts of families, had been forced to move by the dreary financial outlook. Each family that left tore a gaping hole in the social fabric of the community and further isolated the litigants who stayed.

On the seventeenth spill memorial in March 2006, a cadre of townspeople hosted a community potluck, but instead of the usual media, documentary filmmakers and oral historians showed up. Over a plateful of grilled salmon, baked halibut, rice, and salads, I heard one person mutter, "I know this will all be over when they stop coming to study us." Still, I sensed the crowd was grateful for the professionals who told Cordova's story in a way that others could understand.

Together, we watched one such mirror of our story. The documentary DVD, *The Day the Water Died*, captured the human story of unresolved trauma where other films had failed. It triggered an outpouring of personal stories, tears, and songs during the open microphone session afterward. Listening, I realized that Cordova's story was far from over and that it was far greater than the sum of individual tales. There was a common undercurrent of social injustice, legal failings, and lingering harm to the town and environment.

A few days later while watching another documentary, I began to see that our problems had broad social implications. *Endless Fallout* explored the lingering human cost of three of the world's largest technological disasters this century: Union Carbide's chemical accident in Bhopal (India), the nuclear meltdown in Chernobyl (Ukraine), and the *Exxon Valdez* oil spill. The filmmakers showed that, while all these disasters look different from the outside, they looked eerily similar from the inside of "ground zero" communities.

In these cases, the social chaos, collapse, and suffering were very real, yet very different from tangible losses to life, property, and economic opportunity. In Russia, India, and the United States, the corporations and governments— and, in the United States, the courts—never acknowledged or helped repair the social harm. In these cases, the failure to recognize and fix this harm prevented injured communities from healing, from being made "whole," and it contributed to prolonging the chaos.

I spent a few days alone on Eyak Mountain snowshoeing and mulling. What was the flip side of social chaos? What had we taken for granted about our community? Before the disaster, it had functioned relatively smoothly. After, it was chaos for a few years. What had we learned from this disaster, from each other, and from the filmmakers and sociologists who gave us the benefit of a larger framework to view ourselves? Could our lessons benefit other communities struck by disaster or, even better, help prevent these disasters from occurring in the first place? The sociologists counted class litigation as a secondary disaster. Was such litigation avoidable? How could we do things differently?

Shortly after I had framed this new problem, I accepted an invitation to give a talk about it before I left for a family reunion. This was my way of forcing myself to find answers to these questions.

At a tiny cottage in Point Reyes Station in California, I pieced together the story. So as not to intrude on my family's precious time together with our father, who was starting to slow down with the weight of his eighty-five years, I rose early each morning to read from a thick stack of sociology papers on Cordova. My sister would find me lit up like a Christmas tree at 7:00 A.M. each morning, furiously scribbling in a growing pile of notes.

"Was that really the best choice of reading material to bring on vacation?" she asked doubtfully one day. I assured her the reading was oddly cathartic. It helped me make sense of a very emotionally turbulent time.

Community — "You Don't Know What You've Got 'Til It's Gone"

In June when summer days were stretching toward solstice, Malani returned to Cordova, fresh from graduating at Stanford with a college degree in communications and a master's in elementary education in four hectic years. She and Linden regaled me with graduation stories as we drove out "the Road" to the Saddlebag Glacier trail. It was one of the few trails where we could walk side by side. The dogs panted in excitement.

As we shouldered our packs to head into the forest, Malani asked what I had been doing. I told her of my recent speaking engagement—the reason I had missed her graduation.

"Dallas? You went back to *Dallas*?" She looked incredulous.

"Crazy, isn't it? Dr. Rea hosted his twenty-fifth annual symposium. He invited me back to talk about oil spill effects on communities, the psychosocial disaster trauma."

"This is Picou's stuff, right?" Malani had grown up with the sociology study as part of her lexicon.

"Yep, Steve Picou and Duane Gill. The work they did in Cordova shifted scientists' understanding of disaster trauma like a sea change. And it makes sense of what happened to us."

"So what did happen?"

Like other spill survivors in town, Malani was hungry to understand what had turned our town upside down. In understanding, there was an opportunity to clear the rubble, frame a new reality, and move forward.

"Did you ever stop to think about what makes a community work? I mean like what drives a civil society. What makes it 'civil'?"

We hiked in silence as Malani thought a minute. I enjoyed exploring our new relationship as academic peers. Bright green devil's club with spiny stems and leaves grew thick on either side of the trail. Tree roots crisscrossed the forest floor. We had to watch our step.

Finally, Malani said, "Well, law and order, I suppose. But then there're democracies and dictatorships. So there must be more to it."

"Try relationships of give and take."

She frowned. "Like networking?" We split to walk around a tree in the trail.

"Think about it. Your family, your friends—you trust each other; you do things for them; they do things for you. You might form a group with other people to do something specific for your school or church or community. Then you get larger and larger associations right up to state compacts and international agreements."

"So, this doesn't have to be about money."

"Money can be a side benefit, but it's not about money. It's about relationships and trust. More trusting individuals form more and stronger relationships. Well-connected people create healthy communities that can make collective decisions and take directed action. Healthy communities form nations that respect civil liberties and meet high ethical standards. It's like trust and relationships are the grease that keep communities working smoothly. That's what one sociologist said."

"So, what did we lose, exactly, after the spill?" Malani asked.

"A lot of people trusted the oil companies. The TAPS owners promised they wouldn't have a big spill or, if they did, they could clean it up."

"So much for that!"

"Right. It became pretty obvious, pretty fast, that the oil companies had made promises to the people and state that they'd had no intention of fulfilling—and that the state and federal governments had been complacent. No one in charge was prepared or even really knew how to respond to or clean up a large spill."

"So people lost faith in the oil industry and the government," Malani said thoughtfully. "But didn't people still trust each other?"

"At first,' I answered. "We were still a tightly networked community, traumatized, but tight. We took collective action: that city Disaster Response Office that your mom was part of, the battle of Sawmill Bay to protect the hatchery, Sound Love Day."

Linden said, "Sound Love Day was what Cordova was all about. We were united in our grief and we were united against Exxon."

"And that," I said, "created a huge problem for Exxon. It wasn't just Cordova. All the oiled communities were united and furious. So what did Exxon do?"

"The cleanup," said Malani.

"The Money Spill," I said. "Exxon dumped money into all the communities to hire people for its cleanup. Not everyone worked the cleanup. So there were "haves" and "have-nots." A lot of people thought Exxon purposely created division, because people in oiled towns knew the cleanup was mostly a charade. The sociologists say disasters create trauma and mismanaged disasters create social crises."

"So, the Money Spill is what started people fighting?" Malani asked.

"Well, it certainly didn't help. Talk about a mismanaged disaster! But there were at least two other things going on. I mean the spill itself created a huge social trauma."

"I'll never forget when I realized how deeply everyone had been hurt," said Linden. "It was a year later. The city sponsored a healing circle. They brought in a grief counselor. He had this big agenda of what we were going to do. The first thing was to sit in a circle and listen while we each shared our story. Well, that was all we did for three days! And there were only about twenty of us! We cried. We listened. We talked. I remember being just amazed at the depth of the grief and sadness, still, a year later."

"And that trauma was not treated," I pointed out. "That was part of the mismanaged disaster. Steve Picou and Duane Gill tapped into that trauma. They studied how it manifested in our community as arguing, fighting, violence, and abuse. Once they realized what was going on and why, they helped us explore ways to heal from it."

We entered a part of the woods I always thought of as "Gumby Forest." The trees were lean and tall with broken lower branches. Thick green moss draped amputated limbs and hung in long ropy curtains. It was a forest of old trees, born in another time when the soil nurtured plants.

"Part of what was driving some of the fear and uncertainty," I explained to Malani, "was that no one knew when things would actually get better in the Sound. The spill caused instant and lasting chaos. Chief Walter Meganack said it best: 'Never in the millennium of our tradition have we thought it possible for the water to die, but it is true.'"

Linden recalled, "I remember the lost feeling of having no one to turn to for help. It was like we all slid down into a dark hole together." We hiked along in silence for a bit, our footsteps muted by the soft springy forest floor.

Finally, Malani, always one to interject with music, sang, "You don't know what you've got 'til it's gone. . . ."

Then she asked the question that a lot of people do: "Why did it take so long to start getting back on our feet?"

"One reason," I responded, "is that it takes time and certainty to reframe a reality. But there was no certainty, no 'normal,' for a number of years after the spill. Beaches are still oiled. Processors went bankrupt. The science was secret. We didn't know how long the oil would affect the Sound and us. We couldn't regroup. The uncertainty added to the stress."

"Then the pink salmon collapsed," said Malani. "And the herring."

"That ended some of the uncertainty. At least we knew where we stood. Rock bottom."

I kicked a rock off the path. The trail lay across an ancient streambed. Moss covered smooth round river stones. Hikers had pushed most of the loose rocks aside. The others had been trampled underfoot, forming a firm cobbled path.

"If I had to pick a year when we started to reframe our reality as a community, it would be 1993. We figured out the spill had affected the young salmon and herring in 1989 and that's what caused the collapses three and four years later. It took the scientists another five or six years to validate that story, well, really a decade for herring."

Malani thought a minute as we wove around a tree. She asked, "How does the blockade figure into this?"

"Once we agreed upon what had happened, we could take collective action again. Immediately. That was the blockade."

Linden said, "People came back to town after that and they were charged up."

I remembered. "That was when efforts like the SEA Program and the Family Resource Center took off and we were finally all about fixing the community's social and economic problems. Being proactive shifts people from the victim role to the survivor mode." That is the crux of the Peer Listening Circles and Peer Training Program, developed by the sociologists.

"That makes sense," Malani mused thoughtfully.

Linden said, "Cordova is starting to feel more like it did before the spill."

Suddenly, the dogs sprang off the trail and charged through the woods, barking madly.

"Cassie! Bubbie! Come!" Linden yelled. "That better not be a porcupine!"

"Or a bear!" Malani said. The dogs came crashing back through the under-story, leaped onto the trail, and raced away.

We swung down a side trail to the main channel of the outflow from the lake. The dogs tumbled down the bank after us. We stood at the edge of the rushing glacial-fed stream while the dogs took a drink. Then, we climbed back up to the trail.

Malani thought things over. "So that was the sea change you're talking about?"

"The sea change is actually bigger than what happened in our town. Before the 1970s, scientists' understanding of disaster was based on natural disasters or acts of God like floods, fires, and earthquakes. You can't sue God! So survivors would work together to repair damage to their homes and infrastructure. And as we know now, working together helps heal trauma. It restores community and even builds it by people pulling together. Sociologists who observed this thought that disaster trauma was short-lived.

"Then along came human-made disasters like the Three Mile Island nuclear meltdown or toxic neighborhoods in Love Canal and Woburn, Massachusetts, and instead of coming together, people were blown apart by uncertainty, fear, a toxic environment, social problems, drawn-out litigation—the same stuff as here. The trauma was long-lived. One sociologist called these disasters a new species of trouble."

Malani said, "So, now there's a chance to learn from what happened to Cordova to help people avoid this kind of trouble in future disasters."

"Exactly, and that includes the future disaster that's almost upon us," I said. "We're expecting another Money Spill when punitive damages are paid. It will create more haves and have-nots." That is why, I explained, some of us had started the Oiled Regions of Alaska Foundation.

Since this had happened while Malani was at Stanford, I had to further explain the opportunity to forestall this looming disaster trauma. Punitive damages on business claims are taxable. Instead of paying the IRS, the plan was to use charitable giving strategies to direct the money that a person owed in taxes back into their community. I concluded, "The idea is to spread the wealth around the community to lessen divisions and fighting."

Up ahead, the dogs snuffled and barked excitedly at the base of a big spruce. On our first hike on this trail, long ago, I had shown Malani and her brother where squirrels cached spruce cones to feed on during the long winters. Piles of cones and scales lay heaped on the forest floor around three large trees. The midden had settled over time into a spongy mat that supported our weight. It was riddled with holes and tunnels.

A short distance from the squirrel middens, Gumby Forest changed very abruptly into a narrow canyon. Years ago, two large spruce had uprooted and fallen on either side of the trail, exposing enormous root wads that stood like gatekeepers, marking the passage between forest and canyon.

"Oh!" Malani cried, rushing down the trail. "One of the Gatekeepers is gone!" She was tramping around off the trail. "It's not exactly gone," she said. "It's become dirt!" She held up two handfuls of it, brought it over, and sprinkled it on the trail.

We set off single file with Malani in the lead. Sunlight lit up the canyon, filled with sweet-smelling cottonwood and alder, tall grasses, and berry bushes. Waterfalls cascaded down steep walls and small streams coursed across the narrow floor. "This is my favorite part of this trail," said Linden from behind us. "It smells good, it looks good, and it feels good."

"Mine, too," I said.

Malani said, "I bet Steve Picou and Duane Gill like the idea of a community foundation."

"Yeah, they do! They saw the 1989 repeat coming, too. Duane plans to measure our program's success. He thinks it could be a model for other cases with large punitive damage awards."

"We always end up talking about litigation!" Linden said. "I'm sick of the litigation!"

"Exactly! You and all the other claimants. Litigation is the third part of the mismanaged disaster. The sociologists found that litigation dishes out a second helping of Post Traumatic Stress Disorder. They found that people with claims are as stressed out now from the litigation as we all were seventeen years ago from the spill!"

"That's sick!" Linden declared. "The litigation was our only choice."

"I think if lawyers were medical doctors, they would be disbarred for violating the Hippocratic oath: 'Never do harm to anyone.' I've read papers by lawyers, medical doctors, sociologists, psychologists, psychiatrists. . . . They all say the same thing: The legal system doesn't work anymore, especially in cases like ours that involve thousands of claims and complicated science.

"Why have you been wasting your time reading those papers?" Linden asked. "We know it doesn't work. We just sacrificed seventeen years of our lives, for what? A whole lot of headache and woe! A lot of people are going to end up worse off than they were before the spill. They've gone backward into debt!"

"I've been reading those papers to figure out what to do about it," I explained. "We're not the only disaster victims who go through this!"

Linden said in wonder, "You're advocating that we reform the U.S. legal system?"

"Why not, Mom? If it doesn't work?"

"Here's the thing," I said. Corporations are legally obligated to make money for their shareholders. Right now, the legal system allows corporations to profit by stalling. Exxon more than made whatever it will have to pay us by stalling and investing the punitive award in the stock market—the rate of return is so much higher than whatever Exxon will lose in paying interest. Exxon had to stall or the shareholders could have sued the board!"

There were groans in stereo on either side of me.

"Picou made a whole laundry list of corporate strategies to deny or reduce payment to victims (see the table on page 246). If we can change the legal system so there is no financial incentive to stall, then there might be a chance to make injured communities whole."

We hiked along in silence for a bit as we mulled what a new legal system might look like. The problem I found lay deeper than the corporate lawyers. The American justice system is predicated on several underlying assumptions, most of which are no longer valid in adversarial litigation, as we learned through our class action.

Equal treatment under the law? Not possible when those with money use it to influence laws and public perception, or manipulate courts to make punishment moot.

Impartial judges? Not possible when judges are human and often former corporate lawyers.

Decisions based on the whole truth and facts? Not even close. Jurors receive only selective information from judges or court masters who effectively act as gatekeepers, and facts are grossly distorted through corporate-sponsored "science."

The right to a speedy trial? This is guaranteed by the Sixth Amendment, because even 200 years ago people knew that justice delayed is justice denied. Yet nearly five years passed before the *Exxon Valdez* case even went to trial. Cases are time-sensitive. What is considered "just punishment" or punitive at one point in history is based on the science and social ethics of that period. When corporations stall, court decisions are made out of the social context of the times when the accident occurred—and often in conflict with the jury decision.

A trial by peers? The Seventh Amendment of the U.S. Constitution prevents courts from reexamining facts tried by jury. This is to help ensure that justice is imparted by peers, not the educated elite. Punitive awards have been treated as "facts" until recently. When higher courts reexamine punitive awards decided by juries, the "facts" are retried by lawyers—exactly what the Seventh Amendment tries to prevent. The "facts" of monetary punishment are better left to average Americans than corporate lawyers who seek to reduce corporate liability.

I finally said, "Look, take our case. In 1994, the jury decided $5 billion was necessary to punish Exxon—to change corporate behavior, right? In 1994, that was the equivalent of one year's net profit. Last year (2005), Exxon posted net profits of nearly $34 billion. So Exxon's profits are going up at the same time that the legal system is driving the punitive award down, even though it's obvious that $5 billion is no longer punishment—if it ever was. I mean, if Exxon had learned a lesson, it should have been the first oil company to double hull its tankers, not the last."

"No amount of money is ever going to 'make us whole' even if those are the words Exxon used when they promised to do that," Linden said sadly.

"The legal system can't make us whole, because it leaves out process. That's

Some Corporate Defense Strategies in Adversarial Litigation

1. Hire a small army of the best lawyers money can buy. This business cost is written off at taxpayers' expense, while plaintiffs pay lawyers out-of-pocket or on contingency.
2. Limit discovery to hide extent of culpability by claiming thousands of documents are "privileged." This forces plaintiffs to argue for individual documents, a time-consuming and costly burden.
3. Eliminate thousands of claims before requesting class certification. Plaintiffs usually request class certification from the onset to preserve individual claims.
4. Remove the case to court with a politically sympathetic judge.
5. File spurious lawsuits to obfuscate the main case and burden plaintiffs.
6. File a blizzard of motions to hide culpability and wealth from the jury. Plaintiffs must respond to each motion.
7. Try to change standards of evidence (or safety) to increase the chance of prevailing in court.
8. Execute legally questionable and morally deficit secret deals to reduce anticipated losses; e.g., Exxon's secret deal with the Seattle Seven fish processors will return 11 percent of the punitive damage award to Exxon.
9. Eliminate damaging biological and social evidence and witnesses so jurors never know the 'whole truth'—the full extent of harm caused by the accident and the trail of broken promises leading to it; e.g., Exxon successfully denied all non-economic damage claims by preventing studies on mental health trauma and community harm from being admitted as court evidence.

what those papers I read say. People care about how they're treated. It's about respect and dignity and trust. People want to participate, not be sidelined by lawyers or a jury that is only told part of their story. We need a justice system that listens to the injured people and lets us figure out what's fair. Sort of like Picou's Peer Listening training."

"That sounds like mediation," Linden said.

"Exactly. Some African countries use restorative justice and community-wide mediations to restore wholeness. If that can work for war crimes and genocides, why not oil spills?

"Many Africans see our Western justice like the old Western shoot-outs.

10. Fund scientists to assess environmental and other damages. Use corporate-sponsored science to attack credible science; e.g., the illusion of "scientific uncertainty" caused the jury in the *Exxon Valdez* case to reduce damage claims for lost fish harvests.

11. Launch professional and personal attacks to discredit scientists who challenge corporate supremacy in science; e.g., Exxon attacked scientists who disagreed with Exxon's science.

12. Use biased accounting strategies to overestimate costs to corporate defendants and underestimate costs to victims.

13. Fund a comprehensive campaign against punitive damage awards; e.g., such Exxon-sponsored studies found their way into respected law journals and the court itself without mention of their corporate sponsor.

14. Retry the case through appeals. Also through appeals, attempt to reduce or eliminate any large damage awards, using the legal system to stall for time to recoup through investments whatever might have to be paid in awards plus interest.

15. Organize a massive public relations campaign that deconstructs what really happened and reconstructs an all clear signal, pronouncing that damages are gone and all victims (ecological and human) have recovered.

16. Advance rights of corporate "persons."

Source: Adapted from the original with permission from J. Steven Picou, "The Earth Charter and the Exxon Valdez *Oil Spill: Corporate Response to Eco-Social Degradation," keynote, Earth Charter Summit, University of Wisconsin, Oshkosh, September 2002. See also Brent Marshall, Steven Picou, and Jan Schlichtmann, "Technological Disasters, Litigation Stress and the Use of Alternative Dispute Resolution Mechanisms," Law and Policy 26 (2): 289-307, 2004.*

It's all an ego trip for a few people who are trying to outsmart each other and avoid having the truth about their client come out. One tribal advisor in Uganda said, 'You stand up and swear on the Bible to tell the truth, the whole truth, and then it's lies, lies, lies all the way.'"

"Hmmm," said Malani. "Hey, these bridges are new!"

Roughly hewn planks spanned the creek crossing. The old stepping-stones were still in the stream. The dogs waded in and drank deeply from the cool clear water. We set off again.

"So, as part of doing business," Linden said thoughtfully, "the oil companies could agree that any disputes would be settled through mediation. That's a common practice in contracts. We should have made it part of the law that authorized the pipeline!"

"Now you're talking!" I said. "What if all of the original promises for the pipeline had been made law?"

"Maybe no oil spill," said Malani.

Linden was on a roll. "There's something in business called 'liquidated damages,'" she said. "It means damages are predetermined and put in contracts."

"You're thinking we could have liquidated damages for environmental and economic harm? I like it. Besides, if we have to put a price tag on disaster before it happens, it might make people rethink sloppy business practices before it's too late."

"What about paying for mental health trauma?" asked Malani. "We know that's real."

"FEMA covers that in natural disasters," I said. "Oh! How about this? FEMA covers it in all disasters as a cost of doing business borne by American people, unless private damage claims wind up in court. Then corporations pay, regardless of who wins in court. That way, it's an incentive for companies to use mediation."

"I like that!" said Linden. "We could make financial incentives to use mediation to settle disputes. How about if courts were required to escrow damage awards? That would remove a big incentive for corporations to stall."

"Sure would. How about this?" I countered. "Why should Americans pay legal expenses for corporate criminals? We could eliminate the tax deductions for litigation expenses."

"Yeah!" said Linden. "Kelley Weaverling says we should seize the assets of corporate criminals. We do that when people hunt or fish illegally."

Like others who've lived through a corporate disaster, we saw the need to figure this out and soon. Sociologists agree that our society is headed for more of these big class action litigations as we live with the failings of our technology. Think Katrina. Mass asthma from urban traffic. Drought, flooding, and fires from global climate change.

"We're at the lake!" Malani and the dogs ran through the border of thick alders. "*Holy crap!*" she cried. "*Where did the glacier go?*"

We joined her on the narrow cobble beach and looked across the lake. The lake sat in a bowl formed by steep mountains at the head of the canyon. There were hardly any icebergs in the lake or snowfields on the ridges. Saddlebag Glacier was barely visible. It had retreated up the valley.

"Global warming!" Malani and I both chorused.

"Enough, you guys!" said Linden. "Let's enjoy the day."

Six months later, on December 22, the Ninth Circuit cut the original $5 billion punitive award in half to $2.5 billion. The court cited no legal reason for this drastic reduction. The majority of judges simply—and coldly—opined "It is time for this protracted litigation to end."

Fisherman and others thought so too, but not like this.

Community Catharsis: The Shame Pole

On March 24, 2007, the eighteenth memorial of the *Exxon Valdez* oil spill, some 80 people gathered at the Masonic building in Cordova for the unveiling of a Shame Pole dedicated to ExxonMobil. In Native tradition, such totem poles are carved to shame someone for unpaid debts. The last one carved in Alaska was six generations earlier, nearly 150 years ago.

The Shame Pole came to the community by way of Bob Henrichs who had commissioned it, Native carver Mike Webber who had given form to thoughts and feelings, and people who had stopped by Mike's warehouse to share ideas and stories, and to help sand and paint. The Shame Pole was more than retribution to ExxonMobil for failing to make us whole. The Shame Pole was a community catharsis.

Its nine feet of yellow cedar spoke volumes. At the top, the upside-down head of ExxonMobil's retired CEO Lee Raymond spewed the Death Wave down the top third of the pole. Exxon's unfulfilled promise, "We will make you whole," floated on the black oil. The slick was littered with dead wildlife and red dollar signs from the divisive cleanup, painted in the carver's blood. The middle of the pole spoke of lingering harm to the Sound with sick and "disappeared" herring in ghostly outline, and lingering harm to people with boat foreclosures and families that no longer fished together—or at all. Below this, the scale of justice tipped in Exxon's favor, weighed down with time and money to show injustice for all, especially those who died without compensation. A ring of people with linked arms were carved around the pole's base to illustrate our community's long journey of reconnection and healing. The forms had holes for hearts—a play on Exxon's promise to make us "whole." Mike said, Exxon "put a hole in our hearts and they've taken part of our soul as well."

Never Do Harm: Ideas to Restore Justice to America's Legal System

Recognize Potential for Disaster Trauma

1. Incorporate mental health trauma treatment in *all* disaster planning and response, including natural, human-made, and acts of terrorism by requiring the Federal Emergency Management Act to provide short- and long-term mental health counseling for disaster victims through closure of litigation (if any).
2. Require defendants in adversarial litigation to reimburse the federal government (FEMA) for mental health trauma treatment *regardless of who prevails in court.*

Minimize Disputes Upfront

1. Make legally binding all corporate promises made for permits, right-of-ways, and other phases of planning, scoping, development, and post-development restoration.
2. Include in contracts:
    - an immediate *"cessation of contract clause"* if any promises or protective laws are challenged after project startup;
    - a clause that prevents lawsuits based on future lost profits; and
    - a clause that all disputes including those from industrial accidents and exposures will be settled through mediation within 1–5 years.
3. Escrow:
    - any promised funds for future projects such as dismantling and removal of the infrastructure and restoration of the area;
    - liquidated compensatory damages to the environment, people, and communities in advance of a development.
4. Require each party to pay their own legal fees except for public interest lawsuits.

Create Incentives to Resolve Disputes through Non-Adversarial Mechanisms

1. Require the losing party in adversarial litigation to pay the attorney fees and expenses of the prevailing party.

2. Require parties in private lawsuits to mediate before trial *and* before arguing any appeals.
3. Do not allow new government contracts for parties in adversarial litigation *and* through the period of time equal to that of the duration of the litigation.
4. Freeze and replace government contracts of corporate defendants involved in adversarial litigation.
5. Eliminate tax-deductible write-offs of expenses for adversarial litigation.
6. Eliminate tax-deductible write-offs of expenses for corporate-sponsored "science" conducted by perpetrators of environmental crimes including global climate change.
7. Seize assets of corporate defendants involved in adversarial litigation, *and their parent corporations,* and place in the custody of shareholder-stakeholder group created by the court through the duration of the litigation.
8. Require damage awards assessed in adversarial litigation cases that are not closed within five years of jury decisions to automatically *double every five years* to compensate for unanticipated long-term harm.

Hasten Closure of Disputes in Court

1. Require punitive damage awards be escrowed when entered in court so neither party benefits from stalling case closure.
2. Fulfill intent of punitive damages:
    • Link punitive damages to net profits of parent corporations, rather than compensatory awards, to ensure punishment is meted out fairly to all sizes of corporations;
    • In cases where punitive damages are equivalent to a proportion of the net profit of the defendant, require awards to *be that proportion at the time of case closure, or* the original award, plus interest, *whichever is greater.*
3. Create a federal tax law option in which the entire tax-deductible portion of any punitive damage award may gifted to charity organizations within the region affected by the disaster.

During the dedication, I thought back to one of my visits in Mike's warehouse when he was carving the pole. I remembered seeing the pain in his eyes as he worked. Mike said, "I didn't think this would be so hard. But it's bringing back all the memories." He spoke of his divorce and how he missed fishing as a family. He had fished different gear throughout the seasons, long-lining for cod, setting pots for crab or shrimp, seining for herring and salmon, and gillnetting. He had done well in some fisheries, he said, okay in others, but that had been enough—until the spill. Some of those fisheries like herring, crab, and shrimp had never recovered. His life had slowly unraveled. His new boat, built especially for gillnetting herring, had never had a herring aboard. What is a fisherman without fish? After a fishing accident, he embraced his Native ways and learned to carve, which, he said, had felt more like *remembering* how to carve.

Writing did the same thing to me, I finally told him. It stirred up memories. But once released, I found they never settled back as deeply again. Stirred enough, it became a matter of living with them, rather than them living you. At that point of release, I had found it possible to work with them and transform them into stories. The blank uncut parts of the pole reminded me of blank pages of an unfinished story. How would the memories on this pole take shape? When I left Mike, shavings of yellow cedar were falling again on the warehouse floor like snowflakes falling quietly in the forest.

After the dedication, I thought about the ring of figures encircling the base of the Shame Pole and I saw Community. I suddenly realized there was another lesson from the spill—and it was linked to our stubborn dependence on fossil fuels.

CHAPTER FIFTEEN

A NEW CONSCIOUSNESS

2007–2008

For me, the arm-in-arm figures at the base of the Shame Pole held the key to solving a much larger social problem. I saw parallels between Cordova's disaster and the looming disaster of global climate change.

We had learned from the spill that communities polarized by issues or hamstrung by trauma are not able to make collective decisions or take action to save themselves. Yet, when people set aside their differences and focus instead on what they have in common, relationships and trust grow and it becomes possible to work together to resolve mutual concerns.

What we share in common in Cordova are deep core values so central to being human that many are recognized as human rights in either the U.S. Bill of Rights or the more inclusive Universal Declaration of Human Rights. The latter was drafted by a United Nations committee chaired by Eleanor Roosevelt. Her committee was the first to articulate basic economic, social, and cultural rights. Values spelled out as rights can then be codified into laws.

For example, in Cordova, the values of a job with living wages, a safe home, and a family are reflected as the universal right to life, liberty, and security of persons; and the right to work and to form and join trade unions, among others. The values of civic engagement and social diversity translate into the universal right to freedom of opinion and expression; and the right to freedom of peaceful assembly and association, among others. The values of opportunity and the opportunity to make choices are coded into the universal right to be free from slavery or servitude; and the right to freedom of thought, conscience, and religion, among others. The values of health and a healthy environment are recognized as the universal right to a standard of living adequate for health and well-being, among others.

These values and rights frame the foundation of Franklin Delano Roosevelt's four freedoms: freedom of speech and expression; freedom of religion; freedom from want; and freedom from fear. Taken together, these frame a sustainable future. I saw people in Cordova as wanting no more or no less than other Americans—or other people on the planet.

Holding the Cordova experience as a mirror, I saw reflected on the surface of America a nation of people so polarized by issues or hamstrung by politics that we could not make collective decisions or take action to save ourselves. The map of red and blue states, sharp in relief of political divides, stuck in my mind. However, in community after community, and region after region, people were linking arms and putting aside differences to work together on the central threat to our survival—global climate change.

By 2007, the stakes in the choice of energy futures had gone up. Getting it wrong or moving too slowly would mean catastrophe for hundreds of millions of people and jeopardize all life on the planet. Scientific evidence that we needed to break our oil dependency within the next ten years to literally save ourselves was falling like hard rain. In an unprecedented meeting of minds, thousands of scientists around the world had reached consensus that Earth's climate is dangerously overheating from human-made causes, primarily burning fossil fuels. A buildup of carbon and other "greenhouse gases" in the atmosphere are destabilizing the climate and threatening Earth's life-support systems.

As if that wasn't enough, burning fossil fuels is also poisoning people. Medical doctors had found that oil pollution in urban air kills more Americans annually than car accidents through heart attacks, asthma, emphysema, and hardened arteries, among other things. On top of that, the world has reached peak oil—the experts' best guess for the top of the mountain of plentiful, relatively cheap, and easily-extractable oil. After peak oil, it's all downhill. A looming future of wars over ever shrinking resources, exorbitant prices, and environmental destruction lies ahead for those who tarry too long on the fossil fuel path.

Despite this ugly picture, oil companies and their industrial alliances are still pressing to wrest the last drops of oil from shelves deep offshore and from shales and sands under mountain and forest. It is past time to get off oil. Yet the people's movement for a sustainable world has run smack into an entrenched Corporate–State block that is loath to begin a transition to clean fuels, even ones well within reach of our technology.

How had corporations grown so big that they could no longer be held accountable to the people? It was a question that I had heard in Cordova. I resolved to find out, because in the answer lay the key to social justice, transitioning off oil, and achieving a sustainable future.

American Civics Revisited

When I started down this trail in fall 2005, my inquiry led me to contemporaries who were tilling the muck of time and lore for clues to this question. They in turn pointed me to a long line of visionaries, patriots, and ordinary people who had asked this question back to the very beginnings of our country.

Still, my pursuit took well over a year. At the center of it was a fresh look at American civics as taught by Thomas Linzey and Richard Grossman in the Daniel Pennock Democracy School. Linzey and Grossman brought alive a chapter of history not taught in secondary schools—the evolution of large corporations from short-lived, single-purpose entities, chartered for the common good, into conglomerates that dictate drafting of law and policy to support one and only one purpose: profits for their investors. This slice of history was served with stories of people's movements to counter the growing corporate control over human lives and community futures. I read, wrote, took trainings, and finally felt enough ownership of the story to share it.

During summer 2007, I practiced my new legacy story on groups of visitors who stayed at Orca Adventure Lodge in the remodeled cannery that had been a victim of the oil spill. Girl Scouts, Outward Bound groups, classes of traveling students, ecotours, scholars, sports fishermen and hunters, and people from other countries sat with fishermen and friends who came to listen to our evolving story. Questions and discussion opened up more areas to explore. This crosssection of humanity helped hone and sharpen the story until the reaction was pretty much the same every time: What can we do to help?

One day in late August, Linden called to invite me over. "Malani's in from fishing and she had the afternoon off. I've told her a little about your talk, but she wants to hear it from you. She's making brownies. We're having the seine crew for dinner. . . ."

I jumped at the chance to see Malani. She had cut her first solo CD[7] with original songs during the winter in Santa Cruz. She had returned to crew with her father, both working for a close family friend who shared a love of music. I had hardly seen her all summer and I missed our talks. Her life was changing and would pull her to new places and adventures. She knew it. Her title song was a good-bye to Cordova. "Can I invite the film crew to dinner? I'll pick a salad from the garden."

"Sure! They're family now."

I picked a mix of salad greens, herbs, carrots, snap peas, and a couple zucchinis from my neighbor's raised beds, packed the harvest in my knapsack, and set off on my bike. Pedaling past Eyak Lake, I got a light, intoxicated feeling and realized that suddenly, finally, I was relaxed.

I had been "on" all summer, giving lectures or shooting scenes with the Quebec film crew, working on the successor to their earlier documentary, *Endless Fallout*. They had chosen my "character" as central to their feature film. At first I had no idea what that meant, but quickly learned it was cameras, microphones, lights, commotion, questions, and direction everywhere I went—Iceworm Festival, Salmon Jam, the Fourth of July picnic, hikes, my home or other people's homes, the harbor, even other states. . . .

Townspeople would see me coming with the "paparazzi," as my father called them, and turn away, but as the year wore on, people realized this film crew was different. They hung out with us, trying to get a real sense of the community. They came back. They cared about the town. They offered us a chance to tell our story in our own words—no faceless, honeyed voice narrating the scenes into a story scripted by people who didn't live the spill and didn't understand what had really happened.

The film crew offered me the gift of deep healing. Friendships blossomed with time and shared work. The vulnerable and deeply hurt parts of my psyche that I had masked with "Dr. Ott the scientist" became exposed. A hidden hurt festers. A hurt examined with loving intent heals. Like a mother kissing her child's cut, I was able to soothe my trauma. I found my human voice. I became reconnected to that solid calm core that lies at the center of all beings. My perception of other people's emotions deepened as my awareness of my own inner landscape grew. It was a priceless gift.

I was greeted by silence as I swung into the O'Tooles' yard. Both dogs had gone deaf as they aged. I ran up the hill and steep steps, pounding hard on each plank. The vibrations alerted Cassie to a visitor and she swung sightless eyes in my direction. She caught my scent and stood up, wagging her tail and barking hoarsely. Malani opened the door. We laughed and hugged as Bubby charged out, barking.

I asked the standard Cordova question: "How's fishing?"

"There are so many fish! Everyone is catching fish."

"So the film crew wasn't too much trouble?" I had prevailed upon my friends to fulfill the crews' need for fishing footage.

"No, but it was a little more exciting than we planned. The wind picked up and it twisted the bag full of fish before we could bring it on deck. It almost pulled us over. Waves were washing over the stern and side! Mike was shouting orders. They just kept filming!"

"God. That crew is so lucky with good weather, good fishing. . . ."

"And a good story!" said Linden. "When do they think the film will be done?"

"A year from now. Same time as my book."

"That's what I want to hear about!" said Malani. "Mom says you have a new ending for your book, but you have to explain it. I just put the brownies in the oven. They take forty minutes. Let's talk before everyone else gets here."

Linden poured tea as Malani and I sat at the kitchen table. She said, "I'm going to clean up for tonight. I've already heard your talk twice. Malani hasn't."

Linden put a big pot of rice on the stove to cook and disappeared into the living room. I grabbed a piece of scrap paper and a pen. "What did you learn in high school civics about our form of government?" I asked Malani.

She said, "There're three branches of government and a system of checks and balances, but that doesn't seem to be working so well right now."

"Hang on. We'll get there." I drew a triangle on the paper. I wrote "Legislative" below the left-hand corner of the triangle and "Bureaucracy" in the right-hand corner. I turned the paper so Malani could see it.

"The legislative branch makes the law." I pointed to the bureaucracy. "The executive branch administers the law and the judicial branch interprets the law." I drew a double-headed arrow below the triangle and pointing to the two corners. "Here's our system of checks and balances."

"What's at the top?"

I wrote "We, the People" to the left of the top corner and drew a circle around the words. "There it is: our sovereign self-governance. Look familiar?"

Malani nodded. "That's what I was taught in school."

"This is what we're all taught. But our system has been hijacked." I slashed a line through "We, the People" and drew another larger circle to the right of the upper point. In it, I wrote in large block letters, "CORPORATE PERSONS" and below in smaller letters, "Natural Persons." "And the hijackers are large transnational corporations," I explained.

"How did that happen?" asked Malani.

"It was a setup—and people weren't paying attention."

Our conversation wound back 230 years to the American Revolution. The past year and a half of research had landed me on a soapbox. "We fought to throw off the twin yokes of oppression: the British monarchy and the big transnational corporations at the time like the Hudson Bay Company and the East India Company," I exclaimed.

"The Boston Tea Party!" Malani chimed in. We clunked our tea mugs together.

"But our Founders wanted to build an empire to rival the British Empire. Our Constitution is actually set up to facilitate property and commerce."

"What about 'All men are created equal' and 'Liberty and justice for all'?"

"That was the Declaration of Independence. That was never codified into law."

"Oh, yeah," said Malani. "But it is funny to hear you talk about this instead of oil."

"All roads lead to oil. We'll get there." Malani grinned.

"When Benjamin Franklin stepped out of the Philadelphia Convention, a lady asked whether the framers had 'given' the people a Monarchy or a Republic. He replied, 'A Republic, Madam, if you can keep it.'"

"I've heard that."

"But have you thought about it? When you create something, you know its weaknesses. I think what our Founders foresaw was that the Republic could be destroyed if rights of commerce became more important than rights of people."

"That's what's happening with the *Exxon Valdez* case!" Malani looked down at the triangle I had drawn. "How did we get Corporate Persons?" she asked.

"It turns out there are two ways to amend the Constitution: formally in Congress through people-made law, which has been done now twenty-seven times; and informally through the federal judiciary by judge-made law—or rather through interpretation of the law."

"Uh-oh."

"Yeah, *big* uh-oh," I said. So, now we're to the Civil War."

"Okay."

"After the Civil War, we passed the Civil Rights Amendments—the Thirteenth, Fourteenth, and Fifteenth."

"I know the Fourteenth Amendment—due process and equal protection under the law!"

"But did you know that one became a favorite target of corporations? During the first forty years after it passed, there were 307 lawsuits brought under the Fourteenth Amendment. Of these, nineteen dealt with African Americans and 288 with Corporations trying to claim these privileges."

"That's crazy!"

"Well, persistence paid off. In 1886 a federal court ruled that a railroad corporation's 'rights' of due process had been violated. Since you have to have rights before they can be violated, the *Santa Clara* ruling implicitly created corporate 'persons.'"

"What?! It took women another thirty-four years to become recognized as persons!"

"Good point. Of course, when one corporation has 'rights,' they all do. You know, 'equal protection under the law'? And once corporations usurped one right intended for persons, they went after others."

"Through the courts instead of Congress!"

"Yep. So for the last 120 years, rights intended for natural persons have been usurped by corporate challengers through the federal judiciary."

"Like what rights?"

I shrugged. "The First Amendment. Corporations gained the 'right' to protect political and commercial contributions as 'free speech.'"

I reached for the triangle figure and drew an arrow pointing from "Corporate Persons" to "Legislative." I put dollar signs over the arrow.

"Corporations have overwhelmed citizen participation in politics and elections."

"They sure have!"

"The Fourth Amendment. Corporations gained the 'right' of protection against 'unreasonable search and seizure.'" I drew another arrow pointing from "Corporate Persons" to "Bureaucracy." "If food inspectors, or the EPA, or safety inspectors have to obtain a warrant to search for violations, how will they catch problems?"

"They won't—not a lot anyway."

I nodded. "The Fifth Amendment. Corporations gained the 'right' to protection against governmental regulations that result in a 'taking' of corporate property or a diminishment of its value. That's what Exxon argued to bring the *Exxon Valdez* back to the Sound."

I crossed out "Checks & Balances."

"Now Congress can pass a law, and the President can sign it—and corporations can challenge it, if it interferes with future profits."

"That's insane!"

"That's globalization."

"This is all upside down and backward of what I learned in school," Malani wailed.

"It's amazing what a little history and a class action lawsuit does for one's perspective. I think there's a good reason we're still taught the illusion of democracy in school," I said grimly.

"What do you mean?"

"We claim to be spreading democracy all over the planet, but we're really spreading that." I pointed to the marked-up triangle (fig 5).

"What is that?"

"I can tell you what other people call it. Franklin Roosevelt said, "The liberty of a democracy is not safe if the people tolerate the growth of private power to a point where it becomes stronger than their democratic State itself. That, in its essence is Fascism—ownership of government by an individual, by a group, or any controlling private power."

"*No!*"

"A lot of our leaders saw what was going on," I said. "But here's my favorite quote. Guess who said, 'Fascism should more appropriately be called Corporatism because it is a merger of state and corporate power.' The clues are: not a U.S. leader and World War II."

"Fascism is Corporatism? Jeez. Um, Churchill?"

"Enemy not ally."

"Hitler?"

"Close!"

"Mussolini?"

"Yep, Benito Mussolini—and he should know!"

"No kidding! But wait. This doesn't feel like fascism. I mean, we still have all our rights and elections and stuff."

"Yeah, but it looks like fascism. And it's a lot more subtle than what my Dad fought in World War II. It's almost like Oz where 'We, the People' have the illusion of power, but behind the curtain, the corporations are pulling levers and operating our government."

"It wasn't so subtle with Dick Cheney's energy task force!"

"Well, other things are more subtle." I ticked off a list. "Privatizing health care, privatizing the commons—water, seeds, genes, airwaves. War profiteering, prison profiteering—we've got the highest rate of incarceration in the world! Haves and have-nots: 20 percent of Americans live in poverty while the richest 1 percent own over one-third of the nation's property and stocks."

"This can't go on."

"It doesn't need to. Other democratic, developed nations have done far better with far less. European countries have managed to grow thriving economies with healthy educated people, intact families, and social parity—and with less spending on military, prisons, healthcare, and education. America can do better, but the *human* People need to be in charge."

The Power Behind the Curtain
Democracy...

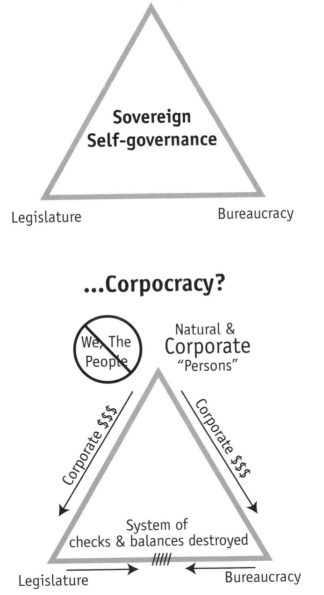

Figure 5.

"What can we do about all this?" she demanded.

"Well, we can't have a participatory democracy if people don't participate."

"What do you mean? Like voting? Because less than half the country is voting."

"No. Not just that. The relationship thing. If people don't network with each other, they don't get involved in their community. They don't participate in the democratic process in its most elemental form: community. If you're networking, you're familiar with local problems and solutions. And the local process mirrors the regional and national process. If you're not plugged into your community, you're not plugged into the country. One heartbeat for all."

"People aren't networking?"

"Not like we used to in the first half of last century. Remember in the 1960s when people began staying home to watch television? That's called cocooning now."

"Nope. That was before my time!"

"Oh. I forget you're a kid! Well, the 1960s cocooning ended a very long run—a tradition almost—of American involvement in politics, government, and civics. After the '60s, people dropped out. Television is the number one cause of civic *dis*-engagement."

"So, turn off television and save the Republic?"

"That's a good one," I laughed. But basically, yes. We need to spend our leisure time doing things. We need to plug into our family and neighbors and country and work on solutions to our climate crisis."

"What can people do?"

"Lots, actually. But it's about more than reusing, restoring, recycling, and rescuing the Republic. People in Pennsylvania and California are asserting local self-governance by defining 'persons' as 'natural.' That makes the 'Corporate Person' illegitimate."

"Illegal!" Malani laughed.

"Both actually. And I think we need to push that idea from the top down as well by passing the Twenty-eighth Amendment to the Constitution: the separation of corporation and state. People-made law trumps judge-made law."

"The Twenty-eighth Amendment to the Constitution?!" I smiled at the flush of excitement this idea brought to Malani. It was the same flush it brought to other audiences. Real patriotism was not dead in America. It was dormant. It was not about flag-waving and shopping to boost the economy. The flames of resistance to tyranny and oppression actually do burn in our blood. We just need a rekindling.

"Look, we've done this before. When Abolitionists faced the legality of slavery, the citizenry launched a movement and drove the Civil Rights Amendments into the Constitution," I explained. "When Suffragists faced the legality of women as property, the citizenry launched a movement and drove the Nineteenth Amendment into the Constitution.

"Now, we're facing the legality of Corporate Persons, so we need to launch a movement to separate corporation and state and to clarify that all references to 'persons' in our founding documents and amendments refer to 'Natural Persons' in perpetuity."

"You're going to start a movement?" Malani did not look convinced.

"No, I'm joining it. Lots of people are already thinking like this. Have you seen Robert Reich's new book, *Supercapitalism*? He was Clinton's labor secretary. He says, 'Separating supercapitalism and democracy is the only constructive agenda for change. All else is frolic and detour.'"

"Wow!" said Malani, pushing back her chair. "I love it. Exxon thinks this whole oil spill story will be over with the Supreme Court decision. I mean, what's a few billion dollars in fines when you're making $40 billion or more a year in profit?

"But this takes the issue to a whole new level. We have to get off oil, because it's killing us and the planet. And we have to fix the U.S. legal system so corporations can't keep polluting for profit. And we can turn the *Exxon Valdez* oil spill into a civil rights movement! We've got to amend the Constitution so people's rights count over corporate rights!"

She looked at me, convinced now, with a bright smile. "What can I do to help?"

"You're going to be teaching our future leaders! You can teach them that another, better way of living is possible. What might the world and their community and lives look like without fossil fuels? The kids need to learn to live in this new world order, which means *you* need to figure it out, too, so you can teach them. But for starters," I smiled, "civil rights movements need songs."

As Malani went to take the brownies from the oven, we heard truck doors slam, and dinner guests spilled into the house. After the salmon barbeque, as the evening wore on, Sam reached for his guitar and others reached for their instruments. We sat in a circle of song just as we had done for the past two decades, except for the crew filming quietly from the corner. Eventually, they put down their cameras as the music drew them, too, into our circle.

Who Rules? A Clash of Values

I knew exactly the very instant I made up my mind.

It was February 26, 2008, the day before the Supreme Court hearing of the *Exxon Valdez* case. I was in Washington, D.C., with Lisa Marie and the Quebec film crew. The day had wound "Hill visits" with congressional delegates and staff, and media events, organized by Cordova fishermen. As dusk turned into dark, we caught up with the fishermen again for a candlelight vigil on the mall. Rumor was that the local placeholder agencies were fully booked for the Supreme Court hearing. These agencies literally hire people to stand in line for popular events, including hearings and trials, so that highly paid lobbyists, lawyers, or other professionals would not have to compete with the public for seats. That's when I felt the rebellious kindling that had smoldered by day.

We drove by the Supreme Court on our way back to the hotel. There on the sidewalk, backlit by the courthouse floodlights, two people stood waiting for tomorrow's hearing—staking out a place in line before the coming of the rumored placeholders. I felt a rising surge of fire. *Who were they?* I needed to know. We stopped so I could hail them. It was the former mayor of Kodiak in 1989 and his teenage son, born after the spill.

"Riki, is that you?" Bob Brodie clasped my hand through the car window. That's when I knew I would be spending the night on the sidewalk right along with them, holding a place in line so we could actually get into the courtroom at our own hearing.

On the ride back to the hotel, Lisa Marie and the cameraman spoke of gourmet foods, cooking, and fine wines, while the two producers argued in French or agreed in English as they navigated streets. I made plans for a long night. I would wait for Zak, who was flying in from squid fishing in California to join us.

When Zak learned of the placeholders, he simply said, "I didn't come all this way not to hear our lawsuit." He put on extra layers of clothing and was ready to go. When the producer, Robert, learned of our plans, he insisted on driving us into town, instead of letting us take a cab.

We arrived at 11:30 P.M. to find three people in line. Marge Salmon, a former Cordova fisherma'm, settled into her sleeping bag as Zak and I set up camp on the curb. I had brought knapsacks to use as "sit-upons" to insulate us from the cold concrete. There would be light snow showers before dawn. Five young students walked up with blankets and pillows. I looked at the fresh young faces.

"Placeholders?" We asked each other. No, they said, pre-law students from Lipscomb University in Tennessee to see the "trial of our lifetime." Each of our groups made phone calls to recruit members. Unbeknownst to me, the students, who were excited to be with "real" plaintiffs, also called their professor, who told them to sit with us and ask questions.

By midnight, our ranks had swelled to fifty. After establishing a place in line, bundled forms regrouped into three clumps. Nine pre-law students gathered around Zak and me, while others sat reading textbooks under the glow of streetlamps. Downstream from them, fishermen had pulled camp chairs into a tight circle and were playing Trivial Pursuit.

The students pelted Zak and me with questions about the spill, fishing, our case. Zak listened patiently and spoke with a poised grace. Zak was about the same age as these law students, but he was light-years apart from them in experience. He had lived what his scholarly peers could only absorb from books and oral history. Under their examination, Zak and I became cocounselors, trying our case before the nine student-judges. The impartiality of the student-judges, initially stated, dissolved in heart-told stories that stitched together nearly nineteen years of lost livelihoods, hopes and dreams; estranged friendships and broken families; and a sick Prince William Sound still struggling to recover from the toxic shock and resulting loss of life.

When the questions turned to effects on the Native community, I drew Sven Haakanson, Jr., into our cocounsel. Sven, an Alaska Native from Kodiak, had joined Bob and his son. In his quietly understated way, Sven explained that the spill had torn a generation-wide hole in their subsistence culture. Their culture depends upon continuity of teaching a respectful coexistence with a healthy environment. Lacking both, the culture had stumbled. Whether Elders could buffer the fall with generations as yet unborn remained to be seen.

When the student-judges asked Zak what he thought was the central issue raised by this case, he didn't hesitate. "We have to separate corporations and democracy. Corporations have become too big to be held accountable to the people and government."

This unexpected answer drew a new line of questioning. I drew imaginary triangles on the blackboard of a dark night's sky to explain how our democratic process had been corrupted by a consolidation of wealth and power through "Corporate Persons."

Inspired by the rapt audience, I added one more element that had coalesced since my talk with Malani. I etched three circles into imaginations, intertwined like Olympic rings. The three circles represented economic, environmental, and social wealth.

At the center, where the circles overlapped, was the "triple bottom line," a new accounting system that measures the health of our economy against social and environmental factors, not simply as money exchanging hands. A triple bottom line is good for business, good for people, and good for the environment—unlike our current economic measure, the Gross Domestic Product, which thrives on a sick society. By its count, wars, pollution, prisons, divorces, and cancers and other chemical-derived diseases result in exchanges of money that are "good" for a suicide economy. But a living economy needs a new measure of true wealth, a measure of progress toward a sustainable future for all, grown in local self-reliant communities.

I found myself on my soapbox again, this time with a league of law students listening. In a democracy, I explained, human values count and are codified into law. In a "corpocracy," corporate values count and are codified into law. Corporations exist for one purpose: to make a profit for shareholders. This was decided by a state court in 1919 and it's still the most frequently cited decision in courts of law by corporations defending their actions. Without the counterbalance of human needs and human rights, we could never achieve a sustainable future. The choice is with us—The People—as it always is in a true democracy. (figure 6)

When the icy wind picked up at 2 A.M., the outside hearing abruptly adjourned. The nine lay judges merged into one solid lump of blankets, pillows, and bodies—more to conserve heat than sleep. They reminded me of meerkats huddled for warmth.

The circle of fishermen downstream from us called friends to send more sleeping bags, camping pads, warm jackets, hats, and coffee. When arriving taxis disgorged the gear, fishermen fortified their circle against the wind and resumed their game of Trivial Pursuit, which lasted through the night.

I zipped my $5 thrift store jacket up to my neck and caught a plastic grocery bag as it blew past. I tied the bag on my head like a scarf, pulled my cap down on top of it, and pulled my "smoke ring"—a neck gaiter made with musk ox underwool, warm and light as smoke—around my face. Zak grinned, shook his head, and wandered down to the bulky circle to join the game.

Staring alternately at America's capital, lit by floodlights, and the dark sky, lit by a waning half-moon and an ocean of stars, I thought about the issues we had raised before the wind dampened our court. It all boiled down to whether American people would have the courage to embrace basic human

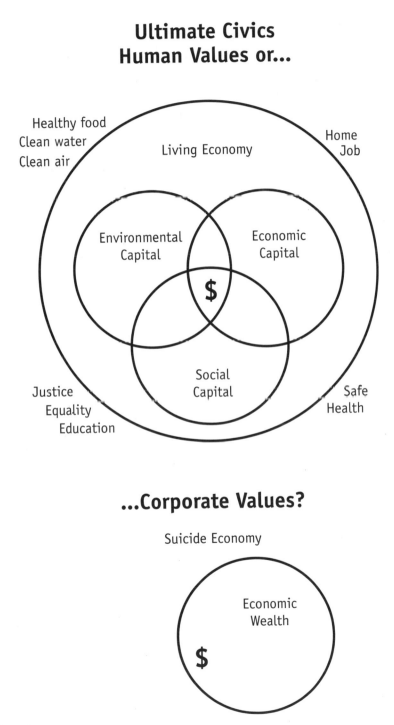

Ultimate Civics
Human Values or...

Healthy food
Clean water
Clean air

Living Economy

Home
Job

Environmental
Capital

Economic
Capital

$

Social
Capital

Justice
Equality
Education

Safe
Health

...Corporate Values?

Suicide Economy

Economic
Wealth

$

Figure 6.

rights as 155 other nations had done. All of the industrialized countries except the United States had ratified the Universal Declaration of Human Rights, as had many countries far poorer than the United States. We had considered it once, but the Cold War with its labels of "Marxist," "Socialist," and "Communist" had driven compassion from reason.

As the moon arced slowly across the night sky over the White House, I wondered, would American people find in their hearts the courage to ratify the simple truth that the phrase "liberty and justice for all" meant exactly that?

Dawn brought the film crew with hard-boiled eggs, yogurt, and apples. It brought the Capital police with orders to break camp and form a single line. It brought the sun with its promise of warmth. It brought the hope that our highest court would shed laws rooted in past centuries to meet the changing times and changing needs of human persons.

Unlike the midnight court, which had rendered its decision before daylight, we would have to wait for the Supreme Court's decision. I could only hope the professional judges would rule as The People's court had done—in our favor.

EPILOGUE

The phone rang at 6:07 A.M., Alaska time, on June 25, 2008. "Riki, have you heard?" It was Yereth Rosen with Reuters.

"No." I cringed at the tone in her voice. Everyone in Cordova had been on pins and needles. The Supreme Court had a recess on the horizon, and the judges needed to rule on the *Exxon Valdez* case before they departed. The final word would be coming any day now.

"Then I'm sorry to have to tell you. The court reduced the punitive award to $507.5 million and. . . ."

I didn't hear the rest of what she said. My mind went blank. This was devastating news for all the fishermen and other people whose lives had become like storm-tossed ships at sea ever since we heard the news of the spill, some nineteen years ago.

"Riki? Riki?" Yereth's voice caught my attention again.

"How could they? What else do you know?"

"It's all sketchy right now. I'll call back once I know more." She hung up.

I stared out the window at a scene that suddenly matched my mood: gusty gray clouds and a rainsquall. $507 million was just 10 percent of the original jury award. This would mean bankruptcies, foreclosures, homes sold, fishing businesses lost, and friends moving. I wasn't eager to pick up the phone to call Linden and others, but I didn't want them to have to learn the news from the media.

Six hours later, a group of us gathered on Main Street to paint our opinions of the Supreme Court decision on Tyvek sheets to post on walls of willing businesses. Our nucleus of activity attracted others. There were no countercurrents in the discussion or mood. We all understood what we had lost. But did others?

Imagine if the primary industry in your community was wiped out by the actions of another. If you owned a business that depended on that primary industry, wouldn't you feel entitled to a damage claim as well? Yet we knew of hundreds of such damage claims that had been thrown out, casualties of legal battles.

Imagine if the equity in your home was wiped out by the actions of another. Wouldn't you feel entitled to damage claims for that loss? Yet some of the banner painters among us had lost hundreds of thousands of dollars in equity in fishing permits that had not counted in court.

Imagine if you were owed substantial damages from another's actions, but only a fraction of the harm was provable in court at the time of the trial. But mortgages were due and living expenses had to be paid in the intervening years as the case dragged on. Would you have signed over your future claims to bankers and loan managers in trade for debt relief as many fishermen were forced to do? If so, then you might understand why we do not consider ourselves made whole by an amount of money that does not even get us back to where we were twenty years ago—much less to where we might have been absent the harm.

In strong brushstrokes, bright orange, deep blue, and bold yellow letters distilled our disappointment into short phrases. "EXXON MADE $/ WE PAID $." "MOM & POP LOSE / CORPORATIONS WIN."

Our talk turned from money to matters of law. The Supreme Court had ruled that a one-to-one ratio of compensatory to punitive damages was sufficient punishment under maritime law. In hard cash this meant the jury award of one year's net profit in 1994 was reduced to four days of net profit in 2008. This was not punishment. ExxonMobil would feel this sting like an elephant feels a mosquito bite. But worse, we reasoned, it was just a matter of time before this ratio was tested in other cases in other communities harmed by another giant corporation seeking to reduce its liability.

"WHO'S NEXT?" one of us penned on a sheet, while others painted, "GUILTY UNTIL PROVEN WEALTHY."

We all felt the justice system was broken. The threat of big punitive damages act to deter giant corporations from bad conduct. Without this threat, we worried corporations would compromise public health, worker safety, and the environment for profit. One of us scripted, "ARE CORPORATIONS ABOVE THE LAW?" in solid orange as we wove our worries toward the springboard question in Cordova, the question that sprung talk into action.

What are we going to do now?

It was a question I had heard my whole life in circles of people gathered to problem-solve. It brought the teachings of my father full circle from the DDT battles in Wisconsin to the emerging global battle over civil rights—human rights versus corporate "rights"—or Ultimate Civics.

"We could go to Congress to have this overturned," I suggested, reminding everyone that the oilmen had done this thirty-five years ago when the fishermen had taken their case to block the pipeline terminus in Port Valdez to the Supreme Court and won. Smiles lifted the gloom. So there was a way forward!

Armed with painter's tape and a ladder, we split into teams to post our handiwork as the talk turned to how to pitch this idea to the American people and Congress.

Later, inspired by the resilient mood, Malani wrote a song of protest over the Supreme Court's sell-out to big business at the expense of the "little guys." It was a lament of lost justice and lost civil rights—and it was a call to action.

Does the Supreme Court's decision bring closure to the Cordova community? Not really. And, if not, then what will? This is a question often asked by media. For each person who suffered the spill's devastating effects firsthand, there is a different answer, because closure means different things to different people.

What of the grandparents who were robbed of precious time with grandchildren because they lost their retirement security and had to keep fishing to pay bills long into their "golden years"?

What of Native Elders who felt their culture skip a beat because they were not able to teach an entire generation of youth the traditional ways of living with respect for and in harmony with the land?

What of those of my generation, who felt the peak years of our lives were lost to circumstances beyond our control and then to a global corporation that conspired to pretend everything was back to normal when it was not? It is uncomfortable living another's lie and, in a great irony of our times, it can be even more uncomfortable trying to correct the corporate-state lore.

What of the spill children, who struggled at a young age to cope with a big hurt that could not be comforted by a parent's hug?

For the Cordova community, there is no single event that will bring full closure, but rather a combination of at least three events. The Supreme Court decision brought one element of closure to a legal quagmire that had gone on for far too long. We also need to see the herring population return to its pre-spill glory, signaling that the Sound is back to normal. And, finally, we'll need to rebuild confidence and trust in ourselves and our institutions; we need to feel confident that such an event will not happen again, and that if it does, the systems set up to protect us will not falter to favor corporate interests. For this final assurance, we the people, so to speak, must be able to hold the government and oil industry accountable to the law and lore of the land. That will require changes in the legal system and our founding charter to reflect a shift in priorities from economics to human rights and community values. It will require the participation of citizens in other parts of the country to help enact these changes to avert tragedy in their own backyards.

Closure for individuals is a different story. Those who lean heavily on the Supreme Court's decision may close this chapter of their lives soon after the court makes a ruling. Those who wait for the herring to rebound may be waiting years or decades. Those who died—over 6,000—while their cases churned through the judiciary system will never have had the peace of closure. And for those who work to hold the government and industry accountable to the people, there will never be an "all clear," because such is the basic work of democracy. Democracy is like a campfire: It needs to be constantly tended or it will die. Our spill experience will forever drive our work in the world.

Four months before the Supreme Court ruling, while we were in Washington, D.C., I was inside the courthouse at the small café, warming up after our night vigil on the sidewalk and eating with Zak and a dozen or so other fishermen. Sylvia Lange from Cordova rejoined us after freshening up in the restroom. Rubbing her still-cold hands, she told us that she had spoken in the ladies' room to two very stylish and expensively turned out women with fine briefcases. Her black eyes twinkled mischievously. According to Sylvia, one of the fine ladies had said, "Oh, you must be from *that* town."

As we all shared a laugh, I felt how good it was to be from *that* town. That town had been through a lot. We had stumbled, fallen, and recovered. Now we could get back to the business of being a community. And, maybe, somewhere in our story, there are lessons to break the falls of other communities and to speed their recovery so that, community by community, we can work together to rebuild a nation that, too, has stumbled.

TIMELINE

1968

January............ ARCO discovers America's largest oilfield on Alaska North Slope, triggering "Black Gold" Rush.

1969

Oil forces gather to support pipeline south from Prudhoe Bay. Cordova fishermen, alarmed over big oil spills in California and Massachusetts, oppose pipeline terminus and tanker terminal in Port Valdez.

January............ Santa Barbara oil well blowout (200,000 gallons)
September....... Buzzards Bay, Mass,, heating oil spill (185,000 gallons)

1970

National environmental awareness, triggered by Santa Barbara spill and other events, fans opposition to Alaska pipeline and supports suite of public health, worker safety, and environmental laws.

January 1......... National Environmental Policy Act (NEPA)
August 14 .... BP, ARCO, Humble (now ExxonMobil), and five other oil companies form consortium, Alyeska, to build and operate Alaska pipeline and tanker terminal
December 29 .. U.S. Occupational Safety and Health Act

1971

Despite massive public opposition to Alaska pipeline, federal and Alaska governments steadily press project. Cordova fishermen's lawsuit is consolidated with environmental and Native lawsuits to become first major test of NEPA.

March............. Cordova fishermen sue Department of the Interior
July .... Alaska legislature creates Dept. of Environmental Conservation (ADEC) to oversee construction of Alaska pipeline and oil development in general
December 18 .. Alaska Native Claims Settlement Act clears land issues for Alaska pipeline

1972

Oilmen and/or Nixon administration repeatedly promise that state-of-the-art construction, tankers, navigational procedures, and oil spill response equipment will make "operations at Port Valdez and in Prince William Sound the safest in the world."

January............ Federal judge rules Department of the Interior in compliance with environmental requirements; Cordova fishermen appeal
October 18...... Federal Water Pollution Control Amendments (predecessor to Clean Water Act) establish pollution discharge permits and spill-response planning process

1973

President Nixon authorizes Alaska pipeline after tied vote in Senate broken in favor by Vice President Agnew. Act forecloses further legal action. Few promises are codified into new law; oilmen start lobbying against double-bottom tankers.

February 9 ...... U.S. District Court of Appeals, Washington, D.C., rules in fishermen's favor, blocking Alaska pipeline project
April 7 .... U.S. Supreme Court upholds ruling
November 16 .. Trans-Alaska Pipeline Authorization Act

1974

Urged by Cordova fishermen, Alaska passes laws to enact salmon hatcheries in Prince William Sound.

December 30 .. Prince William Sound Aquaculture Corporation forms

1975

Construction of Alaska pipeline starts. Within six months, news stories report violation of state and federal permits and laws, faulty construction, embezzlement, bribery, and other irregularities.

March .... First section of pipeline laid

1976

At urging of Cordova fishermen and others, Alaska passes laws to increase tanker safety, reduce risk of pollution from tanker terminal, and generally codify oilmen's promises in light of sloppy construction and environmental cost-cutting measures on Alaska pipeline.

May .... Alaska passes tanker safety and pollution discharge laws
June 21............ Congressional oversight hearings on Alaska pipeline quality control and other issues

1977

Alaska pipeline completed as Clean Water Act and Clean Air Act pass to regulate oil and other pollution.

May 31 .... Pipeline construction done
June 20............ Oil flow startup
August 1 .... First tanker loaded and leaves terminal
September 16 .. Chevron and other oil companies sue to overturn Alaska tanker safety and pollution discharge laws

1979

Oil companies prevail in state court, breaking promise of double-bottom tankers, among others. Alaska opts to repeal its tanker safety and pollution control laws, but, at urging of Cordova fishermen, it appeals single provision to regulate tanker ballast water discharge. EPA finds Alyeska is polluting Port Valdez in violation of discharge permit.

1983

January............ EPA reauthorizes Alyeska's discharge permit, allowing more pollution into Port Valdez.

1984

Alaska wins appeal to regulate ballast water discharge from tanker terminal and receives warnings that Alyeska is not prepared to respond to big spill. Hundreds die and thousands sickened in poisonous gas leak in Bhopal, India, shocking world with realization that corporations recklessly risk lives on a massive scale for profit.

May .... State employees warn Alyeska cannot handle a big spill
December .... State employees warn again of shortcomings in Alyeska's spill response
                 program
December 3 .... Bhopal poisonous gas leak

1985

EPA investigation confirms oil pollution from tanker terminal. Cordova fishermen sue EPA even as many Alaska residents grow complacent after receiving first annual Permanent Fund dividend from investment of share of oil revenues.

May .... Fishermen sue EPA over Alyeska discharge permit
July .... EPA issues Alyeska compliance order for discharge permit

1987

Department of the Interior recommends opening Arctic National Wildlife Refuge for oil and gas exploration, while quashing agency reports of harm to wildlife from Prudhoe Bay oil fields. *Glacier Bay* oil spill in Cook Inlet heightens Cordova fishermen's concerns over Alyeska operations.

July .... *Glacier Bay* oil spill in Cook Inlet; response inadequate; Cook Inlet fishermen
                 sue
November 5 .... EPA hearings in Valdez on reauthorizing Alyeska's discharge permit

1988

Prudhoe Bay oil field production and tanker traffic in Port Valdez peak; EPA lists Port Valdez as toxic-impaired water body from oil pollution, yet closes four-year investigation of Alyeska air quality with no enforcement action. Value of Prince William Sound fishing permits soars with high prices for salmon and herring harvests and in anticipation of full hatchery production.

1989

Failed initial response to *Exxon Valdez* grounding results in most damaging oil spill in U.S. history, hundreds of lawsuits for damages, congressional probes into Alaska pipeline operations, citizen oversight groups of oil operations, and concerted effort by Exxon and Alyeska to minimize perceptions of damage. Fisheries closed from Prince William Sound to Aleutian Peninsula. Mismanaged cleanup results in health concerns for workers and secondary disaster in oiled communities as high-level trauma and social dysfunction ensues.

January............ Two tanker spills at terminal warn of problems with cleanup and single-hull
                 tankers
March 24 .... *Exxon Valdez* oil spill
April .... Spill declared hazardous waste cleanup; feds approve Exxon's request to provide
                 only minimal safety training for workers
June .... Alyeska and fishermen create predecessor to Regional Citizens' Advisory
                 Council; fishermen and environmentalists form Oil Reform Alliance to
                 advocate stronger spill prevention and response laws

July .... EPA reauthorizes Alyeska's discharge permit, reducing permitted amounts of
                pollution
July 10 .... Alyeska creates ship escort system for tankers (seventeen years after promised)
August .... Sociologists start case study in Cordova of spill trauma
September 9 .... Cordova fishermen stage protest in Port Valdez over failed cleanup; 6,722
                workers file claims for respiratory illnesses; Exxon dismisses as "Valdez Crud,"
                fails to report claims to feds/OSHA

1990

Behind-the-scenes stories of political and legal efforts to hold oil companies accountable reveal
strong corporate influences and system biases. Public pressure drives passage of stronger oil
spill prevention laws. Congressional probes of Alaska pipeline operations continue, triggering
backlash against critics. Massive community-level trauma documented in all oiled communities;
leaked reports of extensive harm to wildlife feed uncertainty and stress. Cleanup continues on
oiled beaches; fishery closures persist in Prince William Sound from oiled beaches.

February .... Alyeska targets critics with spy operation
February 14 .... Federal and Exxon criminal plea agreement collapses
May .... Alaska passes seven new laws strengthening oil spill prevention and response
                measures
August 18 .... Oil Pollution Act passes, codifies many pre-pipeline promises into law,
                mandates double-hull tankers by 2015, creates Trustee Council to manage
                restoration projects, mandates citizens' advisory councils
October .... Alyeska fires first whistleblower snared in spy operation
December .... Alaska pipeline owners shut down spy operation
December 14 .. Federal judge denies class certification; state judge certifies first of several
                classes

1991

Feds and Alaska settle Exxon's criminal and civil spill fines, creating pot of funds for restoration
and construction projects. Citizens uncover illegal dumping of oil wastes in Port Valdez,
triggering government hearings and investigations. Beach cleanup continues as disastrous pink
season in Sound causes bankruptcies; angst mounts over worry of oil damages and perceptions
that judges' personal biases influence legal decisions. Exxon and Alyeska delay and eliminate
private damage claims.

February 8 ...... Federal judge rules private damages are maritime tort, preempts state law, and
                clears way to eliminate thousands of claims; State judge earlier preserved claims
                under state law
March .... Alaska hearings on Ballast Watergate, state and federal investigations start
March 25 .... Plaintiffs file $50 billion in damage claims against TAPL Fund
August .... "Humpy Dump" in Sound
August .... Fishermen win *Glacier Bay* lawsuit; lead trial lawyer shifts to *Exxon Valdez* case
October 8 .... Federal judge approves criminal plea agreement, despite earlier rejecting similar
                one
November .... Congressional hearing on Alyeska spy operation; Alyeska fires more
                whistleblowers/quality control inspectors

1992

Citizens demand accountability of oil spill fines when EVOS Trustee Council cuts popular
studies that document harm to wildlife. Exxon employs legal tactics to dismiss, delay private

damages case as evidence mounts of harm to workers and wildlife; cleanup declared "complete." Members of the public and the oil lobby clash over attempts to legalize air and water pollution from tanker terminal in Port Valdez, weaken new spill-prevention standards, and gut state water quality standards. Citizens and quality control inspectors warn of imminent failure of Alaska pipeline, trigger congressional hearings and audits; illegal dumping of ballast water halts, Port Valdez water quality slowly improves.

January–
February .... Alyeska fires more whistleblowers
April .... News stories break on sick cleanup workers
May .... Hickel vetoes popular bill to use spill fines for habitat acquisition
June 12............ Oil spill cleanup declared "complete"
June .... Citizens challenge Alyeska air quality study; initiate efforts for vapor recovery
August .... Wild and hatchery pink salmon populations collapse in Sound
September....... Federal scientists start seminal "fish-tox" study to determine effects of low
                       levels of oil on eggs, young salmon, and (later) herring
December .... Alyeska fires supervisor of fired quality control inspectors; triggers
                       congressional interest

1993

Stress and anger build in Cordova with release of studies showing extensive harm to wildlife, Exxon's denial of harm, collapse of herring population, suicide of former mayor, and second collapse of pink salmon population. Fishermen link fish collapses to spill and blockade tanker traffic to focus attention on ailing Sound. Citizens demand accountability with oil spill money, want funds for habitat acquisition and restoration studies; Congress orders pipeline audit, based on whistleblowers' concerns. Plaintiffs' lawyers secretly outmaneuver Exxon to settle private damages with Alyeska, leaving Exxon to fight alone.

January............ EVOS Trustees/publicly-funded spill studies released, show massive and
                       on-going harm
April .... Exxon releases studies showing minimal harm, rapid wildlife recovery from
                       spill as herring population collapses in Sound and fisheries canceled
May .... Former Cordova mayor Bobby Van Brocklin commits suicide
July .... Alyeska settles with whistleblowers, agrees to rehire; Congressional hearing on
                       Alaska pipeline quality control problems; feds order audit
July .... Alyeska settles private spill damages for $98 million; Exxon files injunction
August .... Wild and hatchery pink salmon populations collapse in Sound; fishermen
                       blockade Valdez Narrows and gain federal promise for ecosystem studies
September....... Public planning process for first ecosystem study on salmon and herring starts;
                       first acoustic survey of herring by PWS Science Center
September....... File-stuffing incident (creating false documents) reported during federal audit
November....... Congressional hearing on Alaska pipeline quality control and audit findings;
                       pipeline owners promise fixes, but blacklist whistleblowers
December .... Invasion-of-privacy lawsuit settles for Alyeska spy operation; Alyeska
                       whistleblowers file more charges

1994

Empty tanker accident in Sound shows need for improvements; citizens successfully press Coast Guard for reforms. Events around five-year spill memorial rock town but Cordovans, empowered by blockade, become proactive in solving lingering social, economic, and environmental problems from spill and start to heal dysfunction. Scientists start ecosystem studies to understand effects of oil on salmon and herring. Federal trial for private damages yield highest punitive award in history; Exxon vows to fight "unjust verdict." Citizen oversight group on Alaska pipeline forms in wake of company insiders reporting continuing problems with quality control and repairs.

January 4......... Empty tanker *Overseas Ohio* rips open hull on iceberg in PWS
January............ Cordova town meeting series on fiscal reality
April .... First ecosystem study (SEA Program) funded by Trustee Council; planning process for second study (NVP Program) to look at effects of oil and food on key coastal species
April .... Herring fisheries in Sound canceled
April .... More Alyeska whistleblowers file charges, report problems
May .... *Exxon Valdez* trials start in federal district court
June 13............ Federal jury finds Exxon and Hazelwood reckless
August 11....... Federal jury awards plaintiffs $287 million in compensatory damages
September 16 . Federal jury awards plaintiffs $5 billion punitive damages
October .... Exxon and Hazelwood file twenty-two posttrial motions to stall payment, overturn decision
November....... Coast Guard rule requires more, improved tug escorts, weather restrictions

1995

Cordovans vie over different visions of "progress" as alternatives to large-scale resource extraction projects on Copper River Delta are sought to diversify faltering fish-based economy. Exxon uses legal tactics to stall, dismiss, or reduce awards in private damages case; fishermen, Natives, and others undertake divisive Damage Matrix to divide awards among all claimants. Cordova, Kodiak sue state to protect areas left out of first tanker response plans under new laws.

January............ District court denies all of Exxon's posttrial motions; Exxon appeals
April .... Herring fisheries in Sound canceled
June .... Exxon charges jury misconduct to stall, overturn punitive award; district court holds interviews and hearings
July .... Group of international artists visit Cordova to promote sustainable uses of area
September 6.... Exxon files motion for new trial claiming jury tampering
September....... Pressed by citizens, EPA orders vapor controls on two tanker-loading berths
October .... Cordova, Kodiak appeal tanker response plans
November....... Planning process for third ecosystem study (APEX) to look at effects of climate on seabird and marine mammal populations

1996

Sociologists conduct trainings to alleviate community-level social trauma; trainings become national model. Plaintiffs' lawyers flush "nefarious plot" to kickback punitive award of "Seattle Seven" processors to Exxon; plaintiffs and lawyers fight to preserve punitive award in Exxon case and from state and federal tort reform efforts; Supreme Court rules to limit punitive damages. Cordovans explore sustainable development options amid debates over logging, mining, and oil development; other citizen-driven efforts track lack of repairs on Alaska pipeline and need for better tanker escort system in Sound. Federal scientists conduct beach dig in Sound, find virtually fresh toxic oil buried in biologically-rich intertidal zone.

January–
February .... Sociologists and citizens conduct peer listening and training programs
March............. Exxon's Seattle Seven object to Damage Matrix, revealing scheme to kickback processors' punitive award to Exxon
March............. Exxon files lawsuits to overturn tanker ban, return *Exxon Valdez* to Sound

April .... Herring fisheries in Sound canceled
May .... Supreme Court reverses punitive damage award in *BMW v. Gore* as "grossly
                    excessive"
June .... District court approves Damage Matrix and Phase IV damage claims
June .... Beach dig finds lots of fresh toxic oil from spill; feds initiate four-year survey
September....... First purchase of Native lands in Sound with oil spill funds
September....... Exxon's Seattle Seven appeal kickback scheme to Ninth Circuit
September....... District court enters judgment on $5 billion jury verdict, starting interest
October 8........ Exxon stalls by arguing to amend judgment on punitive damages
October .... Native corporation unveils major resource extraction project on Copper River
                    Delta, tied in with use of oil spill funds for access road and deepwater port

1997

First herring fisheries in four years yield disappointing harvest; federal scientists confirm link
between oil spill and salmon collapses. Cordovans link with residents in Copper River watershed
to discuss options for sustainable development based on community values. Exxon's assault on
punitive damage award continues; determined citizens thwart attempts to return old *Exxon
Valdez* to Sound and dodge double-hull tanker requirements.

January............ Exxon files lawsuits to return old *Exxon Valdez* to Alaska trade
January–
  February .... District court rejects Exxon's motion on punitive damages; Exxon appeals
April .... Herring fisheries in Sound yield few small and immature fish
May .... Group of international artists visit Cordova for bird migration
May .... Alaska passes tort reform law, exempts *Exxon Valdez* case
June .... D.C. District court transfers Exxon's lawsuit to return banned *Exxon Valdez* to
                    Sound to Alaska district court
August............ PWS Native corporation sells land through EVOS Trustee Council
September 23 . Exxon files motion for new trial, based on jury tampering
December .... Exxon and other shippers "reconfigure" several tankers to stall double-hull
                    requirement before Congress closes loophole

1998

Cordovans engage in community-based tourism planning to grow economy compatible with
commercial fishing. Disappointing herring fishery becomes last as fisheries closed indefinitely for
stock recovery. Fishermen prevail in response planning process, gain protection for Copper River
Delta as drive to open Delta for resource extraction falters. Major spill drill shows high level of
response preparation, but resurrects old battle over dispersant use; citizens oppose dispersants
and the oil industry and Coast Guard press for its approval. Exxon appeals continue.

January 5......... Ninth Circuit stays proceedings, orders limited remand of Exxon's motion for
                    new trial
March............. Vapor controls operational on two berths at tanker terminal
April .... Herring fisheries in Sound yield few small and immature fish
June .... District judge upholds law, *Exxon Valdez* remains banned from Sound; Exxon
                    appeals
July .... State court fines Hazelwood, sentences him to community service
July–August ... District court denies Exxon's motion for a new trial based on jury tampering;
                    Exxon appeals
October .... BP conducts major spill drill; Coast Guard hearings on dispersant use
December .... Tanker *Ericka* oil spill off France (3 million gallons) creates successful

international drive for double-hull tankers, ending attempts to circumvent law in United States

1999

Mental health trauma spikes in Cordova with ten-year spill memorial; citizens protest ExxonMobil merger. Federal scientists find low levels of oil harm young salmon and herring, call for revisions of federal laws and energy policy to reflect new science; EPA lists small oil particles in crude as threat to human health, wildlife. Citizens begin drive to reopen civil settlement, work to link lingering harm to wildlife and workers with Exxon's spill. Ninth Circuit hears arguments in private damages case; Hazelwood starts community service sentence in Anchorage. Major improvements in spill prevention and response achieved in Sound twenty-seven years after promised.

January............ First new tractor tug arrives in Sound, second in May
March............. "Valdez Crud" news story on chronic respiratory problems of cleanup workers
May 3 .... Ninth Circuit hears arguments on consolidated appeals
June 21 .... Hazelwood starts 1,000 hours of community service
April .... Herring fisheries in Sound canceled
September....... SEA Program, federal fish-tox study completed
October .... First new double-hull tanker for Alaska trade built
November 30.. Merger of Exxon and Mobil approved

2000

Scientists link buried oil with lingering harm to wildlife in Sound; link with herring collapse and lack of recovery still not confirmed. BP ARCO merger ends drive for oil leasing on Copper River Delta. More shippers order double-hull tankers, but not ExxonMobil.

March 16 .... Ninth Circuit denies Exxon's appeal for new trial based on alleged jury tampering; Exxon appeals
April .... Herring fisheries in Sound canceled; PWS Science Center starts Steller sea lion surveys, notes coincidence of herring
April 13 .... BP ARCO merger approved
September....... Second ecosystem study (NVP Program), federal beach survey complete
September ...... BP orders three new double-hull tankers for Alaska trade
October 2........ U.S. Supreme Court upholds decision on jury tampering
October 12...... Ninth Circuit rules Exxon's Seattle Seven, other processors entitled to share of punitive damages; also reinstates claims of tender boat operators and crew, processor crews, others

2001

Final ecosystem study shows effects of climate on wildlife populations as distinct from oil effects. First new double-hull tanker in service; Hazelwood completes community service sentence. Ninth Circuit remands punitive award, orders district court to reduce award in light of Supreme Court ruling. Citizens in oiled region take proactive steps to reduce social trauma anticipated from punitive award. Public process for reauthorization of Alaska pipeline starts despite failure to adequately deal with quality control issues.

April .... Herring fisheries in Sound canceled
July 11............. First new double-hull tanker reaches Sound
August 17 .... Hazelwood completes 1,000 hours of community service
September....... Third ecosystem study (APEX) completed

November 5 .... "Valdez Crud" investigative news story triggers congressional concern as similar "Crud" reported in 9/11 workers

November 7 .... Ninth Circuit vacates, remands $5 billion punitive award as excessive in light of *BMW v. Gore*; also rejects Exxon's motion that punitive damages are barred under Clean Water Act

2002

State undermines citizens' efforts to require shippers to demonstrate that spill response plans work in practice; EPA proposes rule to exempt vapor recovery at tanker terminal, citizens oppose. *Exxon Valdez* permanently banned from Sound. District court reduces punitive award; decision appealed.

February 1 ...... Alaska Supreme Court rules shippers must demonstrate that spill response plans work

April .... Alaska law overturns Supreme Court ruling, declares shippers must only prove response plans work *on paper*

April .... Herring fisheries in Sound canceled

May .... Spill response plans include areas outside Sound

June .... State court trial on municipalities' claims

October 11 ...... Oral arguments held on punitive damages remand

October 31 ...... *Exxon Valdez* banned from Alaska oil trade; later sold to Chinese company to ship bulk ore

November .... State renews Alaska pipeline right-of-way grant for 30 years

December 9 .... District court reduces punitive award to $4 billion plus interest, states $5 billion constitutionally permissible

2003

Federal/state governments rubber-stamp Alaska pipeline reauthorization permits, ignore public's appeal for citizen oversight. More improvements in Sound with addition of ice-detecting radar. Ninth Circuit remands punitive damages to district court in light of new Supreme Court ruling. New science that oil is more toxic to wildlife than thought in 1970s is widely accepted; Yale study shows chronic illnesses in Exxon workers fourteen years after cleanup.

January............ Department of the Interior renews Alaska pipeline right-of-way grant for thirty years, stipulates audit every three years

January............ High-tech iceberg-detecting radar system operational in Sound

April .... Herring fisheries in Sound canceled

April 7 .... Supreme Court suggests punitive damages should not exceed a "single-digit ratio" or 10:1 punitive to compensatory in *State Farm v. Campbell*

May .... "Valdez Crud" news story; Yale thesis finds chronic illnesses in workers

July 11............. Tender claims settle

August 22 .... Ninth Circuit remands punitive award in light of *State Farm v. Campbell*

August 25 .... EPA keeps rule requiring vapor controls for loading tankers

December 3 .... Oral argument in district court on punitive award

December 19 .. Emerging science on oil toxicity published in *Science*

2004

Decade of acoustic herring surveys and Steller sea lion surveys link population collapses with spill. District court reinstates punitive award.

January 28....... District court approves punitive award of $4.5 billion plus interest, states $5 billion award constitutionally permissible; Exxon later appeals

February .... EPA ruling exempts ballast water treatment plant from vapor controls
April .... Herring fisheries in Sound canceled

2005

Cordova ranks among top ten seaports in nation based on harvest value, regaining ground lost after spill; rise in harvest value largely due to unoiled Copper River fisheries. Prince William Sound seine-fishing permits remain around 10 percent of pre-spill value.

April .... Herring fisheries in Sound canceled

2006

Citizens successfully press federal/state governments to reopen civil settlement for spill damages based on "unanticipated injury," claim additional funds from Exxon for restoration projects. Ninth Circuit cuts $5 billion punitive award in half.

January 27....... Ninth Circuit hears arguments on punitive damages
April .... Herring fisheries in Sound canceled
June 1.............. U.S. Department of Justice and Alaska file preliminary paperwork for reopener
August 31 .... U.S. Department of Justice and Alaska request Exxon pay $92 million under
                reopener
December 22 .. Ninth Circuit reduces punitive damages to $2.5 billion

2007

Combustion of oil and coal widely accepted as life-threatening to humans and the planet, Nobel Peace Prize awarded to politicians and scientists working to disseminate this information. ExxonMobil tries unsuccessfully to stall punitive decision; case moves to Supreme Court.

January 12....... Exxon petitions Ninth Circuit for rehearings; denied; appealed
April .... Herring fisheries in Sound canceled

2008

Cordovans unanimously request and receive share of oil spill funds for community center and oil spill library instead of divisive access road and deepwater port. Supreme Court hears *Exxon Valdez* case, sets precedent to cap all punitive damages, reduces original jury award over 98 percent from equivalent of one year's net profit, ending longest-running maritime punitive damage case in history. Coalition of citizens continues to press for oversight of Alaska pipeline, reform of worker protection laws, and overturning Supreme Court decision.

February .... ExxonMobil posts net profits of $40.6 billion for 2007
February 27 .... Supreme Court hears *Exxon Valdez* case
April .... Herring fisheries in Sound canceled
April .... Cordova receives oil spill funds for civic center and library
June 9–10........ State court hears arguments over Alaska pipeline response plans, brought by
                citizens, over failure to protect Copper River and Delta from pipeline spill
June 25............ Supreme Court reduces punitive award to $507.5 million, legislates cap of 1:1
                punitive to compensatory in maritime cases

NOTES

ABBREVIATIONS

NOTE: Volume no. and starting page number for *Exxon Valdez Case, Exxon Shipping Company, et al. v. Grant Baker, et al.*, ___S.Ct. ___, 2008 WL 2511219 (US) not available as of book publication.

Preface
xv **"happened to ours"**: *Voices of the Sound* (Anchorage, Alaska: Film Center for the Environment, 1990), VHS.

Chapter 1: A Place to Stand
Firsthand experience and the following resources provided general background material for this chapter: Jim Lethcoe, *An Observer's Guide to the Geology of Prince William Sound, Alaska* (Valdez, Alaska: Prince William Sound Books, 1990); Nancy Lethcoe, *An Observer's Guide to the Glaciers of Prince William Sound, Alaska* (Valdez, Alaska: Prince William Sound Books, 1987); Jim Lethcoe and Nancy Lethcoe, *A History of Prince William Sound, Alaska* (Valdez, Alaska: Prince William Sound Books, 1987); Prince William Sound Science Center, Conservation International, Copper River Delta Institute, and Ecotrust, "Prince William Sound, Copper River, North Gulf of Alaska: Ecosystem" (Cordova, Alaska: Prince William Sound Science Center, 1991); Riki Ott, *Artists for Nature in Alaska's Copper River Delta* (Seattle: University of Washington Press; Wormer, the Netherlands: Inmerc bv, 1998).

10 **lived locally**: Kristin Smith, *Copper River Riches: What Makes Us Special?* vol. 2, *Making the Most of Copper River Resources*, ed. Kristin Smith (Cordova, Alaska: Copper River Watershed Project, 1998), E-3.

10 **fish harvesting or processing:** Niel Fried, "A Trends Profile—City of Cordova," *Alaska Economic Trends* 14(6) (1994): 1–4.

11 **largest salmon ranching program in the world:** PWSAC, www.pwsac.com.

13 **the entire Lower 48:** Pete Isleib and Brina Kessel, *Birds of the North Gulf Coast—Prince William Sound, Alaska,* Biological papers of the University of Alaska, No. 14 (1973; repr., Fairbanks: University of Alaska Press, 1992). See also www.swivel.com/data_columns/ spreadsheet/3801069. The Endangered Species Act, Bald and Golden Eagle Protection Act, and national ban on DDT, among other things, contributed to full recovery of the bald eagle population in the Lower 48. The Department of the Interior delisted bald eagles as an endangered species in June 2007. By federal counts, there are about 10,000 nesting pairs in the Lower 48 and 50,000 to 70,000 bald eagles in Alaska.

13 **each with distinct sounds:** Craig Matkin, *An Observer's Guide to the Orcas of Prince William Sound* (Valdez, Alaska: Prince William Sound Books, 1994).

Chapter 2: Politics of Oil

In fall 1989, the *Anchorage Daily News* ran a series of articles investigating the actions and history of Exxon, Alyeska, the Coast Guard, and the State of Alaska to show the spill was not simply the world's biggest drunk-driving accident. Articles in the series, "Blueprint for Disaster," include: Stan Jones, "Empty Promises. Coast Guard Bowed to Industry Pressure," and "Alyeska Whistleblower Was Left Out on a Limb," *ADN,* October 15, 1989; Stan Jones, "Fighting Flares Agnew. Industry's Scare Tactics Don't Hold Up," *ADN,* October 16, 1989; Patti Epler, "Paper Tiger. Department Leaders Put No Real Heat on Alyeska," October 22, 1989; Craig Medred, "The Commissioner. Kelso Turns from Quiet Diplomacy to Public Battles," *ADN,* October 23, 1989; Patti Epler, "Too Little, Too Late. Promises Ring Hollow. Alyeska: Company Failed to Fulfill Early Promises," *ADN,* October 29, 1989; Richard Mauer, "Big Blunder. Until Spill, Exxon Was Ghost in State," *ADN,* November 5, 1989.

20 **filling in the gaps:** Ross Mullins (Cordova fisherman), interview with author, November 19, 1999.

20 **open up the Arctic for oil exploration:** Peter Coates, *The Trans-Alaska Pipeline Controversy: Technology, Conservation, and the Frontier* (London: Associated University Presses, Inc., 1991), first paperback ed. (Anchorage: University of Alaska Press, 1993), 164–165.

20 **"rendezvous of our dreams":** Coates, *TAPS Controversy:* quote, 179; "The Trans-Alaska Pipeline Controversy: 1, 1969–1971," 175–216.

21 **low levels of oil:** www.whoi.edu/oceanus/viewArticle.do?id=2471.

21 **"in a real fix":** Sheelagh Mullins, conversation with author, July 23, 1998.

22 **for the alternative Canadian route:** Coates, "The Trans-Alaska Pipeline Controversy: 2, 1971–1974," in *TAPS Controversy,* 217–250.

22 **"give a damn":** James Payne, "Our Way of Life is Threatened and Nobody Seems to Give a Damn: The Cordova District Fishermen's Union and the Trans-Alaska Pipeline" (unpublished manuscript, Alaska Humanities Forum, Anchorage, October 1985).

22 **"boats will get":** S. Mullins, interview.

23 **"in the world":** "Alyeska Reports," vol. 1(3) (1971), 16, in "The Promises Issue: Commitments and Representations by Alyeska and Its Owner Companies Regarding the Trans-Alaska Pipeline Issue," prepared for Chuck Hamel and Dan Lawn by Townsend Environmental, Otis, Ore., 1994, 3, www.alaskaforum.org (Archives: Reports).

23 **"at the terminal":** U.S. Department of Interior, TAPS Hearings, in Washington, D.C., 92nd Cong., 1st sess., February 16, 1971, exhibits submitted by witnesses, vol. II, exhibit 11, "APSC, exhibit 1, Department of Interior Hearings," tab 7, "Oil Spills," 7, in "Promises," Townsend Environmental, 15.

23 **"for this area":** Emery A. Winkler (ARCO fleet captain), testimony, U.S. Department of Interior, Hearing in Respect to Environmental Impact of Proposed TAPS, in Anchorage, Alaska, 92nd Cong., 1st sess., February 24, 1971, 489, in "Promises," Townsend Environmental, 10.

23 **"dealing with oil spills.":** L. R. Beynon (Alyeska owner company official from BP), testimony, U.S. Department of Interior, Hearing, 507, in "Promises," Townsend Environmental, 14.

23 "get that [authorization] permit. . . .": Jack Roderick, *Crude Dreams: A Personal History of Oil &* *Politics in Alaska* (Fairbanks: Epicenter Press, 1997), 296.

23 to enter Port Valdez: Rogers C. B. Morton (Secretary of the Interior), testimony, U.S. House, Joint Economic Committee and Committee on Interior and Insular Affairs, Subcommittee on Public Lands, 93rd Cong., 1st Sess., in Washington, D.C., June 22, 1972, 143–150 in "Promises," Townsend Environmental, 53.

24 discharge into Port Valdez: Ibid., 53.

24 regulate tanker traffic and control port pollution: Chapter 266, 1976 Alaska Laws: Tank Vessel Traffic Regulation Act and Oil Discharge Prevention and Pollution Control Act. See also Alison Rieser, "Federal Preemption Considerations for State Oil Spill Prevention and Response Arrangements," vol. 3, appendix M, no. 4.2, 16–22, in *Spill. The Wreck of the Exxon Valdez. Implications for Safe Transportation of Oil*, Final Report, 4 vols., AOSC (Juneau: State of Alaska, 1990).

24 sued the state to overturn it: *Chevron v. Hammond*, 726 F. 2d 483 (9th Cir. 1984).

24 tanker and oil terminal safety inspections: AOSC, *Spill*, 138–139; Larry Persily, "ADEC Budget History," vol. 1, appendix E, in *Spill*, AOSC, appendix.

25 fulfill this mandate: Rieser, "Federal Preemption Considerations," 19.

25 promised vigilance by oversight agencies: Stan Jones and Larry Campbell, "Countdown to Disaster. The Events before the Grounding," *ADN*, May 14, 1989; Charles McCoy, "Broken Promises: Alyeska Record Shows How Big Oil Neglected Alaskan Environment; Pipeline Firm Cut Corners and Scrapped Safeguards, Raising Risk of Disaster; Allegation of Fabricated Data," *Wall Street Journal*, July 6, 1989.

25 mandated by the pipeline act: U.S. Department of Interior, Agreement and Grant of Right-of-Way for Trans-Alaska Pipeline between the United States of America and Amerada Hess Corporation, ARCO Pipe Line Company, Exxon Pipeline Company, Mobil Alaska Pipeline Company, Phillips Petroleum Company, Sohio Pipe Line Company, and Union Alaska Pipeline Company, January 23, 1974, 5–6, 14–15.

26 in uncontrolled quantities: U.S. EPA, *Performance Evaluation of Ballast Water Treatment Plant in Valdez, Alaska*, prepared by Ihor Lysyj (Seattle, Wash., 1985); Balden Environmental Management, Inc., report to Michele Brown, Assistant Attorney General (Juneau: State of Alaska, July 25, 1988); Patti Epler, "Report: Not All Pollutants Limited in Alyeska Permit. Discharge Flows into Port Valdez, but Effect on Environment Unknown," *ADN*, October 3, 1985.

27 back up his claims: Bob Blake, conversation with author, November 1, 1999.

27 into Port Valdez: Mohammad J. Hameedi, "The Ballast Water Treatment Plant," in *Environmental Studies in Port Valdez, Alaska: A Basis for Management*, vol. 24, eds. David Shaw and Mohammad Hameedi (Berlin: Springer-Verlag, 1988).

27 three feet deep: Patti Epler, "Scientist Says Valdez Harbor Pollution Poses Serious Threat to Environment," *ADN*, February 22, 1986. See also Epler, "Slipping Through the Cracks: Wastewater from Terminal Eludes Agency Control," *ADN*, October 27, 1985.

28 Chuck Hamel's allegations: Andy Pasztor and Robert Taylor, "Unsafe Harbor: Alyeska Pipeline Firm is Accused of Polluting Sea Water Since 1977 – Alyeska Documents Support Claims of Lax Procedures at Water-Treatment Plant – Company Insists It Complies," *Wall Street Journal*, February 20, 1986. See also U.S. EPA, Compliance Order No. 1085-07-350309A, Region 10, Seattle, Wash., July 12, 1985; U.S. EPA, Action Items for Valdez Ballast Water Treatment Plant, Region 10, Seattle, Wash., October 29, 1985; U.S. EPA, Amendment to Compliance Order No. 1085-07-35-309A, Region 10, Seattle, Wash., November 6, 1985; U.S. General Accounting Office, *Water Pollution: EPA Controls over Ballast Water at Trans-Alaska Pipeline Marine Terminal*, report to U.S. House, Committee on Energy and Commerce, Subcommittee on Oversight and Investigations, GAO/RCED-87-118, Washington, D.C., June 1987.

Chapter 3: Prelude to Disaster

29 consummate wheeler-and-dealer: Patti Epler, "One Man's Battle Against Alyeska. Former Oil Broker Lays Siege to Pipeline Consortium," *ADN*, September 15, 1985.

29 **brokering insider information:** Hamel's motivation for his actions was revealed as part of Alyeska's covert surveillance operation and congressional oversight hearing (U.S. House, *Draft Report of the Committee on Interior and Insular Affairs on Alyeska Covert Operation, Part I*, 102nd Congr., 2nd sess. (Washington, D.C.: U.S. Government Printing Office, 1992), 59–62.

30 **public's turn to testify:** Patti Epler, "Fisherman Takes on Alyeska," *ADN*, February 21, 1988.

33 **contaminated with low levels of hydrocarbons:** Patti Epler, "Scientists Say Port Valdez Fish Contaminated. Federal Researchers Find Bottom-Dwelling Fish Tainted with Hydrocarbons from Oil Pollution," *ADN*, October 2, 1988; Patti Epler, "Port Valdez Study Stirs Controversy. Report Finds No Pollution; One Scientist Doesn't Buy It," *ADN*, July 29, 1988.

34 **the cheapest option:** Balden Environmental Management, Inc., report to Michele Brown, Assistant Attorney General, Juneau, Alaska, July 25, 1988.

34 **compliance with the discharge permit:** Woodward-Clyde Consultants, "Ballast Water Treatment Facility Effluent Plume Behavior, A Synthesis of Findings," prepared for APSC, Valdez, Alaska, March 1987; Woodward-Clyde Consultants, "Data Report, Port Valdez Receiving Water Study, Ballast Water Treatment Facility, 1985–86," 2 vols., prepared for APSC, Valdez, Alaska, 1987.

34 **73 percent of the time:** Mark Benjamin, Responses to Questions posed by Mary Pinkel, Assistant Attorney General, State of Alaska, Juneau, Alaska, April 17, 1988; ADEC, *ADEC Review of Alyeska's Data*, prepared by Dan Lawn, Juneau, Alaska, 1986.

34 **criminal counts of air pollution:** *Valdez Vanguard*, "Alyeska Fined for Criminal Pollution," February 18, 1987; Bob Ortega, "DEC Says Oil Terminal Fouls Air, Claims Alyeska Fails to Keep Control," *Anchorage Times*, December 8, 1987; Bob Ortega, "EPA Verifies Pipeline Air Pollution, Valdez Emissions Confirmed High," *Anchorage Times*, March 6, 1988; Bob Ortega, "Records Verify Pipeline Emission, Pollution Control Flawed for Years," *Anchorage Times*, April 7, 1988; Bob Ortega, "System Snafu Forces Valdez Shutdown. Pipeline Pollution System Will Need Major Overhaul," *Anchorage Times*, July 31, 1988.

34 **in the country:** Yereth Rosen, "Hazardous Air Emissions Go Unregulated in Alaska, EPA Misses Deadline to Set Rules for Oil-Tanker Terminals," *Christian Science Monitor*, December 4, 1992.

34 **"pollute the environment":** Patti Epler, "EPA Closes Investigation of Alyeska. Agency Says No Action Due Against Pipeline Company," *ADN*, August 17, 1988.

34 **fishermen didn't believe it:** Riki Ott, "Applying Science at Alyeska: The Good, the Bad, and the Ugly," paper presented on behalf of CDFU at the American Fisheries Society Annual Meeting, Anchorage, September 1989.

34 **a prickly issue:** James Butler and James Payne, eds., *Using Oil Spill Dispersants on the Sea* (Washington, D.C.: The National Academies Press, 1989).

35 **approve the plan two weeks before Exxon's spill:** Alaska Regional Response Team, Alaska Federal and State Preparedness Plan for Response to Oil and Hazardous Substance Discharges and Releases, Unified Plan, vol. 1, Oil Dispersant Guidelines for Alaska, Annex F, F-11–F-13. www.akrrt.org/UnifiedPlan/F-Annex.pdf and http://www.akrrt.org/UnifiedPlan/index.shtml; Nancy Lethcoe and Lisa Nurnberger, eds., *Prince William Sound Environmental Reader: 1989–T/V EVOS* (Valdez, Alaska: PWS Conservation Alliance, 1989), 41–43.

35 **harvest value:** U.S. Department of Commerce, NOAA, NMFS, "Fisheries of the United States," http://www.st.nmfs.noaa.gov/st1/commercial/landings/lport_yeard.html.

35 **Area E skyrocketed:** Hal Bernton, "High Cost of Casting. Soaring Permit Prices Create Fishing Elite," *ADN*, December 18, 1988; Alaska Limited Entry Commission, Prince William Sound: salmon drift gillnet permits, http://www.cfec.state.ak.us/pmtvalue/x_s03e.htm; salmon seine permits, http://www.cfec.state.ak.us/pmtvalue/x_s01e.htm.

36 **double that of other oil companies:** According to a 1991 tally of major U.S. corporations in the *Fortune* 500 (April 20, 1992), Exxon and ARCO averaged an 18.4 percent return on stockholders' equity over the ten-year period from January 1982 to December 1991. During this period, the average return for the oil industry was 9 percent and the average return on the S&P 500 was about 12 percent, according to economist Richard Fineberg. Richard Fineberg,

"North Slope Profits and Production Prospects," prepared for the Alaska State Legislature Senate Finance Committee, Juneau, Alaska, November 12, 1992.

36 **oversee the terminal and tankers:** Bob Ortega, "Shortages Limit Agency Monitoring," *Anchorage Times*, April 7, 1988; Larry Persily, "ADEC Budget History," appendix F, in *Spill*, AOSC.

36 **even a moderate spill:** Patti Epler, "Officials Say Cleanup Skills Weak for Years," *ADN*, March 27, 1989.

36 **pollution of critical wetlands:** U.S. Fish and Wildlife Service, *Comparison of Actual and Predicted Impacts of the Trans-Alaska Pipeline System and Prudhoe Bay Oilfields on the North Slope of Alaska*, draft report, Washington, D.C., 1987; Douglas Lee, "Oil in the Wilderness: An Arctic Dilemma," *National Geographic*, December 1988, 858–871; U.S. House, Committee on Interior and Insular Affairs, Subcommittee on Water, Power and Offshore Energy Resources, *Manipulation of Science and the Regulatory Process Affecting Oil and Gas Development in Alaska*, 101st Cong., 2nd sess., in Washington, D.C., May 3, 1990.

36 **notorious problem in the North Gulf coast trade:** U.S. Coast Guard, *Report of the Tanker Safety Study Group*, prepared by Admiral H. H. Bell and others (Washington, D.C.: U.S. Department of Transportation, October 6, 1989); U.S. Coast Guard, *Report of the Tanker Safety Study Group*, chairman H. H. Bell (rear admiral, USCG, retired), (Washington, D.C.: U.S. Department of Transportation, 1990). See also Eric Nalder, *Tankers Full of Trouble: The Perilous Journey of Alaskan Crude* (New York: Grove Press, 1994). The chief investigative reporter for the *Seattle Times* won a Pulitzer Prize for National Reporting for his series on TAPS tankers.

37 **from that spill:** Patti Epler, "Blueprint for Disaster: Changing of the Guard," *ADN*, October 29, 1989.

37 **that evening at the terminal:** Stan Jones and Larry Campbell, "Countdown to Disaster."

38 **warning that I had given before:** Riki Ott, "Spilled Oil and the Alaska Fishing Industry: Looking Beyond Fouled Nets and Lost Fishing Time," presented at the International Oil Spill Conference, Open Ocean and Coastal Spill Panel, San Antonio, Tex., February 12–15, 1989.

38 **to avoid icebergs:** AOSC, *Spill*, vol. 4, appendix N (Day Minus One), 7, 10, 14.

38 **before sailing:** Ibid., 12.

38 **series of errors:** Ibid., 13–14.

38 **or left side:** Ibid., 18.

38 **"in serious trouble":** Ibid. (Day One), 2.

Chapter 4: Taking a Stand

For interested readers, the *Anchorage Daily News* maintains an archive of spill stories and images at www.adn.com/evos/pgs/intro.html.

41 **"We're fucked":** Tom Horton, "Paradise Lost," *Rolling Stone Environmental Reader*, 154.

41 **littered the reef:** The author and others organized a diving expedition to Bligh Reef on July 26, 1991, to find the grounding site. The mission was successful and the team returned with pieces of metal from the tanker hull. One piece was gifted to the Anchorage Museum of History and Art, another to the Cordova Museum.

41 **"for awhile":** Jones and Campbell, "Events Before Grounding." The National Safety Transportation Board put the exact time of the grounding at 12:04 A.M.; Hazelwood's lawyer put it at 12:16 A.M. Hazelwood notified the Coast Guard at 12:27 A.M. This opens the question of what Hazelwood did for up to twenty-three minutes before notifying the Coast Guard of the grounding.

41 **stricken tanker:** AOSC, *Spill*, vol. 4, appendix N (Day 1), 10.

41 **"into the night":** Ibid., 26.

41 **he later insisted:** Ibid., 10; Wells and McCoy, "Out of Control: How Unpreparedness Turned the Alaska Spill into Ecological Debacle," *Wall Street Journal*, April 3, 1989; Patti Epler, "The Events After the Grounding," *ADN*, May 14, 1989.

42 **record is silent:** AOSC, *Spill*, vol. 4, appendix N (Day 1), 27–8; Horton, "Paradise Lost," 153–154.

42 **into the sea:** AOSC, *Spill*, vol. 4, appendix N (Day 1), 34.

44 **"240,000 barrels [of oil]":** APSC, Emergency command center telephone recordings, transcripts, Anchorage, Alaska, March 24–29, 1989, KWY00104–1752, 2275, 1580, http://www.arlis.org (keywords: Alyeska transcript).

44 **on-the-water application:** Riki Ott, *Sound Truth and Corporate Myth$: The Legacy of the EVOS* (Cordova, Alaska: Dragonfly Sisters Press, 2005), 10–14, 21–24.

44 **"for show and tell":** COC, "Testimony in Washington, D.C.," *CFS*, April 28, 1989.

44 **"catching oil or not":** APSC, telephone transcripts, KWY001042012.

44 **streams of misinformation:** Ott, *Sound Truth*, 22–23; Nancy Lethcoe and Lisa Nurnberger, *Prince William Sound Environmental Reader* (Valdez, Alaska: PWS Conservation Alliance), 44; AOSC, *Spill*, vol. 4, appendix N (Day 2), 11–12.

45 **the high-end estimate:** R. Hennelly, "Split Wide Open: Did the *Valdez* Spill 11 Million Gallons—or 27 Million?" *Village Voice*, January 2, 1990; Hal Spence, "Was the Spill 38 Million Gallons?" *Homer News*, April 12, 1990.

45 **forty miles into the Sound:** AOSC, *Spill*, vol. 4, appendix N (Day 4), 1–2. See also Timothy Egan, "Exxon Concedes It Can't Contain Most of Oil Spill," *New York Times National*, March 30, 1989.

46 **"on their part":** U.S. House, Committee on Interior and Insular Affairs, *Oversight Hearing on Investigation of the EVOS, PWS, Alaska*, 5 vols., *Part I: Investigation of the EVOS, PWS, Alaska*, 101st Cong., 1st sess., in Cordova, Alaska, May 5, 1989, and in Valdez, Alaska, May 7–8, 1989, serial no. 101-5, 101.

46 **"public relations nightmare":** APSC, telephone transcripts, KWY001042258.

46 **"the way I feel":** APSC, telephone transcripts, KWY001042258–59.

47 **"we will compensate it":** Ross Mullins, *We Will Make You Whole* (Cordova, Alaska: Ross Mullins, 1989), VHS.

48 **to testify:** U.S. House, Committee on Merchant Marine and Fisheries, Subcommittee on Coast Guard and Navigations, *Hearing re: H.R. 2158–To Provide Better Maritime Safety for PWS, Alaska, and for Other Purposes*, 101st Cong., 1st sess., Washington, D.C., May 11, 1989; U.S. Senate, Committee on Environment and Public Works, Subcommittee on Environmental Protection, *Hearing on the Adequacy and Effectiveness of the Oil Spill Cleanup in PWS, Alaska*, 101st Cong., 1st sess., Washington, D.C., April 19, 1989.

48 **"should drink milk":** COC, "In Union We are Strong," *CFS*, April 24, 1989. See also COC, "Sound Love," *CFS*, May 9, 1989.

49 **role in oversight:** Jonathan Wills, *A Place in the Sun*, Social and Economic Studies, No. 41 (St. John's, Newfoundland: Institute of Social and Economic Research, Memorial University of Newfoundland, 1991).

49 **stories of the charade:** Ott, *Sound Truth*, 24–26, 29–35; COC, "Testimony in Washington, D.C.," *CFS*, April 28, 1989.

50 **with its fancy skimmers:** Art Davidson, *In the Wake of the Exxon Valdez: The Devastating Impact of the Alaska Oil Spill* (San Francisco: Sierra Club Books, 1990), 112.

50 **eroded social solidarity:** ADEC, *The Exxon Valdez Oil Spill, Final Report, State of Alaska Response*, Juneau, Alaska, June 1993, 114–119; Impact Assessment, "Ecconomic, Social, and Psychological Impact Assessment of the EVOS, Final Report," prepared for the Alaska Conference of Mayors, Oiled Mayors' Subcommittee, Anchorage, November 15, 1990, 121–123; John Russell and others, "Psychological and Social Impacts of the EVOS and Cleanup," AFSS 18 (1996): 867–878, on 875–877; Davidson, "Shorelines" and "How Clean is Clean?" in *In the Wake*, 179–218; John Keeble, *Out of the Channel: The EVOS in PWS*, 10th ed. (Spokane, Wash.: Eastern Washington University Press, 1999), 204, 231, 258–59; National Wildlife Federation (NWF) and others, "The Day the Water Died: A Compilation of the November 1989 Citizens Commission Hearings on the EVOS," available through NWF, Washington, D.C., 37–47; Michelle Mayer, *All the King's Horses: Community Response to the EVOS*, honors thesis, Arizona State University Honors College, 1993.

50 **to function effectively:** COC, "One-fifth of Labor Force Lost to Spill," *CFS*, May 20, 1989.

50 **overwhelmed by trauma:** Impact Assessment, *Oiled Mayors' Report*, 4–5, 10–16, 39–49; Keeble, *Out of the Channel*, 261.

51 **"a 200,000-barrel spill"**: U.S. House, *EVOS Investigation, Part I*, 148.

51 **"since Moby-Dick"**: Reuters, "Alaska Officials Press Complaints Against Exxon on Cleanup of Oil," *New York Times*, May 10, 1989, http://query.nytimes.com/gst/fullpage.html?res=950DE0D61730F933A25756C0A96F948260.

52 **"trying to save it"**: Clyde Robbins (U.S. Coast Guard Vice Admiral), "Overview of Cleanup Methods and Operations," paper presented at the Alaskan Oil Spill and Human Health Conference, Seattle, Wash, July 28–30, 1989, 2–3. See also Ott, *Sound Truth*, 29–32, 203–204; ADEC, *Final Report*, 119–127, 151 n. 57.

52 **"its public image aspects"**: Davidson, *In the Wake*, 201.

53 **state health officials**: Ott, *Sound Truth*, 57 (figure 2), 66–67.

53 **seven boats and gear**: COC, "More Fishing Districts Open," *CFS*, July 29, 1989; COC, "All Fishing in Prince William Sound Halts," *CFS*, August 1, 1989; COC, "Fishermen Angry," *CFS*, August 3, 1989.

53 **"predicted it would be"**: COC, "Stevens Expects Normal Fishing and Tourist Seasons," *CFS*, April 26, 1989.

54 **keep the product out of watercourses were ignored**: Exxon, "MSDS, Inipol EAP22," Houston, Tex., July 28, 1989; Exxon, "MSDS for Corexit 9527," Houston, Tex., June 14, 1992; Ken Wells and Charlie McCoy, "Exxon Confronted by Mutiny in Ranks of Cleanup Workers. Shore Crews Refuse To Spray New Chemical On Shore. Safety May Be a Concern," *Wall Street Journal*, August 9, 1989.

54 **Inipol EAP22**: ADEC, *Final Report*, 69–72, 73–82; Ott, *Sound Truth*, 32–34, 425–426.

54 **attention of local government**: T. McDowell, Seldovia Town Meeting with Spill Agency Representatives, August 24, 1989, VHS. ARLIS, Anchorage, Alaska, seven videos.

55 **loading oil**: COC, "Boaters Join in Protest Regatta," *CFS*, September 12, 1989.

55 **stopped trading hands**: H. Radtke, C. M. Dewees, and E. J. Smith, "The Fishing Industry and Pacific Coastal Communities: Understanding the Assessment of Economic Impacts," Pacific Sea Grant College Program, Marine Advisory Program publication UCSGMAP-87-1 (1987); Neal Fried, "Trends Profile—The City of Cordova," *Alaska Economic Trends*, March 1994, 1–5.

55 **across the oiled region**: Impact Assessment, *Oiled Mayors' Report*, 3–4, 130–34.

57 **intensified the trauma**: Ibid., x–xiv, 15.

57 **"of this community"**: Ibid., 12, 15.

57 **air and water quality**: McCoy, "Broken Promises."

58 **about the spill and cleanup**: Riki Ott and Jeannine Buller, "The EVOS: Accidental or Symptomatic?" presented on the East Coast lecture tour to sixteen academic institutions, November 9–December 8, 1989. See also Riki Ott, "Oil in the Marine Environment," in *Prince William Sound Environmental Reader*, eds. Lethcoe and Nurnberger, 30–35.

58 **reaching the public**: Ken Wells, "Exxon, Alyeska Seek to Keep Spill Evidence Secret," *Wall Street Journal*, December 29, 1989; Keeble, *Out of the Channel*, 313.

59 **problem with Exxon's loss formula**: Patience Andersen Faulkner (Alaska Native, Cordova resident), interview with author, November 28, 1999.

59 **objections from our many lawyers**: William Hirsch, "Justice Delayed: Seven Years Later and No End in Sight," in *The Exxon Valdez Disaster: Readings on a Modern Social Problem* (Dubuque, Iowa: Kendall/Hunt Publishing Company, 1997), 271–303, on 272; D. Hevesi, "Alaska Judge in Exxon Case 'A Decent Man,' Friends Say," *Seattle Post-Intelligencer*, April 25, 1991.

59 **lawyer Dave Oesting**: Dave Oesting (lead cocounsel for plaintiffs in *Exxon Valdez Case*), interview with author, December 1, 1999.

60 **colead the plaintiffs' team**: David Lebedoff, *Cleaning Up: The Story Behind the Biggest Legal Bonanza of Our Time* (New York: The Free Press, 1997), 106–9.

Chapter 5: Virtual Reality

62 **start dripping down**: COC, "Heavy Sheens," *CFS*, March 19, 1990; ADEC, *Final Report*, 136.

62 **oiled beach debris**: ADEC, *Final Report*, 135–47; COC, "NOAA Recommendation for Cleanup" and "ADF&G Prepares Spring Cleanup Priorities," *CFS*, March 12, 1990.

62 **"oil on those beaches"**: COC, "Heavy Sheens," *CFS*, March 19, 1990.

62 **"adulterated by oil"**: COC, "PWS Salmon Harvest Task Force Meeting in Cordova," *CFS*, April 9, 1990. See also COC, "ADF&G and ADEC Memo of Understanding," *CFS*, April 18, 1990.

65 **"keep up with [Riki]"**: Stan Stephens, Comments, "Prevention, Response, and Oversight Five Years After the EVOS," proceedings of an International Conference, sponsored by Alaska Sea Grant College Program, University of Alaska, Fairbanks, Anchorage, March 23–25, 1994, 25.

65 **"of a rupture"**: George Frost and Patti Epler, "Special Report: Pitted Pipeline Corrosion Along 800-Mile Trans-Alaska Pipeline Could Result in a Multi Billion Dollar Repair Bill Depleting the State Treasury," *ADN*, February 25, 1990.

65 **from 1969 through 1987**: Edward Deakin, "Oil Industry Profitability in Alaska 1969–1987," prepared for the Alaska Department of Revenue, Juneau, Alaska, March 15, 1989.

65 **one million dollars a day**: Richard Fineberg, "Hidden Billions: The TAPS DR&R [Dismantling, Removal, and Restoration] Provision," prepared for Stan Stephens, Valdez, Alaska, 1992.

66 **terminal, Sullom Voe**: Scottish Eye, *Slick Operators* (Scotland: Skyline Film and Television Productions, 1990).

66 **"TAPS owner organizations"**: U.S. House, *Draft Report on Alyeska Covert Operation*, 36–37.

66 **and Alyeska**: John Connolly, "Inside the Shadow CIA," *Spy Magazine*, September 1992, 46–54, www.americanpolitics.com/sc1992209connolly1.html; Connolly and Erzc Reguly, "Badlands," *Spy Magazine*, April 1992.

66 **hounds of hell**: U.S. House, Committee on Interior and Insular Affairs, *Oversight Hearings on Alyeska Covert Operations*, 102nd Congr., 2nd sess., Washington, D.C., November 4–6, 1991, serial no. 102–13, 612. "Call off the dogs!" is a reference to the spy team that was made in handwritten notes at an Alyeska owner company meeting on September 25, 1990, in Denver, Colo.

66 **"healthy and productive"**: U.S. House, *EVOS Investigation, Part IV: Cleanup and Damage Assessment*, 101st Cong., 2nd sess., Washington, D.C., March 22 and April 24, 1990, 74–75.

66 **"egg, alevin or fry"**: U.S. House, *EVOS Investigation, Part IV*, 180–81. See also Charles Wohlforth, "Hot Water Spill Cleanup Kills Shorelife. Tests Show High Death Toll for Organisms on Beach and Those Under Water Near Shore," *ADN*, February 17, 1990; Charles Wohlforth, "Spill Scientists Frustrated," *ADN*, March 4, 1990; David Whitney and Craig Medred, "State Says Oil Spill Studies Provide Ominous Results, *ADN*, March 23, 1990.

67 **"that's the case"**: U.S. House, *EVOS Investigation, Part IV*, 175.

67 **"field observations"**: Exxon, "Environmental Recovery in PWS and the Gulf of Alaska. Field Observations of Jenifer Baker, Robert Clark, and Paul Kingston," a supplement to the authors' scientific review: "Natural Recovery of Cold Water Marine Environments After an Oil Spill," paper, presented at the 13th Arctic and Marine Oil Spill Program Technical Seminar, Edmonton, Alberta, June 6, 1990, 1. The package was widely distributed to schools and universities.

67 **to add scientific credibility**: Otto Harrison, Exxon Corporation, lecture to the Institute of Petroleum, London, March 4, 1992, in "The *Exxon Valdez*: A Case of Corporate Virtual Reality," Andrew Rowell, 25 n. 262.

67 **Erickson told Congress**: U.S. House, *EVOS Investigation, Part IV*, 178.

67 **"years to come"**: COC, "Jim Hermiller Now Honored Cordovan," *CFS*, May 15, 1990; *CT*, 1990. See also Terry Wilson, "Spill Response Disaster Sparks Evolution of SERVS," *Valdez Vanguard*, March 10, 1999.

68 **"many rough spots and several holes"**: COC, "CDFU Signs Contract with Alyeska," *CFS*, June 1, 1990; COC, "Oil Spill Drill 'Successful'," *CFS*, June 29, 1990.

68 **seven spill bills into law**: ADEC, *Final Report*, 156.

68 **response performance criteria**: AS.46.04.030. Oil Discharge Prevention and Contingency Plans.

68 **"post-traumatic stress disorder"**: COC, "Social and Psychological Study Results Released," *CFS*, April 26, 1990, in "Stress and Disruption in an Alaskan Fishing Community: Initial and Continuing Impacts of the EVOS," Steven Picou and others, *Industrial Crisis Quarterly* 6 (1992): 235–257.

69 **major source of stress:** William Freudenburg, "Contamination, Corrosion and the Social Order: An Overview," *Current Sociology* vol. 45(3) (1997): 19–39 on 27–29.

69 **Open Meetings Act:** James MacPherson, "Complaints Served at Council Meeting," *CT*, June 14, 1990. See also James MacPherson, "City May Join Suit," *CT*, June 21, 1990; Don Adams, "OMA [Open Meetings Act] Lawsuit in Full Swing," *CT*, August 2, 1990; Don Adams, "City Becomes Party in Meeting Dispute," *CT*, August 30, 1990; Don Adams, "Group Tries to Oust Councilman Taylor," *CT*, September 20, 1990; Don Adams, "Council to Continue Lawsuit," *CT*, October 11, 1990; Don Adams, "Affidavit Filed," *CT*, November 26, 1990; Don Adams, "Exxon Papers Being Sought," *CT*, November 22, 1990; Don Adams, "Council Sets Recall Vote," *CT*, December 13, 1990.

70 **stress from the spill:** Terry Wilson, "Spill Study Says City Still Suffers Stress," *CT*, reprinted from *Valdez Vanguard*, July 26, 1990; Robert Donald and others, "The Stress Related Impact of the *Valdez* Oil Spill on the Residents of Cordova and Valdez, Alaska: A Comparative Study Conducted by the Valdez Counseling Center," Valdez, Alaska, 1990

71 **oil can stunt growth:** Brian Bue and others, "Pinks in Peril: Declining Wild Stocks in PWS," *Alaska's Wildlife* January–February 1993, 34–36; Ott, *Sound Truth*, 256–257.

72 **in the Mediterranean:** COC, "*Exxon Valdez*," *CFS*, April 9, 1990; David Sedeno, "*Exxon Valdez* Gets New Duty and New Name," *ADN*, July 7, 1990.

73 **"those of the [federal] government":** ADEC, *Final Report*, 30–43, quote on 42.

73 **"it's covered up":** Don Adams, "Team Leaders Claim 'Cover-Up'," *CT*, October 25, 1990.

73 **"It's the same thing":** COC, "Coast Guard Chief Calls for More Cleanup in '91," *CFS*, August 10, 1990.

73 **the ad declared:** Exxon, "Sound Progress," ad, *CT*, September 20, 1990.

74 **"in the soul's journey":** Clarissa Pinkola Estés, *Women Who Run with the Wolves: Myths and Stories of the Wild Woman Archetype* (New York: Ballantine Books, 1992), 15.

74 **avoidance behavior as an indication of lingering spill trauma:** Steven Picou and Duane Gill, "Disruption and Stress in an Alaskan Fishing Community: Initial and Continuing Impacts of the *Exxon Valdez* Oil Spill," *Industrial Crisis Quarterly* 6 (1992): 235–257.

74 **in Prince William Sound and Cook Inlet:** *Oil Pollution Act of 1990*, Public Law 101-380, 101st Cong., 2nd sess. (August 18, 1990). OPA 90 preserved the ability of states to set stricter spill prevention and response standards than the federal government; required the Coast Guard to establish several national response centers to stage oil spill cleanup and response equipment along the nation's coastline; and replaced the dysfunctional TAPL Fund, an industry-controlled bottleneck that severely limited monetary settlements to parties injured by oil spills, with a $1 billion national fund to pay for future cleanups and to compensate injured parties.

75 **light on Bligh Reef:** David Whitney, "Oil Spill Bill Wins Approval: House Senate Panel Reaches Compromise," *ADN*, July 27, 1990.

75 **there had been compromises:** These included weakening states' authority to enforce spill cleanup; allowing a twenty-five-year phase-in period for double-hull tankers; not requiring citizen oversight of the entire TAPS; and allowing the spiller to negotiate spill studies with the federal government and, failing consensus, to default to 1970s test protocol—ninety-six-hour bioassays that fail to detect long-term harm from oil. In other words, the latter compromise locks oil spill science into the old understanding that oil only causes short-term harm.

75 **"documents to prove it":** AP, "EPA Warns of Valdez Cancer Risk," *ADN*, May 26, 1990.

75 **to reduce vapor emissions:** Terry Wilson, "EPA, Alyeska Have Oil Showdown," *CT*, reprinted from *Valdez Vanguard*, July 26, 1990; Kim Fararo and George Frost, "Alyeska Slows Pipeline Flow, Air Pollution Dispute Prompts Action; Normal Operation Resumes after a Judge's Order," *ADN*, July 20, 1990.

76 **Alyeska lied with statistics:** Terry Wilson, "Air Quality is Topic at Meeting," *Valdez Vanguard*, September 26, 1990; AP, "Alyeska, State Settle Disputes over Air Pollution," September 21, 1990; APSC, "Report on Valdez Tanker Loading Vapor Emission Testing and Evaluation," October 22, 1990.

76 **stolen from his home:** U.S. House, *Draft Report on Alyeska Covert Operation*, 17–18, 27–32.

77 **in state court:** Hirsch, "Justice Delayed," 272, 275; Marilee Enge, "Judge in Oil-Spill Case Refuses to Permit Class-Action Lawsuits," *ADN*, December 21, 1990.

77 **all the injured individuals:** Hirsch, "Justice Delayed," 274–75.

77 **in federal court:** COC, "Judge: Use Fund for Oil Spill Suits," *CFS*, September 29, 1990.

78 **one hundred claims still in court:** Lebedoff, *Cleaning Up*, 91.

78 **over admissible evidence:** Oesting, interview; Hirsch, "Justice Delayed," 273–274, 281.

79 **"three or four years":** Hirsch, "Justice Delayed," 294 n. 31.

Chapter 6: Tricks of the Trade

80 **for squabbling:** Don Adams, "Petition Filed," *CT*, January 3, 1991; "Spat Makes State News!," *CT*, January 10, 1991; Charles Wohlforth, "Suit Over Cordova's Spill Decisions Divides Its People, Drains Its Savings," *ADN*, January 3, 1991.

80 **ill-tempered bickering:** "Meeting to Air Future," *CT*, January 24, 1991; "Recall Vote Due," *CT*, February 14, 1991; "Councilwoman Recalled," *CT*, February 21, 1991; Don Adams, "Council Stalled on Vote Certification," *CT*, February 28, 1991.

80 **worth without the spill:** Don Adams, "Pinks Set Record," *CT*, September 20, 1990; Maurice Cohen, "Economic Impacts of the *Exxon Valdez* Oil Spill," in *Exxon Valdez Disaster*, eds. Picou, Gill, and Cohen, 133–160.

80 **diversify the local economy:** Don Adams, "Town Facing 'Slump'" and "City to Mull Port," *CT*, January 31, 1991; Don Adams, "Council Eyeing $13 Million Port," *CT*, February 28, 1991.

83 **adamantly denied in 1985:** Chuck Hamel, letter to William Reilly (Administrator, U.S. EPA), Washington, D.C., February 12, 1991; William Coughlin, "The Other Oil Pollution Menace; Chronic Discharges are Poisoning Oceans, Scientists Say," *Boston Globe*, February 25, 1991; Don Adams, "Toxic Wastes Said Being Dumped Here," *CT*, January 17, 1991; "New Ruling Made," *CT*, February 14, 1991; "EPA Hearing Sought," *CT*, February 21, 1991.

83 **"that kind of discharge":** Allanna Sullivan, "Exxon Confirms Waste Water Charges. Move May Impede a Valdez Settlement," *Wall Street Journal*, February 19, 1991.

83 **property dispute against Exxon:** Stan Jones, "Hamel Suit Says Exxon Lied About Oil Find," *ADN*, March 19, 1997; Stan Jones, "Expert: Exxon Paid Half," *ADN*, March 25, 1997; Stan Jones, "Exxon Sues Hamel, CFM Corp. for Legal Fees in Failed Lawsuit," *ADN*, April 22, 1997.

84 **minimize pollution at sea:** MARPOL 73/78 is the International Convention for the Prevention of Pollution by Ships, 1973, as amended by Protocol in 1978. Annex I, ratified by the U.S., concerns oily ballast.

84 **"no one did something about it":** Kim Fararo and Hal Bernton, "Tankers in Valdez Dump Waste Along with Ballast, Report Finds," *ADN*, August 29, 1991.

84 **for six weeks:** Riki Ott, "Debriefing Notes for the House Special Committee on Oil and Gas, *Hearing on Alyeska Ballast Water Treatment and TAPS Operations*," with attachments, including subpoenaed records showing EPA had confirmed Hamel's 1985 complaints (#1), records of suspect activities from *Exxon Valdez* (2/28/89) and *Overseas New York* (7/16/88) (#2), *Baton Rouge* (4/16/89) and *Exxon Houston* (2/21/89) (#3), and *Exxon Bernicia* (5/10/89) (#4), and summary of comments from technical citizen advisory groups (#5), Juneau, Alaska, March 25, 1991, revised April 19, 1991. See also Richard Fineberg, "Alyeska Pipeline Terminal Ballast Water Treatment and Northbound Shipments: Final Report," prepared for the PWS RCAC," May 1991.

84 **filed for bankruptcy:** Don Adams, "Local Reaction Guarded," *CT*, March 7, 1991; Sue Laird, "Co-op Bankrupt," *CT*, March 7, 1991; Don Adams, "Chugach Bankruptcy Shocks Cordovans," *CT*, March 14, 1991.

84 **drop in pink prices:** Alaska Seafood Marketing Institute, *Salmon 2000*, Juneau, Alaska, 1991; "Salmon Markets Down," *CT*, April 18, 1991; Nancy Griffin, "Sustainable Yield–Alaska Wild Salmon Fishery Survives Global Competition, Low Prices," *The Working Waterfront*, web edition, September 12, 2006, at www.workingwaterfront.com/article.asp?storyID=20040903.

85 **tax evasion scam:** In 1986, Congress, at the urging of Alaska Senator Ted Stevens, reopened a federal tax loophole to create huge "net operating losses" or NOLs, solely for the use

of Alaska Native corporations. Stevens's shortsighted economic solution to stem Native corporate bankruptcies cost taxpayers over a billion dollars in losses the first year, instead of the anticipated $60 million. Congress closed the loophole in 1988 but the damage was done. About a million acres of ancestral Native land in the spill region was at risk. To consummate the existing NOL transactions, the forest had to be clear-cut. The logging provided little or no direct cash benefits to shareholders, while destroying life-giving subsistence opportunities. Thomas Berger, *Village Voice: The Report of the Alaska Native Review Commission* (New York: Hill & Wang, 1994); John Strohmeyer, *Extreme Conditions: Big Oil and the Transformation of Alaska* (New York: Simon & Schuster, 1993); Ecotrust and others, *An Atlas of People and Place, Part 1: Natural Forests and Native Language of the Coastal Temperate Rain Forest* (Portland: Interrain Pacific, 1995).

86 **the deal imploded:** Barbara Rosewicz and Allanna Sullivan, "Exxon and U.S. in Talks to Settle Certain Charges. Pact on Criminal Allegations over 89 Alaska Oil Spill Could Cut Firm's Costs," *Wall Street Journal*, February 14, 1990.

86 **economic and emotional appeals:** Gerald Masolini, "The Salmon Used to Splash in the Creek," guest opinion, *CT*, March 21, 1991; Becky Chapek, "Middle People," LTE, *CT*, March 28, 1991; Pam Smith, "My Trees," LTE, *CT*, May 2, 1991; Don Adams, "Native Schism Erupts," *CT*, May 16, 1991; Don Adams, "Dissidents Call for Halt to Eyak Logging," *CT*, June 6, 1991; "Eyak Indians Hold Meetings to Halt Logging Operations," *CT*, June 13, 1991.

86 **or lingering harm:** ADEC, *Final Report*, 1993, 168–69.

86 **three to eight billion dollars:** Charles Wohlforth, "Information Believed to be in Spill Studies," *ADN*, March 31, 1991.

86 **"any of our plans":** Keith Schneider, "Judge Rejects $100 Million Fine for Exxon in Oil Spill as Too Low," *New York Times*, April 25, 1991; John Lancaster, "Exxon Plea Bargain Thrown Out by Judge, $100 Million Oil Spill Fine Called Too Lenient," *Washington Post*, April 25, 1991.

87 **"lost our ability to trust":** Joe Sonneman, "All Trust Gone, Mayor Tells Committee," *CT*, April 18, 1991.

87 **summary of injury:** Charles Wohlworth and David Hulen, "Study Worsens Spill Damage Estimates," *ADN*, April 9, 1991. See also Don Adams, "Natives Angry over Exxon Claims," *CT*, March 14, 1991; Don Adams, "Fishermen Oppose Settlement" and "Report Shocks Cordova," *CT*, April 18, 1991.

87 **"effectively cleaned":** Exxon, "Exxon Says Published Studies Show Significant Environmental Recovery in Alaska," press release, April 17, 1991. See also Exxon, "Summary of Published Studies on the Effects of the *Exxon Valdez* Oil Spill on Natural Resources," press release, April 16, 1991.

87 **fine was too low:** ADEC, *Final Report*, 170; Allanna Sullivan, Charles McCoy, and Paul Barrett, "Judge Rejects Exxon Alaska-Spill Pact; Net Income Rose 75% in First Quarter," *Wall Street Journal*, April 25, 1991.

88 **under the TAPL Fund:** Faulkner, interview.

88 **State Ombudsman's office:** Ralph Thomas, "Ombudsman Says Spill Rules Preview Unethical; Report Says DEC Commssioner's Hand Delivery to Alyeska Appears 'Much Too Cozy,'" *ADN*, August 28, 1991.

90 **lawsuit was a maritime tort:** Oesting, interview; Hirsch, "Justice Delayed," 273.

91 **no revival possible:** Don Adams, "PWS Communities in Midst of 'Ongoing Disaster'" and "Soul Has a Price," editorial, *CT*, June 27, 1991.

92 **ballast water treatment plant:** PWS RCAC, "Ballast Water Treatment Program Underway," *The Observer*, fall 1991.

92 **law turned off:** U.S. EPA, *Oil Tanker Waste Disposal Practices: A Review*, January 1992; ADEC, Dan Lawn (Environmental Engineer III), *Analysis of TAPS Trade*, 1991; ADEC, Svend Brandt-Erichsen (Regional Administrator Southcentral Region), *Ballast Water Handling*, 1991. See also Kim Fararo and Hal Bernton, "Tankers in Valdez Dump Waste Along with Ballast, Report Finds," *ADN*, August 29, 1991; Riki Ott, "Politics Prevent Honest Appraisal of Valdez Oil Pollution," *ADN*, October 11, 1991.

92 **to its treatment plant:** Mark Moran, "Alyeska Fined Over Dumping. EPA Seeks $20,000 for Alleged Release of Tanker Ballast at Valdez," *ADN*, August 22, 1991.

93 **was a disaster:** Don Adams, "Pinks May Jeopardize Hatcheries, Canneries," *CT*, August 15, 1991; Adams, "Fishermen Call for Disaster Declaration, Ouster of Tillion" and "No Buyers for 3 Million Pink Salmon, Corporation Says," *CT*, August 22, 1991.

94 **"victory of democracy":** Don Adams, "Governor Offers Surplus Pink Salmon to Soviets," *CT*, August 22, 1991. See also Adams, "Salmon Giveaway Underway," and "Thanks to Many People, Disaster Turns to Triumph," *CT*, August 29, 1991; Wesley Loy, "Exxon Tape: Sound's Nearly Recovered," *ADN*, September 17, 1991.

96 **wreaked havoc in the community:** Don Adams, "Fishermen Lament 1991 Season, Year of the Fish Spill," *CT*, August 29, 1991; Dan Murphy, "Salmon Industry in Turmoil: Processors Want Hatcheries out of Sales," *Valdez Vanguard*, September 5, 1991; John McMullen, "Hatcheries Explain Their Side of '91," guest commentary, *CT*, September 12, 1991; Don Adams, "Alaska Fishing Industry Needs to See the Big Picture," *CT*, September 12, 1991; Adams, "PWSAC Faces Industry Crisis: Hatcheries Consider Preselling 100% of Cost Recovery Fish," *CT*, September 19, 1991; Adams, "Co-op Shuts Down: Hard Times Hit Another Cannery," *CT*, October 10, 1991; Adams, "CAMA gets New Life after Disastrous 1991 Fishing Season," *CT*, November 21, 1991.

97 **identical to the earlier one:** *State of Alaska v. Exxon* (1991); Memorandum of Agreement and Consent Decree for Civil Action A91-081CV in *USA v. Alaska* (1991); *USA v. Exxon Corporation* (1991); *USA v. Exxon Shipping* (1991). See also George Frost, "Second Spill Settlement Looks Like the First. Exxon Agrees to $125 Million Criminal Fine for the 1989 Spill," *ADN*, October 1, 1991.

98 **high levels of stress:** Steven Picou and Duane Gill, "The EVOS and Chronic Psychological Stress," *AFSS* 18 (1996): 879–893; Duane Gill and Steven Picou, "The Day the Water Died: Cultural Impacts of the EVOS," in *The Exxon Valdez Disaster*, eds. Picou, Gill, and Cohen, 167–187.

98 **marketing strategy:** "Governor Sends Commission Out to Assist Fishers," *CT*, September 26, 1991; "State Visits Cordova to Aid Fishers" and "Contingency Funds Used," *CT*, October 3, 1991; Don Adams, "Team Looks into PWS Fishing Plan," *CT*, November 14, 1991.

99 **in the process:** *United States v. Billie Garde*, 673 F. Su604, 604 (D.D.C.) 1987.

99 **congressional subpoenas and hearing:** U.S. House, *Report on Alyeska Covert Operation*, 40–43.

99 **endangering national security:** Ibid.: extortionist, 59–62; privileged, 42.

100 **"single trip to the public library":** U.S. House, *Oversight Hearing on Alyeska Covert Operation*, 12.

100 **avoid legal pitfalls:** Ibid., "A Report to the Owners' Committee of APSC," submitted by Paul, Hastings, Janofsky & Walker, January 22, 1991, 5–602.

100 **diagrams of the phone tap networks:** Ibid., 449–450.

100 **"based on demerits":** Ibid., 612; U.S. House, *Report on Alyeska Covert Operation*, 46–51.

100 **"receiving inside info–Pat":** U.S. House, *Oversight Hearing on Alyeska Covert Operation*, 661.

101 **citizens were violated:** U.S. House, *Report on Alyeska Covert Operation*, 62–86.

102 **fees and costs:** "Council Meets over Taylor-VanBrocklin," *CT*, November 7, 1991; Don Adams, "Reversal of Taylor Case Shocks City: Judge Michalski Says City Must Pay for Ex-Councilwoman's Attorney Fees," *CT*, December 4, 1991; "Council Rejects Taylor's Offer," *CT*, December 11, 1991; Adams, "City Council Holds on to Appeal Option in Taylor Case," *CT*, December 18, 1991; Adams, "Fishermen Call for Disaster Declaration," *CT*, December 23, 1991.

102 **"shaken to their roots":** Don Adams, "Fishermen Call for Disaster Declaration," *CT*, December 23, 1991.

102 **collateral attack on *Chevron v. Hammond*:** Hirsch, "Justice Delayed," 276; Oesting, interview.

Chapter 7: When Right Makes Might

104 **"how to build it":** Don Adams, "Attorney General Tells Community Road Will Be Built," *CT*, January 15, 1992. See also Tom Kizzia, "Pitfalls Along the Road to Cordova. Town at Odds Over Route to Happiness," *ADN*, January 19, 1992.

105 **services were cut:** Don Adams, "Cordova Will Pay Court Costs," *CT*, January 2, 1992; "Cordova Budget in Crisis," and "Library Asks for Help with Adopt-A-Book Program," *CT*, January 29, 1992; "City Starts Four-Day Week in Effort to Save Money," "Cordova City Finance Director Explains Budget Shortfall, Inadequate Accounting, Oil Spill, Taylor Case are Some of Reasons Offered for Problem," and "State Spending Declines in Entitlement Programs," *CT*, February 19, 1992.

105 **live in Seattle:** Jacques Picard, "Cordova is Sixth Highest in State Among Surveyed Communities," *CT*, January 15, 1992.

105 **no extra money in town:** Don Adams, "Odiak Child Development Center Closes Doors," *CT*, January 15, 1992; "Cordova Budget in Crisis," *CT*, January 29, 1992; "Two Cordova Bars May Have to Close for Not Paying Taxes," *CT*, March 4, 1992.

106 **in the paper:** Allanna Sullivan, "Alyeska Pipeline Service Criticized by an Ex-Inspector," *Wall Street Journal*, March 17, 1992; Kim Fararo, "More Ex-Staff Critize Alyeska Safety, *ADN*, April 10, 1992.

107 **reports on whistleblowers:** Philip Jos, Mark Tompkins, and Steven Hays, "In Praise of Difficult People: A Portrait of the Committed Whistleblower," *Public Administration Review*, November/ December 1989, 552–561.

108 **Dan lost his job:** Daniel Lawn (ADEC district office supervisor, Valdez), interview with author, June 6, 1998; Daniel Lawn, memo to Bill Lamoreaux (ADEC regional supervisor), December 19, 1984, in U.S. House, *EVOS Investigation, Part I*, 874; Daniel Lawn, memo to Bob Martin (Environmental Quality Office), May 1, 1984, in U.S. House, *EVOS Investigation, Part I*, 890; Dan Lawn, memo to Steve Zrake (ADEC Anchorage), July 13, 1982, in U.S. House, *EVOS Investigation, Part I*, 893; Patti Epler, "Memo Puts DEC Decision in New Light," *ADN*, August 11, 1989; Patti Epler, "New Job for DEC Manager. Some Say State Bows to Alyeska," *ADN*, August 3, 1989; Terry Wilson, "DEC Cuts Lawn from Valdez Office," *Valdez Vanguard*, October 31, 1990; AFER, "The Dan Lawn Story," *Alaska Forum*, winter 1996.

109 **"treatment plant at Valdez":** William Coughlin, "Exxon Issues New Dumping Rules," *Boston Globe*, March 7, 1992. See also Alyson Pytte, "Tanker Dumping Rules Tightened," *ADN*, January 4, 1992.

109 **under the Oil Pollution Act:** PWS RCAC, "State Spill & Prevention Regulations Look Good," *The Observer*, January 1992; "Negotiators Struggle to Define "Maximum Extent Practicable" on Federal Vessel Regulations," *The Observer*, April 1992; "Proposed Regs to Implement Stricter Laws of Federal Oil Pollution Act of 1990," and "Response Requirement Caps Set Too Low," *The Observer*, July 1992.

109 **inside or outside the Sound:** PWS RCAC, "Liability of Response Contractors Big in '92," and "Fish Group Reps Review Nearshore Response Plans," *The Observer*, January 1992; PWS RCAC "Nearshore Response Plan Looks Good, but Some Gaps," *The Observer*, September 1992.

109 **whistleblower protection bill:** Alaska, House Labor and Commerce Committee, *Whistleblower Protection for Employees of Private Employers: Hearings on HB 570*, 17th legislature, 2nd session, scheduled for April 14, 1992 (canceled). See also Mary Alice McKeen, "[Prepared] Testimony of the Government Accountability Project on Whistleblower Protection for Private Sector Employees (HR 570) before the House Labor and Commerce Committee, Alaska State Legislature," April 14, 1992; Billie Pirner Garde, "[Prepared] Testimony before the House of Representatives, State of Alaska, Labor and Commerce Committee," April 14, 1992.

110 **whistleblower conference in Washington, D.C.:** Association of Forest Service Employees for Environmental Ethics and Government Accountability Project, "Protecting Integrity and Ethics in Management of Natural Resources Report," Georgetown Conference Center, Washington, D.C., March 27–28, 1992.

110 **"a legal iceberg":** William Coughlin, "Illness Tied to Exxon Cleanup is Cited in Spate of Lawsuits," *Boston Sunday Globe*, April 12, 1992.

110 **used on the spill:** Exxon Company, MSDS, Crude Oil, Houston, Tex., May 15, 1988; Exxon Company, MSDS, Inipol EAP22; Exxon Company, MSDS, Corexit 9527.

110 **"need to wake up":** William Coughlin, "Doctor Says Oil, Cleanup Toxins Fatal. Mixture of

Chemicals Responsible for Illness and Death from Alaska Spill, Suits Claim," *Boston Globe*, May 10, 1992.

111 **Chugach shareholder Sylvia Lange:** Don Adams, "Chugach Alaska Corporation Plans Sale of Cannery Equipment," *CT*, March 25, 1992.

111 **Norquest Seafoods:** Don Adams, "Processor Reopens Plant, Creates 'Silver Lining' in Cloudy Job Market," *CT*, April 1, 1992; "Gloomy Salmon Market Looks Brighter in 1993," *CT*, April 1, 1992; "PWSAC Anticipates Good 'Pink' Year," *CT*, June 3, 1992.

111 **"like last year":** "'92 Fishing Season Could Mimic '91 Fiasco, State Study Says," *CT*, July 8, 1992.

111 **for payroll expenses:** Don Adams, "Council Oks Bank Loan to Meet Monthly Payroll," *CT*, May 13, 1992.

111 **requested capital grants:** Don Adams, "Voters Pass Four Bonds, but Nix Patching City Roof," *CT*, May 6, 1992; "Bond Sale Sends Message," *CT*, May 20, 1992.

111 **the worst looked imminent:** Don Adams, "Pink Season Looks Like a Quandary," *CT*, July 22, 1992.

112 **to buy trees:** "Bill Targets Oil Spill Settlement Money," *CT*, April 29, 1992; David Whitney and Hal Berton, "Hickel Wants Spill Funds Held Back; Governor Against Bill Targeting Money for Timber," *ADN*, April 8, 1992; Ralph Thomas, "Veto Kills Timber Buyouts; Hickel's Capital Budget Cuts Disappoint Environmentalists," *ADN*, July 16, 1992.

112 **beach cleanup was complete:** Roanne Pigano, "Cleanup Crews Start Fourth, Likely Final, Year on Spill," *ADN*, May 14, 1992; ADEC, *Final Report*, 146–147.

114 **settled under the TAPL Fund:** Lebedoff, *Cleaning Up*, 99–100.

114 **Holland's court:** Ibid., 84–100.

114 **broke laws:** U.S. Congress, House, *Report on Alyeska Covert Operation*, 1992, 3–5.

115 **too-full water balloon:** Tony Bickert, "Painter Barely Escapes Electrical Shock," *Valdez Vanguard*, July 30, 1992; Allanna Sullivan, "Slippery Slope. Alaska Pipeline Gets 'Sham' Safety Checks, Former Workers Say. They Contend That Alyeska Resorts To Intimidation To Weaken Inspections. Consortium Defends Actions," *Wall Street Journal*, August 4, 1992; Kim Fararo, "Ex-Alyeska Inspector Complains to D.C.," *ADN*, March 17, 1992; Kim Fararo, "More Ex-Staff Criticize Alyeska Safety," *ADN*, April 10, 1992.

115 **main source of air pollution:** PWS RCAC, "Review of the Valdez Air Health Study," Anchorage, Alaska, August 25, 1992; PWS RCAC, "Independent Review of Air Study Disputes Alyeska Findings," *The Observer*, September 1992; Kim Fararo, "Study Absolving Alyeska Flawed, Air Experts Say," *ADN*, August 27, 1992.

116 **one processing plant:** Don Adams, "Pink Salmon Season the Worst Since 1978," *CT*, August 26, 1992.

116 **to pay their debts:** Don Adams, "PWSAC Seeks Loan Deferral," *CT*, September 23, 1992; Adams, "PWSAC Committee to Re-Examine Cost-Recovery Policy," *CT*, October 8, 1992; Judy Lietzau, "Fishermen Told Not to Ignore Financial Problems," *CT*, October 15, 1992.

116 **community against itself:** Don Adams, "200 Vent Anger Over Cordova's Annexation Plan," *CT*, July 22, 1992; Adams, "City Answers Annexation Criticisms," *CT*, September 16, 1992; Gary Lewis, "Pro: Why is Annexation Desirable?" and Christine Honkola, "A Bitter Pill for Many Residents," *CT*, December 10, 1992.

116 **further divided the community:** "State Funds Deep-Water Port Study, Results Due in October," *CT*, July 8, 1992; "Alaska Pipeline Settles Suit Over Valdez Spill," *New York Times*, November 26, 1992; Marc Cowart, "Alyeska Settlement to Fund Shepard Point Road, Dock," *CT*, December 3, 1992.

116 **struggled for control:** "Settlement Money on Council Agenda," *CT*, January 2, 1992; Chris Casati, "Sherstone Tells Trustees Timber Buyback Plan is OK," *CT*, January 15, 1992; Don Adams, "Loggers Unite Against Settlement Timber Buyback," *CT*, February 12, 1992; Adams, "Loggers, Environmentalists Go Back to Work," *CT*, March 11, 1992; Adams, "Eyak Corporation Elects Nine New Members to Board," *CT*, May 6, 1992; Adams, "Environmental Concerns Bring Business to Loggers" and "Eyak Corporation Gets Land-Trade Deal with Feds," *CT*, June 24, 1992; Adams, "Anti-Loggers Protest with Blockade," *CT*, July 29, 1992;

Margy Johnson, guest opinion, "Whiners Drown Out Future Leaders," *CT*, August 12, 1992; Marie Smith Jones, community view, "Help Save Our Land," *CT*, September 16, 1992; "Court Halts Logging on Ancestral Lands," *CT*, September 23, 1992; Adams, "Eyak Logging Resumes After Judge Lifts Restraint," *CT*, September 30, 1992; Dune Lankard, LTE, "Fight Goes On," *CT*, October 15, 1992; Adams, "Crane Sabotage" and "Scientists Eye New Methods of Tree Harvesting," *CT*, November 12, 1992; Marc Cowart, "Mud Slide Kills Logger," *CT*, December 3, 1992; Ross Mullins, LTE, "Muddy Situation," *CT*, December 10, 1992.

117 **to find answers:** "Low Survival Rate of Pink Salmon Fry Mystifies PWSAC," *CT*, September 2, 1992; "Meeting Spotlights Pink Reports," *CT*, September 16, 1992; Riki Ott, "Fish" and "Fish and Oil Toxicity" in *Sound Truth*, 249–269, 343–369.

117 **educators and policy-makers:** *Scientists and the Alaska Oil Spill, The Wildlife, the Cleanup, the Outlook* (Houston: Exxon Company, 1992), VHS.

117 **state's water quality standards:** Kim Fararo, "Dollar Has New Clout with ADEC, New Water Rules Weigh Jobs Against Health Risk," *ADN*, September 13, 1992; Kim Fararo, "EPA Says Looser Pollution Rules May Pose Hazard," *ADN*, October 24, 1992.

117 **mine tailings disposal:** In 1993, Sierra Club Legal Defense Fund and National Wildlife Federation successfully sued the EPA over the conversion of waterbodies issue, based on the argument that Alaska could not arbitrarily change the definition of "waters of the United States," a fundamental principle of the Clean Water Act, to "treatment works."

117 **opposing the proposed changes:** United Fishermen of Alaska and Cordova District Fishermen United, ad, "Action Alert: Commercial Fishing Under Fire from ADEC," *CT*, August 12, 1992; Jerry McCune, "New Regulations will Lead to Degradation of Fish Habitat and Long-Term Reductions in Fish Populations," *CT*, September 23, 1992; Kim Fararo, "Pollution Philosophy Changing. DEC Wants to Weigh Job, Danger to Health," September 13, 1992; "DEC Extends Water-Quality Review," *CT*, November 5, 1992.

118 **Middle Rock in Valdez Narrows:** Kim Fararo, "Near Miss in the Narrows. Tanker's Tugboat Escort Puts Itself in a Hard Spot: Between Middle Rock and a New Disaster," *ADN*, November 22, 1992.

118 **compromised by Alyeska's actions:** David Whitney, "Alyeska Facing Tough Panel, Congressional Hearing Expected Next Year on Safety Charges," *ADN*, December 5, 1992; "Alyeska Critic Has Attention of D.C. Panel," *ADN*, February 26, 1993.

118 **couldn't do both:** Oesting, interview.

Chapter 8: As Bad as It Gets

120 **Library and Information Services in Anchorage:** Alaska Department of Law, ACE Investigation Files 1989–1991, ARLIS, Anchorage; Ott, *Sound Truth*, 6–7.

120 **still poisonous four years after the spill:** The technical science papers presented at the *EVOS* Symposium, sponsored by the EVOS Trustee Council, University of Alaska Sea Grant College Program, and the American Fisheries Society, Alaska Chapter, in Anchorage, February 2–5, 1993, were published in *Proceedings of the EVOS Symposium*, eds. Stanley Rice and others (Bethesda, Md.: American Fisheries Society, 1996). For a general discussion, see *Alaska's Wildlife*, January–February, 1993. See also Ott, *Sound Truth*: sea otters, 215–221; harlequin ducks, 239–246; river otters, 308–312.

121 **were also having problems:** Ott, *Sound Truth*: pink salmon, 249–259; herring, 259–266.

121 **previous year's prediction:** *Times* staff, "'93 Pink Return Looks Promising," *CT*, January 21, 1993; *Times* staff, "Record Herring Harvest Possible," *CT*, March 4, 1993.

122 **$17 to $86 million:** Maurice Cohen, "The Economic Impact of an Environmental Accident: A Time Series Analysis of the EVOS in Southcentral Alaska," *Sociological Spectrum* 13 (1993): 35–63; Maurice Cohen, "Economic Impacts of the EVOS," in *The Exxon Valdez Disaster*, eds. Picou, Gill, and Cohen, 133–163.

124 **Sound was recovering rapidly:** In the opinion of this author and other scientists who were not funded by Exxon, the conclusions by Exxon scientists of little damage and rapid recovery are not supported by their study designs. For a general discussion on manipulation of spill studies, specific to the species mentioned in this section, see Ott, *Sound Truth*: background oil, 364–369;

sea otters, 215–221, 228, 300–304, 315–316;salmon, 249–259, 266–267, 289; and herring 267–269. Exxon's technical spill papers were published in *EVOS: Fate and Effects in Alaskan Waters*, eds. Peter Wells, James Butler, and James Hughes (Philadelphia: American Society for Testing and Materials, 1995).

124 **simply vanished:** Marc Cowen, "Mystery Disease Plagues Herring," *CT*, April 22, 1993.

126 **Van Brocklin took his life:** *Times* staff, "Former Mayor Found Dead, Cordova Loses a Friend," *CT*, May 6, 1993.

126 **"to forgive ourselves":** Michelle O'Leary, "A Dear Friend Leaves Us with a Parting Gift," guest opinion, *CT*, May 6, 1993. See also Marilee Enge, "Cordova Mourns Yet Another Loss: Suicide Touches Nerve Left Raw by Oil Spill," *ADN*, May 17, 1993.

127 **protect salmon streams:** Jerry McCune, "Fund Fishing Resources Now—Or Pay Later," guest editorial, *CT*, April 8, 1993; Marc Cowen, "Trustees Told to Restore Sound," *CT*, May 6, 1993; Karl Becker, "Research Fisheries," LTE, *CT*, May 6, 1993.

127 **"most confusing budget process . . . ever":** Soren Wuerth, "Cost of Living Goes Up," *CT*, July 1, 1993.

127 **newly annexed residents:** Marc Cowen, "Commission Says Yes to Annexation," *CT*, January 7, 1993; "75 Sue to Block City Plan," *CT*, February 11, 1993; "Opponents Lose Battle to Halt Plan," *CT*, March 11, 1993; "Annexation Task Force Appointed," *CT*, March 11, 1933; "Annexation Now Official; Taxes, Lawsuit Pending," *CT*, April 8, 1993; "Resolution Asks Council to Resign," *CT*, May 13, 1993; Marc Cowen, "Two Council Members Refuse to Resign," *CT*, June 3, 1993.

127 **no support from Governor Hickel:** Marc Cowen, "Hickel's Project List Skips Cordova," *CT*, April 8, 1993; Cathy Sherman, "Plain Stupid," LTE, *CT*, April 22, 1993.

127 **city manager warned:** Ann Chandonnet, "Council Sets Mill Rate at 11," *CT*, June 24, 1993. See also Marc Cowen, "Council Gives Ultimatum to Tax-Owing Businesses," *CT*, March 25, 1993; Cowen, "Budget Boggles Council;" Wuerth, "Cost of Living Goes Up;" Soren Wuerth, "Garbage Rate Rises to $33.70," *CT*, July 22, 1993.

128 **"I resent it":** Stanley Samuelson, "Hatchery Disaster," LTE, *CT*, July 1, 1993. See also Ellen Lockyer, "Fishermen Forgo Pink Run to Help Out Valdez Hatchery," *Maritime Alaska*, July 7–8, 1993.

128 **reports were disheartening:** Soren Wuerth, "No Seining Until More Pinks Arrive," *CT*, July 22, 1993; Laine Welch, "Will Pinks Pull a No-Show?" *Maritime Alaska*, August 5–6, 1993; Ellen Lockyer, "PWS Pinks Late–Again," *CT*, August 12, 1993; Laine Welch, "State Help Sought in Sound Pink Disaster," *Maritime Alaska*, August 19–20, 1993.

129 **"spill stress data":** "Exxon Wins Look at Spill Stress Data," *ADN*, May 26, 1993; Marilee Enge, "Scientist, Exxon Fight Over Data: Sociologist Guarding Cordova Confidentiality," *ADN*, May 26, 1993; Enge, "Scientist Fears for Career if Judge Forces Him to Reveal Spill Research," *ADN*, May 27, 1993; E. Marshall, "Court Orders 'Sharing' of Data," *Science*, July 16, 1993, 284–286.

130 **screamed at each other:** Soren Wuerth, "Timber Falls in 'Off-Limits' Land," *CT*, July 29, 1993; "Protesters Decry Clear-Cuts," *CT*, July 22, 1993; "Loggers Rally, Employees Air Fears About Lost Jobs from Land Buy-Out," *CT*, July 29, 1993.

130 **"Coca Cola for a year":** Marilee Enge, "Alyeska to Pay $98 Million to Settle Exxon Spill Claims," *ADN*, July 14, 1993. See also Soren Wuerth, "Cordovans Feel Cautious, Optimistic," *CT*, July 15, 1993.

131 **spread quickly in town:** Soren Wuerth, "Fishermen Blame Spill for Disaster, Plan Protest," *CT*, August 19, 1993; Tom Kizzia, "Measuring Up the Sound. Biologists Cannot Explain Collapse of Pink Runs: Fishermen Blame Spill," *ADN*, September 5, 1993.

132 **"bunch of fishermen":** Tony Bickert, "Protest Shuts Port," *CT*, August 26, 1993. See also Soren Wuerth, "Officials Seeking Antidote for Area's Ailing Economy," *CT*, August 26, 1993; Rick Steiner, "Oil's Toxic Shock to System to Blame," guest opinion, *CT*, August 26, 1993.

132 **disbanded the blockade:** Soren Wuerth, "ARCO, BP Plan Compensation," *CT*, September 2, 1993; Tony Bickert, "Coast Guard: No Fines for Fishermen Protesters," *CT*, October 14, 1993.

132 **General Accounting Office:** U.S. General Accounting Office, *Natural Resources Restoration: Use of EVOS Settlement Funds*, briefing report to the Chairman, Committee on Natural Resources, U.S. House, GAO/RCED-93-206BR, August 1993.

132 **everything except restoration:** Natalie Phillips, "Oil Spill Trustees Rebuked. GAO Study Criticizes Settlement Spending," August 23, 1993; AP, "Trustees Livid Over GAO Report," *ADN*, August 24, 1993; "New Trouble in PWS," editorial, *New York Times*, August 25, 1993.

133 **mood in town shifted:** Soren Wuerth, "Depression Worse Than Ever, Picou Says," *CT*, September 9, 1993.

133 **"the energy of the blockade":** Torie Baker (Cordova fisherma'm), interview with author, Cordova, Alaska, November 19, 1999.

133 **least profitable on record:** Soren Wuerth, "Empty Nets, Statistics Get More Dismal," *CT*, September 2, 1993; Cindy Stimson, "Future Looks Grim for Commercial Fishers," *CT*, September 2, 1993.

133 **inflated permit prices:** Ed Crane (Commercial Fishing and Agriculture Bank president), interview with author, November 30, 1999.

133 **$98 million Alyeska settlement:** AP, "Exxon Sues Alyeska to Block Deal Settling Spill Claims," *ADN*, September 3, 1993.

136 **'early retirement':** Kim Fararo, "Hermiller Leaving Alyeska. Chief Brought Reforms, but OK'd Spy Activity," *ADN*, February 6, 1993; Bruce Melzer, "Alyeska's Security Chief Calls It Quits," *ADN*, February 11, 1993.

136 **rehire list:** David Whitney, "Ex-Workers Reach Deal with Alyeska. Charges Still to Be Studied," *ADN*, May 29, 1993.

136 **"déjà vu all over again":** U.S. House, Committee on Energy and Commerce, Subcommittee on Oversight and Investigations, *Oversight Hearings on Trans-Alaska Pipeline*, 103rd Cong., 1st sess., Washington, D.C., serial no. 103–83, July 14 and November 10, 1993, 1–3; U.S. House, Committee on Interstate and Foreign Commerce, Subcommittee on Energy and Power, *Oversight Hearing on Alyeska Oil Pipeline: Problems Concerning the General Lack of Quality Control in the Welding During the Construction of the Trans-Alaska Pipeline*, 94th Cong., 2nd sess., Washington, D.C., serial no. 94–125, June 21, 1976.

137 **audit confirms the whistleblowers' stories:** David Whitney, "Audit Slams Pipeline Operation. Wiring, Welds, Records Call Safety into Question," *ADN*, November 10, 1993.

137 **'File Stuffing Incident':** U.S. House, *Oversight Hearing on the Trans-Alaska Pipeline*, 185–186.

137 **more lawsuits:** Billie Pirner Garde (attorney, Hardy & Johns), letter to Stan Stephens, Valdez, Alaska, re: U.S. Department of Labor (USDOL) Complaints, Bureau of Land Management Investigation, the Dept. of Transportation Inspector General's Investigation, and Other Concerns, plus attachments, including USDOL Complaints for Michael Shelton-Kelly, #4; James Schooley, #7; R. Glen Plumlee, #8; Robert Plumlee, #10; Kenneth Hayson, #12; and Richardo Ray Acord, #12, among others.

137 **"do not touch":** U.S. House, *Oversight Hearing on Trans-Alaska Pipeline*, 156; Steve Rinehart, "ARCO, Contractor Dennounce Blacklisting," *ADN*, November 13, 1993.

137 **"concerns of the public interest":** Ibid., 160.

137 **"their luck runs out":** Ibid., 177.

138 **a people's judge:** Julie Cohen, "Big Oil's Slippery Slope. On the Eve of Trial, Alyeska Pipeline Faces Uphill Battle Against Whistleblower," *Legal News* 16 (26), week of November 15, 1993.

138 **learned what had happened:** Kim Fararo, "Alyeska Still Hunting for Leakers, Hamel Says This Time in Court," *ADN*, August 5, 1993; Fararo, "Judge Solicits Notes, Oil Whistle-blower Told to Open Files," *ADN*, August 17, 1993; David Whitney, "Judge Denies Alyeska's Requests to Uncover Hamel's Sources," *ADN*, October 9, 1993; Whitney, "Alyeska's Laywers Rile Federal Judge," *ADN*, November 20, 1993.

138 **primary author of RICO:** David Whitney, "Judge Says He'll Decide Taping Issue. Legality of Alyeska's Tapes of Hamel Ruled Not for Jury," *ADN*, November 18, 1993.

138 **illegal but it was an accident:** David Whitney, "Witness: Taping Illegal. Spy Takes Stand at Hamel Hearing," *ADN*, November 23, 1993; Whitney, "Hamel Judge Orders Talks. Events Indicate Whistle-blower, Oil Firms May Settle," *ADN*, December 14, 1993.

139 **pleading the Fifth like crazy:** David Whitney, "2nd Agent Takes Fifth in Hamel Case," *ADN*, November 24, 1993.

139 **over on Solstice:** David Whitney, "Hamel, Alyeska Sign Settlement. Agreement Terms Keep Secret How Much Money Pipeline Company Critic Will Be Paid," *ADN*, December 21, 1993; Charles McCoy and Richard Schmitt, "Alyeska Settles Suit by a Whistle-Blower," *Wall Street Journal*, December 21, 1993. See also *Management Information Technologies, Inc., et al. v. APSC, et al.*, No. 92-1730-CV (SS), U.S. District Court, District of Columbia, December 20, 1993; Frank DeLong, Stan Stephens, Dan Lawn, Robert Swift, Fredericka Ott, and Roy Dalthorp v. APSC, James Patrick Wellington, The Wackenhut Corporation, Wayne Black, Richard Lund, BP Pipeline (Alaska), Inc., Exxon Pipeline Company, ARCO Transportation Corp., 3AN-92-6608-CV, State of Alaska Superior Court, Third Judicial District, December 21, 1994.

Chapter 9: Decisions

143 **piece of paper:** "Ice Damages Empty Tanker, No Oil is Spilled," *CT*, January 6, 1994. See also Hal Berton, "Tankers to Get Escorts in Ice-Laden Sound," *ADN*, January 18, 1994.

143 **"therapy for residents":** Soren Wuerth, "Town Meeting Offers Therapy for Residents," *CT*, January 27, 1994.

143 **pittance from state lawmakers:** Soren Wuerth, "Trouble Times Ahead for City," *CT*, January 13, 1994.

143 **won by one vote:** Soren Wuerth, "Recount Secures Johnson's Victory," *CT*, October 21, 1993.

144 **town meeting:** COC, *Town Meeting Report*, Cordova, Alaska, 1994.

145 **"time to move on":** Cinthia Stimson, "Funeral Aims to Bury the Blues About the Spill," *CT*, February 24, 1994.

145 **"murdered by negligence":** Rich Septien, "Bogus Burial," LTE, *CT*, March 3, 1994. See also Cinthia Stimson, "Blues Processional Canceled," *CT*, March 17, 1994.

145 **billions of dollars:** AP, "Judge Holland Sides with Exxon Over Native Damage Claims" and "Judge: Fishermen Can't Claim Lost Boat Values," *CT*, March 31, 1994; Hirsch, "Justice Delayed," 278–280 nn. 53–54. Based on a subsequent appellate court decision, tendermen, fish processors, cannery workers, and municipalities were able to refile their claims in state court.

146 **"consequences of an accident":** *Exxon Valdez Case,* Order No. 189, 13.

146 **in trade for operating permits:** Townsend, "Promises."

147 **my report, Sound Truth:** Riki Ott, "Sound Truth: Exxon's Manipulation of Science and the Significance of the *Exxon Valdez* Oil Spill," Greenpeace Report (Anchorage, Alaska), March 24, 1994.

147 **without their beloved coach:** "Cordova Judo Team Claims State Crown," *CT*, March 31, 1994.

147 **two more ecosystem studies:** These were the Alaska Predator Experiment and the Nearshore Vertebrate Predator Program: www.evostc.state.ak.us/Projects/titlesearchstart.cfm, "APEX" and "NVP" for project titles. Results of the NVP Program are discussed elsewhere in this book. For a general description of the APEX studies, see Ott, "Apex Predators," in *Sound Truth*, 317–341.

147 **direct stake in the litigation:** Rosanne Pagano, "Cordova Not Ready to Forgive or Forget: After a 5-Year Wait, an Angry Fishing Town's Day in Court with Exxon Approaches," *ADN*, March 25, 1994.

149 **in the paper:** David Hulen, "Captain's Record Shows 3 Alcohol Arrests," *ADN*, March 28, 1989; AP, "Skipper's Mother Confirms He Had a Drinking Problem," *ADN*, March 29, 1989; David Hulen, "Investigator Says Alcohol Smelled on Skipper's Breath," *ADN*, March 30, 1989; AP, "Suit Charges Captain was Heavy Drinker: 18-Month-Old Court Papers Say Hazelwood was Regularly Drunk," *ADN*, April 10, 1989. These articles are just a sampling of those available in the *ADN* spill archive: www.adn.com/evos/pgs/sp5.html.

149 **Judge Holland's objections:** Lebedoff, *Cleaning Up*, 279–280; Natalie Phillips, "$5,000,000,000. Jury Sets Oil Spill Damages," *ADN*, September 17, 1994. In spite of Judge Holland's implorings, jurors gave in-depth interviews to two reporters. See Emily Barker, "The *Exxon Valdez* Trial: A Do-It-Yourself Jury," *American Lawyer*, November 1994, 68–77, and Natalie Phillips, "The Exxon Decision. 'We Did the Right Thing' Jury Foreman Recounts Long Haul to Judgment," *ADN*, September 18, 1994, www.adn.com/evos/stories/EV407.html.

150 **"in our company"**: Barker, "Do-It-Yourself Jury," 71, 73–74.

151 **you and I are responsible**: Natalie Phillips, "Jury Finds Exxon, Joe Reckless," *CT*, June 14, 1994.

151 **"dancing . . . in the streets"**: Sandra Medearis, "Residents Take News Positively," *CT*, June 16, 1994.

151 **"in the courtroom"**: Oesting, interview. After the trial, this money, along with personal contributions from Oesting and O'Neill, was used to send the trial team staff and paralegals on a fishing charter in Homer.

152 **revolutionized courtroom technology**: M. Lassiter, "Multimedia Trial Presentation Systems Win Cases," *National Law Journal*, October 10, 1994; K. Dewey, "Slick Trial Tactics. Plaintiffs' Council in Exxon Case Won Big by Going High-Tech," *Los Angeles Daily Journal*, September 18, 1995.

153 **"boggled my mind"**: Mullins, interview.

153 **"PhDs can't even agree on"**: Barker, "Do-It-Yourself Jury," 74.

154 **"livelihoods are completely different"**: Natalie Phillips, "Damage: $287 Million. Fishermen Unhappy; Exxon Says It's Pleased," *ADN*, August 12, 1994.

154 **"restitution can be accomplished"**: Street Talk, *CT*, August 18, 1994.

154 **only part of the whole**: Steep declines in harvest of wild foods in 1989 and several years thereafter by Natives in Prince William Sound are well documented by ADFG, as are the effects on the Natives' way of life or culture. See James Fall and Jay Field, "Subsistence Uses of Fish and Wildlife Before and After the EVOS," *AFSS* 18 (1996): 819–836; Christopher Dyer, "Tradition Loss as Secondary Disaster: Long-Term Cultural Impacts of the *EVOS*," *Sociological Spectrum* 13(1) (1993): 65–88; Christopher Dyer, Duane Gill, and Steven Picou, "Social Disruption and the *Valdez* Oil Spill: Alaskan Natives in a Natural Resource Community," *Sociological Spectrum* 12(2) (1992): 105–126; Gill and Picou, "The Day the Water Died." On August 29, 1994, the United Nations adopted a definition of cultural genocide that included "prevention of or redress for" loss of resources: "(b) Any action which has the aim or effect of dispossessing them [indigenous people] of their lands, territories or resources." http// en.wikipedia.org/wiki/Cultural_genocide.

155 **against a large punitive award**: *Exxon Valdez Case*, Order No.: spills, 240; indemnity, 245; material effect, 246.

155 **mandatory punitive action class**: Ibid., Order No. 204 and 204 Supplement. According to Dave Oesting, Judge Holland's decision contained an irony of significance in legal circles. He explained, "The punitive damages claim that went to the jury, was tried under the aegis of the *Airport Depot Diner* case to resolve Exxon's counterclaim, not our claim for punitive damages." Judge Holland had stayed the *Airport Depot Diner* case in 1991 as a legal mechanism to allow him to retain control of all the punitive damage claims.

155 **voluminous jury instructions**: Hirsch, "Justice Delayed," 283–284.

156 **$0 to $20 billion**: Barker, "Do-It-Yourself Jury," 76.

157 **"being a community again"**: Sandra Medearis, "Exxon Verdict Sends Message," *CT*, September 22, 1994.

157 **"overturn this unjust verdict"**: Phillips, "$5,000,000,000."

159 **"to buy T-shirts"**: Dennis McQuire, LTE, *CT*, August 11, 1994.

159 **'the Doberman of watchdog groups'**: Tony Bickert, "New Watchdog Group Has Teeth," *Valdez Vanguard*, September 7, 1994.

159 **working in the Sound**: PWS RCAC, "RCAC Asks Alyeska to Continue Role as Contingency Plan Holder for Sound," "Nearshore Strike Team Demonstration in Seldovia," "Nearshore Response Dril and Exercises Planned," "Decision on Vapor Control System Expected in June," *The Observer*, spring 1994; "Special Report: Follow Up on *Eastern Lion*," summer 1994; "New Federal Rule Yields Escort Changes," "Towing Study Key to Changes," "Why Tractor Tugs?" "Ballast Water Monitoring Program Underway at Terminal," "Specifics of Vapor Control System Due Out in Spring," *The Observer*, fall 1994; "ADEC to Shippers: Beef Up Tanker Escorts Through Valdez Narrows," *The Observer*, fall 1995; "Eastern Lion Springs Leak, Oil Spreads in Port Valdez," *CT*, May 26, 1994; Kim Fararo, "EPA May Force Alyeska to Cut Emissions," *ADN*, May 18, 1994; Tony Bickert, "EPA Proposes Vapor Regulations for the Terminal," *Valdez Vanguard*, May 19, 1994.

160 **worse than the feds claimed**: Richard Fineberg, *Pipeline in Peril: A Status Report on the Trans-Alaska Pipeline*, prepared for Alaska, Valdez, September 1996, 3.19

160 **by the end of next year**: Ibid., 4.3–4.7.

160 **federal or congressional investigations**: Billie Garde letter to Stan Stephens with 22 attachments; David Whitney, "Alyeska Ordered to Help Whistleblower," *ADN*, September 10, 1994; Whitney, "Feds Rap Alyeska for Not Rehiring Whistleblowers," *ADN*, October 26. 1994.

160 **throw out the punitive award**: Natalie Phillips, "Exxon Verdict's Fate in Air. Attorneys Hope for $5 Billion Decision by Year's End," *ADN*, November 3, 1994.

161 **on specific projects**: Riki Ott, "Plan Can Be Made Better To Fit Cordova's Needs," commentary, *CT*, June 16, 1994.

Chapter 10: Stepping-stones

162 **"might be significant"**: ADNR, "Preliminary Best Interest Finding Regarding Proposed Oil and Gas Lease Sale 79, Cape Yakataga," 1994.

163 **Thea Thomas said**: Cinthia Stimson, "Fishermen Face Another Spring Without Herring," *CT*, February 2, 1995.

163 **bars sat empty**: Cinthia Stimson, "Another Lean Season," *CT*, February 9, 1995.

163 **"in the Mona Lisa"**: Cinthia Stimson, "Eyaks, EVOSTC [EVOS Trustee Council] at Stalemate, Trees Still Up for Grabs," *CT*, March 2, 1995.

163 **shareholders sued**: Cinthia Stimson, "Council Endorses Shepherd Point Road Project," *CT*, January, 26, 1995.

163 **"financial siege"**: Margy Johnson, "Budget Time Means Facing the Cuts That Are on the Way," commentary, *CT*, May 4, 1995.

163 **pay the taxes**: Cinthia Stimson, "Third Time's a Charm for Town Meeting," *CT*, March 9, 1995; "Voters to Decide Tax Rate," *CT*, April 13, 1995; "Voters Pass Sales Tax Increase," *CT*, May 11, 1995; "Council Raises Property Taxes Despite Sales Tax Hike," *CT*, May 25, 1995.

163 **adult population in town**: Cinthia Stimson, "Cordova Speaks Out, Residents Protest Oil and Gas Lease Sales," *CT*, April 27, 1995.

163 **city and fishermen sued**: Cinthia Stimson, "Council Considers Coastal Program," *CT*, April 27, 1995; Karen Collins-Dollente, "Lawsuit Pending on Lease Sale 79," *CT*, June 15, 1995.

164 **was pure magic**: Jane Crarer, "Cordova Artists Continue to Produce World-Class Work," special to the *Times*, *CT*, July 6, 1995; Crarer, "Artists Working for Future of Delta," special to the *Times*, *CT*, July 20, 1995; Sandi McDaniel, "Art for Nature's Sake: International Project Draws Attention to Threatened Copper River Delta," *ADN*, July 30, 1995.

164 **compatible with our fisheries**: Jane Crarer, "Inspiring Art Kicks Off Copper River Delta Project," special to the *Times*, *CT*, August 3, 1995; *Earthscape: Artists on the Copper River Delta* (Anchorage: Baker-Jennings Films, 1995), VHS, http://shenandoahfilms.com/Earthscape.asp.

166 **"attitude in Cordova"**: Margy Johnson, commentary, "The Cordova I See: A Candid Reflection," *CT*, September 28, 1995.

167 **"that testosterone factor"**: Mullins, interview. Claimants in the Damage Matrix process included commercial fishermen, processors, tenders, cannery workers, aquaculture associations, area businesses, municipalities, Alaska Natives, and Alaska Native corporations. The fishermen's class alone had thirty-five subdivisions based on fishery, area, and gear type.

168 **Sea Program to nonscientists**: Riki Ott, "Sound Ecosystem Assessment (SEA) Program," in *Sound Truth*, 273–291.

168 **Exxon's posttrial motions**: *Exxon Valdez Case*, Order No. 264–275; Sheila Toomey, "Judge Upholds Exxon Award. Holland Says Evidence Supports Damages; Oil Giant to Fight On," *ADN*, January 28, 1995.

168 **"accepts its findings"**: *Exxon Valdez Case.*, Order No. 267, 30.

169 **tried to commit suicide**: Natalie Phillips, "The $5 Billion Jury. For 18 Weeks, the *Exxon Valdez* Trial Jurors Listened, Argued, Laughed and Sometimes Even Dozed Off," *ADN*, January 22, 1995.

169 **"exaggerated account of the events"**: *Exxon Valdez Case*, Order No. 308, 19.

169 **in the punitive award**: Ibid., Order No. 317; Natalie Phillips, "3.5 Million Settles Last Exxon Suit," *ADN*, January 18, 1996.

169 **owing Exxon money:** Hirsch, "Justice Delayed," 286–287.

170 **by spilling oil:** *Exxon Valdez Case,* Order No. 297, 10, 46.

170 **share in the jury award:** Ibid., Order No. 297, 34–38.

170 **in his earlier rulings:** Ibid., Orders No. 289–292; Hirsch, "Justice Delayed," 276.

170 **to heal spill trauma:** *Times* staff, "Community Education Program Set for 1996," *CT,* January 4, 1996.

171 **spirits of participants:** *Times* staff, "Let the Healing Begin: Talking Circles Focus on Native, Community Issues," *CT,* January 18, 1996; Belen Cook, Native Village of Eyak, personal communication, January 5, 2007.

171 **Peer Listening Training:** PWS RCAC, "Mental Health Pilot Programs Well Received," *The Observer,* spring 1996; Steven Picou, "The 'Talking Circle' as Sociological Practice: Cultural Transformation of Chronic Disaster Impacts," *Sociological Practice: A Journal of Clinical and Applied Research* 2(2) (2000): 77–97.

171 **lack of fish:** "Herring Season Canceled," *CT,* January 25, 1996.

171 **seven Seattle processors:** Oesting, interview; *Icicle Seafoods v. Exxon,* A94-208-CV (D. Alaska, May 13, 1994). The Seattle Seven included Icicle Seafoods, Inc., Peter Pan Seafoods, Inc., Seven Seas Corp., Stellar Seafoods, Inc., Ocean Beauty Seafoods, Inc., Wards Cove Packing Co., Alaska Boat Co., North Pacific Processors, Inc., ADF, Inc., dba Aleutian Dragon Fisheries, Trident Seafoods Corp., and North Coast Seafood Processors, Inc.

172 **share of the punitive damage award:** *Exxon Valdez Case,* Order No. 317, 18, 20, and 22 (quotes), and 18–31 (background Seattle Seven); Hirsch, "Justice Delayed," 288–289.

172 **"fraud on the court":** Charles McCoy, "Exxon's Secret Valdez Deals Anger Judge," *Wall Street Journal,* June 13, 1996.

172 **"deplorably in private":** *Exxon Valdez Case,* Order No. 317, 30.

172 **"negate its verdict":** Ibid., Order No. 317, 30. See also Alex Salpukas, "Exxon is Accused of 'Astonishing Ruse' in Oil Spill Trial," *New York Times,* June 14, 1996; Charles McCoy and P. Fritsch, "Exxon Defends Its 'Novel' Approach to Reducing Valdez Punitive Damages," *Wall Street Journal,* June 14, 1996; Natalie Phillips, "Judge Thwarts Exxon. Oil Giant's Maneuver Sought Part of Award," *ADN,* June 13, 1996.

172 **through the seafood processors:** Rosanne Pagano, "Processors Appeal Oil Spill Ruling," *CT,* November 21, 1996.

172 **"greed, plain and simple":** Oesting, interview; *Exxon Valdez Case,* Order No. 317, 32–49.

172 **bombed in state court:** Rosanna Pagano, "Court Bars Payments to Natives. Exxon Owes Nothing," *ADN,* March 31, 1995.

173 **"fair, adequate, and reasonable":** *Exxon Valdez Case,* Order No. 317, 43 n. 66, 44–45, 49.

173 **in the Pacific Northwest:** Due to budget cuts, Alaska had fewer than three full-time habitat biologists to monitor logging practices on the state's 129 million acres of forested land in 1995. By comparison, Washington State had eleven to twelve full-time-equivalent positions for its 20 million acres of forested lands. To match Washington's effort, Alaska would have needed to employ seventy-four full-time habitat biologists. ADFG, *1995 Report to the Board of Forestry,* January 16, 1996.

173 **supporting this effort:** Riki Ott, "Sustainable Development and Cordova," commentary, *CT,* March 7, 1996; Riki Ott, "Share Your Ideas on March 23," LTE, *CT,* March 14, 1996.

173 **to attend the workshop:** Copper River Delta Project, special project of Alaska Clean Water Alliance, ad, *CT,* March 7, 1996.

174 **"coming together":** Kristin Smith, "Cordova Community is Coming Together," commentary, *CT,* March 28, 1996.

174 **to the local paper:** Riki Ott, "Dreamscapes," LTE, *CT,* April 4, 1996.

175 **on wildlife and fish:** Dick Borer, "Back Talk," and David Werner, "Another Opinion on the Same Topic," LTE, *CT,* April 11, 1996; John Carnes, "Misconceptions Lead to a Dead, Dark Forest," LTE, *CT,* April 25, 1996; Timothy Tirrell, "Forget the Trees and Build Malls," LTE, *CT,* May 2, 1996; David Werner, "Dispute Goes On," LTE, *CT,* May 16, 1996.

175 **honest economics:** Thomas Michael Power, *Lost Landscapes and Failed Economies: The Search for A Value of Place* (Washington, D.C.: Island Press, 1996).

175 **logging in the Sound would stop:** *Times* staff, "Trustees Agree to Buy Tatitlek Lands," *CT*, September 5, 1996; Jennifer Strange, "Eyak Corporation May Sell 75,000 Acres of PWS Land to EVOS," *CT*, July 3, 1997; Marybeth Holleman, "Sound Investment: Oil-Spill Settlement Buys Shoreline Crucial to the Recovery of Damaged Wildlife Populations," special to the *Daily News*, *ADN*, August 17, 1997; EVOS Trustee Council, *1997* and *1998 Status Report*s, Anchorage, Alaska.

175 **with the logging letters:** Steven Picou, "Technological Disasters: Why Are They Different?," special to the *Times*, *CT*, April 11, 1996; "Man-Man Disasters Linger," *CT*, April 25, 1996; "Technological Disasters: Letting Go of Chronic Depression," *CT*, May 9, 1996; "Chronic Stress and Alcohol Consumption Figure in Disasters," *CT*, May 16, 1996; "Technological Disasters: Talking to Children in Stressful Situations," *CT*, May 23, 1996; "The Mood-Food Connection and Stress," *CT*, June 13, 1996; "Chronic Stress and Cancer—Could There Be a Link?" *CT*, July 3, 1996.

176 **"will help people heal":** Steven Picou, "Communities Learn to Cope," *CT*, July 11, 1996.

176 **glut from farmed salmon:** Jennifer Strange, "Cordova Seiners Ask for Price Negotiations," *CT*, July 17, 1997; "Seiners Say No to Pink Prices," *CT*, July 31, 1997; "Seiners May Settle For Less," *CT*, August 7, 1997; "Seiners Agree to the Prices, Get Back on Water," *CT*, August 14, 1997.

176 **$295 million per year:** Natalie Phillips, "There's Intense Interest. When Does Meter Run on $5 Billion?" *ADN*, September 24, 1994.

176 **made into banners:** Jennifer Strange, "It's a Banner Year for Cordova," *CT*, May 1, 1997.

177 **delinquent taxpayers this spring:** Cinthia Stimson, "Harbor Rates Increase for Storage Users," *CT*, January 18, 1996; Becky Shipman, "Flush Your Toilets or Buy Groceries?" LTE, *CT*, March 7, 1996; Debbie Knight, "Experience Left Taxpayer Hurt and Degraded," LTE, *CT*, May 23, 1996; Scott Janke, "Paying Bills Benefits Us All," LTE, *CT*, May 30, 1996.

177 **in the first place:** APSC, "Oil Spill Prevention Measures for the TAPS," 1973, in *Promises*, Townsend Environmental, 19; PWS RCAC, "New Weather Monitoring Equipment Installed in Sound," "Spill Prevention Scores Big One with New Vessel Traffic System," *The Observer*, summer 1995; "Regulators OK Alyeska Pipe Replacement Plan," "Terminal and SERVS Report on Activities," *The Observer*, spring 1996; "Risk Assessment Pinpoints Ways to Make Oil Transportation Safer," "Shippers Announce Plans, Changes," winter 1996–1997.

178 **lip service to the contrary:** APSC, Jim Hermiller (Alyeska president), "State of the Trans-Atlantic Pipeline: A Report to the People of Alaska," ad, *ADN*, February 4, 1996, B4; Staff, "Heard on the Street," February 16, 1996; Richard Fineberg, "TAPS Employee Concerns and Employee Concerns Programs," in *Pipeline in Peril*, 11.1–22.

178 **Carbon Mountain Project:** Cinthia Stimson, "Chugach Corp. Unveils Project," "Chugach Expects 15-Year Project," and Koncor Forest Products, Co., "Philosophies to Work By," ad, *CT*, October 24, 1996.

Chapter 11: Gaining Ground

179 **back into the Sound:** David Whitney, "Exxon Tries to Overturn Tanker Ban," *ADN*, January 17, 1997; "Alaskan to Rule on Ex–*Exxon Valdez*," *ADN*, January 31, 1997.

179 **unconstitutional taking of property:** David Whitney, "Exxon Wants Notorious Tanker Back on Duty," *ADN*, April 5, 1996.

180 **disposing of the stuff:** AFER, *Poisoning the Well*, Valdez, Alaska, January 1997; Helen Jung, "Improper Rig Waste Probed. Doyon Drilling Injected 2,000 Gallons of Chemicals, BP Says," *ADN*, January 10, 1996; Kim Fararo, "Illegal Dumping Lasted for Years. EPA Investigates Endicott Practices," *ADN*, January 20, 1996.

180 **expensive fixes for last:** Richard Fineberg, "Pipeline in Peril: Alaska at Risk on the 20th Anniversary of the Trans-Alaska Pipeline," prepared for AFER, June 1997, www.finebergresearch.com/reports.html.

180 **all the time:** Richard Fineberg, "How Much is Enough? Estimated Profits from Alaska North Slope Production and Associated Pipeline Operations 1993–1998 (Preliminary Report), prepared for Oil Watch, www.finebergresearch.com/reports.html.

180 **defeat the bill last year:** Linden O'Toole, "Cordova's Exxon Damage Awards at Risk!," LTE, *CT*, April 17, 1997; Jennifer Strange, "Tort Reform Could Damage Oil Spill Plaintiffs' Cases," *CT*, March 27, 1997; Strange, "City Lobbies Hard Against Caps on Punitive Damages," *CT*, April 10, 1997.

180 **evident in the bill:** Jennifer Strange, "Revised Tort Reform Bill Goes to Knowles," *CT*, April 24, 1997; Brian Shaw, "Veto Tort Reform Bill," and Dorne Hawxhurst, "CDFU Nixes Tort Reform," LTE, *CT*, June 6, 1996; Kate Troll (executive director UFA), "Tort Reform," LTE, *CT*, May 8, 1997.

181 **earliest coastal plans in Alaska:** The Alaska Coastal Management Program is a joint effort by the federal, state, and local governments and the private sector to manage activities along America's coasts. It is authorized under the Coastal Zone Management Act (CZMA), which is the only federal environmental program that requires a balance between economic development and resource protection within the coastal zone.

183 **"a fiasco":** Stan Hamuelson, "The Herring Season," LTE, *CT*, May 8, 1997. See also "Sitka Rolling in Herring," *CT*, March 20, 1997; "Herring are Here, But Samples Show Immature Fish, Low Egg Count," *CT*, April 3, 1997.

184 **"control the speed of . . . [development]":** Jennifer Strange, "Workshop Explores Tourism Strategies," *CT*, May 29, 1997.

186 **project in Alaska:** CRWP, "Making the Most of Copper River Resources," 4 vols., Cordova, Alaska, April 20, 1998.

186 **phased in double-hull tankers:** Riki Ott, "State Taking Wrong Side in Spill Prevention," letter to Governor Tony Knowles and LTE, *CT*, November 28, 1997.

186 **mandated in federal law:** Stan Jones, "2 New Tankers Planned: Both ARCO Ships Get Double Hulls," *ADN*, July 30, 1997.

186 **reconfiguring them:** "Oil Shippers Find Way to Keep Single Hulls Afloat," *CT*, December 12, 1997.

187 **district court in Anchorage:** Natalie Phillips, "Judge Demands Evidence of Oil-Spill Jury-Tampering," *ADN*, January 27, 1998.

188 **"extraordinary newly discovered documents":** Natalie Phillips, "Guard Tainted Oil Spill Trial, Exxon Claims," *ADN*, October 14, 1997.

188 **and Louisiana crude:** Ott, *Sound Truth*, 423–424.

189 **dog is as welcome as you are:** John Atwood (editor-in-chief, *Sports Afield*), www.rivers-edge.com/content/view/44/57;"50 Best Outdoor Sports Towns," *Sports Afield*, February 1998.

189 **vigorous civic debate:** Charles Wohlforth, "Three Gems: Discover a Trio of Towns That Time Forgot—Just Off the Tourist Track," *Alaska Magazine*, February 1998, 53–59, quotes on 53, 55.

190 **Cordova and Chitina:** Jennifer Strange, "Cordova Residents Say Copper River Trail Plan Not What They Expected," *CT*, January 29, 1998; Elizabeth Saavedra and Jennifer Strange, "Trail Talk: Residents Voice Concerns About Copper River Trail," *CT*, February 19, 1998.

191 **art book:** Ott, *Alaska's Copper River Delta*.

192 **keeping Cordova afloat:** Area Management Reports, www.cf.adfg.state.ak.us/region2/pwshome.php

192 **"for . . . non-public roads":** "Murkowski Angry," *CT*, June 11, 1998.

192 **leeway for carelessness:** "Activists Plan 'Action Camp' as Loggers Start Carbon Mt. Project," *CT*, June 18, 1998.

192 **across the wetland:** Jennifer Strange, "Activists Hold Up Road Project," *CT*, June 25, 1998. The five activists were convicted of resisting arrest, disorderly conduct, criminal trespass, and criminal mischief and sentenced to one year in jail, which was suspended, and forty hours of community service. Strange, "Protesters Found Guilty," *CT*, March 25, 1999.

192 **Interior appropriations bill:** Jennifer Strange, "Congress Taking Sides in Carbon Mt. Road Issue," *CT*, July 23, 1998; Strange, "CAC [Chugach Alaska Corp.], Forest Service Debate Value of Rider," *CT*, July 30, 1998; AP, "House Members Vote Down Two Anti-Road-Building Amendments," *CT*, July 30, 1998.

193 **play for real:** "BP Plans Fall Spill Drill in Sound," *CT*, August 13, 1998; BP Spill of National Significance Drill, ad, *CT*, October 8, 1998.

193 **get it on their skin:** U.S. Coast Guard, Summary Report of Public Workshop: Scheduled Increase in Mechanical Recovery and Potential Changes to Dispersant Planning Requirements, remarks by Dick Lessard (Exxon), Washington, D.C., September 15, 1998, www.USCG. mil/?VRP/reg/dc.shtml#issues.

194 **ill-fated ship:** Natalie Phillips, "Oil Tanker Still Barred from Sound. Judge Refuses to Remove Restriction on *Exxon Valdez*," *ADN*, June 18, 1998; David Kravets, "*Exxon Valdez* Ban Upheld," *ADN*, November 2, 2002. In January 2008, ExxonMobil sold the tanker to a Chinese shipping company that plans to convert it for hauling bulk ore—and rename it: *Dong Fang Ocean*. Erika Bolstad, "End of the *Exxon Valdez* Case is in Sight," *ADN,* February 26, 2008.

194 **community service in Alaska:** Marilee Enge, "Hazelwood Sentenced to Cleanup. Judge Gives Him 1,000 Hours on Oiled Beaches," *ADN*, March 24, 1990; Linda Deutsch, "Hazelwood Gets Two Charges Dismissed," *ADN*, July 26, 1990; C. Solomon, "Hazelwood, Grounded by Notoriety, Confronts Valdez Hardships on Land," *Wall Street Journal*, September 20, 1994; T. Badger, "Hazelwood Case Has 2nd Go in Appeals Court," *ADN*, May 10, 1995; Liz Ruskin, "Hazelwood Conviction Tossed Out. Definition of 'Negligence' Criticized; State to Appeal," *ADN*, March 16, 1996; Liz Ruskin, "Hazelwood Conviction Reinstated," *ADN*, October 4, 1997; Daniel Coyle, "The Captain Went Down with the Ship," *Outside Magazine*, October 1997; Rosana Pagano, "Appeals Court Upholds Hazelwood Sentence," *ADN*, July 3, 1998; Eric Nalder, "*Exxon Valdez* Captain: Was He Villain or Victim?" *Seattle Times*, March 14, 1999. See also *ADN* archives www. adn.com/evos/pgs/sp5.html. As of 2008, Hazelwood is a consultant and claims adjustor for Chalos and Brown, the law firm that represented him during his trials. Bolstad, "End in Sight."

194 **Judge Holland agreed:** *Exxon Valdez Case,* Order No. 348.

194 **no "mathematically bright line" had been drawn:** *BMW of North America, Inc. v. Gore*, 517 U.S. 559 (1996).

194 **single-digit ration favored by the high court:** *Cooper Industries, Inc. v. Leatherman Tool Corp, Inc.*, 532 U.S. 424 (2001)

195 **"bizarre and shocking":** *Exxon Valdez Case,* Order No. 339, 17, 23. See also Natalie Phillips, "Exxon Verdict Stands. Jury Tampering Claim Rejected," *ADN*, August 1, 1998; Natalie Phillips, "Exxon Adds Jury Coercion to Appeal," *ADN*, November 13, 1998.

Chapter 12: Moving On

198 **approved by Judge Holland:** "Exxon Supplemental Claims Program; Claims Process Moves Forward for 11 Claim Categories," *Business Wire*, September 24, 1998; "Exxon Supplemental Claims Program; Claims Process Moves Forward for 19 Additional Claim Categories," *Business Wire*, July 1, 1999.

198 **jettisoned their claims to move on:** Jennifer Strange, "Spill Memories Are Still Fresh for Many," *CT*, March 4, 1999.

198 **wrote to Senator Murkowski:** Jennifer Strange, "Cordova Group Opposes Exxon-Mobil Merger," *CT*, January 28, 1999; Strange, "Murkowski Responds to Cordova Oil Merger Concerns," *CT*, February 18, 1999; Marla Jean Adkins, LTE, "Lawmakers Should Oppose Exxon-Mobil Merger," *CT*, February 25, 1999; Steve Conn, LTE, "Exxon Has Not Kept Its Promise," *CT*, March 4, 1999; Richard Septien, LTE, "Get Your Ducks In a Row Before Second-Guessing," *CT*, March 11, 1999; Strange, "Gorton Voices Objection to Exxon-Mobil Merger," *CT*, March 11, 1999; Strange, "Knowles Rejects Anti-Merger Resolution," *CT*, March 18, 1999.

198 **give them the world:** Jennifer Strange, "The Exxon-Mobil Merger at a Glance," *CT*, January 28, 1999.

198 **double-hull tanker petition:** Jennifer Strange, "Cordovans Lobby D.C. to Keep Double Hull Tanker Requirements," Area Update, *CT*, January 21, 1999; PWS RCAC, "Council Opposes Industry Request to Extend the Life of Single-Hull Tankers," *The Observer*, March 1999.

198 **according to the Coast Guard:** U.S. Coast Guard, *Report of the Tanker Safety Study Group* (1989, 1990).

199 **were not fully trained:** Tony Bickert, "SERVS Comes Up Short in Surprise Spill Drill," *Valdez Vanguard*, January 24, 1999; T. A. Badger, "Alyeska Spill Workers Aren't Ready, State Says," *ADN*, February 11, 1999.

199 **painful memories it evoked:** Jennifer Strange, "10 Years After: Media Returns to Document Lingering Effects of *Exxon Valdez* Spill," *CT*, February 25, 1999; Jennifer Strange, "Spill Memories are Still Fresh for Many Cordovans," *CT*, March 4, 1999."

200 **"a check's not going to do it":** Jennifer Strange, "Cordova Residents Talk About 'Life After the Spill,'" *CT*, March 11, 1999. See also Steven Picou, "At A Glance: Effects of Natural vs. Technological Disasters," *CT*, March 25, 1999.

200 **continued social upheaval:** Times Staff, "Cordova Youths Take 1st, 3rd in Essay Contest," *CT*, April 1, 1999; Sean Sjostedt, "*Exxon Valdez*," *CT*, April 1, 1999; Brian Johannessen, "We Learn, We Remember," *CT*, April 1, 1999.

200 **"tell their children of these tales":** Marilyn Honkola, "Confronting a Steel-Hearted Corporation," *CT*, April 1, 1999.

201 **cover them up:** Jennifer Strange, "Alaskans Find Little Balance with Oil Industry at Conference," *CT*, March 11, 1999.

201 **by 90 percent:** Tony Knowles, Commentary, "Vigilance is the Legacy of the *Exxon Valdez* Oil Spill," *CT*, March 25, 1999.

201 **of a century earlier:** Tony Bickert, "Guardians of the Sound: Lawn, Stephens, Ott Still Going Strong 10 Years After Oil Spill," *Valdez Vanguard*, March 3, 1999; Richard Fineberg, "Praise the Pipe and Pass the Money: Facts and Reflections on Big Oil in Alaska Ten Years After the *Exxon Valdez* Spill," prepared for Research Associates, Ester, Alaska, March 1999. www.finebergresearch.com/reports.html.

201 **tractor tugs and advance radar:** Wills, *Place in the Sun;* Scottish Eye, *Slick Operators.*

201 **permit reauthorization process:** The reauthorization permit for the Trans-Alaska Pipeline was granted in 2002 after four years of public hearings and process, mostly held in Alaska. This was in sharp contrast to the original pipeline hearings, which had been held nationwide. Richard Fineberg, "The Emperor's Big Hose: How Big Oil Gets Rich Gambling with Alaska's Environment," prepared for the AFER, June 2002, www.finebergresearch.com/reports.html.

202 **taken their toll:** Malani O'Toole, "What Exxon Means," *'Til Now*, CD, © 2007 Malani.

202 **documentary division in 1999:** John Tracy, Tim Woolston, and Eric Sowl, "America's Biggest Oil Spill: 10 Years After," March 24, 1999, KTUU-TV.

202 **"okay with me":** Jennifer Strange, "Cordovans Go Coast to Coast to Talk About EVOS," *CT*, March 25, 1999.

203 **pleading for sanity:** Patty Kallander, "Small-town Cordova Not Immune to Big City Social Problems," commentary, *CT*, January 28, 1999; Steve Walters, "Domestic Violence is a Demon," LTE, *CT*, February 11, 1999; Shelly Chisum and Dorthy Shepard, "Compassion Should Take the Place of Judgment," LTE, *CT*, March 11, 1999.

204 **Interfaith Center for Corporate Responsibility:** Jennifer Strange, "Groups Pressure Exxon to Pay Up Before Merger," *CT*, May 27, 1999.

205 **Dallas County cops:** Jennifer Strange, "Ott Arrested for Protesting Exxon-Mobil Merger," *CT*, June 3, 1999.

207 **hours of community service:** Staff, "Hazelwood Wraps Up 1,000 Hours of Community Service at Bean's," *Alaska Digest*, August 17, 2001.

207 **in the winter months:** Jody Seitz, "Family Brings Heli-Sports to Cordova," *CT*, March 11, 1999.

207 **last of those big cruise ships:** Alberto Cagliano, "End of a Dynasty," *CT*, September 9, 1999.

207 **Leopold legacy conference:** Riki Ott, "Cultivating Conservation in Our Conscious and Our Communities: Reflections from the Field," presented on behalf of CRWP at the Leopold Legacy conference, Wisconsin Academy of Sciences, Arts and Letters, Madison, Wis., October 4–7, 1999.

208 **spill memorial:** Natalie Phillips, "Still Painful. 10 Years Later, Front-Line Spill Workers Link Physical Ailments To Cleanup Work," *ADN*, March 23, 1999.

209 **cleanup workers:** PWS RCAC, "Council Visit to French Spill Shows Readiness Still Crucial," "French Tanker Accident Provides a Refresher Course in Oil-Spill Lessons," *The Observer*, March 2000.

209 **ahead of the United States:** PWS RCAC, "Council to Visit French Spill."

Chapter 13: Leaving the Oil Age

215 **gold mine of information:** *Garry Stubblefield and Melissa Stubblefield v. Exxon Shipping Company, Exxon Corp., VECO, Inc., and Norcon, Inc.* 3AN–91–6261 CV, Alaska Superior Court, Third Judicial District at Anchorage (1994).

215 **for occupational asthma:** Ott, *Sound Truth*, 55–56.

215 **medical records and air quality monitoring data:** Exxon, "Clinical Data On Upper Respiratory Infections," 1989, *in Sound Truth*, Ott, 57, figure 2; Med-Tox, "Air Monitoring Results For Oil Mist and PAHs," and "Statistical Summary of Industrial Hygiene Monitoring," 1989, in *Sound Truth*, Ott, 64–66, 450–451.

215 **Valdez Crud:** Susan Stranahan, "The Valdez Crud: Are Crude Oil and Chemicals to Blame for the Health Problems of Workers Who Cleaned Up Exxon's Mess?" *Mother Jones*, March/April 2003.

216 **where people breathed it:** Ott, *Sound Truth*, 55–67.

216 **reasons Exxon's program had failed:** Ibid., 39–53.

216 **read his books:** William Rea, *Chemical Sensitivity*, 4 vols. (Boca Raton, Fla: CRC Press, Lewis Publishers, 1992–1997). See also Nicholas Ashford and Claudia Miller, *Chemical Exposures: Low Levels and High Stakes*, 2nd ed. (New York: John Wiley & Sons, 1998); Ott, *Sound Truth*, 73–83.

217 **Phyllis La Joie:** Riki Ott, "Phyllis 'Dolly' La Joie," in *Sound Truth*, 85–95. See also 148–151.

217 **Ron Smith:** Ott, "Ron Smith and Randy Lowe," and "Toxic Torts and Justice Denied," in *Sound Truth*, 71–83, 139–156.

218 **literature review:** Ibid., 159–164.

218 **fetal-toxin:** www.westp2net.org/janitorial/tools/haz2.htm.

218 **and watercourses:** Exxon, MSDS for Corexit 9527 and Inipol EAP22, in *Sound Truth*, Ott, 12–13; Sunshine Makers, Inc., MSDS for Simple Green, version no. 1007, Huntington Harbour, Calif., 2002, in *Sound Truth*, Ott, 13.

218 **Donnie Moeller and Captain Richard Nagel:** Ott, *Sound Truth:* Moeller, 101–108; Nagel, 118–121.

218 **liability waiver that Exxon circulated:** Exxon, "Partial Release Form for Indemnity from Adverse Health Effects from Cleanup Work, 1989," in *Sound Truth*, Ott, 33, figure 1.

220 **designed to protect workers:** Ott, *Sound Truth*, 125–138.

220 **work-related illnesses:** U.S. Department of Labor, OSHA, "Determination of Work-Relatedness; Recording and Reporting Occupational Injuries and Illness, Subpart: Record-Keeping Forms and Recording Criteria, 29 CFR 1904.5, Subpart C, Section 1904.5(b)(2)(viii), 2004. One criteria states: "Exclude from record keeping those injuries/illnesses that do not provide information useful to the identification of occupational injuries and illnesses and thus would skew natural injury/illness data." Exemption number (viii) specifically states: "Colds and flu will not be considered work-related."

220 **"of the oil spill":** U.S. Dept. of Health and Human Services, National Institute of Occupational Safety and Health, *Health Hazard Evaluation*, prepared by R. W. Gorman, S. Berardinelli, and T. R. Bender, HETA 89-200 and 89-273-2111, Exxon/Valdez Alaska Oil Spill, May 2004, 30; Ott, *Sound Truth*, 135–138.

220 **crude oil mists and particles:** Ott, *Sound Truth*, 62–63.

220 **health care institutions:** Riki Ott, "Vanishing Claims," and "Toxic Torts and Justice Denied," *Sound Truth*, 125–138, 139–156. See also 167–176; Linda Price King, *Chemical Injury and the Courts: A Litigation Guide for Clients and Their Attorneys* (Jefferson, N.C.: McFarland & Company, 1999).

221 **with that tragedy had realized:** Ed Masry (Masry & Vititoe, partner), Erin Brockovitch (Masry & Vititoe, researcher), Mike Schneider (lawyer, Anchorage), and Riki Ott (AFER), letter to U.S. Senator Hilary Clinton (D-NY), Senator Harry Reid (D-NV), Congressman George Miller (D-CA), and Congressman Major Owens (D-NY), re: Protecting Cleanup Workers, Lesson Learned from *Exxon Valdez*, November 21, 2001.

222 **basis for the Clean Water Act:** Ott, *Sound Truth*, 181–184.

222 **like a narcotic:** Ibid., 224.

223 **still buried on beaches:** Ibid., 361–364; Rachel D'Oro, "*Exxon Valdez* Oil Won't Vanish Soon. Federal Study: Crude from 1989 Spill Will Continue to Foul Beaches for Decades," *ADN*, February 1, 2007.

223 **produce viable offspring:** Ott, "Fish and Oil Toxicity," in *Sound Truth*.

223 **fast-swimming fish:** Ott, "Nearshore Vertebrate Predator (NVP) Project," in *Sound Truth*, 293–316.

224 **young fish in 1989:** Thomas and Thorne, "Acoustical-Optical Asssessment of Pacific Herring and Their Predator Assemblage in PWS, Alaska," *Aquatic Living Resources* 16 (2003): 247–253. See also Richard Thorne and Gary Thomas, "Acoustic Observation of Gas Bubble Release by Pacific Herring," *Canadian Journal of Fisheries and Aquatic Sciences*, 47 (1990): 1920–1928; Gary Thomas and Richard Thorne, "Night-Time Predation by Steller Sea Lions," *Nature* 411 (2001): 1013.

225 **wiped out the fish:** Ott, *Sound Truth*, 259–266, 350–355.

226 **harm from the spill:** Ibid., 196–198. As noted in this section, Exxon's statistical gyrations to keep average levels of oil below the state's water quality standards defy physics and common sense.

226 **and they die:** Ibid., 219–221, 228, 300–304.

226 **statistical no-no:** Ibid., 210.

226 **on oiled beaches:** Ibid., 212–213.

227 **"toxic pollutants":** U.S. EPA, Emergency Planning and Community Right-to-Know Act, Section 313, Guidance for reporting toxic chemicals: Polycyclic aromatic compounds category, Final, Washington, D.C.: U.S. EPA, EPA 260-B-01-03, August.

228 **according to the EPA:** U.S. EPA, *1999 Persistent, Bioaccumulative and Toxic Pollutants Initiative (PBTI) Report*, Pollution Prevention Information Clearinghouse, Washington, D.C., 2000, www.epa.gov/pbt/accomp99.htm.

228 **exhaust particles:** National Research Council, *Oil in the Sea III: Inputs, Fates, and Effects* (Washington, D.C.: National Academies Press, 2002).

228 **chemical sensitivities:** Terry Tamminen, *Lives per Gallon: The True Costs of our Oil Addiction* (New York: Island Press, 2006); David Ewing Duncan, "The Pollution Within," *National Geographic*, October 2006, 116–143.

228 **master's thesis at Yale:** Annie O'Neill, *Self-Reported Exposures and Health Status Among Workers from the EVOS Cleanup*, master's thesis, M.P.H. Yale University, Department of Epidemiology and Public Health, May 2003.

228 **sick from Exxon's cleanup:** Ott, *Sound Truth*, 164–167. Chronic respiratory problems were more recently documented in cleanup workers from the *Prestige* oil spill off the coast of Spain in 2002: Jan-Paul Zock and others, "Prolonged Respiratory Symptoms in Clean-Up Workers of the *Prestige* Oil Spill," *American Journal of Respiratory and Critical Care Medicine* 176 (2007): 610–616.

228 *Science* **magazine:** Charles Peterson and others, "Long-Term Ecosystem Response to the *Exxon Valdez* Oil Spill," *Science*, December 19, 2003, 2082–2086. See also Ott, *Sound Truth*, 392–396.

228 **"slippery science":** Lila Guterman, "Slippery Science: 15 Years After the *Exxon Valdez* Oil Spill, Researchers Debate Its Lingering Effects with $100-Million on the Line," *Chronicle of Higher Education*, September 24, 2004, http://chronicle.com/free/v51/i05/05a01201.htm.

230 **statewide news in Washington and Alaska:** Professor William H. Rodgers, Jr., and the Seminar on Natural Resource Damages, Law B585, Univ. of Washington, School of Law, winter 2005 (J. B. Crosetto, C. A. Holley, T. C. Kade, J. H. Kaufman, C. M. Kstelec, K. A. Michael, R. J. Sandberg, and J. L. Schorr), "The *Exxon Valdez* Reopener: Natural Resources Damage Settlements and Roads Not Taken," May 2005; Robert McClure, "UW Helps on *Exxon Valdez* Claim," *Seattle Post-Intelligencer*, May 2, 2006; Meeghan Black, "Clock Ticking to Claim *Exxon Valdez* Money," *King 5 Television*, May 26, 2005; Angela Unruh, "*Exxon Valdez* Funds Likely to Go Unused," *KTUU Television*, May 26, 2005.

230 **"oncoming climate catastrophe":** "Put a Tiger in Your Think Tank," *Mother Jones*, May/June 2005, http://www.motherjones.com/news/featurex/2005/05/exxon_chart.html; Bill McKibben, Chris Mooney, and Ross Gelbspan, "As the World Burns," Bill McKibben, "Climate of Denial,"

Chris Mooney, "Some Like It Hot," and Ross Gelbspan, "Snowed," *Mother Jones*, May/June 2005, http://www.motherjones.com/toc/2005/05/index.html. See also Union of Concerned Scientists, *Smoke, Mirrors & Hot Air: How ExxonMobil Uses Big Tobacco's Tactics to Manufacture Uncertainty on Climate Science*, Washington, D.C., January 2007, www.ucsusa.org/global_warming/science/exxonmobil-smoke-mirrors-hot.html.

231 **as "recovered":** EVOS Trustee Council, *EVOS Restoration Plan, Update on Injured Resources and Services 2006*, Anchorage, Alaska, www.evostc.state.ak.us/Publications/injuredresources.cfm.

231 **decades to come:** Dan Joling, "Greater Exxon Damage Alleged," *ADN*, May 17, 2006; Rachel D'Oro, "*Exxon Valdez* Oil Won't Vanish Soon," *ADN*, February 1, 2007; Jeff Short and others, "Slightly Weathered *Exxon Valdez* Oil Persists in Gulf of Alaska Beach Sediments After 16 Years," *Environmental Science and Technology* 41(4) (2007): 1245–1250, http://pubs.acs.org/cgi-bin/sample.cgi/esthag/2007/41/i04/pdf/es0620033.pdf. See also Riki Ott, PhD, "Testimony to U.S. Senate Environment and Public Works Committee Hearing on the EPA SPCC [Spill Prevention, Control, and Countermeasure] Plan," Washington, D.C., December 14, 2006.

231 **remove buried oil from beaches:** U.S. Department of Justice, Environment and Natural Resources Division, Sue Ellen Wooldridge (Assistant U.S. Attorney General) and David Marquez (Alaska Attorney General), letter to Charles Mathews (general counsel, ExxonMobil) and others, re: Demand for Cost of Restoration Under Reopener for Unknown Injury in *United States v. Exxon Corporation*, et al., Nos. 3:91-0082 & 3:91-0083 (D. Alaska), August 31, 2006; Felicity Barringer, "$92 Million More is Sought for *Exxon Valdez* Cleanup," *New York Times*, June 2, 2006.

Chapter 14: "A New Species of Trouble"

236 **one of those cases:** John Platt, "Exxon's Deadly Legacy Lives on for Fishermen," *AlterNet*, March 24, 2008, www.alternet.org/water/80476/.

236 **Maxwell family as well:** Robert Maxwell, Jr., interview with author, April 26, 2001.

237 *The Day the Water Died:* Brave New Films in association with Sierra Club Productions, 2006, www.sierraclub.org/tv/episode-exxon.asp.

237 *Endless Fallout:* Montreal, Canada: Robert Cornellier with Macumba International Films, 2006, documentary DVD, www.macumbainternational.com/english/.

239 **psychosocial disaster trauma:** Riki Ott, "Toxicological Paradigm Shifts after the *EVOS*" and "Sociological Paradigm Shifts after the *EVOS*," keynote presentations at the twentieth annual international symposium on Man and His Environment in Health and Disease, sponsored by the American Environmental Health Foundation and the American Academy of Environment and Medicine, Dallas, Texas, June 7–10, 2007.

239 **relationships of give and take:** Robert Putnam, *Bowling Alone: The Collapse and Revival of American Community* (New York: Simon and Schuster Paperbacks, 2000).

240 **one sociologist said:** Ibid., 288. See also Christian Bjornskov and Gert Tinggaard Svendsen, "Measuring Social Capital—Is There A Single Underlying Explanation?," Department of Economics, Aarhus School of Business, Working Paper 03-5, ISSN 1397-4831, 2003.

240 **mostly a charade:** ADEC, *Final Report*, 119–127; Michelle Mayer, *All the King's Horses*; Patrick Daley and Dan O'Neill, "'Sad is Too Mild a Word,' Press Coverage of the EVOS," in *The Exxon Valdez Disaster*, eds. Picou, Gill, and Cohen, 239–250.

240 **huge social trauma:** Steven Picou, Duane Gill, and Maurie Cohen, "The EVOS as a Technological Disaster: Conceptualizing a Social Problem," in *The Exxon Valdez Disaster*, eds. Picou, Gill, and Cohen, 3–21; Impact Assessment, *Oiled Mayors' Report*; National Wildlife Federation and others, "The Day the Water Died." See also Christopher Dyer, Duane Gill, and Steven Picou, "Social Disruption And The EVOS"; Duane Gill and Steven Picou, "The Social Psychological Impacts of a Technological Disaster: Collective Stress and Perceived Health Risks," *Journal of Hazardous Materials* 27 (1991): 77–89; Lawrence Palinkas and others, "Community Patterns of Psychiatric Disorders After the EVOS," *American Journal of Psychiatry* 150 (1993): 1517–1523; Lawrence Palinkas and others, "Ethnic Differences in Stress, Coping, and Depressive Symptoms After the EVOS," *Journal of Nervous and Mental*

Disease 180 (1992): 287–293; Steven Picou and Duane Gill, "The *Exxon Valdez* Oil Spill and Chronic Psychological Stress," *AFSS* 18 (1996): 879–893; Steven Picou and others, "Stress and Disruption in an Alaskan Fishing Community: Initial and Continuing Impacts of the *Exxon Valdez* Oil Spill," *Industrial Crisis Quarterly* 6 (3) (1992): 235–257; Mari Rodin and others, "Community Impacts Resulting from the EVOS," *Industrial Crisis Quarterly* 6 (1992): 219–234; John Russell and others, "Psychological and Social Impacts of the EVOS and Cleanup."

241 "but it is true": Chief Walter Meganek, Port Graham Native Village, Kenai Penninsula, Alaska, in National Wildlife Federation and others, "The Day the Water Died."

241 uncertainty added to stress: Catalina Arata and others, "Coping with Technological Disaster: An Application of the Conservation of Resources Model to the *Exxon Valdez* Oil Spill," *Journal of Traumatic Stress* 13(1) (2000): 28–39.

242 Peer Listening Program: Steven Picou, "The Talking Circle as Sociological Practice.

242 "new species of trouble". Kai Erickson, *A New Species of Trouble: The Human Experience of Modern Disasters* (New York: W. W. Norton, 1994). See also Michael Edelstein, *Contaminated Communities: Coping with Residential Toxic Exposure* (Boulder, Colo.: Westview Press, 2004), 2nd edition.

243 Oiled Regions of Alaska Foundation: www.orafoundation.org/.

244 third part of the mismanaged disaster: Brent Marshall, Steven Picou, and Jan Schlichtmann, "Technological Disasters, Litigation Stress and the Use of Alternative Dispute Resolution Mechanisms," *Law and Policy* 26(2) (2004): 289–307; Steven Picou, Brent Marshall, and Duane Gill, "Disaster, Litigation, and the Corrosive Community," *Social Forces* 82(4) (2004): 1497–1526; Steven Picou and Cecelia Martin, "Long-Term Community Impacts of the EVOS: Patterns of Social Disruption and Psychological Stress Seventeen Years after the Disaster," final report to National Science Foundation, Office of Polar Research, Washington, D.C., Award Number: 0002572, April 2007.

244 legal system doesn't work anymore: Andrew Baum and India Fleming, "Implications of Psychological Research on Stress and Technological Accidents," *American Psychologist*, 48(6) (1993): 665–672; Larry Cohen and Joyce Vesper, "Forensic Stress Disorder," *Law and Psychology Review* 25 (2001): 1–27; Mardi Horowitz, "Stress Response Syndromes: Character Style and Brief Psychotherapy," *Archives of General Psychiatry* 31 (1974): 768–81; Robert Kagan and Lee Axelrad, eds., *Regulatory Encounters: Multinational Corporations and American Legal Adversarialism* (University of California Press: Berkeley, 2000); Paul Lees-Haley, "Litigation Response Syndrome," *American Journal of Forensic Psychology* 6(1) (1988): 3–12; Luther Munford, "The Peacemaker Test: Designing Legal Rights to Reduce Legal Warfare," *Harvard Negotiation Legal Review* 12 (spring 2007): 377–414; Tamara Relis, "Civil Litigation from Litigants' Perspectives: What We Know and What We Don't Know About the Litigation Experience of Individual Litigants," *Studies in Law, Politics, and Society* 25 (2002): 151–212; Daniel Shuman, "When Time Does Not Heal: Understanding the Importance of Avoiding Unnecessary Delay in the Resolution of Tort Cases," *Psychology, Public Policy, and Law* 6 (2000): 880–897; Larry Strasburger, "The Litigant-Patient: Mental Health Consequences of Civil Litigation," *Journal of the American Academy of Psychiatry Law* 27(2) (1999): 203–11.

244 for their shareholders: *Dodge v. Ford Motor Co.* 170 N.W. 668 (1919).

245 corporate-sponsored science: There is a huge and growing body of literature on this topic. See Sharon Beder, *Global Spin: The Corporate Assault on Environmentalism* (White River Junction, Vt.: Chelsea Green Publishing Company, 1998); Kenneth Foster and Peter Huber, *Judging Science: Scientific Knowledge and the Federal Courts* (Cambridge: MIT Press, 1999); Peter Huber, *Galileo's Revenge: Junk Science in the Courtroom* (New York: Basic Books, 1993); Everett Koop, *The Cigarette Papers* (Berkeley: University of California Press, 1999); Chris Mooney, *The Republican War on Science* (New York: Basic Books, 2005). For more technical papers, see David Egilman and Susanna Rankin Bohme, eds., *Corporate Corruption of Science*, Special Issue, *International Journal of Occupational and Environmental Health*, 2005 (11).

246 mediations to restore wholeness: Abraham McLaughlin, "Paths To Forgiveness: Africa After War," 4-part series, *Christian Science Monitor*, October 23–26, 2006.

247 **"lies all the way"**: Abraham McLaughlin, "Ugandans Welcome 'Terrorists' Back," *Christian Science Monitor*, October 23, 2006.

248 **failings of our technology**: Fran Norris and others, "The Range, Magnitude, And Duration Of Effects Of Natural And Human-Caused Disasters: A Review Of The Empirical Literature," National Center for PTSD, 2002, www.ncptsd.va.gov/ncmain/ncdocs/fact_shts/fs_range.html?opm=1&rr=rr48&srt=d&echorr=true. See also Christine Bevc, Brent Marshall, and Steven Picou, "Environmental Justice and Toxic Exposure: Toward a Special Model of Physical Health and Psychological Well-Being," *Social Science Research* 36 (2007): 48–67; Brent Marshall and Steven Picou, "Postnormal Science, Precautionary Principle, and Worst Cases: The Challenge of Twenty-First Century Catastrophes," *Sociological Inquiry* 78(2) (2008): 230–247; Brent Marshall, Steven Picou, and Duane Gill, "Terrorism as Disaster: Selected Commonalities and Long-Term Recovery for 9/11 Survivors," *Research in Social Problems and Public Policy* 11 (2003): 73–96. Steven Picou posts key papers on his web site: http://stevenpicou.com/selected_publications.html.

249 **time for this protracted litigation to end**: Brandon Loomis, "Exxon Fine for Oil Spill is Slashed on Appeal. Huge Cut: Punitive Damages Drop to $2.5 Billion from $4.5 Billion," ADN, December 23, 2006. Earlier, Judge Holland had reinstated the punitive award to $4.5 billion and returned it to the Ninth Circuit after considering the Supreme Court's most recent decision at the time on punitive damages in *State Farm Mutual Automobile Insurance Co.v. Campbell* (01-1289) 538 U.S. 408 (2003) ___ P.3d ___, reversed and remanded.

249 **"our soul as well"**: Alex Demarban, "Shame Pole Unveiled On Anniversary Of *Exxon Valdez* Spill," *ADN*, March 25, 2007, http://dwb.adn.com/news/alaska/ap_alaska/story/8738967p-8640635c.html.

Chapter 15: A New Consciousness

253 **basic economic, social, and cultural rights**: "Is the U.S. Ready for Human Rights? *Yes!* spring 2007, www.yesmagazine.org/default.asp?ID=203. For an abbreviated form of the Universal Declaration of Human Rights, see "The Universal Declaration" at this web site.

254 **primarily burning fossil fuels**: The Norwegian Nobel Foundation awarded its 2007 Nobel Peace Prize to the Intergovernmental Panel on Climate Change and Albert Gore for their work to build up and disseminate knowledge about human-made climate change and potential solutions.

254 **threatening Earth's life-support systems**: There is a huge and rapidly growing body of literature on this topic for all levels of readers. Articles and photos in *National Geographic* are accessible and revealing: See Tim Appenzeller and Dennis Dimick, "The Heat is On"; Daniel Glick, "GeoSigns"; Fen Montaigne, "Ecosigns"; and Virginia Morell, "TimeSigns," *National Geographic*, September 2004, 2–75; Tim Appenzeller, "The Case of the Missing Carbon," *National Geographic*, February 2004, 88–117; Bill McKibben, "Carbon's New Math" with map supplement "Changing Climate," *National Geographic*, October 2007, 32–37; Paul Nicklen, "Life at the Edge" and Tim Appenzeller, "Big Thaw," *National Geographic*, 32–71. *Yes!* magazine, published by Positive Futures Network, maintains a user-friendly website for high school students and activists: see "Stop Global Warming Cold," *Yes!* spring 2008, www.yesmagazine.org/default.asp?ID=245.

254 **hardened arteries, among other things**: Adam Voiland, "The Smallest of Pollutants are Linked to Outsize Health Risks," *U.S. News and World Report*, February 27, 2008, http://health.usnews.com/articles/health/2008/02/27/the-smallest-of-pollutants-are-linked-to-outsize-health-risks.html; Tamminen, *Lives per Gallon*.

254 **entrenched corporate–stateblock**: Dana Milbank and Justin Blum, "Document Says Oil Chiefs Met With Cheney Task Force," *Washington Post*, November 16, 2005, www.washingtonpost.com/wp-dyn/content/article/2005/11/15/AR2005111501842.html; Mike Allen, "GAO Cites Corporate Shaping of Energy Plan," *Washington Post*, August 26, 2003, www.washingtonpost.com/wp-dyn/articles/A44891-2003Aug25.html; Chris Mooney, "Some Like It Hot," *Mother Jones*, May/June 2005, http://www.motherjones.com/news/feature/2005/05/some_like_it_hot.html; and Union of Concerned Scientists, "Smoke, Mirrors, and Hot Air: How ExxonMobil

Uses Big Tobacco's Tactics To Manufacture Uncertainty On Climate Science," January 2007, www.ucsusa.org/global_warming/science/exxonmobil-smoke-mirrors-hot.html.

255 **Daniel Pennock Democracy School:** www.celdf.org.

255 **first solo CD:** *'Til Now*, CD, © 2007 Malani.

257 **film will be done:** *Black Wave: The Legacy of the* Exxon Valdez (Montreal, Canada: Perception Cinema and Macumba International, 2008), feature film.

258 **"if you can keep it":** Benjamin Franklin, www.bartleby.com/73/1593.html.

258 **claim these privileges:** Mary Zepernick, "Human Rights vs. Corporate Rights," in *Defying Corporations: A Book of History and Strategy* (New York: Apex Press, 2001), ed. Dean Ritz, 198–199; Howard Zinn, interview in *The Corporation* (Canada: Mark Achbar, Jennifer Abbott, and Joel Bakan, producers, 2003), www.thecorporation.com/index.cfm?page_id=2.

258 **had been violated:** *Santa Clara County v. Southern Pacific Railroad Co.* 118 U.S. 394 1886; Richard Grossman and Frank Adams, "Taking Care of Business: Citizenship and the Charter of Incorporation," in *Defying Corporations*, ed. Dean Ritz, 59–71; Greg Colrldge, "March of Folly: Corporate Perversion of the Fourteenth Amendment," in *Defying Corporations*, ed. Dean Ritz, 106–107.

259 **went after others:** Thomas Linzey, "Turning Defense into Offense: Challenging Corporations and Creating Self-Governance," plenary presentation at Bioneers conference, Marin, Calif., 2006, DVD, https://www.bioneers.org/.

259 **free speech:** Jane Anne Morris, "Speaking Truth to Power about Campaign Reform," in *Defying Corporations*, ed. Dean Ritz, 190–197.

259 **how will they catch problems:** Charlie Cray and Lee Drutman, *The People's Business: Controlling Corporations and Restoring Democracy* (San Francisco: Berrett-Koehler, 2004), 57.

259 **diminishment of its value:** Richard Grossman, "Justice for Sale: Shortchanging the Public Interest for Private Gain," in *Defying Corporations*, ed. Dean Ritz, 110–115.

259 **interferes with future profits:** Cray and Drutman, *The People's Business*, 60.

259 **that's globalization:** Howard Mann, *Private Rights, Public Problems: A Guide To NAFTA's Controversial Chapter On Investor Rights* (Winnipeg, Canada: International Institute for Sustainable Development and the World Wildlife Fund, 2001), 15, www.iisd.org/publications/pub.aspx?id=270. International trade agreements like NAFTA and GATT give corporations legal authority to undermine state and local laws. For example, chapter 11 of NAFTA is modeled after the Interstate Commerce Clause in the U.S. Constitution. It allows corporations to sue foreign governments over *perceived threats to future profits*, including laws passed to protect public health and the environment.

260 **"any controlling private power":** Franklin Delano Roosevelt, address to Congress, April 29, 1938, http://current.com/items/88932748_franklin_d_roosevelt_growth_of_private_power_could_lead_to_fascism.

260 **"merger of corporate and state power":** http://thinkexist.com/quotation/fascism_should_more_appropriately_be_called/163211.html.

260 **looks like fascism:** Laurence Britt, "Fascism Anyone?" *Free Inquiry* 23 (2), 2003, www.secularhumanism.org/library/fi/britt_23_2.html.

260 **more subtle:** "5,000 Years of Empire: Ready for a Change?" *Yes!* summer 2006, www.yesmagazine.org/default.asp?ID=179; "Stand Up to Corporate Power," *Yes!* fall 2007, www.yesmagazine.org/default.asp?ID=231; "Health Care for All," *Yes!* fall 2006, www.yesmagazine.org/default.asp?ID=189; Elizabeth Docteur and Howard Oxley, "Health Care: A Quest for Better Value," Organization for Economic Co-operation and Development, *OECD Observer* No. 238, July 2003, www.oecdobserver.org/news/fullstory.php/aid/1054/Health_care:_A_quest_for_better_value.html; "Superpower? Get Over It," *Yes!* summer 2008, www.yesmagazine.org/default.asp?ID=203; www.globalissues.org/Geopolitics/ArmsTrade/Spending.asp; www.demos.org/inequality/numbers.cfm.

260 **far better with far less:** Ed Diener and Martin Seligman, "Beyond Money: Toward an Economy of Well-Being," *Psychological Science in the Public Interest* vol. 5(1) (2004): 1–31, www.psych.uiuc.edu/~ediener/hottopic/papersonline.htm; "The Economist's Intelligence Unit's Quality of Life Index," *The World*, 2005, www.economist.com/markets/rankings/displaystory.cfm?story_

id=9753089; Ronald Colman, ed., "Why We Need New Measures of Wellbeing," *Reality Check: Canadian Journal of Wellbeing*, vol. 1(1) 2001, www.gpiatlantic.org/realitycheck/index.htm.

262 civic *dis*-engagement: Putnam, *Bowling Alone.*

262 **Pennsylvania and California:** List of new ordinances: www.celdf.org; Kaitlin Sopoci-Belknap, "Democracy Unlimited: Measure T Bans Corporate Campaign Financing," *Yes!* fall 2007, www. yesmagazine.org/article.asp?ID=1829.

263 **thinking like this:** Jeff Kaplan, "Common Knowledge," *Yes!* fall 2007, www.yesmagazine.org/article.asp?ID=1830.

263 **"frolic and detour":** Robert Reich, *Supercapitalism: The Transformation of Business, Democracy, and Everyday Life* (New York: Alfred A. Knopf, 2007).

266 **most frequently cited decision:** *Dodge v. Ford Motor Co.* 170 N.W. 668 (1919). In 1919, the Michigan Supreme Court established "shareholder primacy" by ruling, "A business corporation is organized and carried on primarily for the profit of the stockholders. The powers of the directors are to be employed for that end." This is still the leading case cited on corporate purpose. www.everything2.com/index.pl?node_id=1768159.

Epilogue

269 **reduced the punitive award to $507.5 million:** "Erika Bolstad, "'This is It; It's Done'," *ADN,* June 26, 2008; David Biello, "Prince William Sound and Fury: Oil Giant Dodges Punitive Damages for Valdez Spill," *Scientific American,* June 28, 2008.

269 **opinions of the Supreme Court decision:** Wesley Loy, "Decision Torments Cordova Fishermen," *ADN,* June 26, 2008.

270 **not punishment:** Joel Connelly, "Exxon's Slap on the Wrist," *Seattle P-I,* June 26, 2008; staff, "That Activist Court Spills Oil on Logic," *Seattle Times,* June 27, 2008.

271 **American people and Congress:** Editorial, "A Punitive Ruling: Supreme Court Strayed When It Reduced Punitive Damages Pail to *Exxon Valdez* Oil-Spill Victims," *Houston Chronicle,* June 30, 2008.

272 **from *that* town:** Sylvia Lange, "Proud to be from 'That' Town," *CT,* May 1, 2008.

GLOSSARY

Area E: A commercial fishing management district that includes Prince William Sound and the Copper River Delta, as designated by the Alaska Department of Fish and Game

ballast water: seawater carried in the hold of an empty oil tanker to give the craft increased stability

bar: a submerged bank of sand between two islands, the water over which is deep enough, at certain times, to allow boats to navigate safely over it (as in "crossing the bar")

Can Channel: a shallow tidal slough, originally marked by buoys or "cans" (now poles), landward of Egg Island on the Copper River Delta that is navigable only at certain stages of the tide by shallow draft boats

Chinook: *See* king salmon.

chum salmon: *Oncorhynchus keta* is a type of Pacific salmon that has wide distribution in the Pacific Rim nations, lives three to six years, and is a traditional source of dried fish for winter use; a.k.a. "dog" salmon.

closure: a varying period of time when commercial salmon fisheries are closed to allow upriver escapement

coho salmon: *See* silver salmon.

corked: when commercial fisherman "A" sets his net too close to fisherman "B" and intercepts salmon that would have been caught by fisherman B (as in "You corked me!")

dog salmon: *See* chum salmon.

drift gill net: a type of gill net that drifts with the tide or currents

escapement: a percentage of the total anticipated return of a salmon species that is allowed to pass upriver (i.e., to escape the commercial fisheries) for upriver users and for spawning and propagation of the species

the Flats: the approximately seventy mile stretch of coastline along the Gulf of Alaska between Cape Saint Elias and Orca Inlet that is renowned for shifting barrier islands and sandbars, notorious weather, and dangerous maritime conditions; a.k.a. the Copper River Delta

gill net: a type of fishing net that is vertically suspended in the water and catches fish by entangling them in meshes

gillnetter: a boat or person engaged in fishing with a gill net

highliner: a commercial fisherman who excels at his or her trade by catching consistently more fish than the average fisherman

herring pound: a type of commercial fishing gear that involves a vertically suspended mesh enclosure in the water, like an underwater corral, to hold mature Pacific herring until they have spawned on the sea plants also suspended in the corral structure

humpy: *See* pink salmon.

inside: geographic area landward of the open ocean and breaker patches that is sometimes open to commercial fishing or travel by shallow draft boat (as in "We fished 'inside' Grass Island" or "They went 'inside' instead of crossing the bar")

jitney: overpowered skiff used to launch a purse seine from a seine boat

king salmon: *Oncorhynchus tshawytscha* is the largest of Pacific salmon; it often exceeds thirty pounds and lives four years; a.k.a. "Chinook."

Loran: LOng RAnge Navigation is a land-based navigation system that uses low-frequency radio and multiple transmitters to determine location and speed of the receiver

Lower 48: Alaskan term for the 48 contiguous states; *See also* Outside

net hanger: person who builds new fishing nets by attaching lines and corks to webbing

offsets: advance payments for losses, received from the Exxon Claim Program, the Alyeska settlement, and the TAPL Fund, which were to be deducted from any compensatory damage award in the *Exxon Valdez* case

on step: traveling in a boat on plane at a high speed, where the boat hull rises partly out of the water and draws less draft

opener: a varying period of time when commercial salmon fisheries are open to allow harvest

Outside: Alaskan term for geographic locations beyond the state itself (as in "the family traveled 'Outside' for three weeks")

out the Road: heading east out of Cordova on the Copper River Highway (as in "They went for a drive out the Road")

permit: a license to participate in a particular fishery and gear type in a specific management district; the value of a commercial fishery limited entry permit fluctuates, depending on the health of the fisheries and market demand (as in "She held a salmon seine permit for Prince William Sound")

pink salmon: *Oncorhynchus gorbuscha* is the smallest of the Pacific salmon, averaging three to four pounds, and it lives for two years; a.k.a. "humpy" for the pronounced laterally flattened hump, which develops on the back of adult males before spawning

processor: cannery; plant that employs crews to prepare raw seafood to can, flash freeze, fillet, or otherwise treat fish, shellfish, and other seafood for wholesale and retail markets

Racetrack: an extremely shallow tidal slough, marked by buoys, landward of Copper Sands and Grass Island on the Copper River Delta that is navigable only at high water by shallow draft boats, traveling at high speed on step

red salmon: *See* sockeye salmon.

seine, specifically, **purse seine:** a type of fishing net that is vertically suspended in the water, towed into a circle around a school of fish, then drawn closed at the bottom to form a bag that catches the fish; fish captured in the bag or "purse" are then transferred to a fish hold either by pumping the fish aboard or by bringing the entire bag aboard and releasing it directly into the hold

seiner: a boat or person engaged in fishing with a purse seine net

set net: a type of gill net that is deployed in the water perpendicular to a beach and is anchored in place

setnetter: a boat or person engaged in fishing with a set net

silver salmon: *Ocorhynchus kisutch* is the second largest of Pacific salmon; lives two to four years; a.k.a. "coho."

sockeye salmon: *Oncorhynchus nerka* is a type of Pacific salmon that lives four years; a.k.a. "red" salmon for the bright red color of its flesh and because it turns a bright red color when swimming upriver to spawn

spawn: to mass release and deposit eggs and sperm to propagate the species

spillionaire: name for a person who made a lot of money on the oil spill cleanup

whistleblower: an employee who reports workplace wrongdoing, usually noncompliance with worker safety or environmental laws, to media and policy-makers with the specific goal of holding the institution accountable to protective laws

ABOUT THE AUTHOR

Riki Ott received her master's and doctorate in marine pollution before becoming a commercial salmon fisherma'am in Alaska. After witnessing firsthand the ecological destruction and social chaos from the *Exxon Valdez* oil spill in Prince William Sound, Alaska, she retired from fishing to cofound three nonprofit organizations to deal with lingering social, economic, environmental, and judicial fallout from the spill disaster. She draws on her academic training and experience to educate, empower, and motivate students and the general public to address the climate crisis and our energy future through local solutions. Ott has written two other books: *Artists for Nature in Alaska's Copper River Delta* (Seattle: University of Washington Press, 1998) and *Sound Truth and Corporate Myth$: The Legacy of the* Exxon Valdez *Oil Spill* (Cordova, Alaska: Dragonfly Sisters Press, 2005). She lives in Cordova, Alaska.

INDEX

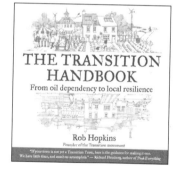